MW00994599

A John Hope Franklin Center Book

Post-Contemporary

Interventions

Series Editors:

Stanley Fish and

Fredric Jameson

DARK CONTINENTS

Psychoanalysis and Colonialism

RANJANA KHANNA

Duke University Press

Durham and London 2003

2nd printing, 2004

©2003 Duke University Press

All rights reserved

Printed in the United States of

America on acid-free paper ∞

Typeset in Bembo by Tseng

Information Systems, Inc.

Library of Congress Cataloging-

in-Publication Data appear on the

last printed page of this book.

For my parents
Shyam Krishna Khanna
and
Prem Khanna
(1935–1992)

Contents

[As] the mute outside that sustains all systematicity; as a maternal and still silent ground that nourishes all foundations—she does not have to conform to the codes theory has set up for itself.—Luce Irigaray, *Speculum of the Other Woman*

Freud infamously referred to women's sexuality as a "dark continent" for psychoanalysis. Within the continent of psychoanalysis made present by Freud lay this other continent that remained concealed. The map of it was yet to be drawn, or at least a sketchy map needed to be filled in. Not quite absent, it was present only in concealment and mysteriousness.

This study takes Henry Morton Stanley's metaphor for Africa and Freud's metaphor for women's sexuality and considers what it means to make colonialism and women the starting point of an investigation of psychoanalysis. *Dark Continents* makes use of psychoanalytic theory to perform this examination. What is at stake here is the status of psychoanalysis. While at times it is the object of investigation, it is also the preferred theoretical mode of analysis. Reading psychoanalysis symptomatically allows me to understand it as a masculinist and colonialist discipline that promoted an idea of Western subjectivity in opposition to a colonized, feminine, and primitive other. Placing psychoanalysis in the world, and understanding the problematic differentiations that psychoanalysis fails to acknowledge, allows me to reconfigure its politics. If psychoanalysis at its Freudian inception and in various other incarnations presents the reader with a story of subjectivity in Western Europe, as I argue, placing it in the world allows for an understanding of the ideological strife engendered in its language and the concepts it projected into existence. Far from rejecting psychoanalysis, *Dark Continents* shows the importance of psychoanalysis in the world today as a reading practice that makes apparent the psychical strife of colonial and postcolonial modernity. I argue that psychoanalysis itself is a colonial discipline, and that, as such, it provides mechanisms for the critique of postcoloniality and neocolonialism. I call this critique critical melancholia. Critical melancholia is an affect of coloniality as well as a reading practice that makes apparent the decentered nature of the psychoanalytic paradigm.

In his essay "Contradiction and Overdetermination," Louis Althusser commends Antonio Gramsci for being the only theorist to adequately "follow up on the explorations of Marx and Engels" in order to understand how "superstructures" are overdetermined by a multitude of factors, and do not have their sole origins in the economic base. Outlining an epistemological break between the young Marx's humanism and the mature Marx's science of dialectical materialism, Althusser emphasized the decentered nature of superstructures, or social formations. He considered that this decenteredness was undertheorized. As if haunted by the "dark continent" himself, Althusser wrote of this undertheorization thus: "Like the map of Africa before the great explorations, this theory remains a realm sketched in outline, with its great mountain chains and rivers, but often unknown in detail beyond a few well-known regions. Who has *really* attempted to follow up the explorations of Marx and Engels? I can only think of Gramsci."[1]

Offering a critique of early Marx, Althusser writes a new Marxist theory, and he does this through mapping Marx's explorations, exploring the unknown regions, and offering a cartography of the previously sketchy structures that overdetermined the thought of early Marx. To break from the humanist structures that overdetermined his theory, Marx had to develop a critique that constituted a science unrestricted by the ideological force of those structures. For Althusser, "Marx established a new *science:* the science of the history of 'social formations.'"[2] Drawing a comparison to the roles of Thales in the development of mathematics and Galileo in physics, Althusser claimed that Marx opened up a new "continent," and in doing so, "'induced' the birth of a new theoretically and practically revolutionary philosophy." To understand the relevance of this birth today, a "long theoretical labour and long historical maturing are required before they can acquire an explicit and adequate form."[3] Gramsci had gone through this labor and developed the idea of hegemony to supplement that of ideology. Althusser would develop an idea of antihumanism to understand how occurrences and perceptions were overdetermined by a variety of structures rather than solely economics or Hegelian inversion.

Althusser considered Marx to have induced the birth of a new science, and I would say the same of Freud. Following Althusser's terminology, one could say of Freud that a whole continent was opened up by him: the science of the Western self in its relation to modern nation-statehood, even as a "dark continent" lay within its realms. But master narratives of European modernity (like psychoanalysis) caused what Aimé Césaire reinscribed as "colonial trauma," a concept of pain emerging in writing that is somewhat different from Fredric Jameson's concept of the "hurt" inflicted by history's grand narratives.[4] Following Kaja Silverman, "colonial trauma" can be understood in terms of "historical trauma." Taking her cue from Freud's writings on "war trauma," Silverman conceived historical trauma as the interruption and deconstitution of master narratives or "dominant fictions."[5] Trauma begins to undo these fictions in a manner that turns the cause of trauma into a spectral presence interrupting the fiction of mastery and questioning the transparency of the prose that informs it. Freud's notion of selfhood began, as he neared World War II, to change and fragment in a manner that recognized how trauma could not be accommodated. Its affective form, which can be witnessed in Freud himself symptomatically as well as theoretically, was melancholia.

Dark Continents is divided into three parts: "Genealogies," "Colonial Rescriptings," and "Haunting and the Future." The first part follows a Foucauldian approach, tracing the genealogy of psychoanalytic development and linking it to other colonial disciplines that emerge in the same paradigmatic moment. This genealogical exercise reveals how melancholia was first theorized and then lived as the affect of political disenchantment in Freud's work. The second part, "Colonial Rescriptings," moves away from the strictly genealogical style to consider how psychoanalysis was parochialized in the colonies, but this time through the critical lens of melancholia. Coloniality demands a reading practice alert to the symptom of melancholia, just as it requires an understanding of how melancholia was contemporaneously conceived as a category of analysis. The final part is more speculative in its style, largely because it looks toward the future even as it is haunted by various melancholic specters. Each section's style implies a different notion of temporality and historicity that is informed by the nature of the particular affect at hand.

Postcolonial theory has frequently rejected psychoanalysis, objecting with some justification that it imposed a uniform notion of self onto the world. On the occasions when psychoanalytic theory has been employed in postcolonial analysis, it has been for the most part Lacanian. While there is a sustained engagement with the work of Jacques Lacan in the latter half of this book, *Dark Continents* is not a Lacanian study. *Dark Continents* proposes a concept of colonial melancholia that has no place within a Lacanian structuralist framework. Here colonial melancholia is presented as a politics of affect and as a form of individuated critique. This involves understanding the contingency of psychoanalysis vis-à-vis colonialism, neocolonialism, and nationalism. In fact, psychoanalysis, reconfigured through its location as a colonial discipline, and read against the grain, becomes the means through which contingent postcolonial futures can be imagined ethically.

Acknowledgments

Where does one start with acknowledgments for a first book? There are, of course, many people to thank for my early intellectual formation, the most prominent of these in my mind is Susheila Nasta. Some of the early research for the first two chapters was conducted when I was doing doctoral work in women's studies at the University of York in Britain. There, Nicole Ward Jouve and Joanna Hodge supervised the development of questions that continue to inform my thinking. Mary Jacobus, Laura Mulvey, and Tim Murray also helped me along the way, as did Dinah Dufton, Deniz Horrocks, and Misha Kavka.

Although my work is usually a solitary process, I have many friends and students to thank at the University of Utah, University of Rochester, University of Washington, Cornell University, and Duke University for being interested in the project, and patiently listening as I tried out ideas on them. Among those who deserve special mention for both their institutional support and friendship are Carolyn Allen, Karen Brennan, Marshall Brown, Lisa Cartwright, Karen Engle, Fred Jameson, Tom Lockwood, Bette London, Ileana Porras, Maureen Quilligan, Laurie Sears, Steve Shaviro, Nikhil Singh, Henry Staten, Steve Tatum, Priscilla Wald, and Alys Weinbaum. Two feminist writing groups deserve special mention. The participants included Madeleine Yue Dong, Carol Mavor, Uta Poiger, Jan Radway, Lynn Thomas, Alys Weinbaum, and Teresa Vilaros. Special thanks for the comments, encouragements, and meals during my year at the Society for the Humanities at Cornell University go to Mieke

Bal, Anne Berger, Mitchell Greenberg, Eleanor Kaufman, Natalie Melas, Tim Murray, Jim Siegel, and Marie-Claire Vallois. Tim Brennan and John Mowitt also gave helpful comments on an earlier version of the manuscript. Thanks also go to my editor, Reynolds Smith, for advice, generosity, and patience during the process.

Thanks to all those who kept asking whether the book was yet finished, especially my family old and new (Mona, Sunil, Aditya, Shefali, Srimathi, Dorai, Krishna, Seetu, Aditi). Obviously this book would not have been possible without my parents (Shyam and Prem Khanna), who probably taught me the most important things in life (and in death). My biggest thanks goes to my very favorite companion in all things, Srinivas Aravamudan. His thoughtfulness, brilliance, and joyfulness have brought pleasure to and changed the meaning of intellectual pursuit, the quotidian, solidarity, and friendship.

A section of Chapter 1 was previously published as a section of "The Construction of the Dark Continent: Agency as Autobiography," in *Women's Lives/Women's Times,* ed. Treva Broughton and Linda Anderson (New York: SUNY Press, 1997), 103–20. An earlier version of Chapter 5 was previously published as "Ethical Ambiguities and Specters of Colonialism: Futures of Transnational Feminism," in *Feminist Consequences: Theory for the New Century,* ed. Elisabeth Bronfen and Misha Kavka (New York: Columbia University Press, 2000).

Dark Continents

Introduction. Worlding Psychoanalysis

In "Geopsychoanalysis," Jacques Derrida comments on the blindness of psychoanalysis to most of the earth, and of what it inscribes on the earth through "its ongoing worldification," that is, a textualization, and the violent event of imposing a way of being in the world.[1] His project is to criticize polemically the politics of the International Psychoanalytic Association, and the treatment of what is dismissed by it as "the rest of the world," in which "*Homo psychoanalyticus* is unknown or outlawed."[2] The IPA was established in 1913, although its conception took place nearly a decade earlier. Psychoanalytic institutes developed internationally, some with the blessings of the IPA, some more independently. The majority, predictably, was in Europe and the United States, a minority in Central and South America, but very few institutes were established in "the rest of the world"—in Africa, Asia, and Australia. Since its inception, the association has claimed a nonpolitical agenda. Today this claim is in evidence, for example, in the statements by the IPA on the U.N. World Conference against Racism, and on the terrorist attacks on the United States, both in September 2001. Concerned about the accusation of anti-Semitism in the reporting of the conference in the United States, and mindful of the necessity of making a psychoanalytic response to the attacks on the World Trade Center and the Pentagon, the president of the IPA, Professor Daniel Widlöcher, issued the following statement:

> The purpose [of attending the U.N. conference] is to consider, advise, and promote contributions that the profession of psychoanaly-

sis might make in areas of international concern. . . . Our Committee was not engaged in political issues. . . . It has been the view of the IPA Executive Committee that it is in the interest of the IPA to participate in the United Nation's system. So far the expansion of personal contacts, and information about psychoanalysis, have proved to be a potential avenue of international outreach that we need to maintain and strengthen. In addition, given the present terrorist assault on the United States, and the growing concern of the international community on the relationship between fundamentalist ideologies, terrorism, and the outbreak of primitive violence, psychoanalysis has an important role in contributing to the understanding of the psychodynamics of violence at the level of the individual and social groups.[3]

The defensiveness concerning involvement in international politics produces a notion of the nonpolitical. Understanding the psychodynamics of forms of violence named "primitive," "terrorist," "fundamentalist," and "ideological" is rendered apolitical. Such claims to neutrality in psychoanalysis need to be understood textually, that is, through the rhetorical processes that deny political complicity.

Dark Continents does not, for the most part, discuss the particular politics and dynamics of the International Psychoanalytic Association. But much of its work does lend to an analysis of statements such as the one above. The IPA claims to be apolitical. Considering the strife that characterized the emergence of psychoanalysis, the politics of an institution offering international outreach can be thought through more critically, rather than, for example, internationalist coalition or analysis of the status and relevance of psychoanalytic thought in different contexts. This allows, for example, a critical reconceptualization of the term "primitive violence" used in modern political contexts of global late capitalism. Dark Continents proposes that the concepts of self and being that came into existence in psychoanalysis were dependent on strife or violence, that is, on the politics of colonial relations.

While Derrida's criticisms of the politics of the IPA are pertinent in understanding its political complicities, my project is somewhat different. The development of psychoanalysis brought into existence a new way of being in the world for men and women across the globe in its rendition of modern national selfhood. Just as some were spoken into existence through the discipline, others were created, or worlded, as its underside, rendered as the earth, or as primitive beings against which the modern European self, in need of psychoanalysis, was situated.

Worlding

Worlding, writes Martin Heidegger in "The Thing" and in "The Origin of the Work of Art," is the production of art in the space between earth and world. "Production" and "work," that is, the imaginative and ontological labor performed in art objects, are the essence of art because art objects do the work of opening up the world so that one can imagine a way of being within it. While the process of transformation from raw materials (paint, canvas, clay) into painting or sculpture are part and parcel of any consideration of art, the ontological shaping constituted through the art less frequently contributes to an understanding of "the work." And yet forms of being brought into the world in art, the best example of which is poetry for Heidegger, are twofold:

> Projective saying is poetry: the saying of world and earth, the saying of the arena of their strife and thus of the place of all nearness and remoteness of the gods. Poetry is the saying of the unconcealedness of beings. Actual language at any given moment is the happening of this saying, in which a people's world historically arises for it and the earth is preserved as that which remains closed. Projective saying is saying which, in preparing the sayable, simultaneously brings the unsayable as such into a world. In such saying, the concepts of a historical people's essence, i.e., of its belonging to world history, are performed for that people.[4]

> The world presences by worlding. That means: the world's worlding cannot be explained by anything else, nor can it be fathomed through anything else. . . . As soon as human cognition here calls for an explanation, it fails to transcend the world's nature, and falls short of it.[5]

If "actual language" is "the happening of this saying," then art is not so much an object that represents something already existing. Rather, it is an event or a condition for the possibility of coming into being. Worlding performs the "unconcealedness of being" because it brings a new way of being in the world, along with the attendant concealedness of the earth that occurs simultaneously. This simultaneous projection of unconcealedness in the world and closure into the earth constitutes the process and the work of worlding. It is an act of strife between being and nonbeing, or more accurately, between being-in-the-world and concealment in the earth, marked as invisible to the world. Worlding is not the representation of an opposition between self (in the world) and other (concealed in the earth and absent from the world). Worlding is an event through which the participants are brought into temporality and history, or, conversely, excluded from these and concealed timelessly into the earth.

If for Heidegger art and technology brought the world into uncon-cealedness, *Dark Continents* proposes that a social science like psychoanaly-sis does something similar in the event of its projective saying. Science in the Althusserian sense is the introduction of a conceptual apparatus into the world rather than an analysis of empirical elements. For Althusser, science, and particularly a science of sciences like Marxism, is opposed to ideology. The concept of "worlding" shares something with the notion of science, but it is a process and an event, indicated by the turning of the noun into a participle and at times a verb by Heidegger. Worlding is a projection into existence of certain elements in the world which now become unconcealed. As some things are made visible in the world, or as they are brought out of the raw material of the earth, they simulta-neously remainder others as earth. The process of worlding is one of strife between the unconcealed (worlded) and the concealed (earthed), and it is one that I understand as profoundly ideological.

Gayatri Chakravorty Spivak has reinterpreted (or, in her words, delib-erately vulgarized) Heidegger's concept of worlding through understand-ing the violence ("strife") Heidegger describes in the passage from earth to world as the establishment of colonial control of space through map-ping, land appropriation, and the transformation of the raw materials of the earth into the politico-economic and geographical category of "world." If Heidegger claimed that the art work allowed a sense of the unsayable, Spivak translates those terms as the projecting of the colonized as "other," nonself, or as the unsayable of colonial selfhood.[6] The colo-nized thus become the "closed," the "concealed," or the "earth" through the establishment of the world. To understand not only the world as it is brought into unconcealedness, but also the strife in its inception, allows us to see how the earth itself is changed forever through the creation of the world. "Worlding" involves a creation of strife; understanding world-ing involves an analysis of that strife—critically worlding the processes of the previously earthed, thereby seeing the historical, political, and economic dynamics of strife through its unconcealment. If Heidegger saw the processes of naming as bringing being into the world and into history, Spivak locates that history more specifically in coloniality. She wrests the metaphor of earth into world from timeless abstraction, tying it into the historico-political contingencies of Enlightenment colonial Europe.

Worlding, for me, is the process of understanding the violence of the production of psychoanalysis in the world. Less pure than science, this process looks to worlding and earthing in the context of coloniality, as an epistemic violence. Both what was made possible and impossible to think in the projective saying that constitutes psychoanalysis restructured the sense of being in coloniality. More than "contextualization," worlding allows us to understand the scientific event in the production of language that threw something into the world, and simultaneously captured another as earthly raw material. Psychoanalysis now has to be read in terms of the way it contributed to the project of worlding. It also means reading that worlding against the grain, and positioning the previously earthed as the point of entry into inquiry. My project of "worlding psychoanalysis" is therefore twofold. It documents the world events through which psychoanalysis was produced, and it also offers a critical reading practice which itself is a product of that initial violent projective saying. Worlding is the understanding of global strife in the production of textuality. It understands history as an utterance projected into the world and understands the world, and not only the local context, as profoundly shaped into unconcealment through that event of saying. History is given to the world and the earth from which psychoanalysis emerged. History is returned to the world through reading for the way in which earthed specters exert pressure on that which is unconcealed.

It may seem strange to render psychoanalysis an art form for which poetry is an archetype. Foucault cited Freud as a rare example of an author who genuinely engendered a new discourse. Freud's standing as a poet in Heidegger's terminology is, however, distinct from his establishment as an author. The poet, after all, brings about events in which a more fluid movement of disclosure and concealment takes place as beings become textualized into a technology of understanding through projective saying.

If psychoanalysis was instrumental in projecting an idea of a "historical people's essence," that is, the essence of selves at the turn of the twentieth century in Europe, it did this equally in a colonial relation. The national self in Europe is structured in psychoanalysis as a modern counterpart of the primitive colonized. In its profoundly European constitution, it expresses the unsayable: the impossible achievement of selfhood for the colonized, who remain primitive and concealed, and the simultaneous tenuousness of the metropolitan colonizer's self once decolonization is in place and the strife that sustains the colonized as primitive is over. "Worlding psychoanalysis" means understanding the twofold nature of this constitution: understanding what psychoanalysis makes possible as said and as unsayable in coloniality, that is, in the world in history and in temporality.

Psychoanalysis is a colonial discipline. A colonial intellectual formation disciplines a way of being as much as it establishes a form of analysis based in the age of colonialism and constitutive of concepts of the primitive against which the civilizing mission could establish itself. It brought into the world an idea of being that was dependent on colonial political and ontological relations, and through its disciplinary practices, formalized and perpetuated an idea of uncivilized, primitive, concealed, and timeless colonized peoples. As a discipline, it formalized strategies to normalize a form of civilized being constituted through colonial political dynamics. In the space between the earth and the colonizing world of late-nineteenth and early-twentieth-century Europe, a national-colonial self was brought into existence, or perhaps more accurately, into unconcealment. And it situated itself, with fascination, in opposition to its repressed, concealed, and mysterious "dark continents": colonial Africa, women, and the primitive.

This becomes apparent through the textuality of strife. Worlding, now a critical approach analyzing the work performed in the creation of the sayable and the unsayable, takes the universalism out of discourses of modernity like psychoanalysis, and considers their function and manifestation in the world. While the metropolitan discipline maintained its notion of civilized being, discrepant versions began to emerge at the borders of the world coming into being.[7] Understanding psychoanalysis as a colonial discipline allows us to see how nation-statehood for the former colonies of Europe encrypts the violence of the European nation in its colonial manifestations. The development of psychoanalysis itself constitutes an ethnography of nation-statehood. It embodies the violent inception of colonial being and reveals its colonial specters, which are at once the call of justice—the by-product of reading strife—and the forms of violence it engenders.

Psychoanalysis has been criticized for its universalizations, its elitism, and its ahistoricism. Its relevance has been questioned for analyses of the social. While psychoanalysis and colonialism occupy separate realms—that of the psyche, sometimes reduced to the personal in the case of psychoanalysis, and that of the political and economic expressed as the public in the case of nationalism and colonialism—they do not constitute entirely discrete entities. Evaluated in feminist terms, psychoanalysis is revealed to be contingent upon the forms of European colonial nationalism at the turn of the last century. Changes within colonial and gender politics, in turn, have reformulated the use of psychoanalysis, and made more apparent the way in which it came into being in the historico-political world it made for itself. While most historical accounts of psychoanalysis taking politics into account center on the notion of race in terms of Judaism, *Dark Continents* situates this idea of race alongside that of coloniality and the forms of concealment and unconcealment it engendered as it came into existence.

Some thirty years ago, Carl Schorske wrote that Freudian psychoanalysis exemplified political disempowerment. His analysis centered on the early text *The Interpretation of Dreams*. Schorske disclosed the political drama encrypted in the dreams used as the bedrock of Freud's study. Political disempowerment arose with the historical increase of anti-Semitism during Freud's lifetime. For Schorske, politics in *The Interpretation of Dreams* became "an epiphenomenal manifestation of psychic forces" that showed "the counterpolitical ingredient in the origins of psychoanalysis."[8] He noted another crisis in Freud's life at the time. Freud's father died in 1896, and as Schorske remarks, this loss was dramatized in dreams as professional failure and political guilt. Schorske, therefore, draws a parallel between Freud and Hamlet: "To lay his father's ghost to rest Freud had either, like Hamlet, to affirm the primacy of politics by removing what was rotten in the state of Denmark (a civic task) or to neutralize politics by reducing it to psychological categories (an intellectual task)."[9] In Schorske's estimation, Freud chose to reduce his own political past and present to that of the primal conflict between father and son. Freud "gave his fellow liberals an ahistorical theory of man and society that could make bearable a political world spun out of orbit and beyond control."[10]

Schorske confines his account of the political and historical conditions of the growth of psychoanalysis to fin-de-siècle Vienna. But he neglects the larger discourses of archaeology and anthropology which inform Freud's language, as well as affects of his physical, emotional, and phantasmatic mobility. These must be considered when analyzing the discipline and practice of psychoanalysis in relation to national and colonial politics.

The rhetoric of psychoanalysis tells the story of a Europe and its colonies in a process of transition, and one could say the same of Hamlet, who hovers in Schorske's analogy and to whom we shall return shortly. In a textual analysis, psychoanalysis does not simply choose the intellectual at the expense of the political, but rather dramatizes the disempowerment of the psychoanalytical subject as coterminous with the expansion of the European nation-state. Freud does not, therefore, simply choose the epiphenomenal (or the secondary symptom) over the political. The political hovers over Freud's writings in a symmetrically opposed manner to that of King Hamlet's specter disclosing the conjugal pollution that infects the body politic. No more than Oedipus, who unwittingly caused the pollution of the city and the marriage bed, can Hamlet separate the political from the filial. By inverting the structure he analyzes, Freud's writings carry the specter of politics with them.

Reading psychoanalysis not only gives us the story of the political transformations in Europe. It also shows us the psychical changes in both metropolitans and colonials that took place as a result of the transition from European nationalist discourse to state hegemonic appropriation of that discourse. Whereas Tom Nairn has suggested that " 'nationalism' is the pathology of modern developmental history, as inescapable as 'neurosis' in the individual,"[11] his analogy normalizes a more contingent and dynamic relationship between the two, which Freud's work demonstrates. Psychoanalysis helps us understand how the state's reliance on the nation is about different forms of representation, whether in terms of textualization, print capitalism, or representational politics. Psychoanalysis describes the processing of subjects into the larger groups that constitute nation-states. This processing moves the subject from earth to world, reproduction to production, emotion to signification, and filiation to affiliation at the same time that it makes visible the strife that haunts those representational teleologies.

Psychoanalysis does this through a language laden with colonial discourse. Much of the work that employed psychoanalytic language to analyze decolonization allowed room for those specters, or perhaps caused those specters to emerge. Albert Memmi used both psychoanalysis and Marxism to understand decolonization and colonialism, seeing them as the analytically discrete entities that they are, but using the techniques of one to supplement the shortcomings of the other. Others, like Fanon, eventually prioritized political analysis to identify the source of the mental strife he saw in the clinic. In Marxism, this trajectory led to an analysis of the economics of coloniality, and of neocolonialism, the depletion of natural resources, the need for decolonization as a precursor to the international revolution of workers, and the work on the communist tricontinental.[12] In psychoanalytic terms, studies of the effect of coloniality on individuals and on groups, and the failings of existent concepts of self to understand anything other than products of European modernity based in Europe, led to revisionist work as well as reassessments of mental health and the political consequences of new forms of selfhood brought about in various contexts because of European modernity and coloniality.

In the field of postcolonial studies, from such diverse disciplines as literary criticism and theory, history, education, international law, and anthropology, and following Edward Said's comment that "imperial concerns [are] constitutively significant to the culture of the modern West,"[13] many have argued that the relationship of nineteenth-century disciplines to the colonies is more the result of a constitutive effect of the colonial encounter than merely an imperial imposition onto those colonies through education, research, economics, and policy.[14] Seen in this light, psychoanalysis cannot be understood adequately in any context without considering how it was constituted both in Europe and in its colonies, in other words, how it was constituted as a colonial discipline through the economic, political, cultural, and epistemic strife in the transition from earth into world.

Understanding the strife at the heart of worlding allows us to see the necessity of bringing two apparently disparate critical and disciplinary traditions together. Psychoanalysis is a technical and clinical field that investigates mental phenomena. It has been used in studies of society and culture since its inception, with Freud turning to readings of war, anti-Semitism, or Shakespeare alongside his writings on clinical issues like obsessional neurosis. Colonialism is a series of historical events with political and economic repercussions for the globe. In its full-fledged European form, colonialism manifested itself as imperialism: the imposition of one nation-state, itself coming into being, onto large areas of the world, the control of which was assumed along with mastery over their inhabitants for the purpose of economic gain and more global political power. But psychoanalysis could emerge only when Europe's nations were entering modernity through their relationship with the colonies. The concept of self and the event of being that emerge in psychoanalytic theory, even in its many variations that have come into existence in the post-Freudian period, developed in relation to the concept of the European nation-state. This factor makes psychoanalysis crucial for the understanding of postcoloniality and decolonization.

It is the project of demonstrating the contingency of Europe's grand narratives with coloniality, including concepts of modernity's self, civilization, and nationhood, that allows for a reading of psychoanalysis as a colonial discipline. Many have cautioned that a critical reading of these narratives does not simply call for an outright rejection of modernity and the disciplinary models that accompany it.[15] That would fail to acknowledge the strife of worlding, and the profound global change in forms of knowing brought about in these narratives and the economic relations they sanctioned.

In spite of the many criticisms of psychoanalysis, it persists internationally, with varied amounts of influence in different parts of the globe, as a mode of clinical and cultural analysis. Importantly, it is influential not only among peoples in the West who bear some resemblance to the Vienna of the turn of the century, sharing with it, for example, Semitic religions, nuclear families, hyperindividualism, middle-class urban centers, a history of Western disciplinary knowledge, racism, and repressive concepts of sexuality. It also remains a mode of analysis in parts of the world that share only partially in those characteristics. With this in mind, it seems pertinent to consider the development of psychoanalysis not only contextually, but also, as Mary Anne Doane has suggested, ethnographically, in order to understand what could be said and unsaid through the projective saying of its disciplinary poetics.[16]

Understanding psychoanalysis ethnographically involves analyzing its use, both by Europeans and by the colonized. If the idea of worlding and the earth seems to kill off the colonized, or to turn the people who make up that category into concealed earth existing only as a by-product of coloniality, some sense of the parochiality of various psychoanalyses will help temper that sense, giving life to uses of psychoanalysis differing from that formed by Freud in its metropolitan center. The project of worlding as the analysis of strife involves understanding parochialization and rejection, and also provincializing a language that presented itself as universal.

Partha Chatterjee has written extensively on the parochialization of metropolitan discourse, or an adaptation to suit a different environment and group dynamic. Chatterjee was writing about postcolonial nationhood in India to develop this notion of parochialization as the complete refashioning of the European model of nation-statehood in the colonial outreach in the postindependence era. For these reasons, his critical practice is equally relevant for psychoanalysis. Chatterjee's parochializations refer to forms of nation-statehood in India that came into being in quite varied ways, depending on one's relation to (future) state power. Peasants, women, and outcasts had a very different sense of nationhood than did the elite, and they shunned the false sense of community that elite nationalists envisioned before official independence in 1947. This sense of an "imagined community," even if it was projected by the elite, was an almost impossible undertaking. The discrepant forms of imagining independence from colonial powers highlighted the struggle between capital and community. The universality of nationalist discourse was disavowed in the varied forms of parochialization that took place.[17]

But these forms of parochialization will be inadequate for an understanding of colonial worlding without a simultaneous understanding of the contingency of European modernity with coloniality. Dipesh Chakrabarty's idea of "provincializing Europe" is helpful in this regard, and distinct from Chatterjee's comparative analyses of distinct modernities in the colonies. Chakrabarty focuses on the constitutive nature of European modernity in colonial rule. He writes specifically about the discipline of history and the difficulties associated with those areas deemed "nonmodern" in colonial historiography. This idea of the nonmodern can be extended to the anthropology of the primitive so attractive to Freud in works such as *Totem and Taboo*. Chakrabarty notes that the modern (in his case exemplified best in Enlightenment colonial historiography, and in my case in the evolutionary logic that informs Freud's sense of the growth of repression in "civilization") will always seem inadequate in its rendition in the colonies, as it is precisely the difference between the colonies and Europe that renders the colonies primitive. The logic of evolutionary and teleological temporality that already rendered the colonies "unmodern" thus fails to fully grasp the discrepant modernity that emerges in the colonies. The idea of the discrepant modern in *Dark Continents* draws on these theories of worlding-in-the-world and the provincialization and parochialization of psychoanalysis. My critique is developed through a psychoanalytic theory reformulated, read against the grain, and mindful of the strife at its center—between capital and community, between individual and group, between primitive and civilized, between particular and universal, and between singular and ideal.

Temporality and Nationhood

While the relationship between the individual citizen or subject to the state has frequently been understood as that between memory and history, the unconscious dimensions of national subjecthood have rarely been explored in any systematic fashion. I am suggesting that the affect of colonialism, understood as the spectral remainder of the inassimilable colonial structure of the modern nation-state, informs and shapes the temporality of contemporary nation-statehood.

Clearly, not all forms of memory or forgetting need a psychoanalytic lens to interpret them. In 1882, when Ernest Renan famously talked of the need to "remember to forget" the prehistory of nation-statehood, he had no psychoanalytic concept of that selective and collective amnesia in mind.[18] The nation had to be willed into existence, and this willing was conceived by Renan as a *daily plebiscite*. In contemporary terms, this finds its apotheosis in our age of "rememoration."[19] More recently, historians like Pierre Nora in his edition of the new French national history, *Les lieux de mémoire* (Realms of Memory), has suggested that "the new history is purely transferential history."[20] What he means by this is that the individualization of memory and the individual's responsibility to *remember* historical events for the sake of group cohesion or conflict (in this case national) enables "successive generations to mediate their cultural myths by inculcating them with their desires."[21] The past is thus individualized, and the citizen's own responsibility to the group or nation is to *remember to forget* in order that the future can be willed into existence. National formation is understood as the assimilation into a narrative of self or of history, the past of the nation.

Anthropologists, for example in Richard Werbner's edited volume

Memory and the Postcolony: African Anthropology and the Critique of Power, or writers, such as Wole Soyinka in *The Burden of Memory, the Muse of Forgiveness,* have employed varied concepts of memory and forgetting to write about nation-statehood and the resonance of the past in the present. These range from critiques of national nostalgia, analysis of the state denial and disappeared bodies that mark memories, and state or counter-hegemonic memorialization, to the ethics of memory construction. Werbner et al. suggest that the "historical approach to memory takes it as problematic that intractable traces of the past are felt on people's bodies, known in their landscapes, landmarks and souvenirs, and perceived as the tough moral fabric of their social relations—sometimes the stifling, utterly unwelcome fabric. The very passion in, for and against memory, keeping it alive, burying or killing it, disclosing, registering, textualising and recreating it, is also problematic."[22] Clearly, when memory is called upon to claim or disclaim an official past, its resonance as counterfactual narrative becomes extremely important, especially in conditions of the suppression of truth. When official narratives show that the state has chosen to forget the uncomfortable past of those it claims to represent, the political use of memory is to right a wrong, make visible the invisible, or give knowledge where ignorance has reigned. Here, the terms *memory* and *forgetting* are employed as inscription and erasure.

Wole Soyinka implores us to consider the shortcomings of forgiveness for the attempt to give justice as a counter to that which burdens the memory of colonial exploitation in Africa. Once again, memory is understood as the responsibility to understand the historical burden of colonialism that affects everyday life in most African countries. To understand contemporary political and economic problems in Africa in terms of colonialism is to draft memory as the genealogy of the present. Soyinka's motivation for writing is both the inadequacy of national apologies for colonial impoverishment of Africa and the notable absence of such apologies in an age in which they appear to be a large part of political discourse (Clinton apologizing for slavery; the pope for the wrongs of the Vatican; Blair for the Irish potato famine). The burden of memory translates to the ongoing exploitation of Africa in terms of the politics of aid, as much as the effect of colonialism more generally.[23]

Others, especially those working on the Holocaust and the Holocaust archives (for example, Shoshana Felman and Dori Laub), have employed the concept of trauma, developed through Pierre Janet, and then Freud and psychoanalysis, to understand the structure of narrative and narrative temporality in recollecting historical and personal events.[24] Cathy Caruth's work on trauma has led the way in this kind of analysis.[25] Psychiatrist Vamik Volkan and psychoanalyst Sudhir Kakar, for example, have sought to understand how the remainder of psychical trauma manifests itself as that which exists beyond a "chosen trauma" of a group.[26] A collective "chosen trauma" is the group response to an event apparently experienced by a group in a fairly uniform fashion, and apparently with fairly uniform results. For psychoanalysis, trauma is experienced (or blocked from experience) in individuals and in the everyday. It is certainly true that individuals are part of groups, and that trauma is connected to group relations. But the "chosen trauma" is something conceived as an event that the group experienced together with particular group affective responses, often employed by groups to consolidate a sense of collective identity. One could say, in fact, that no individual event took place that resulted in a trauma, and that the trauma is indeed only an affect resulting from group identification (whether individually willed, or imposed externally). Chosen trauma is, perhaps, akin to the *Annalistes'* conception of the historical event in the *longue durée* of historical time. The chosen trauma, or the event qua event, takes on a particular resonance for the history of the people, their most deeply felt cultural affiliations and anxieties, and collective symbols of a community.[27]

In *Imagined Communities*, Benedict Anderson writes of the time of the nation as being that of empty time rather than messianic time. He takes his terms from Walter Benjamin's essay "Theses on the Philosophy of History," in which Benjamin writes of the Angelus Novus, the Janus-faced angel who always looks back while looking forward, and thus conceives the present in terms of the past before and the future ahead. Messianic time is marked by ritual experienced as the reenactment of an event, rather than an annual commemoration; thus Easter, for example, is relived as the death and rising of Christ rather than as an occasion to remember that moment. Benjamin works hard to invest the present with Messianic time to foreground the "nowness" of the present rid of its causal logic. There is thus a simultaneity suggested with diachronic moments, rather than a synchronous and spatial sense of simultaneity conceptualized as occurring in "empty time." And this is similar also to the difference between the storyteller in Benjamin's terms, the novelist, and the journalist. Information supplied on a "weekly" or "daily" basis by the journalist marks the distinctiveness of that day, rather than, as in the novel, "carry[ing] the incommensurable to extremes in the representation of human life."[28] It is the solitude of the novelist that marks his distinctiveness from other fiction creators, because there is no oral framework that subtends it, as there is for the storyteller. The storyteller works within a messianic time, the novelist in empty time.

Anderson takes this up to discuss the time of the nation as empty time, because, in rather anonymous fashion, community is created through this idea of simultaneity within national borders within which the newspaper, or indeed the novel, is distributed. The temporal framework of the "meanwhile" thus introduces a spatial component into the understanding of time. Homi Bhabha contrasts the time of the nation discussed by Anderson with one marked by *Nachträglichkeit*—a psychoanalytic concept of deferred action that Bhabha understands as a time-lag—which he finds typical of postcolonial nations. He identifies the splitting that interrupts and causes a time-lag within the temporal synchronicity of the present, and locates this as the midpoint between a linear concept of time that progresses causally.[29]

All these concepts of memory tied to the nation-state are clearly important in understanding the role of individuated concepts of history in nation-state formation. Most, however, assume a concept of homogeneous, empty time in their understanding of the relation of the past to the present. The function of the archive—whether official or one that is challenged through differing narratives of memory, suppressed information, new evidence, or reinterpretation—is nonetheless to inscribe the authority of the *archon* as something made available to the people of the nation through news or research as a past shared either then or now. *Dark Continents* departs from the idea of homogeneous and empty time through the concept of melancholia. In developing an idea of postcolonial melancholy, simultaneity and homogeneity are challenged.

Encrypted figures that initiate a process of haunting disrupt the linearity of time leading up to the shared present. Haunting relates to this temporal framework, but adds something to it, for it locates melancholia rather than simply *Nachträglichkeit* at its core. And what is lost is not marked only by a repression that emerges in the same form at a later date, but also one that is lost and swallowed whole, incorporated. While some specters may be put to rest permanently through the work of a genealogy of the present, others are endemic to the structure of nation-statehood's colonial inception.

Dark Continents ends with *Hamlet,* which ironically gives us a lesson on the function of the specter for the postcolonial intellectual. If Hamlet struggled with specters of political and conjugal violence, the Freudian reading concerning his repressed admiration for Claudius tells the story of the inevitable movement of history within which Hamlet finds himself. The attempt to avenge his father's murder leads him into the ethical quandary witnessed in the first four cerebral acts of the play, before the genre of the time, revenge tragedy, takes over in the final act. Killing is not Prince Hamlet's business, but the time of the play runs toward its murderous conclusion. If the movement of modernity (or "civilization" in Freud's terms) is one in which increased repression reigns, then Hamlet is indeed left with an ethically impossible situation, one that continues to haunt us, thus disturbing the temporality of the play. The ghost haunts us despite the revenge, and revenge seems botched and inadequate, even if inevitable. If this *trauerspiel,* to employ Benjamin's term for *Hamlet,* gives us a spectral sense of the past that melancholically introduces a different temporality to Hamlet's ethical universe, so colonial melancholy and the specter of colonialism inform the work of seeking justice in the period after colonialism.

Critical Melancholy and the Intellectual

In *Dark Continents,* the idea of colonial melancholy offers a way of reconceptualizing the intellectual. The intellectual has been a crucial category in postcolonial studies since its inception, because colonialism's intellectual projects—orientalism and the disciplinary formations that came into existence with it—needed reconceptualization. Once the formerly colonized became agents of the disciplinary endeavors that had previously worlded them as others, the status of the intellectual and the political stakes of representation and disciplinary formation became sites of contestation. Marxism, especially that espoused by Gramsci, became a crucial tool in the rethinking of intellectual endeavor. In what follows, I briefly describe some debates concerning the status and work of the intellectual in postcolonial studies, and I then explain why "colonial melancholy," an idea with its basis in a psychoanalysis refashioned through the lens of colonialism and feminism, is an important intervention in postcolonial studies. While melancholy alone could be conceived as an affectation presenting the wrongs of colonial suppression, melancholia is an affective state caused by the inability to assimilate a loss, and the consequent nagging return of the thing lost into psychic life. Theorizing melancholia involves theorizing a relationship to the other, and the manner in which the other is manifested. What is at stake in formulating an idea of the affective melancholia of postcolonials, however, is not only an understanding of the different psychic lives of postcolonials. In what follows, I outline the forms of intellectual work enabled by the intimate forms of critique manifest in colonial melancholia.

In his 1953 essay "Notes on Hamlet," C. L. R. James identified Hamlet as an organic intellectual.[30] This term, "organic intellectual," is now suffused for us with Gramscian connotations, especially as it has become one of the mainstays of postcolonial criticism from Edward Said's invocation of it in his introduction to *Orientalism* (1978) to the ongoing work of India's historians of the subaltern in the colonial archive.[31] However, while James is clearly not making the Gramscian distinction between the traditional and the organic intellectual, he nonetheless places this unlikely figure, a Danish prince, at the heart of a Shakespearean reconceptualization of government and politics. James identifies the split in Hamlet's mind as one that characterizes all intellectuals between "the communal change from the medieval world to the world of free individualisation."[32] The communal change — perhaps this can be read as the communal strife — manifests itself in Hamlet's mind, of course, as a ghost. If the ghost is the remainder and the reminder of the medieval, in the move from the feudal to free individualization, or the feudal to the bourgeois, it has broader implications for social critique. Gramsci's focus on the identity of the organic as opposed to the traditional bourgeois intellectual moves in the opposite direction, from the traditional bourgeois to the communal nature of the organic popular.[33]

But what does it mean to call Hamlet an "organic intellectual"? And what are the implications of this Jamesian and Gramscian attribute for psychoanalytic studies of colonialism? Is it useful to think of psychoanalytic implications of the Marxist term "organic intellectual," a figure who emerges from the people rather than from political society, and who does the work of finding forms of representation rather than seeking consent to one already formulated? Returning to the point of entry of psychoanalysis in the context of colonialism, what does it mean to foreground individuated memory when writing of social contexts? and what political use could be made from writing of ghosts (entities differentiated from "forgotten" or suppressed histories, or from what could colloquially be named "skeletons in the closet")? If Gramsci informs postcolonial scholarship's concept of the "organic intellectual," it was also he who reminded us of the central Socratic ethical imperative to "know thyself" before embarking on any critical analysis, and to create an inventory of oneself before beginning. What the Marxist humanist assumed has since been thrown into doubt not only by antihumanists like Foucault, or Derrida, but also by psychoanalysis. The creation of an inventory through which we can know ourselves has been shown to be an impossible task, because parts of oneself may not be known of, may be unconscious, or inaccessible, even as the attempt to know oneself may be crucial.

Reading James and Gramsci through the lens of psychoanalysis, however, allows us to consider another foundation for the intellectual: a spectral one. It allows us to consider what is necessary for postcolonial critique: recognizing that the organic intellectual emerges not only "from the people" but also from what James Joyce's Hamlet, Stephen Dedalus, called *limbo patrum,* the limbo of the fathers. In *limbo patrum* is encountered the filiations and affiliations that haunt, and the affective iterations to which this haunting gives rise. If this *limbo* had a national language, it would be one made of prosopopoeia, giving face to the dead or figure to the absent, rather than trope, and one in which the spectral is even more pertinent than the strictly etymological.

Gramsci's writings are notoriously challenging when it comes to offering a synthesized concept, largely because they appear, and were written, in fragments of notebooks when he was imprisoned for his communist antifascist allegiances. But the role of the intellectual was nevertheless fundamental to the way Gramsci conceived of civil society. Traditional intellectuals functioned as the disseminators of political society's ideas, introducing them into civil society through education, policy, religion, morality, and everyday institutions. They played an indispensable role in creating and maintaining hegemonic concepts, that is, concepts that became dominant through the creation of consent within civil society. In Gramsci's formulation, traditional intellectuals were a holdover from earlier class formations, and existed in *bad faith,* thinking of themselves as autonomous and independent, and embodying reason beyond any kind of class allegiance. But they consciously or unconsciously hid their class interests.

The organic intellectual, on the other hand, emerged from the people, possibly from the proletariat with an already constituted class consciousness, but possibly also from a subaltern group. Subaltern groups are not conjoined by class consciousness, are not privy to the rights afforded to members of civil society, and potentially erupt into incidents of spontaneous insurgency on the margins of civil society. Gramsci emphasized that this is a cause of great concern to political society, which has no way of reacting to them other than through brute force. Organic intellectuals emerging from such a group would be responsible for creating something of a class consciousness among the disparate elements of the subalterns, and would thereby introduce them to the possibility of rights and representation. They introduce the group into the consciousness of civil society with the hope of seeking representation for them, and possibly eventually creating a counter-hegemony. Gramsci adds that the history of the subaltern "classes" could thus be written only after they had ceased to be "subalterns." Given his commitment to membership of the Communist Party, the ideal trajectory for this is to become part of political society that could, in turn, maintain a hegemony within civil society, thus creating the Communist Party as "modern prince." The subaltern therefore comes to be a remainder, necessarily betrayed as it enters the world of civil society. And it leaves something behind that cannot be accounted for, remains unknown, and can only be imagined, in the strife created by worlding. Reading how that melancholic remainder manifests itself through haunting allows for the haunting justice affectively summoned by the unrepresentable subaltern.

The problematic distinction between the two concepts of intellectual has been highlighted recently by David Lloyd and Paul Thomas, who argue that the "traditional intellectual" and his or her structural similarity to or differentiation from the "organic intellectual" is inadequately explained in the context of modern hegemony.[34] As holdovers from earlier class formations, and of the culture of apparent political "disinterestedness" associated with it, the traditional intellectual would presumably be transformed by the dispersed nature of hegemonic civil society, whose "common sense" absorption of ideas in anonymous and independent contexts within nation-states would produce a different distinction between intellectuals than that found in earlier class formations. Intellectuals today are organically produced and differentiated, and would lack unity, or even a uniform manifestation of ideology that could be demystified. In this sense, the modern prince, or the scholarly ruler, would be both traditional and organic, rather like Fanon's bourgeois intellectual in *The Wretched of the Earth*.

In postcolonial studies, the concepts of the organic intellectual and the subaltern have been very influential, particularly in creating oppositional discourse rather than reigning ideology, hegemony, or counterhegemony. The Subaltern Studies group early on committed itself not to studying the hegemonic story of India's nationalist movement and its road to independence from Britain in 1947 but rather to reading the colonial archive for traces of other stories of resistance to the colonial regime. Whether organized or not, many of these stories of such occurrences as peasant insurgencies, or, for example, the role of rumor in mutiny within the army, became the focal point of identifying subalternity once the history of its effect was completed.

In *Orientalism,* Edward Said, a teacher and a bourgeois intellectual, employed the term "organic intellectual" to describe his own role in critique of mostly nineteenth-century European texts that perpetuated and continue to perpetuate through repetition an idea of the Orient that then brought that Orient into existence for the purposes of policy as well as cultural impressions. For Said, the "strategic location" of the author in relation to his text, that is, the manifest content of his orientalism, needed to be read alongside the larger "strategic formation" of the various texts that went into the construction of the orientalist model—the underlying or latent content that underpins any textual variation.

By employing the terms *latent* and *manifest content* from Freud's dream analysis for describing hidden ideology and stated denotation, Said altered their meaning. For Freud, the latent content of a dream was constituted by the way various repressed (unconscious) desires are condensed and displaced onto figures residing in the preconscious, that is, inhabiting, through condensation or displacement, a figure (of speech or otherwise) that holds certain associations from the recent and remote past. These "refigurations" occur, then, in conscious speech when the speech is narrated, and may form meanings that run counter to the "manifest content," or the apparent meaning of the words. In Said's terms, the manifest content corresponds with the "strategic location" of the author to the text, and the latent content would then respond to his or her "strategic formation." In the Foucauldian terms he employs, this strategic formation is the network of discourses that contribute to a dominant paradigm. These paradigms in turn cause certain words, images, and other forms of discourse to carry meanings that relate to other texts existing at the moment. There seems, of course, nothing very psychoanalytic about this use of Freud's terms latent and manifest content. Not only do they suggest the social rather than the individual; they also draw on Foucault's idea of a "positive unconscious," which allows the analyst to read a level of meaning that eludes consciousness but is a constitutive part of it. This is almost a replay of Marxist demystification, one that runs counter to the organic yet dispersed understanding of individuated hegemony evident in Gramsci's, or, indeed, James's, work. Said's use of the latent and manifest reintroduces a strictly archaeological format to the unconscious that is disputed in the Freudian framework. Said's reading of psychoanalysis into Gramscian terminology fails to grasp the affective manifestations brought about through the process of worlding, indeed through the process of strategic formation he seeks to elaborate.

The psychoanalytic reading of organic intellectual and subaltern in the final part of *Dark Continents* extends the concepts of Freudian melancholia and of colonial melancholy. My understanding of the terms is elaborated through the forms of critical nationalism that emerge in melancholic remainders. The remainders are nonidentificatory, and are not driven by a conscious desire for nationhood or community. They do not build a sense of belonging, and are not employed in the service of community building through establishing shared histories or memories. On the contrary, they manifest an inability to remember, an interruption, or a haunting encryption that critiques national-colonial representation. It is the work of the organic intellectual to read critical agency manifested melancholically and spectrally in order to understand a form of nonrepresentational critique, one that cannot be represented but nonetheless alerts to a different form of disenfranchised, subaltern call for justice.

In his important essay "Mourning and Melancholia," Freud distinguished between these two closely related psychical states. Both states are responses to a loss, of a person, or indeed of something as abstract as an ideal, a country, or of liberty.[35] What distinguishes melancholia is a state of dejection, and a form of critical agency that is directed toward the self. Successful mourning involves the psychical work of narcissism, much in the way that infants need to direct all their energies inward (or *cathect* onto oneself, to use the military metaphor Freud employed to talk about the "occupation" of the object with psychical energies) so as to rebuild oneself by taking in the lost object and effectively assimilating it and the feelings of loss associated with it. Some forms of mourning may become pathological in instances when a known lost object is not released, but is constantly mourned as lost, and comes to constitute part of the character of an individual or group.[36]

In melancholia, such assimilation is not possible, and the lost object is swallowed whole. It does not replenish the ego, and narcissistic regeneration does not occur. Having swallowed the lost object whole (to use the metaphor Freud derives from the orality of narcissism as an infant replenishes itself through self-satisfaction), the subject is effectively stuck with the lost object, and therefore begins criticizing it, even though the subject *cannot recognize* and *does not know* what it is she or he criticizes. This means that the subject criticizes him or herself for attributes one would associate more readily with the lost object. While melancholia is paralyzing in Freud's terms, the inassimilable paradoxically becomes the site of what Freud calls "critical agency." This form of agency, he suggests, is rather like "conscience." The concept appears in Freud's essay "On Narcissism" to explain how the energies associated with self-building eventually have to be turned away from the self and directed toward an ideal. If a child initially directs its energies toward itself in order to fulfill its ideal self-image, it later directs them toward an ego-ideal, the combination of an idealized self-image and the values of the parents or collective. If such an ideal were lost, it follows, then, that such critical agency, manifested as anger, would be turned inward if the loss could not be assimilated by performing the work of mourning successfully. This critical identification with the lost object constitutes the burden of melancholia, and indeed the traumatic undoing of self and lost object as a result. Given that the concepts of mourning and melancholia concern loss and the manner in which loss manifests itself, they are also bound to the notion of temporality—the loss of something in time and how one is affected by that in the present and for the future.

We could think of this failure of narcissism through the mythological language of psychoanalysis, and call this critical agency Echo. Gayatri Chakravorty Spivak's criticism of psychoanalysis as an imposition of one model of self onto an entire world calls us to think through the mythologies at the heart of psychoanalysis, and the spurious gendering implied.[37] Whereas *narcissism* is a derogatory term usually applied to women, Spivak sees masculinity inscribing itself and once again failing to hear the distinction of Echo, fated at once to repeat and also be out of synch with the voice she repeats. Thinking of Echo as both a mythological figure and as one who shows how "the time is out of joint," she manifests as the spectral once again who gives a different sense of the temporality of nationhood. If Narcissus could exist through Echo alone, the narcissism of European nationalism and of the consolidated ego could perhaps give way to a discrepant temporality of nationhood sustained through the intellectual work of melancholic Hamlet and his ghosts. What Echo was to Narcissus, melancholia is to mourning. And if Freud would eventually transfer the critical agency found in melancholia into the normalizing function of the superego, I would salvage it, putting the melancholic's manic critical agency into the unworking of conformity, and into the critique of the status quo.

My concept of colonial melancholy is an adaptation from the work of the colonial psychiatrist Antoine Porot, who worked in Algiers and who determined that Algerian Muslim men suffered from what he called "pseudomelancholy." Whereas melancholy theorized in European psychiatry usually led to introspection and moral growth, Porot considered the melancholy quite distinct from that found in Europeans, or indeed in Berbers. In his estimation, Algerian Muslims' melancholy gave rise to violent behavior. Porot attributed this to physical difference in the brain. Working through the writings of Octave Mannoni and Frantz Fanon, as well as the work of Nicolas Abraham and Maria Torok on melancholia, pseudomelancholy can be understood quite differently. This is not least because the violent behavior to which Porot refers can be understood as a form of political protest rather than moral degeneracy. That is not to say that this political protest follows a teleology of its own that is unencumbered by psychical processes of melancholia. On the contrary, political revolutionary violence is a form of melancholia in unconscious response, perhaps, to the loss of an ideal. The ideal, in this context, is the right of subjecthood and the right not to be exploited, both of which lay in the rights of man that the French in Algeria ostensibly endorsed.

Melancholy and *melancholia* are critical terms refashioned and endorsed in this book as analytic tools for critiquing colonialism and its aftermath: the imperium of neocolonial late capitalism. The melancholic "critical agency" theorized by Freud is central to this retheorization, but critical agency is refashioned through the work of Abraham and Torok. Unlike Freud, Abraham and Torok, drawing on Sandor Ferenczi, distinguished between "incorporation" and "introjection." Introjection refers to the full psychical assimilation of a lost object or abstraction. They see introjection (rather like Freud's "mourning") as an ongoing process that allows for the assimilation of events in one's life ("lost" through the passage of time) into a self-generating life-story. Incorporation, on the other hand, refers to unsuccessful mourning. Incorporation, like the swallowing whole described above, can be the cause of the breakdown of signification in Abraham and Torok's terms. This breakdown blocks assimilation and manifests itself linguistically in terms of silence or demetaphorization. This block can be carried through generations as a phantom that haunts speech, unbeknownst to its carrier. For Abraham and Torok, the work of psychoanalysis is to identify the phantom, and bring it back into unhindered signification through assimilation.

The latter part of the argument (which constitutes the aim of a curative psychoanalysis) is inadequate to the task of social analysis. Abraham and Torok's work in the clinic may be quite a different case, but for the analysis of social issues, it goes against the spirit of Freudian analysis. Like Derrida, I find the analytic distinction between introjection and incorporation (and indeed between mourning, pathological mourning, and melancholia) of great importance, and yet the purported "success" of the work of mourning is tenuous because there will always be some remainder of the lost object.[38] In fact, to do away with this remainder would be an impossible and unethical assimilation of otherness, a denial of loss and of an engagement with the damage brought about by that loss. Abraham and Torok's theorization allows for a more extensive understanding of the work of mourning as a whole and of assimilation as a form of narcissism that can be linked to the dominant fiction of nationalism. But the inaccessible remainder is the kernel of melancholia, unknown, inassimilable, interruptive, and present.

Abraham and Torok's concept of demetaphorization, theorized as a symptom of melancholia, allows for an understanding of the material affect of loss as it manifests itself in language. Understanding affect is necessary for an understanding of the materiality of language.[39] Freud borrows the term, in pre-psychoanalytic writings, from German psychology. It refers to the emotion initiated by a traumatic event that subsequently gets detached from that event and attaches itself in another form in the psyche. "I know three mechanisms: transformation of affect (conversion hysteria), displacement of affect (obsessions) and . . . exchange of affect (anxiety neurosis and melancholia)."[40] The separation of the emotion, and its circulation and varied attachments, makes it quite an independent and yet evasive entity. And this is precisely why the recognition of the traumatic event is insufficient to "cure" all that it has brought about in the welfare of the analysand. In suggesting that it manifests itself in language, I am proposing that an inassimilable loss has brought about a manifestation in language.

Demetaphorization is one such manifestation. It involves an emptying out of the process of language and meaning formation from the word. A symptom of melancholia, in Abraham and Torok's work, demetaphorization is the phenomenon of antimetaphorical understanding and use of language. They suggest that language that makes sense only figuratively and suggestively will be translated into its most literal and unidimensional meaning, thus taking the dynamism out of language. The reason for this is an elaborate burial, or a secret encrypted in the prose of much European philosophy and literature that builds on narrative destruction or erasure. For Abraham and Torok the cause of melancholia is an underlying secret carried by the analysand from previous generations. This gives rise to the inability to assimilate successfully a loss of something. The phantom of the secret manifests itself in language as symptom when the secret is in danger of being revealed.

Encryption is a symptom of the illness of mourning, and haunting is a symptom of melancholia. Haunting occurs at the moment when encryption is in danger of being deciphered. Haunting constitutes the *work of melancholia*. Whereas Freud wrote of the work of mourning as the work of assimilating the lost object, the work of melancholia has a critical relation to the lost and to the buried. It manifests, sometimes in paralysis, stasis, or demetaphorization, loss, and it thus calls upon the inassimilable remainder. It does not merely call for inclusion, assimilation, reparation, or retribution. It calls for a response to the critical work of incorporation, and the ethical demand that such incorporation makes on the future.

In the context of new formerly colonized nation-states, the critical response to nation-statehood arises from the secret embedded in nation-state formation: that the concept of nation-statehood was constituted through the colonial relation, and needs to be radically reshaped if it is to survive without colonies, or without a concealed (colonial) other. The specter of colonialism (and indeed its counter—the specter of justice) thus hangs over the postcolonial independent nation-state. The critical melancholic relationship may manifest itself in a form of demetaphorization, a form of loss of the dynamism of representation necessitated by colonial politics (and this can be extended to capitalist economics). Such systems necessitate revolutionary binarism for subjectivity and the right of representation to be achieved. In the terms of Octave Mannoni, the "colonial situation" needs to be understood as a process through which people are constituted as the colonized and the colonizer in a manner that demands conceiving them as proper names that evade the process of their formation. In terms of power relations, as Albert Memmi insists, the binary relation inevitably comes into play, even though there may be forms of radical differentiation in class terms within these groups who, in revolutionary terms, must be locked in combat and who appear to have absolutely opposed interests.

The manner in which the specter looms over independent nation-state politics in terms of nativism, tribalism, and even fundamentalism may be informed by the manner in which the national self is conceived. And it could be illuminated by understanding how the psychoanalytic ego is problematized as nation-state subjecthood is recognized as psychically conflicted.

The Argument of *Dark Continents*

Dark Continents addresses Freud's use of national and colonial archaeology and anthropology to develop his concepts of the unconscious, the evolutionary trajectory of human civilization, and the origins of repression. It thereby establishes the grounds for reading psychoanalysis as a colonial discipline. Psychology, psychiatry, and psychoanalysis had all been employed by European colonizers in the service of European nation-states to assist in the analysis, pathologization, and repression of colonized peoples, sometimes reworking the basic assumptions of those fields to achieve this. During World War II and after, philosophers and decolonization activists alike began to refashion psychoanalysis to put it to more ethical use. Psychoanalysis offers a reading practice that looks to the haunted present and to the future and allows for a responsible feminist analysis of coloniality.

The argument of the book is not that psychoanalysis is simply a product that represents the spirit of its times; indisputably, that is the case. Nor is it that Freud should be rejected because he was a colonialist. Such an argument does not take us very far in thinking through the relationship between psychoanalysis and colonialism, but rather leads to stasis in the discussion of the mutual imbrication. Such a condemnation hardly addresses why psychoanalysis continues to be employed internationally in clinical applications as well as in theorizations of decolonization and postcoloniality emerging from outside its institutional home in Europe.

In *Dark Continents* Freudian psychoanalysis is resituated by considering the implications of its borrowings, as well as Freud's changing relations to these in the course of his career. Rather than simply an imperial imposition of a model of self onto different cultural and national arenas, the psychoanalytic self was constituted through the specifically national-colonial encounter of the late nineteenth and early twentieth centuries. Freud's borrowings from contemporary archaeology and anthropology document a shifting relationship between self and nationhood understood through those colonial projects. Freudian psychoanalysis documents the self's relationship to memory in a similar way to that in which the national is documented in national history at the height of Europe's colonial endeavors at the end of the nineteenth century.

Freud's linguistic and scholastic involvement in colonial exploration can be seen in his modeling of psychoanalysis on archaeological and anthropological insights. Famously, Freud was a great collector of ancient artifacts, from which he drew inspiration for his idea of the unconscious as something buried beneath layers of repression. Psychoanalysis was written in the discursive fields of these two disciplines that are, perhaps, more easily understood in terms of their colonial interests than psychoanalysis itself.

To say this is not to suggest that Freud should be either blamed or endorsed for his archaeology of knowledge, for his adoption of Darwin's and Frazer's evolutionary models, or indeed, for his erasure of cultural difference, particularly when he writes of women. He has been censured on that level, even though his views can be read as an inevitability of the moment within which he lived. Freud recognized the problem of European genealogy as the death of the synthetic European neurotic ego. He found in its place a destructive splitting. Freud recognized this as his own relationship to his nation changed because of anti-Semitism. It is through the notions of disavowal and melancholy that Freud begins to develop a different notion of self, one that embodies a critical nationalism. The critical nationalism embodied a critique of genealogy as the guiding principle of nation formation.

In addition to tracing the historical development of psychoanalysis through colonial disciplines, *Dark Continents* argues that Freud's own status in relation to the nation-state, the Habsburg Empire, and the Nazi occupation of Vienna brought about a radical reformulation of his concept of the ego through moving from a topographical model of archaeological layers of repression to an economic one concerning drives. The idea of the ego and its historicity changed because of the change in his political status and the subsequent shift in relation to the colonial disciplines he had once employed wholeheartedly. Freud's writings are exemplary documents of late-nineteenth-century Europe's theorizations of nationhood and selfhood as they were developed in response to colonial expansion. Of course, this political function of psychoanalysis was never explicitly stated.

It is this change in Freud's notion of subjectivity that allows for a psychoanalytic critique of the modern nation-state. Reading psychoanalysis against the grain reveals the fissures in modern European nation-statehood that would become more obviously apparent in Europe's colonies, emerging, as they were, in strife.

During the time of decolonization, particularly in the aftermath of World War II, there was widespread adoption of psychoanalytic narratives in both the metropolis and the colonies. They ranged from wholesale endorsement of psychoanalysis to critical partial reinscription of some of its techniques and assumptions. Psychoanalysis during the period of decolonization, and in the era that can optimistically if delusionally be named postcolonial, has been essential to theories of decolonization and postcoloniality, and it has drawn enormously from literary examples and models to develop its theories. As this arises from the contingency of psychoanalysis vis-à-vis narratives of nationalism and colonialism, it is imprudent to throw out the proverbial or indeed parochial baby with the bath water of political and economic colonialism. In France, for example, Jean-Paul Sartre developed an existential psychoanalysis that rejected the idea of an unconscious. For the most part, it has been in the French context that psychoanalysis has been employed in the period of decolonization. In the postwar years, Sartre's psychoanalytic notion of being consolidated the ego. Eventually Sartre would make use of this ontology to discuss the master narrative of colonialism. Many theorists of decolonization followed in his footsteps. Some coupled their praise with at times quite harsh critique, as did Frantz Fanon in yet another reinscription.[41] Others endorsed his commitment to decolonization more wholeheartedly and admired his prefaces to works by Memmi, Fanon, and Senghor, and his writing on the issue of race—Jewish, North African, and pan-African negritude. Sartre's more overtly political writing related to his literary criticism. His anticolonial prefaces give insight into the literary meanings of an existential psychoanalysis in the context of colonialism and of the negritude movement.

In these prefaces, Sartre explicitly introduced (and at times misrepresented) writings by decolonization theorists and activists to a white metropolitan audience. Much negritude writing, however, represents a very different relation to psychoanalysis than that suggested by Sartre, and one that changed considerably over time.

In his essay "Black Orpheus" Sartre claimed in highly androcentric, phallocentric language that the black man has to learn to feel whole again after experiencing colonialist racism.[42] The black man's poetry, Sartre insisted, is the only political poetry of the French language because it represents the antithesis of French colonial racism. In this scenario, the synthesis comes with communist internationalism and unpoetic prose and functions on a trajectory moving toward psychical wholeness. For Sartre, prose is crucial for revolutionary struggle.[43] In spite of its developmental dialectic, the essay was extremely influential among those parochializing psychoanalysis. It was through Sartre's work, and that of Octave Mannoni, that the contingency of the European nation-state and the colonies came into view. And the recognition of this mutually constitutive relationship led to further reinscription of psychoanalysis through the use of concepts like Aimé Césaire's "colonial trauma."

With changes in colonial relations, and also in anthropology, came challenges to the dominant psychoanalytic paradigms. Ellen Hellmann's Malinowskian anthropology would have an impact on Wulf Sachs's psychoanalytic study, *Black Hamlet;* the Ortigues would write *African Oedipus;* Gananath Obeyesekere returned to early Freud in *The Work of Culture;* and Ashis Nandy responded to primitivism with *The Savage Freud.* Underscoring the forms of psychical damage documented through writers like Aimé and Suzanne Césaire, René Ménil, Frantz Fanon, Albert Memmi, and Jacques Derrida, *Dark Continents* argues that the rescripting of psychoanalysis manifested colonial melancholy. If the critical *work of melancholia* manifests in haunting, the specter of colonialism is made apparent through psychoanalysis. The notion of the spectral is conceived as the colonialism affect, which includes the inability to introject the lost ideal of nation-statehood. Provincializing psychoanalysis involved understanding discrepant modernities that emerged in the colonies and also among those who were disenfranchised or abused by the European nation-state. Both psychoanalysis and the subjects it described were reshaped in the project of decolonization historically. But psychoanalysis also participated in the production of postcolonial subjects through European modernity and its manifestation in the world. The "specter" of colonialism produces discrepant versions of postcolonial transnational interactions. Something as elusive as the spectral, manifested in language as a poetics of melancholia, paradoxically grounds intellectual work and demonstrates its organic relation to what Fanon thought essential to the psychical workings of colonialism: the historical and the material.[44] The postcolonial intellectual is haunted by the call of justice for the future.

The final section of *Dark Continents* proposes, through reading works by Simone de Beauvoir and others, a transnational feminism informed by a reconfigured psychoanalysis. The book ends with the Hamlet "myth" in psychoanalysis through a reading of the work of Wulf Sachs, a Lithuanian Jewish "refugee" in South Africa who established the psychoanalytic institute there and who wrote a study of a native doctor introduced to him by Ellen Hellmann in 1937. In this concluding chapter, melancholia represents the ghostly workings of unresolvable conflict within the colonial subject.

Melancholia becomes the basis for an ethico-political understanding of colonial pasts, postcolonial presents, and utopian futures.

GENEALOGIES

1. Psychoanalysis and Archaeology

Is death not that upon the basis of which knowledge in general is possible — so much so that we think of it as being, in the area of psychoanalysis, the figure of that empirico-transcendental *duplication* that characterizes man's mode of thinking within finitude? Is desire not that which remains always *unthought* at the heart of thought? And the law-language (at once word and word-system) that psychoanalysis takes such pains to speak, is it not that in which all signification assumes an *origin* more distant than itself, but also that whose return is promised in the very act of analysis? Is it indeed true that this Death, and this Desire, and this Law can never meet within the knowledge that traverses in its positivity the empirical domain of man; but the reason for this is that they designate the conditions of possibility of all knowledge about man . . . ? — Michel Foucault, *The Order of Things: An Archaeology of the Human Sciences*

Foucault ends *The Order of Things: An Archaeology of the Human Sciences* with a section on "Psychoanalysis and Ethnology," in which he clarifies how the two disciplines, or perhaps more accurately counter-sciences or technologies "[make] possible knowledge about man in general."[1] The fundamental difference between the two is spatial interrelation, suggested in the first instance by the transference between analyst and patient and therefore in interpersonal relations. In the second, "the particular relation that the Western *ratio* establishes with all other cultures"[2] is characterized by the relationship between ethnologist and informant; the ideological parameters of that relationship are determined by the colonial origins of anthropology and nineteenth-century political geography. We will explore the connection between ethnology and psychoanalysis in more depth in the next chapter, in which the association between anthropology and psychoanalysis will be the main topic. Here, the connection between the archaeological and the psychoanalytic will be the focus, along with, following Foucault, the meaning of an *archaeology* of the human sciences. While Freud's language for developing psychoanalytic theories is very obviously highly indebted to the discipline of archaeology, it also reveals archaeology to be a *symptomatic* analysis of the past. Symptomaticity suggests something slightly different from a base structure that inevitably forms disciplinary superstructures as the archaeological metaphor may suggest. The idea of symptomaticity implies an interactive and mutually constitutive structure rather than a relationship between separate orders. Understanding the makeup of Freudian theory through archaeology sheds light on the very specific discursive formation of both.

If archaeology and psychoanalysis are mutually constitutive, then it is through the lens of what Foucault calls the third counter-science—linguistics—that this becomes apparent.

> Above ethnology and psychoanalysis, or, more exactly, interwoven with them, a third "counter-science" would appear to traverse, animate and disturb the whole constituted field of the human sciences; like them it would situate its experience in those enlightened and dangerous regions where the knowledge of man acts out [*le savoir de l'homme joue*], in the form of the unconscious and of historicity, its relation with what renders them possible. In "exposing" it, these three counter-sciences threaten the very thing that made it possible for man to be known. Thus we see the destiny of man being spun before our very eyes, but being spun backwards; it is being led back, by those strange bobbins, to the form of its birth, to the homeland that made it possible. And is that not one way of bringing about its end? For linguistics no more speak of man than do psychoanalysis and ethnology.[3]

This *third term,* which can be read as the counter-science that is linguistics, seems earlier in this study of the human sciences to be articulated somewhat differently as an *archaeology.* For this also is described in terms similar to a counter-science, or a methodology that makes knowledge about Man possible rather than increasing knowledge about Man. It is that sense of place, home, destiny, and time stretching back the threads of those bobbins that find articulation in the archaeological, for the death of those past homes is given relevance in the present because the present is revealed as an evolutionary product of the past. The archaeological, then, seems to be a mode of human science that demonstrates how "the knowledge of man acts out" through discourse, because it locates death and origins in the present through a shared imagined past. That past is mythical in its structure: the bobbins remind us of the Fates, and thus it is feminized. And concrete material evidence is presented as leading back, rather like Ariadne's thread that was supposed to save her from the monster. For Foucault, the counter-science reveals desire that exceeds law-language in its moment of articulation. It reveals how Man creates the knowledge of the group in a similar way to that in which the "I" is constituted.

In his "Foreword to the English Edition," Foucault claims that he calls his methodology archaeological "somewhat arbitrarily perhaps."[4] He distinguishes his text from other histories of science by claiming that they attempt

> to restore what eluded that consciousness: the influences that affected it, the implicit philosophies that were subjacent to it, the unformulated thematics, the unseen obstacles; it describes the unconscious of science. This unconscious is always the negative side of science—that which resists it, deflects it or disturbs it. What I would like to do, however, is to reveal a *positive unconscious* of knowledge: a level that eludes the consciousness of the scientist and yet is part of scientific discourse, instead of disputing its validity and seeking to diminish its scientific nature. . . . I have tried to determine the basis or archaeological system common to a whole series of scientific "representations" or "products."[5]

His archaeological system is one that reveals how *Man acts out,* and this *acting out* causes Foucault to understand archaeology as the quintessential if arbitrarily named locus of a "positive unconscious."

It is this model of archaeology as a *positive unconscious* and psychoanalysis as entailing a reconstructive archaeology that I want to address here, and with that in mind, the quotation that heads this chapter. For if psychoanalysis is an archaeology of the mind in terms of its investment in uncovering the dead and buried desire (*remembering*) and formulating those memories in current symptoms (*repeating and acting out*), it is also about a *working through* of that repressed and symptomatic material. One could identify this *working through* as the distinctive feature of Freudian psychoanalysis as it split off from Breuer's more cathartic model of cure as release of emotion.[6] Psychoanalysis does not merely, then, become a performative speech act that allows something buried to emerge, and to be displayed and repeated in the transferential relationship in a way similar to an archaeological artifact displayed in the museum. It also leads us to engage with, indeed to *work through,* those very depths of desire and mourning that allow us to subsume some of the past, consolidating it into our present-day lives. But as Freud tells us late in life, in 1937 just before he fled Nazi Austria, "the main difference lies in the fact that for the archaeologist the reconstruction is the aim and end of his endeavours while for analysis the construction is only a preliminary labour."[7] The psychoanalytic enterprise, says Freud, is more complex than the archaeological because of the nature of the material: the concrete material of archaeology is far easier to investigate than the psychological material with which the analyst works. Surprisingly, Foucault's emphasis on gauging a *positive unconscious* bears more relation to his contemporary Jacques Lacan than to Freud, who of course is far more explicitly involved in the language of archaeology.

If linguistics, psychoanalysis, and ethnology are disciplines in which Man *acts out,* according to Foucault, then archaeology certainly is as well. The translator's term[8] is indeed suggestive of the tripartite psychoanalytic process never adequately elaborated though sketched out early on in Freud's career: that of remembering, repeating—or acting out—and working through. Both the preliminary terms—*erinnern,* "remembering," and *agieren,* "acting out"—refer to particular relations of the present to the past that are preliminary stages in psychoanalytic work. *Digging up* the past and acknowledging its function in the past's influence on the present is sometimes thought of as the central function of analysis, thanks to pop psychology's celebration of the acknowledgment of sometimes rather dubious childhood memories and the popularization of the cathartic method. And the actions and reactions of a patient to the analyst within an analytic session characterize what Foucault (and at times Freud) see as the distinctive psychoanalytic technology—*transference.* The display for the analysts in the form of an actualization of a symptom or of infantile prototypes is coupled in Freud with a repetition or what could be called *performativity,* following Judith Butler's Foucauldian/Lacanian-influenced study of gender categories.[9]

For Lacan, psychoanalysis "is . . . [the] assumption of his history by the subject, in so far as it is constituted by the speech addressed to the other."[10] This form of repetitive display functions as personal (and perhaps cultural and ideological) trait. Although Lacan spends little effort elaborating Freud's concept of *Nachträglichkeit,* or deferred action, it is a key term for his translation of Freud's work into the arena of post-Saussurean linguistics. Lacan explains that Freud demands "a total objectification of proof so long as it is a question of dating the primal scene, but he no more than presupposes all the resubjectifications of the event that seem to him to be necessary to explain its effects at each turning point where the subject restructures himself—that is as many restructurings of the event that take place, as he puts it *nachträglich,* at a later date."[11] Lacan characterizes Freud as placing emphasis on *acting out* through the form of interlocution known as *transference:* "It is on the basis of this interlocution, in so far as it includes the response of the interlocutor, that the meaning of what Freud insists on as the restoration of continuity in the subject's motivations become clear. An operational examination of this objective shows us in effect that it can be satisfied only in the intersubjective continuity of the discourse in which the subject's history is constituted. . . . The unconscious is that part of concrete discourse, in so far as it is transindividual, that is not at the disposal of the subject in re-establishing the continuity of his conscious discourse."[12] Lacan identifies two stages: the form of performative *acting out* in discourse as it is manifested *nachträglich* (later), which allows a repetition of an event to take on a new form in a different historical context. Speech acts with an interlocutor also allow the patient to constitute his history in discourse in spite of the fact that the language of continuity has an unconscious itself. The work that is executed on the earlier speech reveals its unconscious but does so in another utterance that is also a *Nachträglichkeit* or *deferred action.*

This form of *acting out* can perhaps be worked through by understanding a *positive unconscious* of archaeology and the discipline for which it becomes so influential: psychoanalysis.[13] So as to elaborate this *positive unconscious,* and therefore in order to understand the vexed relationship of psychoanalysis to materiality, it is crucial to examine the ways in which psychoanalysis developed in its own historical context, that is, through the language of colonial disciplines such as archaeology and anthropology.

The emergence of psychoanalysis in the late nineteenth century occurred simultaneously with the theorization of nationalism and at the height of colonial expansion. How it relates to these historical phenomena can be examined through the archaeological approach, which is always collecting concrete materials. But the archaeological, as a model of a *positive unconscious,* also cannot fully account for the psychoanalytic. And further, archaeological theorists Rowlands and Robertson posit that "archaeology, especially in its modernist form, has been formed on the premise of a sense of loss, its subject matter conceived to be the recovery of tradition and a sense of community in contrast to the feeling of disenchantment for the world in which they live."[14] But it is the very departure of psychoanalysis from an archaeology that is symptomatic of that which cannot be accounted for in the nineteenth-century German archaeological approach: one which remembers and acts out, and one which was indeed so instrumental for Freud.

Freud initially identified with the nationalist, colonialist self-constructions of such explorers and archaeologists as Henry Morton Stanley and Heinrich Schliemann. Indeed, his early ideas of a self conceived archaeologically were based on this model of self-retrieval, which shared the paradigmatic structure of an archaeology retrieving its positive unconscious. Later in life, however, Freud was not able to sustain such a theory, or such an identification. This was partly because of the ontological shift brought about by his sense of despair at the violence of World War I, and partly because of his own persecution in anti-Semitic turn-of-the-century Vienna. My claim is not foundationalist. As Freud loses faith in the possibilities of representational politics and the "advance" of civilization, he changes his concept of self and indeed shows symptoms that problematize any notion of an archaeologically conceived ego. Eventually, Freud's concepts of melancholia and disavowal constitute symptoms of this loss of faith and become clearer when read through the lens of postcoloniality.

The Archaeological Metaphor

Freud's interest in archaeology is most vividly encountered in his admiration of Heinrich Schliemann's writings and archaeological work. In an 1899 letter to Wilhelm Fliess, Freud writes of reading Schliemann's *Ilios: The City and Country of the Trojans:* "I gave myself a present, Schliemann's

Ilios, and greatly enjoyed the account of his childhood. The man was happy when he found Priam's treasure because happiness comes only with the fulfillment of a childhood wish. This reminds me that I shall not go to Italy this year. Until next time!"[15] Freud refers to Schliemann's rather hesitant autobiographical first chapter in which he justifies the place of autobiography in the archaeological text. The chapter, which was initially excluded from the English and French editions, was then revised for them. In it, Schliemann assures his readers that he inserts it not "from any feeling of vanity, but from a desire to show how the work of my later life has been a natural consequence of the impressions I received in my earliest childhood. . . . The pickaxe and spade for the excavation of Troy and the royal tombs of Mycenae were both forged and sharpened in the little German village in which I passed eight years of my earliest childhood."[16] The boyhood dream, or the earliest wish, then comes into fruition and creates Schliemann as a modern-day Odysseus. Like Troy, his early wish has been uncovered and has led to a discovery. As it comes to the surface, it connects the text of archaeology and the text of the self. The moment in which the self can be synthesized through the archaeological narrative is also the moment in which Troy comes to life but is also created as a museum piece. Its place within a stratified layer consigns it to prehistory rather than allowing it to intrude apocalyptically upon the present in the guise of myth.

For Freud, the *Schliemanniad* occupies two functions. It serves to recall his own desire for travel to a place of classical antiquity, which leads him to add in his letter to Fliess that Schliemann's quest reminds him rather inexplicably "that I shall not go to Italy this year. Until next time!"[17] Freud articulates his own childhood wish, which will lead him to travel to Italy twenty times during his life in spite of his train phobia, a symptom that came to be known as his "Rome neurosis." He often traveled with his unmarried sister-in-law, Minna, who shared a home with Freud and Martha and was one of his main interlocutors. He showed himself to be a product and admirer of a Latin humanism deeply entrenched in a European aesthetic very different from the Jewish heritage into which he was born.[18] Secondly the aesthetic, as exemplified in the *Schliemanniad,* consigned the past to a stratified layer that defined but could not interrupt a moment of civilization. The preliminary work of civilization, then, would remain either repressed or firmly within the realm of memory. It did not allow for a disturbance of the present, but rather would be accounted for so as not to appear as a symptom in the present. As Freud wrote in "The Question of Lay Analysis," "In the mental life of little children today we can still detect the same archaic factors which were once dominant generally in the primeval days of human civilization. In his mental development the child would be repeating the history of his race in an abbreviated form."[19]

The exploratory endeavors of Schliemann the archaeologist were, however, insufficient to develop the psychoanalytic model. Donald Kuspit reads the archaeological as not only intrinsic to but also representative of the psychoanalytic one, resulting in a system for self-understanding that "absolutizes" the archaic and primitive aspects of the psyche.[20] Discussing both Freud's interest in archaeological finds and his scholarship, Kuspit draws from "Dora," where the analyst is referred to as the "conscientious archaeologist,"[21] and to "Constructions in Analysis," in which the archaeological metaphor is probably developed most fully. Kuspit addresses the confusion between the temporal and the spatial metaphors in Freud's archaeological terminology, which understands a temporal event or a disjuncture in memory as a spatial stratification. He suggests that analysts should be wary of a stratified description of the unconscious in which there is movement from the conscious to the preconscious, under which lies the unconscious.

This idea is repeated in the layering of manifest content and latent content in dream theory, in which, as Sabine Hake has maintained, "the shift from categories of originality (primary, secondary) to categories of representation . . . does not really eliminate such hierarchies."[22] For Freud understood dreams, at least partially, as interpretations of archaeological finds. This is exemplified in this theory he draws from Strümpell: "Dreams sometimes bring to light, as it were, from beneath the deepest piles of débris under which the earliest experiences of youth are buried in later times, pictures of particular localities, things or people."[23]

Seeking out what he sees as an opposition between existentialism and phenomenology, Kuspit calls upon Merleau-Ponty to describe the moment of the present in any perception of the past for both the analysand and the analyst—he calls in fact for an anthropological approach, saying: "The psychoanalyst must become a truly participant observer; must catalyze the patient's own psycho-archaeological awareness. . . . Freud used his antiquities to summon up the spirits of his own underworld and to reflect on them, to question them about himself. There were in effect inside him, instruments of self-analysis. They were transference objects, in which he could read his own prehistory."[24] "The scene of memory" of which he writes necessitates a convergence between the spatial and temporal rather than a stratification—hence the anthropological approach (and indeed metaphor) in Kuspit's own writing. But if it is the case that "archaeology signifies the convergence of collective and individual psychology, and of the phylogenetic and ontogenetic in the psyche" in Freud as well as Jung, then the anthropological memory might do something similar in terms of the state or the group.

One could claim, however, as recent critical archaeological theorists have, that the function of archaeology is similar in its ability to supply the group with a memory that connects the group while acknowledging a distinction between the individual and the group. It exemplifies a way of being in the world, and it turns the hidden and concealed of the earth into the matter of the world. While it is true that Schliemann's autobiographical piece spoke of fulfilling his own childhood desires through the performance of archaeological discovery, those childhood desires themselves were constituted by the group, in this case the "little German village in which [he] passed eight years of [his] earliest childhood." As Michael Rowlands contends, in the field of archaeology too, "the search for cultural origins has successfully organized much archaeological writing in the West until recently precisely because of the appeal of collective identity."[25]

So, while Kuspit's restructuration of the psyche according to an anthropological rather than an archaeological principle is on one level quite appealing, it relies on a reading of Freud that removes ambiguity from his texts, and also on an identification of archaeology that fails to adequately acknowledge its complexity. For Freud's own texts are more ambiguous than Kuspit allows for. The simultaneity of the past in the guise of a symptom reveals, in fact, a Freud who is far more anthropologically inclined in terms of disciplinary spatio-temporality. His explicit love seems to be for archaeology, and yet it is the manifestation of desire in relation to the dead that fascinates Freud rather than the dead (or buried) themselves. It is the desire to unconceal the dead, give figure to the absent, and present a history associated with place and temporal belonging. While Strachey's translation often elides variations and ambiguities for the sake of an authoritative but narrow technical vocabulary of psychoanalysis,[26] there are ambiguities in Freud's texts. After all, the problem of the symptom comes to a head in the concept of the uncanny and of déjà vu and is theorized as one in which the presence of the past in the present is at issue, and there are also texts in which psychoanalysis is very explicitly differentiated from archaeology.

Freud's Beloved Treasures: Schliemann and the Archaeological Paradigm

On the wall of Freud's study in Vienna could be found a photograph of the "Gradiva," a Roman bas-relief. Next to it hung a reproduction of Ingres's depiction of Oedipus interrogating the Sphinx. These, along with many more ancient Greek, Egyptian, Roman, and Oriental artifacts, were found in Freud's house and were transported to London when he was forced to escape Nazi Vienna in 1938.[27] His love for both archaeological treasures and of neoclassical invocation of Greek mythology extended throughout his adult life, not only through his own collection but also in documents from his personal life. In a letter to Martha Bernays in 1885 from Paris on the eve of his first meeting with Charcot, Freud wrote to his "beloved treasure" with great pleasure about his visit to the Greek, Roman, Assyrian, and Egyptian rooms at the Louvre, and the obelisk from Luxor at the Place de la Concorde: "Imagine a genuine obelisk, scribbled all over with the most beautiful birds' heads, little seated men and other hieroglyphs, at least three thousand years older than the vulgar crowd round it, built in honor of the king whose name today only a few people can read and who, but for the monument, might be forgotten. . . . For me these things have more historical than aesthetic interest."[28] And a few months later he writes to Minna: "Paris [is like] a vast overdressed Sphinx who gobbles up every foreigner unable to solve her riddles."[29]

The intellectual climate in which Freud lived had seen a massive increase in interest in antiquities, and particularly in an almost scientific relation to their historical significance. Since 1859 when Man's prehistorical presence was established and when Darwin published his evolutionary theories that were to concretize former evolutionary speculations with biological remains, archaeology's marriage to both science and history was confirmed. In the words of Sir John Lubbock, the most popular archaeologist of the day who was to refine ideas of temporal stratification: "A new branch of knowledge has arisen. . . . Archaeology forms the link between geology and history."[30] While these important changes were going on in the field of archaeology, interestingly Freud focuses not on the popular text by Lubbock, but on works that are more imaginatively inclined than scientifically rigorous. For example, while the texts of Wilhelm Jensen's *Gradiva* and Schliemann's *Ilios* feature very strongly in Freud's work, it is the tension between the past and the present that always seems fascinating to him, rather than the accuracy of the past. In fact, in both the body of Zoë, in *Gradiva,* and of Schliemann, in *Ilios,* it is the relationship between desire and death that is of primary interest.[31] It is giving face to the dead, and giving life to the buried. It is understanding desire as the instrument of worlding.

Schliemann's probably highly fabricated memories[32] of discussing his ambition to unearth Troy with his father (whose love of Homer had rubbed off on his son) cause Freud to marvel at his childhood ambition and his fulfilled wishes. Schliemann, after all, was not initially part of a community of archaeologists either of the academic sort or of the museological. Although by the 1870s archaeology had become a branch of classical studies in Germany, it was not through this sort of academic training that Schliemann arrived at Troy, although of course his love of languages (he knew Latin, Arabic, and a number of modern European languages) and particularly Homer had led him to study Greek, both ancient and modern. It was, rather, through a love of Homer but also through a desire to deny the literary—that is, to read in a demetaphorized manner rather like Freud, who insists, according to Mary Jacobus, on a scientific reading of *Gradiva,* ignoring and dismissing its literary qualities.[33] The Homeric text initiated his desire, and yet it was the imaginative transferential relationship to it that archaeology ostensibly worked against. Restoring the absent is not the same as giving face to the absent figure, or breathing life into the dead. Contradicting his father, who had in childhood maintained that Troy was legendary and not historical, Schliemann sought, with the new archaeological tools and theories around him, to concretize Troy, and to prove it to be historical.

The autobiographical chapter of *Ilios* dramatizes a life wholly and single-mindedly focused on the Trojan excavations. After a difficult childhood (because he was sent away from home when his father the pastor was defrocked for misuse of church funds and probably also for adultery), in his early adulthood, he made much money. Schliemann omits the reasons for his departure from home, focusing more on his childhood love, Minna, with whom he shared an interest in Troy. He eventually left the protection of his uncle and his apprenticeship to travel all over the world as a businessman trading in indigo and gold in Amsterdam (where he was rejected by Minna, who had married someone else), St. Petersburg, and California. Having increased his fortune considerably by exchanging gold dust for coins with the Rothschilds in London, he could take up his first love again, studying archaeology for two years in Paris, where he frequented the Louvre and read and studied with such figures as Ernest Renan and Emile Egger. So all of Europe, and some international trade, went into the making of Schliemann.

The adventurous traveler would eventually return to his first love, Hisarlik, and with the aid of trained archaeologists and his second wife, a Greek woman named Sophia, he discovered what he thought to be Homer's Troy, and from it he created himself as Odysseus the traveler and his wife as Helen, adorning *his treasure* with the jewels of times gone by. His marriage to Sophia, who was seventeen when she wed the forty-seven-year-old Schliemann, had been arranged by his friend and ancient and modern Greek tutor, Archbishop Theoclitus Vimbos. Sophia was his cousin, and he sent Schliemann a photo of her along with a matrimonial prospectus in response to Schliemann's request that he "wanted to marry a girl of pure Greek heritage who resembled Helen of Troy . . . she should be unsophisticated as well as good-looking . . . [like a] docile and obedient plant, clever and intelligent." Thus he could educate her "according to my will."[34] In the autobiographical piece, the first wife is not mentioned, and there is little discussion about his second wife, other than the fact that she accompanies him. This was the moment of display of the childhood dream, to his wife, in his writings and communications with archaeologists, scholars, and the public alike, and eventually in museums.

Schliemann writes the autobiographical chapter as a defense of his own work, and as an assurance to his readers of his love for the artifacts. Having established himself as a wealthy businessman first, his imaginary interlocutor is the skeptical critic who sees him as interested more in capital than in cultural heritage. His single-mindedness seems to be testimony; his children (Sergius and Nadeshda by his first wife, and Agamemnon and Andromache by the Greek Sophia) will be left a fortune "large enough to enable them to continue their father's scientific explorations without ever touching their capital."[35] He adds: "I avail myself of this opportunity to assure the reader that, as I love and worship science for its own sake, I shall never make a traffic of it. My large collection of Trojan antiquities have a value which cannot be calculated, but they shall never be sold. If I do not present them in my lifetime, they shall at all events pass, in virtue of my last will, to the museum of the nation I love and esteem most."[36] Establishing the future waves in scientific exploration and passing them on to the next generation, he narrates a childhood passion in order to justify his actions, and assures his readers not only of a scientific love, but also of patriotism for Germany, in spite of the fact that he had become a U.S. citizen in 1868 (and not in 1850 as he claims in *Ilios*).

Ilios will call upon the expertise of great German anthropologists, linguists, and orientalist philologists like Max Müller to comment on the artifacts, bringing their specialist knowledge of, for example, the auspicious Indo-Aryan symbol of the *svastika* and its inverse, the *sauvastika* found in the "third burnt city." Nineteenth-century archaeology had a mission to *save* the artifacts. It is this discourse of salvation of the past and of the foreign that links the colonial and the archaeological so forcefully. And it is the fantasy of reenactment, bolstered through the wealth of international trade, that fortified this way of being-in-the-world and of claiming historicity and national loyalty.

The models of archaeology changed with Schliemann, at least in popular consciousness. While the archaeological societies may have criticized him in his time and after for his fabrication and his lack of care concerning documentation, his appeal was of course extremely widespread. And with the established veracity of a shared past of classical civilization in the moment of the development of the European nation-states, an assertion of a self with an evolutionary past that can come to fruition in the present through excavation and restoration was also established. For this heroic Odyssean figure did not bring Odysseus to life again by eliding the historical strata in between, but did so by establishing an evolutionary difference between past and present, drawing upon a Romantic model of European civilization with its roots in Ancient Greece. Of course, with the recent work of Martin Bernal, as well as the political debates about where Priam's treasures should be located in the aftermath of World War II and again since the razing of the Berlin Wall, the archaeological has been shown to function in the establishment of nation-states as well as in the structure of the boyhood dream fulfilled as an extension of an evolutionary model.[37] As Grahame Clark was to note as early as 1939, "In totalitarian lands, . . . [archaeology] has been deliberately harnessed to subserve the aims of the State without any necessary regard to objective truth. Under the fascist regimes of both Germany and Italy, the very emblems of which, the swastika and fasces, were derived from antiquity, archaeology has been exploited to subserve odious and predatory aims. . . . It was surely no accident that the Nazi regime in Germany should have encouraged archaeological activities."[38]

Schliemann's boyhood dream locates prehistory as feminine; through adorning his wife with the artifacts, he finds once more his first love, Minna. And this of course is something repeated in Freud. Schliemann's other great find, Mycenae beneath the Athenian Acropolis, plays a part in Freud's theories of female sexuality.

The Archaeological Feminine:
Minoan-Mycenae and the Dark Continent

Die Einsicht in die präödipale Vorzeit des Mädchens wirkt als überraschung, ähnlich wie auf anderem Gebiet die Aufdeckung der minoisch-mykenischen Kultur hinter der griechischen.[39]

[Our insight into this early, pre-Oedipus, phase in girls comes to us as a surprise, like the discovery, in another field, of the Minoan-Mycenaean civilisation behind the civilisation of Greece.[40]]

The contemporary female bears traces of an evolutionary anterior phase, and Freud's discovery of it places him alongside Schliemann, and allows him to exist firmly within a later stage of civilization: the Greek from which he takes his mythology and theory of Oedipus. That which is perceived as primitive in the eyes of both nineteenth-century Europe and by the Greeks is consistently associated with the feminine. Freud's theorization of Medusa, for example, shows this very clearly: "The terror of Medusa is the terror of castration that is linked to the sight of something . . . becoming stiff. . . . Thus in the original situation it offers consolation to the spectator: he is still in possession of a penis, and the stiffening reassures him of the fact. To display the penis (or any of its surrogates) is to say: 'I am not afraid of you. I defy you. I have a penis.' "[41]

The implications of Freud's use of Greek mythology to gain insight into Minoan-Mycenaean civilization are manifold, for Oedipus becomes the model for all men, even if seers like Tiresias, and occasionally Freud, can see them for what they are. The ability to have this insight is also the ability to stand independently of that past, without interruption by the buried Minoan-Mycenaean influence. Peter Rudnytsky notes a similarity in the Greek between the words used for sight, blindness, and castration.[42] And it is the maintenance of insight into the prehistoric that seems closely associated with disciplinary establishment. When Freud's language uses archaeology, he is not simply applying a metaphor to gain acceptance in scientific circles. He is also *acting out*. As the very Oedipus he analyzes, he too fears castration, and the inability to assert a discipline, and to be an important part of an intellectual community. He erects himself as archaeologist of the mind, an image of himself that he will not be able to sustain later in his life. His own insight is an assertion, but it is performed on the backs of femininity and the primitive. His own study of Oedipus and the mythology associated with him becomes a substitute itself for the riddle of the Sphinx, and of a defiance of the riddle of femininity.

Oedipus's symbolic castration is thus substituted for the primacy of his heroism: his erection to power as he solves mysteries. "A study of dreams, phantasies and myths has taught us that anxiety about one's eyes, the fear of going blind, is often enough a substitute for the dread of being castrated. The self-blinding of the mythical criminal, Oedipus, was simply a mitigated form of the punishment of castration—the only punishment that was adequate for him by the *lex talionis*. We may try on rationalistic grounds to deny that fears about the eye are derived from fears about castration. . . . But this . . . does not account adequately for the substitutive relation between the eye and the male organ."[43] Freud's desire to be Oedipus is very clearly stated. Rita Ransahoff tells the following story:

> The small group of his followers in Vienna gave him a medallion with his profile on one side and a Greek design of Oedipus answering the Sphinx on the other. Around it was the line from Sophocles's *Oedipus Tyrannus:* "Who divined the famed riddle and was a man most mighty." When he was presented with this medallion, Freud turned pale. He explained that as a student in the University, he would stroll around the court looking at the busts of former illustrious professors. He had a fantasy that one day his bust would be there, and on it would be inscribed this line of Sophocles. In 1955, years after this daydream, [Ernest] Jones presented a bust of Freud to the University of Vienna to be placed in the arcade. On it was inscribed the line from Sophocles.[44]

Erected as the solver of the riddle of the Sphinx, of the riddle of femininity, of the pre-Oedipal stage of sexuality that he characterizes as the

Minoan-Mycenaean behind the Greek, Freud constructs woman as castrated. And it is through his *performance* as Oedipus that this is accomplished. Schliemann assures his audience through the narration of a childhood dream fulfilled that he is not a cheat like his father, but someone quite different. Filial irreverence established, he erects himself anew.

Neither Schliemann nor Freud conceived their archaeological practices as racial. But given the evolutionary theories of Darwin as well as the obvious tribal routes of Medusa, the primitive figure is racially marked in nineteenth-century archaeology and in psychoanalysis. And the position of women is curiously linked to the racial, both in Schliemann's adorning of his Greek wife, and in Freud's conflation of the Minoan-Mycenaean with woman, the recognition of himself as foreign in relation to the Sphinx, and of course most famously in his appellation of woman as "dark continent."[45] Jean Walton has analyzed the ways in which theorizations of women's performativity from Joan Rivière to Judith Butler have been inadequate to the task of understanding how racial difference plays a seminal role in this performance. Perhaps it is this early conflation of the two and the total erasure of black women within that conflation that gives rise to this in spite of, and perhaps because of, the very different roles assigned to the sexes historically in archaeological, psychoanalytic, and colonial relations — and in spite of the massive discourse in colonial science about the size of black women's genitalia, which, as Sander Gilman and Anne McClintock have shown, reaches its apotheosis in the Hottentot Venus.[46]

When Freud makes use of the metaphor of the dark continent, he is expressing some of his own anxieties about the status of psychoanalysis. It is in "The Question of Lay Analysis" that he writes:

> Vom Geschlechtleben des kleinen Mädchens wissen wir weniger als von dem des Knaben. Wir brauchen uns dieser Differenz nicht zu schämen, ist doch auch das Geschlechtsleben des erwachsenen Weibes ein *dark continent* für die Psychologie. Aber wir haben erkannt, daß das Mädchen den Mangel eines dem männlichen gleichwertigen Geschlechtsgliedes schwer empfindet, sich darum für minderwertig hält, und daß dieser "Penisneid" einer ganzen Reihe charakteristisch weiblicher Reaktionen den Ursprung gibt.[47]
>
> [We know less about the sexual life of little girls than of boys. But we need not feel ashamed of this distinction; after all, the sexual life

of adult women is a "dark continent" for psychology. But we have learnt that girls feel deeply their lack of a sexual organ that is equal in value to the male one; they regard themselves on that account as inferior, and this "envy for the penis" is the origin of a whole number of characteristic feminine reactions.[48]]

"The Question of Lay Analysis" was a defense of Theodore Reik, a member of the Vienna Psychoanalytic Society who was accused of *Kurpfuscherei*—treating patients without having a medical degree. It was also, however, a defense of psychoanalysis as a discipline that rejected the necessity of a medical degree. Freud went so far as to say that a medical degree may even work against successful psychoanalytic treatment. The defense is written in the style of a Socratic dialogue, but without conclusion. Freud's interlocutor is an *impartial person*.

Freud explains that "we need not feel ashamed" about our lack of knowledge of female sexuality, he metaphorizes woman as the "dark continent," and in this blurring of her specificity he transfers the shame that "we need not feel" about our lack of knowledge onto her. She ends up with the shame: for her "lack" of sexual organ; for her "inferiority" with respect to the male; in short, for her envy for the penis. And thus his lack of knowledge has been displaced onto her lack of penis. Perhaps fearing her difference, he makes her other, obliterating the specificity and difference of her body by turning it into a fetishized metaphor of the unknown: "dark continent," and it is defined as lack. Curiously, it is here that the concept of Otherness for Freud is formed. Although the Other is not intrinsically racialized or sexualized, it does seem that travel and exploration are the instigators of a theory of the Other, and in this case, the Other of man and of Europe are constructed as inferior versions of this "self," becoming self in a castrated form.

Leaving the metaphor of the "dark continent" in its original English, Freud grants it a further aura: of colonialism and its projection of a mysterious Africa. The disciplinary blind spot is displaced onto imprecise metaphor: the more it is explored, the more it is shrouded in mystery. The metaphor of the "dark continent" first came into use in H. M. Stanley's explorer's narrative about Africa: *Through the Dark Continent*.[49] Interestingly, Stanley's explorations also manifested a deep anxiety about women. Twice he left for travels abroad that almost inevitably led to broken engagements. The second of these, to Alice Pike, after whom his ship was named, led her to write in an autobiographical novel that she had indeed made it possible for him to travel. Africa's mysteriousness was for Stanley as feminized as it was for Freud. For the former, this would lead to immense cruelty even as it bolstered the explorer's reputation. For the latter, it would lead to projecting his lack of knowledge about women onto his theory of them.[50] Reading Stanley alongside Freud reveals unlikely similarities in their prose. Stanley opens the chapter of his autobiography called "Through the Dark Continent" with:

> In a camp in the heart of Africa, not far from Lake Bangweolo, David Livingstone, the travelling evangelist, lay dead. . . . Let me see: Livingstone died in endeavouring to solve the problem of the Lualaba River. John Hanning Speke died by a gun-shot wound during a discussion as to whether Lake Victoria was one lake, as he maintained it to be; or whether, as asserted by Captain Burton, James McQueen, and other theorists, it consisted of a cluster of lakes. . . . To know the extent of the worth of that lake would be worth some trouble. Surely, if I can resolve any of these, which such travellers as Dr. Livingstone, Captains Burton, Speke, and Grant, and Sir Samuel Baker left unsettled, people must needs believe that I discovered Livingstone!
>
> A little while after the burial of Livingstone at Westminster, I strolled over to the office of the "Daily Telegraph," and pointed out to the proprietors how much remained shrouded in mystery in Dark Africa. . . . Africa includes many dangers from man, beast and climate.[51]

Stanley's trip to the "dark continent" is inspired by the dead Livingstone, and its Dickensian autobiographical posturing is as much based on deceit arising from class anxiety as it is about fantasy. The purpose of his journey is not merely to uncover the truth about the lakes of Africa, but to prove that it was he who found Livingstone. In the guise of a quest for the lake, his real desire is to discover the effect of the lake on the man. The fellow explorer for whom Stanley searched far and wide across Africa had, it seems, been overwhelmed by Dark Africa's shrouded mysteries. Dark Africa, like Medusa, has turned the living to stone.[52] Stanley must overcome the threat of castration by the terrifying Medusa that is Africa, and stand erect as he who conquered her mysteries. David Livingstone and John Speke call out to Stanley from beyond the grave, urging him on, not only to the solving of a mystery but to immortality.

The archaeological narrative is, then, predetermined by an autobiographical myth. Both narratives firmly establish an "I," the autobiographical subject, as their organizing principle. Stanley, whose background was even more modest than revealed in autobiographical writing, takes himself, through colonial exploration, out of the class of the poor house into a class of heroic explorers. At times he presented himself as an American, as if to further dramatize his pioneering persona. And his wife Dorothy aids him in this, not only because of her own superior class background, but also importantly because of her editorship of his autobiography after his death. If archaeology is about loss, and about the reconstruction of the past so as to create the present, so is editorship of an autobiography. Here, the response to the dead is a reconstruction in order that he can be adequately mourned, and introjected, for what else can it mean to write someone else's *auto*biography once they are dead? From Dorothy Stanley, editor and coauthor of the autobiography:

> The pathos of this Autobiography lies in the deprivations and denials of those early years, here recorded for the first time. Yet these sufferings, as he came to realise, were shaping and fitting him for the great work he was to perform; and his training and experiences were perhaps the finest a man could have had, since, day by day, he was being educated for the life that lay before him.[53]

She explains how the book was assembled:

> The first nine chapters of the book are Autobiography, covering the early years of Stanley's life. In the remaining chapters, the aim has been to make him the narrator and interpreter of his own actions. This has been done, wherever possible, by interweaving, into a connected narrative, strands gathered from his unpublished writings.
>
> These materials consist . . . of journals and notebooks . . . a number of lectures, upon his various explorations; these he prepared with great care but were never published. . . . Finally, there are his letters; in those to acquaintances, and even to friends, Stanley was always reserved about himself and his feelings; I have therefore used only a few of those written to me, during our married life.[54]

Dorothy's reconstruction of Stanley demonstrates the desire for completion in response to death that serve in the reconstruction of archaeological myths as national functions. The response to the dead, then, is to build up what is lost in order to sustain a temporal framework of development that Stanley himself compares to the archaeological. In his use of archaeological and exploratory images, Freud echoes Stanley. Witness two archaeological metaphors, drawn from Stanley and Freud respectively: "Forty years of my life has passed, and this delving into my earliest years appears to me like an exhumation of Pompeii, buried for centuries under the scoriae, lava, and volcanic dust of Vesuvius. To the man of the Nineteenth Century, who paces the recovered streets and byeways of Pompeii, how strange seem the relics of the far distant life! Just so appear to me the little fatherless babe, and the orphaned child."[55] And from Freud in his reading of Jensen's *Gradiva:*

> In his last simile . . . —of the "childhood friend who has been dug out of the ruins"—the author has presented us with the key to the symbolism of which the hero's delusion made use in disguising his repressed memory. There is, in fact, no better analogy for repression, by which something in the mind is at once made accessible and preserved, than burial of the sort to which Pompeii fell a victim, and from which it could emerge once more through the work of spades. Thus it was that the young archaeologist was obliged in his phantasy to transport to Pompeii the original of the relief which reminded him of the object of his youthful love. The author was well justified, indeed, in lingering over the valuable similarity which his delicate sense had perceived between a particular mental process in the individual and an isolated historical event in the history of mankind.[56]

Freud's passage reads uncannily like Stanley's; he appears, as does Hanold, the story's protagonist, to be like those men of the nineteenth century of whom Stanley writes. Psychoanalysis as a mode of discursive analysis thus reflects this "nineteenth century" narrative. Formed of this narrative, it is naturally attuned to it, analyzes it wonderfully.

The metaphor of the dark continent, then, signals a similarity between these nineteenth-century narratives: psychoanalytic, archaeological, and colonial explorations. The "dark continent" connotes a great deal, but denotes nothing: it is indefinable, and it is primitive, but it allows its explorers a heroic narrative of discovery and a feminization of the land. David Macey suggests that Freud "appears to be blissfully ignorant of the political connotations of his metaphor."[57] And yet the defense of analysis as another exploratory discipline is politically placed by the analogies that seem relevant. Freud's defense has to function analogically, for the discourse of medical science in which he is trained is inadequate to the task of describing psychoanalysis and developing a language for the mental processes. But the analogy suggests something else as well. The very notion of the Other and of the unknown was made apparent in relation to new-found space and encounters with difference, against which the *sameness* of the self was established. Even mystical Otherness, usually associated with the foreign, was described by Freud as an "oceanic feeling."

But, says Freud in his 1927 postscript to "The Question of Lay Analysis," "Unluckily analogies never carry one more than a certain distance; a point is soon reached at which the subjects of the comparison take divergent points."[58] He says this regarding radiology, but it holds equally in relation to the colonial archaeological language. While Freud's language in "Delusions and Dreams in Jensen's *Gradiva*" is close to Stanley's, his analysis of the text seems to tell another story.

Gradiva

Freud was introduced to *Gradiva* by Jung. In a letter, Freud told Jung that he did not think that it was a particularly fine piece of literature, although he was fascinated by the Pompeiian image, Gradiva herself.[59] The text, like the Gradiva herself, allows Freud a thematization, and a condensation, of the sexual, the mythical, and the archaeological.

The similarities of Jensen's work with the language of both Schliemann and Freud cannot go unnoticed. But what is striking about both *Gradiva* and Freud's own reading of it is the inability to leave the archaeologist as the analogous figure to the psychoanalyst, and indeed in this instance to the literary critic. For the archaeologist is both scientist, and therefore analyst, as well as patient; therefore the obsessive demands of and fascination for the science of the day seem somewhat pathological. The scientific analysis of things lost through historical events or desires lost through the repressions of collective modern living and civilization's superego[60] does not help us with living in the present, with our response to the past and death, or with understanding our desire for the Other.

Gradiva is an impossible text to read through the lens of analogy because the parallels drawn in it are not stable. Mary Jacobus notes those drawn between the role of Gradiva and that of the literary text; between the relation of the marble image to the woman and that between "fiction" to real life; and between "woman" and "theory."[61] But where is Freud in this scenario, and with whom does he identify? Given his interest in archaeology, one might expect it to be Hanold, the archaeologist; but archaeology itself seems to be on the couch, and the analyst is the live version of Gradiva, Zoë Bertgang.

Freud's later note on the limitations of analogy seems important to remember here, for no position is easily identifiable with psychoanalysis even though many analogies seem possible. His analysis of the novella reads like a *phantasm*—an imaginary scenario in which the patient identifies with all the characters. In analyzing the text, Freud acts out the limitations of self-analysis, in which the transferential relationship disappears; thus interpersonal interaction has to be played out through a form of splitting. Phantasm allows different characters made out of one the chance to interact and to play out, or act out the transferential relationship so important to psychoanalysis. There are clearly multiple possible identifications within *Gradiva* that evoke different disciplinary and romantic discourses. In fact, imagining an "I" that is not split would be extremely difficult here in this story that contains many of the prevailing narratives or dominant fictions of the day. Here, *the knowledge of Man acts out* through the partial identifications that go against the construction of the self in the dominant fiction of nineteenth-century archaeology. The archaeologist of Jensen's story, Hanold, has devoted his life to archaeology. His most recent archaeological quest has been inspired by a dream in which he sees a living woman whom he identifies as the Pompeiian bas-relief "Gradiva." "Gradiva" is thus both his inspiration for the journey and its desired end, for he seeks out the bas-relief in his work. He shows no sign of understanding his desire to go to Pompeii. There he meets his next-door-neighbor, whose physical appearance and name (Zoë Bertgang; *Bertgang* can be translated as "Gradiva," and *Zoë* means "living") bear a striking resemblance to the art object.

And so Hanold's archaeological quest is actually a mission in self-discovery. His desire has been sublimated into his work and has literally been turned into stone. For Hanold, as Sarah Kofman has suggested, Gradiva seems like an Athena who bears Medusa on her shield, turning him to stone.[62] For Zoë, archaeology serves the Medusa function, as not a feminized but a highly masculinized discipline. But while Hanold's desire has been sublimated into his science, his science cannot escape the dynamic of his repressed desire. Zoë describes the archaeological quest as being characterized by "the fact of someone having to die to come alive."[63] Hanold does not understand the nature of this sublimation, and it is only Zoë who can tell him that his archaeological interest is sublimated desire for her. This is why Freud sees her as psychoanalyst. It is she who can interpret all Hanold's confusions, and Freud does not need to elaborate on Hanold's language, replete as it is with ambiguities, as Zoë is the first to point these out to Hanold, who is unaware of them.

There may be no better analogy for repression than the Pompeiian eruption in which, unlike the case of Troy, that which is buried is preserved in its original form. But the archaeologist is inadequate to the task of working through those findings so that they make sense of the present. Self-analysis fails here, though with the consequence of putting archaeology onto the couch after it has acted out. But this acting out is not exactly transference, for Zoë is not working exclusively with Hanold but also with supplementary information. Freud explains:

> The emergence of Zoë as physician, as I have already remarked, arouses a new interest in us. We shall be anxious to learn whether a cure of the kind she performed upon Hanold is conceivable or even possible, and whether the author has taken as correct a view of the conditions for the disappearance of a delusion as he has for those of its genesis. . . .
>
> The treatment consisted in giving him back from the outside the repressed memories which he could not set free from inside; but it would have had no effect if, in the course of it the therapist had not taken his feelings into account and if her ultimate translation of the delusion had not been: "Look, all this only means that you love me."[64]

This fantasy is also one in which the analyst herself has a very specific wish to be fulfilled—that Hanold return her love and that it is true that "all this only means that you love me."

Freud wrote his analysis of *Gradiva* in 1907, two years after his visit to the Acropolis, which he will not report to us until thirty-one years later. Harry Slochower and Guy Rosolato have each suggested that "A Disturbance of Memory on the Acropolis" (*Eine Erinnerungsstörung auf der Akropolis*), written by Freud in 1936, is attributable to the sight of the ravaged temple to Athena whose image would have appeared with Medusa on the shield. Freud's feelings at the Parthenon are interpreted through

"The Uncanny" and "Medusa's Head." Rosolato is particularly interested in Freud's relationship to the architecture of the temple to Athena, for architecture, as the inevitable acting out of museological and reconstructive archaeology, is something that Freud addresses in "Construction in Analysis." The construction is only the preliminary for psychoanalysis, though, and perhaps Zoë can be read in this reconstructive role. Commenting upon Freud's feeling of "uncanniness," Rosolato conjectures that this results from more than a confrontation with the Medusa. "As for the Parthenon, the outside seems especially ravaged, being but a shell—but if one can imagine it intact and reconstruct the sacred place (the *cella*) that one enters [*pénètre*] by way of *a* door (which one imagines between the cracks that cover the columns). The place contains the statue of the goddess but does not allow the faithful to congregate within it, as the worship takes place in front of the temple. The unknown is located in the inside. . . . The Virgin, as focal object, phallic body, and the goddess of reason and intelligence, marks out the central cavity and fixes the unknown."[65] Rosolato creates an image similar to that found in Jensen's *Gradiva:*

> Empty and silent, the room lay there, appearing absolutely unfamiliar to the man, as he entered, awaking no memory that he had already been here, yet he then recalled it, for the interior of the house offered a deviation from that of the other excavated buildings of the city. The peristyle adjoined the inner court on the other side of the balcony towards the rear—not in the usual way . . . more splendid than any other in Pompeii. It was framed by a colonnade supported by two dozen pillars. . . . These lent solemnity to the great silent space; here in the centre was a spring with a beautifully wrought enclosure . . . Norbert's gaze passed around, and he listened.[66]

Freud reproduces this architectural awe when he pens a letter to Martha describing a visit to the Vatican: "Think of my joy upon coming across today, at the Vatican, after such a long lonely spell, the familiar face of a loved one. But the pleasure of the recognition was, one sided; I'm speaking of seeing the 'Gradiva' who hung high up on a wall."[67] It is in the temple that Hanold first sees Zoë. Both Freud's and Hanold's relationships to the worlds surrounding them are unhinged by the experience of uncanny feelings as they enter these ancient, empty, enclosed spaces. Both are confused by what they see, and are set at odds with their respective sciences. When Freud experiences this "disturbance of memory," he is unable to apply his scientific formulas in the way he manages to with Jensen's text. In fact, he is unable to retrieve anything positive from the experience of this disturbance.

Harry Slochower sees Freud's déjà vu on the Acropolis as a symbolic relic of *mater nuda*, the time when Freud saw his mother naked.[68] "For the last four days my self-analysis, which I consider indispensable for throwing light upon the whole problem, has proceeded in dreams and presented me with the most valuable inferences and clues . . . later my libido was stirred up towards *matrem*. . . . I must have had an opportunity to see her *nudam*."[69] Slochower's essay is concerned with "what Freud had once seen" as childhood memory; he reminds us that the virgin goddess Athena wears Medusa's head, the mother's genitals, on her shield. *Mater nuda* is very different from a mother clothed with Medusa. Freud's confrontation has been with the body of the mother, and not with a symptom of its repression: a representation of the nude mother (by Slochower) as Medusa. Freud's letter is replete with visual images: "Finally . . . I stood on the Acropolis and cast my eyes around upon the landscape. . . . I could really not have imagined it possible that I should ever be granted the sight of Athens with my own eyes."[70]

While their interpretations concerning the ravaged temple as confrontation with the uncanniness of the mother's body are interesting, neither Slochower nor Rosolato extends the analysis sufficiently. While Slochower reads *Gradiva* as the necessary wish fulfillment that Freud failed to have in his 1904 trip to Athens (when he could not be reunited with *matrem nudam* as Hanold has been with Zoë), this still does not account for the timing of Freud's narration of the disturbance, even if it allows us to see *Gradiva* as an acting out of a trauma instigated initially in 1904.

A Disturbance of National Affiliation

If "Delusions and Dreams" is a wish fulfillment of events narrated in the "Disturbance of Memory," it is also a phantasm that dramatizes the failure of archaeological selfhood. For the idealist figure of the cohesive reflective self in Schliemann's and Stanley's work was not one applicable to Freud's rendition of the analyst, or, indeed to Freud himself. The form of travel that had given Schliemann and Stanley a framework for expressing a narrative of the self allowed an opposition between a self and something else. For Schliemann, it was the past of the recently formulated Western World that nineteenth-century humanist archaeology typically concentrated upon. For Stanley, it was colonial Africa, full of mystery. Freud's 1937 essay "Construction in Analysis" elaborated the piecing together of archaeological finds in the process of reconstruction. Schliemann and Stanley, with the aid and creativity of their wives, constructed narratives of their finds that simultaneously offered a continuous narrative of their selves as they single-mindedly erected themselves as admirable figures, lifting themselves from poverty and becoming the very stuff of national heroism. Their constructions of self created the greatness of Europe, and went into developing what it meant to be European nationals with an ancient past and the power and insight to conquer the colonies.

Freud's early writings shared in some of this grandeur. But articles from his later years show the impossibility of doing so, and therefore they theorize a different relationship to the past and to the dead. If manifestations of *Nachträglichkeit* distorted a sense of a continuous past, the founding subjects of archaeology and colonial travel would be disturbed. As Foucault said in *The Archaeology of Knowledge*, "Continuous History is the indispensable correlative of the founding of the subject: the guarantee that everything that has eluded him may be restored to him."[71] Though Freud's own writing reveals a departure that problematizes the earlier formulations of the ego reflecting a nationalist archaeological exploratory narrative, he is largely remembered as an archaeologist of the mind who guaranteed restoration of lost material through the technology of psychoanalysis. Reading psychoanalysis as counter-science, however, reveals the ways knowledge of Man is made possible by laying bare the process through which the founding subject evolves.

However, in the late writings, psychoanalysis is not so much an opposition to science, or the epistemic rupture of counter-science, so much as a product of colonialist and nationalist ideology that commits an epistemic violence upon those who cannot be founding subjects. Where analogy begins to be only partially adequate, there are "discursive regularities"[72] between the sciences as they begin to break down. As Gayatri Chakravorty Spivak has argued in relation to colonial education, epistemic violence is created out of a double negative—one cannot not want to be a part of a discursive framework that has created the epistemological models in which one is trained.[73] Freud cannot not want to be part of the founding archaeological narrative of nineteenth-century interest in Athens, and yet it is the sight of the Acropolis that causes in him a disturbance, which at first appears to be one from which he can gain nothing positive. I would argue, however, that the message sent to us via Romain Rolland (in the "open letter" that is titled "A Disturbance of Memory on the Acropolis") is a covert message about the relationship of the ego to nationalism. Freud, the messenger, gives us a way here of understanding psychoanalysis as an ethnography of the West, or perhaps more accurately of nineteenth-century European nationalism, and the formulation of the subject. And he is fully aware of our potential resistance to the ethnographic message.

> Between repression and what may be termed the normal method of fending off what is distressing or unbearable, by means of recognizing it, considering it, making a judgement upon it and taking appropriate action about it, there lie a whole series of more or less clearly pathological methods of behaviour on the part of the ego. May I stop for a moment to remind you of a marginal case of this kind of defence? You remember the famous lament of the Spanish Moors "*Ay de mi Alhama*" ("Alas for my Alhama"), which tells how King Boabdil received the news of the fall of his city of Alhama. He feels that this loss means the end of his rule. But he will not "let it be true," he determines to treat the news as '*non arrivé.*' . . . It is easy to guess that a further determinant of this behaviour of the king was his need to combat a feeling of powerlessness. By burning the letters and having the messenger killed he was still trying to show his absolute power.[74]

Neither Rosolato nor Slochower adequately addresses why Freud should return to his disturbance and déjà vu in 1936 in this "Open Letter to Romain Rolland." To write an open letter is, for Freud at this time, highly charged, since his writings were burned and suppressed by the Nazis, "to show that [their] power was still at its full." If Freud the messenger is giving a message about the failure, or at least the shortcomings, of the ego in modern nationalist societies, the pathologies of that ego became apparent in the crisis of a national subject under threat.

Freud had been corresponding with Rolland for some years, mainly about his work on Indian religious figures, Ramakrishna and Vivekananda, and on the "oceanic feeling" (a term that, according to psychoanalytic Sanskrit scholar J. Moussaieff Masson, probably derived from Ramakrishna's reading of the Sanskrit text *Aṣṭāvakrasaṃhitā*),[75] which Freud would later discuss in *Civilisation and Its Discontents* and *Group Psychology*. But he also corresponded with him on the relationship of the individual to society, and the persecution of Jews. An early letter from 1923 allows us to see Freud discussing the mistreatment of Jews in Austria and Germany. Reading this letter, it is difficult to imagine young Freud, the loyal Habsburg subject, touched by imperial charisma, whose mother changed her birthday from the Jewish calendar to the Christian so it would coincide with Franz Joseph's and who would tell her children stories about the emperor.[76] In his 1923 letter to Rolland, he described himself as belonging "to a race which in the Middle Ages was held responsible for all epidemics and which today is blamed for the disintegration of the Austrian Empire and the German defeat. Such experiences have a sobering effect and are not conducive to make one believe in illusions. . . . If in the course of evolution we don't learn to divert our instincts from destroying our own kind, if we continue to hate one another for minor differences and kill each other for petty gain . . . what kind of future lies in store for us?"[77]

"Evolution," if such a word is applicable, into a pacifist mode is something Freud hoped for in many of his postwar texts. He suggests that the "introversion" of aggressive impulses is what is needed, as war runs counter to "the psychic disposition imposed on us by the growth of culture," and he suggests that growth of the intellect that masters instinct will lead to the redirection of aggression. There are, in this earlier letter to Rolland, the beginnings of Freud's theory of the "narcissism of minor differences," which he later elaborated in *Civilisation and Its Discontents*. The ethical and aesthetic changes in our ideals are ultimately organic, and so recomposition of the psyche needs to be accomplished, as he would elaborate in "Why War?" in 1933.[78] He clearly hoped for adequate mourning for the ravages of war even as early as 1915, and thus the restoration of the beauty that, once lost, should have become more apparent. Mourning, which can be understood as assimilation of the desire for the dead and that which is lost, has not been completed though.[79] Witness his misery in 1938: "I came to Vienna as a child of four years from a small town in Moravia. After 78 years of assiduous work I had to leave my home, saw the Scientific Society I had founded, dissolved, our institutions destroyed, our printing press taken over by the invaders, the books I had published reduced to pulp, my children expelled from their professions."[80] So the defense of psychoanalysis in "The Question of Lay Analysis" and the heroic archaeological writing in response to the Other falls apart when all that

Freud has sought in his quest is destroyed, and a splitting occurs. For the Other cannot be external or past, but is very suddenly present. The reason for this is that the self is suddenly conceived as foreign.

A change or a splitting takes place in the Freudian ego that can be understood as a disturbance of national affiliation played out on archaeological sites: the Acropolis and the Alhambra Palace. Even in Freud's own work there seems to be a narrative breakdown that takes place when the ego cannot in any simple way affiliate itself nationally. In an even later fragment of an article written in 1937/38 but published posthumously, "The Splitting of the Ego in the Defensive Process," Freud writes of this splitting:

> Let us suppose . . . that a child's ego . . . is suddenly frightened by an experience which teaches it that the continuance of this satisfaction will result in an almost intolerable real danger. It must now decide either to recognize the real danger, give way to it and renounce the instinctual satisfaction, or to disavow reality and make itself believe that there is no reason for fear, so that it may be able to retain the satisfaction. . . . The two contrary reactions to the conflict persist as the center point of a splitting of the ego. The whole process seems so strange to us because we take for granted the synthetic nature of the processes of the ego. But we are clearly at fault in this. The synthetic function of the ego, though it is of such extraordinary importance, is subject to particular conditions and is liable to a whole number of disturbances [Storungen].[81]

In his earlier psychoanalytic texts, Freud postulates the "synthetic function of the ego." But thirty-two years after his initial moment of splitting, when the instability of his own "openness" or access to writing is thematized, there follows an epistemological shift coterminous with a violation of national affiliation.

Freud's own rationale for writing this text thirty-two years after the trip, and his own understanding of why this disturbed memory has come to disturb him once again, is attributed to age. He says, "I myself have grown old and stand in need of forbearance and can travel no more."[82] While in his early writings there is a definite correspondence between the analyst who excavates the unconscious and the archaeologist who unearths the genealogy of civilization, this late piece seems to speak a more confused relationship to the self who can travel or analyze. In his early days of analysis, splits get displaced, and that Odyssean spirit that reads and travels like Schliemann and Stanley does not cause a faltering or even a disturbance in the rhetoric of the ego, even if closer reading often reveals a rupture. In earlier essays, such as "The Question of Lay Analysis," in which it is the whole of his discipline that is at stake and that needs to be defended, Freud seems to have no problem in retrieving something positive from a moment of splitting. He can attribute quite easily his lack of knowledge of female sexuality, or the confusing "dark continent," to woman's lack of penis.

The Odyssean venture that had led Freud to the Acropolis is considered in the light of his relationship to his father, as well as to the next generation: his daughter, Anna, was currently writing a book that would explain the defensive mechanisms that Freud, among others, was experiencing. The generational changes that Freud considered in old age and at the moment of the birthday are tied to the ability to analyze: when Freud had a more secure sense of place, he could be the explorer of the self and its unconscious. Once his own relationship to the homeland is confused, however, for whom can he explore? The "double conscience" could no longer have the stability of an Odysseus who traveled without worries of borders and passports.

In "The Disturbance of Memory," Freud showed enormous resistance to the trip, assuming, inexplicably, that it will be absolutely impossible. Before he and his brother decided to go to Athens, he considered the potential difficulties: "We assumed . . . that we should not be allowed to land in Greece without passports."[83] He began to doubt what he knew as a child and as an adult who considered class and physical mobility an embarrassment to filial piety, "as though," he says, "excel[ling] one's father was still something forbidden."[84] It is a moment, for Freud, when excelling one's father potentially meant being exiled from the fatherland, rather than replacing one's father as Zeus did to Kronos when he threw him out of heaven and established Mt. Olympus for himself, or as Oedipus did unknowingly to Laius. Freud, rather like Hamlet, demonstrated his filial piety through being haunted by the memory of his father.

As he sat contemplating the Acropolis, Freud was struck by a feeling of déjà vu. This feeling of "derealisation" was accompanied, he wrote, by one of "depersonalisation" (where a part of reality or of oneself seems strange to oneself). Both these feelings he analyses as ones which "serve the purpose of defence; they aim at keeping something away from the ego, at disavowing it."[85]

Freud had earlier proposed that "occurrences of *déjà vu* in dreams have a special meaning. . . . These places are invariably the genitals of the dreamer's mother; there is indeed no other place about which one can assert with such conviction that one has been there before."[86] As Freud's association of the archaeological prehistoric is linked to the riddle of femininity, this déjà vu is a return. But it is also a confused return, and one that is unsure of returning to a place of belonging. It is accompanied by a feeling of derealization, a symptom that led Freud to complain that the world seemed unreal. And depersonalization, when he felt unreal to himself. A feeling of self-awareness and a splitting resulted from this. The first takes reality into consideration, and the second disavows it, or refuses to recognize trauma. This confusion led him to say, "So all this really *does* exist, just as we learnt at school,"[87] as if the existence of this founding monument of Western civilization was in doubt in spite of its archaeological reputation.

The disturbance on the Acropolis caused Freud to reassess his own relationship to generational national affiliation and the changes that occur in that construction. Freud's disturbance came from the confusion of national and cultural affiliation. The cultural and racial heritage that was realized in the ravaged temple caused a disturbance of self that challenged the self modeled on the archaeological dig. That self was always already national and always constructed as complete in opposition to another that was to be analyzed.

The sensation of filial piety occurred in old age when Freud saw his daughter moving onto a necessary theorization of defense strategies for the ego that was in "real danger" of death or exile. The piety of the old man also led him to deny this necessary splitting. In "A Comment on Anti-Semitism," Freud literally split himself in two. Presenting a non-Jew's text on anti-Semitism, he claimed that he could not recall the source of the text, but that he concurred with its sentiments. Jones suggests that it was a text he wrote himself, and that he constructed a dialogue in terms of forgetting, saying: "I am a very old man and my memory is no more what it was."[88] This performance with a ghost is a splitting that took place at the moment of "real danger." Cohesive national and personal security were compromised. If a coherent memory is a necessary component of a nationalist history, this was enacted in Freud as a "real danger" to citizenship and national cohesion when his thrones and altars were in danger: travel, his new science, and his children.

Freud's development of a social science of memory was disturbed by a feeling of national piety, as if he had outshone too greatly the values and selective memories of an age gone by, the age of his father and the Habsburg Empire. The age of colonial travel and exploration was that of Freud's youth. That of his old age was the moment of Nazi suppression. The future, to which he referred when writing of his threatened children, would be that of the split and defensive ego, when a nation-state would be unable to exist without rupture and beyond betrayal. Such a nation threatened death, torture, exile, in other words, "real dangers" to Freud.

Even within Freud's own scholarship, then, there is a change in models of the self as they are adversely affected by national conflicts. If psychoanalysis is read as an ethnography rather than as contextless theory or its opposite, alternative models for the nation-state begin to emerge. These manifest themselves not in an archaeological model in which the stratified unconscious is sometimes confused with the anthropological repressed or prehistoric; rather the "scene of memory" always necessitates a consideration of the splits that come to be acknowledged in the ego, which are like the interferences caused by the memory's insistent confrontation with a false unified and unifying sense of history and the subject. If a concept of the nation-state is implicated in the concept of self, new models of psychoanalysis can tell us about the way the nation-state is being formed. A sense of filial piety, and indeed an epistemic violence, necessitate the maintenance and reinscription of the European colonial discourses of modernity that go into modern formation and lead to different understandings of affiliation with the modern nation-state.

If the colonial nation-state was theorized as an entity that characterized itself through opposition to its colonies and to its Others, the postcolonial nation-state as reflected in formulations of the ego has to repeat that model, though importantly with a difference. The disturbance in a collective and selective memory in which past moments are successfully mourned and assimilated to the synthetic ego or nation splits into an age of a melancholic "politics of despair."[89] Modern subjects cannot not feel filial piety to that construction of nation and ego, which are intrinsic to modern being, but must heed Freud's warning in *Civilisation and Its Discontents*. He recognized the moment of passing of the synthetic European neurotic ego as it gave way to a destructive splitting. The splitting of this synthetic psychoanalytic ego situated the moment of its passing, and it also assessed it critically. Reading the changes in the structure of the ego as a critique of the nationalism from which it originated parochialized the structure of the colonizing nation-state. The epistemic violence enacted on the body and consciousness of Freud puts him into real danger, which forces a questioning of his place in an archaeological mythology that mourns the past by finding a place for it. As Schliemann's good friend Ernest Renan would say in relation to nationalism and nationalist history, this allows us to remember to forget as we selectively document our pasts, and retell them to our interlocutors in a way that masks our differences and constructs our singularities in relation to chosen others.

The double conscience witnessed in Freud is actually more akin to a critical relationship with the past in which a split has occurred within a self that was previously constituted out of a feeling of continuous history. I will name this critical agency "melancholia." This is an important concept, which relates to that of incorporation and critical agency. In melancholia, "dissatisfaction with the ego on moral grounds is the most outstanding feature." The patient has experienced "a loss in regard to his ego."[90] This causes the existence of the *plaint* or a kind of lament. The abandoned object is, however, incorporated into the melancholic self and the complaints are directed toward the object that has been incorporated, thus bringing about a critical agency that seems almost separated from the idea of the ego itself. With this splitting, there is engendered a critical relation to the predominant episteme that went into the very construction of that early archaeological Freudian ego. This double consciousness also does something else: it creates a different dynamic between the analyst and the analysand in spatial terms, and thus between the ego and the unconscious as it acts out in the transferential relationship. A critical agency is thus born out of an epistemic violence that allows us to situate psychoanalysis as a colonial discipline that reveals to us an ethnography of the West.

2. Freud in the Sacred Grove

A comparison between the psychology of primitive peoples, as it is taught by social anthropology, and the psychology of neurotics, as it has been revealed by psychoanalysis, will be bound to show numerous points of agreement and will throw new light upon familiar facts in both sciences.—Freud, *Totem and Taboo*

I am not an anthropologist but a psychoanalyst. I had a right to take out of ethnological literature what I might need for the work of analysis.—*Totem and Taboo*

The colonizing situation is [not] indispensable to ethnology: neither hypnosis, nor the patient's alienation within the fantasmatic character of the doctor, is constitutive of psychoanalysis; but just as the latter can be deployed only in the calm violence of a particular relationship and the transference it produces, so ethnology can assume its proper dimensions only within the historical sovereignty—always restrained but always present—of European thought and the relation that can bring it face to face with all other cultures as well as with itself.—Michel Foucault, *The Order of Things*

The structural parallel between psychoanalysis and ethnology exists, according to Foucault, in the sovereign position of the analyst—sovereign, and calmly violent. The subject matter of the two sciences is quite different. In the psychoanalytical paradigm, individuals are analyzed. In ethnology, cultural groups are the focus and individuals' interactions are important only insofar as they are thought to be representative of the larger cultural group. But the *episteme* through which the psychoanalytical and the ethnological are constituted and to which they contribute relies on the sovereign European subject as prime interlocutor. The sovereign European subject is a modern totem against which transference, often in the guise of taboo, is played out.

The metaphoricity of my claim here brings me back into the arena of analogy, which was discussed in the last chapter, but it also does something else. Like Freud's *Totem and Taboo,* it borrows from a homological theory that ontogeny recapitulates phylogeny, that is, that the development of the individual repeats the stages of the development, or evolution (the term is *Entwicklungsgeschichte* for both in German) of the species. As Ernst Haeckel, Darwin's popularizer, would explain it, "An organism, in developing from the ovum, goes through the same changes as did the species in developing from the lower to the higher forms of animal life."[1] For Freud, however, this will serve more than a metaphorical function; it will mean drawing equivalents between white European children, neurotics, and sometimes women and foreign primitives (children, men, and women alike). Freud can thus name his final chapter of *Totem and Taboo* "The Return of Totemism in Children." The "return" is from the prehistoric and contemporary primitive. Drawing a similar parallel and claiming that we should read *Totem and Taboo* as a "truthful translation of totem into psychoanalysis and taboo into transference," Harold Bloom suggests that Freud gives his fullest account of the *transference* neurosis in this text.[2] More importantly, this reveals a structural parallel between ethnologist and the psychoanalyst that suggests they are part of an episteme. It also suggests that they are responding to the same global political relations.

In the project of *provincializing psychoanalysis,* in the context of colonialism, it is necessary to explain the meeting points of these two disciplines within a colonialist episteme. Foucault is probably correct to claim that colonialism is not crucial for ethnology in spite of the latter's development in the colonial context; and alienation is not necessary for psychoanalysis, in spite of its development in the era of the growing alienation of the subject. However, those moments were pivotal for both. Alienation was crucial for anthropology, as colonialism was for psychoanalysis. In the history of those disciplines and in their current practices, there are remnants of that colonial era of alienation, as well as adjustments to the fields to account for changing models of Europe in the era of postcoloniality.

Though ethnology and psychoanalysis are very different, it has been possible for Mary Ann Doane to propose that "psychoanalysis can . . .

be seen as a quite elaborate form of ethnography—as a writing of the ethnicity of the white Western psyche," and that "repression becomes the prerequisite for the construction of a white culture which stipulates that female sexuality act as the trace within of what has been excluded."[3] Female sexuality, and femininity more broadly, became the trace of cultural loss and enigma in metaphors like the "dark continent" or the "Minoan-Mycenaean." Further, psychoanalysis is dependent on ethnology, and in fact forms a kind of ethnology suitable for the West, from that form of analysis designed for the Rest. Interest in those parts of the world that had been newly colonized relied upon the creation of a European sovereign subject; psychoanalysis is a symptom and mechanism of that creation. If the transferential relationship works through a calm violence, it is that of being hailed as a sovereign subject. The calm violence of this interpellation, like the totemic ritual, forms a social contract that individualizes and individuates members of a group at the same time as it confers upon them group "culture" or "civilization."[4] The very existence of the unconscious may well be the excess of that address to the sovereign subject. As something internal to the sovereign subject, the existence of the unconscious confirms sovereignty and individuation, that is, status as civilized beings. The unconscious must also be accessible to the sovereign subject, *for the time being*. To read psychoanalysis as an ethnography of the West, it is first necessary to give some background to the forms of anthropology Freud read and drew upon. This will allow us to see how psychoanalysis and ethnology participate in the same episteme, one that sustains, through calm violence, the sovereign subject of Europe.

Freud's Anthropological Archive

If the archaeological metaphor showed how the psyche was to be considered stratified in spatio-temporal layering, the anthropological, and particularly the ethnographic or cultural anthropological, show how temporal simultaneity exists within a broader progressive structure. A historical developmental account can be gauged in Freud's anthropological world not simply through the biological evolutionary narratives of Lamarck and Darwin, but also through those of such figures as the cultural anthropologists E. B. Tylor and James Frazer. The etiology of the modern symptom itself, and the necessity of theorizing the difference between the modern and the primitive even when they exist simultaneously, can be seen in Tylor's *Primitive Culture*,[5] from which Freud was to draw extensively for his discussion of animism in *Totem and Taboo*. Tylor's consideration of animism covered information about the place of souls and spirits in "primitive" or "lower" cultures. In order to give examples of the primitive, he combined the temporal and the geographic, and conflated lower peoples living contemporaneously and prehistoric peoples. He set these people against the more "advanced" citizens of Britain.

This parallel was known in both pre-evolutionist and evolutionist circles as the *comparative* method, following Condorcet's 1795 *Sketch for a Historical Picture of the Progress of the Human Mind.*[6] The comparative method employed contemporary primitive peoples to stand in for historical primitives in the absence of adequate historical evidence. Thus, the contemporary "primitive" represented an earlier developmental stage in the species. For Lamarck, this was theoretically possible, as he believed that living organisms could exist simultaneously at different stages of the evolutionary ladder, since they could at any time spring from inanimate and inorganic matter.[7] As Freud later put it, a continuity can be seen between "primitive races . . . in past history or at the present time."[8] The same Humean *associationist* philosophy is at work in Frazer, Freud's other main source: if the mind was constituted through an accumulation of senses that were then associated with each other, so were cultures in Frazer and Tylor's work. Similar patterns could be plotted, and therefore often rather tenuous comparisons and similarities theorized. As Frazer wrote:

> If we can shew that a barborous custom . . . has existed elsewhere; if we can detect the motives which led to its institution; if we can prove that these motives have operated widely, perhaps universally, in human society, producing in varied circumstances a variety of institutions, [and] were actually at work in classical antiquity; then we may fairly infer that at a remoter age the same motives gave birth to the priesthood at Nemi. Such an inference, in default of direct evidence . . . can never amount to demonstration. But it will be more or less probable according to degree of completeness.[9]

Like Frazer's, Tylor's examples are extremely wide-ranging, and draw not from field work but largely from such texts as Adolph Bastian's *Mensch in der Geschichte* and *Die deutsche Expedition an der Loango-Küste,* which refer to many different ethnic, racial, cultural, and national groups.[10] This, according to Tylor, was very relevant to understanding contemporary British life: "We in England hardly hear of demoniacal possession except as a historical doctrine of divines,"[11] he wrote. "Even the despised ideas of savage races become a practically important topic to the modern world. . . . [T]o follow the course of animism on from its more primitive stages is to account for much of medieval and modern opinion whose meaning and reason could hardly be comprehended without the aid of a development-theory of culture."[12]

The development theory of culture, as many anthropological critics have shown, participated in the creation of the colonial paternal authority of Britain.[13] If the particulars of anthropology were not important for colonial reform, broader ideas, such as the unchallenged place of England at the head of the evolutionary chain, were. For Tylor, education was the cause of such advancement: "The educated world of Europe and America practically settles a standard by simply placing its own nation at one end of the social scale and the savage tribes on the other, arranging the rest of mankind within these limits according as they respond to savage or to cultured life."[14] Tylor established a sense of continuity in his developmental project. The developmental theory underlying his treatise on animism consistently caused him to translate the function of animism into contemporary philosophic and cultural narratives of progress and causation. Drawing together numerous examples, without much differentiation between them on cultural let alone historical, geographic, or political terms, Tylor, for example, considered spirits to be "simply personified causes."[15] Tylor quoted from David Hume to explain this primitive creation of causes. According to him, man extends his ideas of the soul, projecting onto objects in the external world and thus creating spirits. "There is a universal tendency among mankind to conceive all beings like themselves, and to transfer to every object those qualities with which they are familially acquainted, and of which they are intimately conscious."[16] Tylor's causal logic translated the animistic into the logic of projective creation. He seems, however, blind to the forms of projective identification in his own work necessary for arguing the psychic unity and singularity of the human species.

Although Freud missed the opportunity of citing Tylor on medical practices, *Primitive Culture* provides a fascinating account of the shift from animistic belief to pathological symptom.

> It has to be thoroughly understood that the changed aspect of the subject [of demoniacal possession] in modern opinion is not due to disappearance of the actual manifestations which early philosophy

attributed to demoniacal influence. Hysteria and epilepsy, delirium and mania, and such like bodily derangement, still exist. . . . [I]t is in the civilised world, under the influence of medical doctrines which have been developing since classic times, that the early animistic theory of these morbid phenomena has been gradually superseded by views more in accordance with modern science, to the great gain of our health and happiness. . . . Yet whenever in times old or new, demoniacal influences are brought forward to account for affections which scientific physicians now explain on a different principle, care must be taken not to misjudge the ancient doctrine and its place in history. As belonging to the lower culture it is a perfectly rational philosophical theory to account for certain pathological facts. But just as mechanical astronomy gradually superseded the animistic astronomy of the lower races, so biological pathology gradually supersedes animistic pathology, the immediate operation of personal spiritual beings in both cases giving place to the operation of natural processes.[17]

The aim of this translation into contemporary terms is explained by Tylor in the conclusion of the two-volume text. Ethnology, for him, was "active at once in aiding progress and in removing hindrance[;] the science of culture is essentially a reformer's science."[18] The reformer, indeed, could rationalize enforced systems of colonial education by drawing on this social-evolutionary ladder. It confirmed sovereignty of the subject, and thus selfhood, as it was conceived in Europe, as the standard. Anything that did not fit the standard would be deemed primitive or pathological.

Unlike Tylor, who saw science as a progression away from complex anterior systems that were to him inadequate, Freud did not perceive medical diagnosis to be at the top of the evolutionary ladder. He saw each passing philosophy, whether it were animism, religion, or science, as something to be understood within its own era, and in possession of its own discrete mechanisms of establishing social order. For Freud, different cultural and social orders dealt with instinct and prohibition in differing ways, depending on the local systems of maintaining that social order. In this respect, Freud was closer to Emile Durkheim. In his 1912 *Elementary Forms of Religious Life,* Durkheim explains

the origin of the ambiguity of religious forces as they appear in history, and how they are physical as well as human; moral as well as material. They are moral powers because they are made up entirely of the impressions this moral being, the group, arouses in those other moral beings, its individual members; they do not translate the manner in which physical things affect our senses, but the way in which the collective consciousness acts upon individual consciousness. Their authority is only one form of moral ascendancy of society over its members. But, on the other hand, since they are conceived of under material forms, they could not fail to be regarded as closely related to material things.[19]

Freud, like Durkheim, understood the differing philosophies of animism or religion within their own terminologies or cognitive forms in order to elucidate the dynamic of a particular social order. If the historian were to give an account of Europe's past, then the pathologization of colonialism would be a stage in itself. A progressive mode remained intact, but without the establishment of science at the top of the ladder. And so "reform" for Freud would have to be considered with some skepticism.

But what did Tylor mean by reform? Was he referring to the greatly exaggerated advisory role of the anthropologist in colonial policy?[20] Was he suggesting a therapeutic function served by this discourse for the subjects of study? Or was he referring to the scientific reform of an evolutionary narrative that conferred superiority on the European, and specifically British, subject? The political work of reform conducted by the anthropologist became an issue within psychoanalysis. And it was the ethics of this reform that began to plague Freud both in *Totem and Taboo* (1913) and later in life in *Civilisation and Its Discontents* (1930), which he had originally named *Das Unglück in der Kultur* (Unhappiness in Civilization).

Culture, Civilization, Cure, and Reform

Tylor was apparently unconflicted in his view that reform of the primitive meant sustaining the British sovereign model of selfhood. Freud's notion of reform, the treatment of pathologies remaining from primitives and from childhood, caused him some conflict concerning the "culture" of the "civilised." The terms *culture* (*Kultur*) and *civilization* are of course highly charged, especially for readers of *Keywords*,[21] in which Raymond Williams wrote of the dual meaning of the term *culture*. It has both an anthropological use as descriptive of the habits and activities of groups; and an evaluative one, in the sense of civilized, meaning advanced. Williams cited Tylor as an important player in the development of the anthropological term, noting that he used the term only in the singular. The comparative method allowed Tylor to write of *primitive culture* as if it were singular. George Stocking, however, has countered the argument that there is such division in the use of the term, making the case that Tylor uses them synonymously.[22] Although Tylor used *culture* in his title rather than *civilization,* in the body of the text he uses the two terms interchangeably when referring to primitive culture. Robert Young has noted that Freud's *Kultur* is suggestive of the Enlightenment concept of civilization, which reaches its apotheosis in Matthew Arnold's distinctions between barbarians and civilized, or cultured peoples.[23] In the German context the very fact that the term *Kultur* could be coupled with *discontent* runs counter to Arnold's usage, and indeed counter to the narrative of beneficial progress associated with the notion of reform.

Although the concept of reform was at work both in psychoanalysis and in anthropology, the nature of this reform is quite different. Psychoanalysis is designed to give people a personal history through which they can come to terms with their lot in life, and a sense of the past that can explain their current existence. It supplies the analysand with a rationalization of that which cannot be accounted for in the guise of the unconscious. On the other hand, an anthropology that is built upon a racist evolutionary philosophy posits the contemporary "primitive" as a version of the early stages of human society, and the primitive can therefore have no history. As Johannes Fabian has reminded us in *Time and the Other*,[24] it erases a sense of the past of its subjects of inquiry. If Tylor was responsible for, or at least contributed to, "the operation of ethnologization" of Africa and other colonies,[25] then Freud, as his counterpart in the world of the Western psyche, was responsible for the pathologization of the West. As V. Y. Mudimbe has written in the context of artifacts, anthropology studies "ethnographic artefacts," and art history "is concerned with its own culture and historical space."[26] Psychoanalysis was to art history as primitivism was to anthropology. But Freud wrote in 1913 that the psychoanalyst works in a model different from that of the anthropologist, whose work has to stress synchronicity within the overall diachronic or evolutionary model. The "primitive" in evolutionary and preevolutionary anthropology, and thus for Freud, has no sense of memory or history: "These peoples possess no tradition and no historical memory, so that any research into their early history is faced by the greatest difficulties."[27] Freud does voice some concern about this idea in an early footnote, stating that

> it must not be forgotten that even the lost primitive and conservative races are in some sense *ancient* races and have a long past history behind them during which their original conditions of life have been subject to much development and distortion. So it comes about that in those races in which totemism exists to-day, we may find it in various stages of decay and disintegration or in the process of transition to other social and religious institutions, or again in a stationary condition which may differ greatly from the original one. The difficulty in this last case is to decide whether we should regard the present state of things as a true picture of the significant features of the past or a secondary distortion of them.[28]

As Edwin Wallace writes, Freud must have been aware of such scholars as Max Müller, who wrote of this form of distortion.[29] And it was anthropologists like Müller who led German anthropology more or less to reject an entirely evolutionist principle that would cause the methodological anxiety expressed by Freud here. But Freud would choose to follow the British evolutionist anthropological scene, which, following a comparative method, did not to the same extent concern itself with whether it was really comparing equivalents or whether there was some perceived similarity between entities that have very little in common as soon as their culturally internal meanings are considered. While the differences between the natural history museums in London, Oxford, and Cambridge—and indeed the presence of Müller at Oxford—made for a conflicted community of scholars seeking to establish different models of anthropology,[30] anthropologists like Tylor or Frazer who were working with broad categories, like magic, animism, primitive culture, or indeed, science, would work with different cultural examples to include in their theories of Man. Figures like Müller, or Malinowski, who were to concentrate their energies and scholarship on specific geographical locations, were inevitably going to pose questions for this armchair comparative approach, which would indeed challenge Freud's chosen schema. Freud's doubts about the comparative model, which pose some interesting questions in the postcolonial context when hybridity, nativism, and secondary processes in models of cultural authenticity rather than primitivism are considered, are left at bay in an early footnote that did not disturb the main text; and of course, as David Nonini has noted, Freud would make no acknowledgment of colonial practices or ideologies so important in the popularity of the evolutionist discourse.[31]

The new science of memory that was being formulated by Freud drew on both the spatial models of an evolutionary anthropology and the temporal models of archaeology that sustained the idea of a stratified past for the modern subject. George Stocking has argued that archaeology had experienced a temporal revolution in the pre-evolutionary 1850s that would free it from the biblical time of such archaeologists as Whewell. Biblical time had limited human existence to a framework that could not account for some of the findings of archaeologists who went further afield than Britain and who found six-thousand-year-old evidence of civilized man. The contemporary foreign savages were previously thought to be those who had declined from a higher degree of ascendance on the chain of being, having passed through a period of degeneration.[32] Given these developments, there was no need to assign mythical or supernatural reasons to changes in intelligent life, for a naturalistic model of causation could be established. It is this breakthrough that allowed for evolutionary Darwinism, which would still be criticized for its partial employment of the Lamarckian principle that acquired characteristics could be inherited.

Changes in archaeology, which led to an interest in proving the actual existence of a past once thought to be mythical and an establishment of the difference between a Western cultural heritage and those of the colonies, paved the way for Darwin. Archaeological work that uncovered links between, for example, ancient India and the third level of Troy, as in Schliemann and Müller's collaboration around the *svastika,* would assist also in the establishment of a theory of one human species rather than the *polygenism* of Cuvierian comparative anatomy that would continue to be so popular in France and had been extremely influential in rejecting Lamarck's evolutionary theories. The comparative model, for example, of Schliemann and Müller would, with post-Darwin anthropologists like Tylor and Frazer, change to one that saw the contemporary "primitive" as a version of the early stages of human society that was still in the process of formation. As George Stocking has argued in his defense of Tylor's evolutionary anthropology as the liberal choice of methodology and theory within an extremely conservative and racist climate, the essential psychic unity of Man could now be posited. Whereas Prichard attempted to prove the singularity of the species, it was for Tylor a necessary concept that allowed him to propose a singular evolution of religion from animism. And Frazer could see the evolution from magic to animism and on to science.

This paradigm of psychic unity sounds Jungian, for through the assembling of beliefs and customs from a variety of cultures certain archetypes can be distilled. But Freud read the contemporary anthropological subject slightly differently than did Jung. For Freud, the primitive was one who "awaits treatment," rather than one who serves a function in the distillation of psychological archetypes.[33] Historically speaking, of course, many of the colonized did "await treatment," as will be seen in later chapters. But Freud's comment serves another function. The gesturing toward the future is a necessary mechanism to sustain the narrative of Progress, which is made possible by an accounting for the past, and importantly, by accounting for a response to and desire for "our own" dead.[34] Accounting for this desire, Freud's sense of public history as a process of private mourning allowed for a conceptualization of desire for the dead, the lost, and the past, since "mourning is regularly the reaction to the loss of a loved person, or to the loss of some abstraction which has taken the place of one, such as one's country, liberty, an ideal and so on."[35] It also provides for an understanding of possibilities for the future once the past event has been assimilated into a narrative of self, or of history—or a history intimately conceived as one's own.

Freud's motivation for writing *Totem and Taboo* is clearly stated in his preface; he wished to engage Wundt's work on taboo and Jung's scholarship, which sought to establish individual psychology from an analysis of social psychology. Both were unsatisfactory. Wundt's explanation that taboo found its origins in fear and belief in demons is totally inadequate for Freud. Comparing the primitive to the neurotic with obsessional prohibition, Freud found the explanation in feelings of ambivalence arising from repression of an instinct and simultaneous performance of a preservation instinct, a theory that he had developed in the prewar and war years and that he would later replace with his concept of the life (sexual) instincts and the death (aggressive) instincts.

His disagreement with Jung was much larger, but not directly engaged. Freud implicitly rejected the notion that there is a collective unconscious determined by and working as a Zeitgeist, or collective spirit of the age, existing alongside an individual unconscious. Jung's *collective unconscious* is made up of character archetypes, inherited contents, and instincts. Freud finds such a model of the unconscious unsatisfactory, and it contrasts quite obviously with his highly individualized descriptions. In *Totem and Taboo*, he used anthropology to understand collectivities or groups of people without proposing a collective unconscious. The model of continuity he chose was the evolutionary progressivist one rather than one of a collective unconscious. This allowed him to make use of a theory of psychic unity and continuity, as well as commonalities among groups of people. But it dispenses with a collective unconscious, forming its argument through a teleological description of the gradual process of individuation through which the subject is formed. Freud's study of the relationship of the modern individual to the group would be continued in his psychoanalytical ethnographic study *Group Psychology and the Analysis of the Ego.*

Broadly following Frazer's understanding of the trends in evolutionary models of magic, animism, and science,[36] Freud posited the first evolutionary phase as one in which there is magic, primitive taboo, shame, and collective working through of contiguous relations. The second is based on animism, religious law and morality, guilt, and personal interactions. The third is structured on science, state enforcement of law, and regulation of mental health, criminality, and pathology or neurosis. And it is, unsurprisingly, the Oedipal overthrow of the father that necessitates the emotions of taboo, shame, and guilt, and in modernity, neuroses; in a model of cultural heredity, the subject relates to the originary slaying of the father, albeit with the dominant cultural patterns of the specific moment in civilization.[37] Like Frazer, who will base his multivolume *The Golden Bough* on the simple question of why Diana's priest in the grove at Nemi should be succeeded by his slayer, Freud gives a kind of foundation myth that he wished to explain as the origin of an individualized social order and, rather problematically, as a conscience in which neurotics bore a similarity to primitives.[38]

Even though Foucault would later suggest that "nothing is more alien to psychoanalysis than anything resembling a general theory of man or an anthropology,"[39] the Freudian struggle to resist this tendency in, for example, Jungian analytic psychology is essential to establishing the *calm violence* of the transferential relationship that will assist in the interpellation of subjects as sovereign. As Freud says, "Taboo is not a neurosis but a social institution. We are therefore faced with the task of explaining what difference there is in principle between a neurosis and a cultural creation such as taboo."[40] Indeed, the recognition that taboo is not a neurosis shows that Freud included in his consideration the ways in which particular ages produce certain social institutions. Tylor too saw primitive cultures as having their own institutions, and yet for him Britain was clearly the top of a developmental ladder. *Totem and Taboo* manifests a more conflicted response to the idea of what in the anthropological field is known as "reform," and in the psychoanalytic, as cure.

Totem and Taboo: The Different Cultural Institutions

Later in *Totem and Taboo,* obviously under the influence of Durkheim, Freud writes: "[The] single comparison between taboo and obsessional neurosis is enough to enable us to gather the nature of the relation between the different forms of neurosis and cultural institutions, and to see how it is that the study of the psychology of the neuroses is important for an understanding of the growth of civilization."[41] The study of neurosis shows a growing distinction between the private and the public spheres that will be central to the constitution of the modern subject. For Freud's thesis about taboo is that it is constituted through a relationship of ambivalence. The public taboo against incest establishes sexuality as a part of a sphere in which the whole clan participates. Freud's naturalized nuclear family ("the real family")[42] is extended to include all other members of a clan, and the principle of exogamy gives rise to vigilance about sexual activity among clan members. Thus, a social order is established through the clan responsibility for its maintenance and is not assigned to individuals with a conscience, but to the entire clan. Shame in the face of other members of the clan governs the behavior of those who make up the group.

Freud adopts Frazer's rather unsatisfactory and tautological argument that the era of magic, in which the magician can manipulate nature and thus control the outcomes of certain actions through the establishment of taboo, declined because it proved to be inadequate. Following this, the era of animism or religion gave a spiritual reasoning for social order. Freud follows the early Durkheim, who suggests the capacity of ritual and religious law to maintain this: "Religion ceases to be an inexplicable hallucination and takes a foothold in reality. In fact, we can say that the believer is not deceived when he believes in the existence of a moral power upon which he depends and from which he receives all that is best in himself: this power exists: it is society."[43] Within Freud's logic, progressing from Durkheim, there are the beginnings of personalization and individuation of actions and a growing conscience in which shame will be replaced with guilt. But this guilt, particularly in the form in which it can be expunged through confession or some other ritual, is less internalized and more formally accounted for in the religious model than in the modern system in which social order is maintained through state enforcement of law and regulation of mental health. The pathologization and criminalization of transgressions of the social order divides completely the subject's world into public regulation and personal, individuated responsibility. Freud's argument suggests that there are neurotics in the modern era because the former mechanisms for maintaining social order have fallen apart. Now, the responsibility of dealing with transgression is turned inward into the psyche with a calm violence. This is most apparent in the control of sexual behavior in which individualized repression splits the subject into private and public, and in mourning rituals, interesting because they express the difficulties of understanding desire in relation to the dead and the past. In the context of sexual repression, the public arena meets out the punishment for transgression, and the individual can rarely balance the opposing draws of the sexual drive and the preservation instinct:

> The clinical history of a typical case of "touching phobia" is as follows. Quite at the beginning, in very early childhood, the patient shows a strong *desire* to touch, the aim of which is of a far more specialized kind than one would have been inclined to expect. This desire is promptly met by an *external* prohibition against carrying on that kind of touching. [Both the desire and the prohibition relate to the child's touching his own genitals.] The prohibition is accepted, since it finds support from powerful *internal* forces [that is, from the child's loving relation to the authors of the prohibition], and proves stronger than the instinct which is seeking to express itself in the touching. In consequence, however, of the child's primitive psychical constitution, the prohibition does not succeed in *abolishing* the instinct. Its only result is to *repress* it.[44]

The ambivalence pertaining to the prohibition is something different from the *taboo* itself, in spite of the apparently oxymoronic concept of taboo as the sacred and the unclean, as well as Freud's Durkheimian definition as "a symptom of the ambivalence and a compromise between the two conflicting impulses."[45] The child's psychical condition, in this context the instinct to masturbate, is understood as primitive, but the social order in which it is understood as primitive is very definitely in *Totem and Taboo* presented by Freud as modern and civilized. The pathological split afforded by individualized repression gives rise to a very *modern* problem.

And perhaps this is not simply a modern problem in the evolutionary sense, but a problem for modernity, as Freud begins to suggest later in *Civilisation and Its Discontents.*

But modernity has to be understood beyond its parochial European context as colonialist. Even in *Totem and Taboo* Freud tells us: "The asocial nature of neuroses has its genetic origin in their most fundamental purpose, which is to take flight from an unsatisfying reality into a more pleasurable world of phantasy. The real world, which is avoided in this way by neurotics, is under the sway of human society and of the institutions collectively created by it. To turn away from reality is at the same time to withdraw from the community of man."[46] This withdrawal from the "community of man" characterizing the isolation of neurotics seems an inevitable outcome of the *illness* of modern society. (As Ernest Gellner, in his refutation of psychoanalysis, which almost acknowledges its anthropological import, exclaimed, "In brief: the news of the plague which is upon us and of its character is, in rough outline, true. The news brought us about the cure is not. *C'est la therapie, et non pas la maladie, qui est imaginaire.*")[47]

Interestingly, Freud assumes a "community of man," in spite of breakdowns in ritual and social orders that link man primarily through identification with the group, in favor of identification through interpellation. I suggested at the beginning of this chapter that one of the central differences between the two disciplines of psychoanalysis and ethnology is the concentration on the one hand on individuals, and on the other on groups. Freud, however, will later write on the group and how the individual participates within it. How the modern group differs from the Darwinian "primal horde," "with which archaeologists endeavor to lighten the darkness of prehistoric times,"[48] will be one of the central questions of *Group Psychology and the Analysis of the Ego,* where the group is not naturalized as an extension of the family, but is very definitely conceived as *artificial.* What this means for individuals' identifications with cultures, civilizations, and nations will be the focus of the next section.

The Modern Individual and the Modern Group

In his destroyed metapsychology paper of which a 1915 draft was discovered in 1985, "A Phylogenetic Fantasy," Freud considers in Lamarckian fashion the way in which mental disorders change depending on the survival needs for mankind. Taking a slightly different direction than that of *Totem and Taboo,* he adds another equation to that of ontogeny recapitulating phylogeny, and considers developmental ages for two particular kinds of mental disorders — transference neuroses, including anxiety hysteria, conversion hysteria, and obsessional neurosis; and narcissistic neuroses, including dementia praecox, paranoia, and melancholia mania. These have adapted as a result of both climatic (for example, the end of the Ice Age) and sociological changes affecting mankind's needs for survival. Freud writes:

> If the dispositions to the three transference neuroses were acquired in the struggle with the exigencies of the Ice Age, then the fixations that underlie the narcissistic neuroses originate from the oppression by the father, who after the end of the Ice Age assumes, continues its role as it were, against the second generation. As the first struggle leads to the patriarchal stage of civilization, the second [leads] to the social; but from both come the fixations which in their return after millennia become the disposition of the two groups of neuroses. Also in this sense neurosis is therefore a cultural acquisition. The parallel that has been sketched here may be no more than a playful comparison.[49]

It is perhaps the playfulness of the comparison that caused Freud to destroy his final draft of the essay, and as Ilse Grubrich-Simitis has suggested, also to abandon the research into the psychological implications of Lamarckian theory of the will or volition that brings about evolution or adaptation, which he had considered pursuing with his Hungarian colleague Sandor Ferenczi. But Lamarck's theories offered him a way to conceptualize the relationship between individual and group without having to share Jung's theories of a collective unconscious. Mental illness as a cultural acquisition that goes through (highly gendered) evolutionary models is suggestive of cultural as well as natural causes for the development of certain mental states. Discussing the onset of the more modern neuroses and the gendered nature of the originary killing of the father who jealously kept the women of the tribe as his own property, and subsequent creation of the homosexual primal horde that eventually would institute exogamy, he will resort to the phylogenetic fantasy in order to consider how cultural heritage is sustained, and how it spreads across genders:

The triumph over the father must have been planned and fantasized through countless generations before it was realized. How the dispositions produced by the father's oppression spread to women seems in itself to create greater difficulties. The vicissitudes of women in these primeval times are especially obscure to us. Thus, conditions of life that we have not recognized may come into consideration. But we are spared the grossest difficulty by observing that we should not forget human bisexuality. Thus women can assume the dispositions acquired by men and bring them to light in themselves.[50]

This puzzle arises for Freud in relation to the reproduction of the primal horde. Men who were responsible for overthrowing the father because he threatened them with castration are bound together by guilt. But how did this horde reproduce? And how did cultural transmission take place? In *Group Psychology,* Freud presents us with modern groups, which he describes as *artificial groups,* suggesting a transition from primal horde to artificial group. The first phase, according to Freud, was patriarchal, but he is unclear how the second phase relates to patriarchy. He suggested the possibility of "new acquisition" and "influences"[51] that exist alongside that which could be literally inherited. If, thanks to biological bisexuality, the *homosexual horde* can reproduce, then men and women who are products of that relationship may inherit a disposition for modern neuroses. But is a group simply bound together by the neuroses they share? And, in terms of the colonial paradigm that interests us, how does *culture* spread within a group in a way that, rather narcissistically, maintains its sense of superiority to the *primitive other*?

If *Totem and Taboo* gave Freud a way of understanding the relationship between historical and individual memory, and thus affiliation to a group, *Group Psychology and the Analysis of the Ego* attempts to understand how the modern group is bound together. If the social contract was based upon collective guilt for the primitive, modern man seems bound together through libidinal ties of a different nature. And it is the theorization of the ego-ideal that allows Freud a way of formulating a modern contract for an artificial group. This ego-ideal allows simultaneously for an understanding of how one becomes a self through the mechanisms of narcissism, and how identification with a group occurs—something that appears, on the surface, as the inverse of narcissism. To explain this, it is first necessary to say something about the psychoanalytic understanding of narcissism in isolation, and then relate this to the sustaining of the ego and identification with others. The idea of sustaining a modern self and a modern group is constitutionally invested in creating a primitive and colonized other. This is both constitutive of a discourse of modern self-hood, and also of the description of the social context that gave rise to modern neurosis.

The Constitution of the Modern Self and the Modern Group: Narcissism and Identification

The term *narcissism* derives from the myth of Narcissus, who directed his love toward an image of himself. This concept became important for Freud centrally in an essay called "On Narcissism" (1914). It is related to the idea of cathexis, an *economic* concept referring to the psychical energy, originating from internal sources, that is attached to an idea or a group of ideas, to a part of the body, or to an object, thus transforming the perception of them. Freud thought it normal to cathect onto objects, thus creating object-cathexes through a process of *object-libido*. He also noted the directing of energy into the preservation of self, when libido is cathected onto the ego. He termed this *ego-libido*. In his early work "Psychoanalytic Notes on an Autobiographical Account of a Case of Paranoia" (1911), Freud thought of ego-libido as something that occurred in an early stage of sexual development, suggesting that a child unifies his or her sexual instincts by taking him/herself as the first love-object. In "Mourning and Melancholia" (1915–17), he began to observe a connection between structural narcissism, as described in "On Narcissism," and a return to an earlier stage of erotic development, because an early form of narcissistic cathexis assists in the unification of the ego. Freud, influenced now by Karl Abraham, in his early work on narcissism (1908), wrote: "We are bound to suppose that a unity comparable to the ego cannot exist in the individual from the start; the ego has to be developed. The auto-erotic instincts, however, are there from the very first; so there must be something added to auto-eroticism—a new psychical action—in order to bring about narcissism."[52]

The very constitution of the ego as something produced out of narcissism caused Freud to understand *narcissistic identification* as a reversion to an earlier stage of development. He associated this with the oral stage in which pleasure is gained through oral satisfaction like sucking at the breast. Sucking becomes more than a means to drink milk. It is also an incorporation of an object into oneself. This emphasis on orality in adult life rather than in infancy is suggestive of a regression for Freud, or of the dissolution of the Oedipus complex. However, by the time Freud wrote *Group Psychology and the Analysis of the Ego,* his conception of narcissism's function in the sustaining of the ego had changed once again. He began to understand narcissism as *structural* and economic rather than developmental. Narcissism became a kind of wall that exists directing all libido toward the ego rather than out toward an object that would, in the older model, be incorporated.

But the formation of a unified ego that was posited in "On Narcissism" required narcissism that must be kept at bay through parental intervention. This, according to Freud, resulted in the formation of an ego-ideal. For Freud, an ego-ideal is a figure combined from narcissism (ego-cathexis—idealization of the ego) and identification with the parents, their substitutes, or their collective values. Thus a separation takes place between ego-ideal and ego, the former being projected as an ideal onto someone or something else. Freud ends "On Narcissism" looking forward to *Group Psychology:*

> The ego-ideal opens up an important avenue for the understanding of group psychology. In addition to its individual side, this ideal has a social side; it is also the common ideal of a family, a class or a nation. It binds not only a person's narcissistic libido, but also a considerable amount of his homosexual libido, which is in this way turned back into the ego. The want of satisfaction which arises from the non-fulfillment of this ideal liberates homosexual libido, and this is transformed into a sense of guilt (social anxiety). Originally this sense of guilt was a fear of punishment by the parents, or, more correctly, the fear of losing their love; later the parents are replaced by an indefinite number of fellow-men. The frequent causation of paranoia by an injury to the ego, by a frustration of satisfaction within the sphere of an ego-ideal, is thus made more intelligible, as is the convergence of ideal-formation and sublimation in the ego ideal, as well as the involution of sublimations and the possible transformation of ideals in paraphrenic disorders.[53]

Paraphrenic (or schizophrenic) disorders aside, the ego-ideal in *Group Psychology* was clearly differentiated from the ego. The subject substitutes another person for the ego-ideal, and this accounts for love of leaders, and also subordination to hypnotists or group leaders, particularly in *artificial groups* like the church or the army. The modern artificial group is based on a convergence of "a number of individuals [who] have put one and the same object in the place of their ego-ideal and have consequently identified themselves with one another in their ego."[54] "Each individual is a component part of numerous groups, he is bound by ties of identification in many directions, and he has built up his ego-ideal on the most various models. . . . Each individual . . . has a share in numerous group minds—those of his race, of his class, of his creed, of his nationality etc.—and he can also raise himself above them to the extent of having a scrap of independence and originality."[55] The artificial group is one that the individual does not realistically have the option to leave (and perhaps one could argue that this is not really the case in the large artificial group known as modern liberal nation state). It is interesting that Freud chose the church and the army as his two examples of modern artificial groups. In the context of missionary action and imperial rule in the colonies aided by the military, they are tied definitionally very closely to the colonizing nation.

In *Group Psychology* Freud analyzed the social nature of the individual. While his main focus was the group, he never lost sight of the individual. He wrote of how individuality came into being through social interactions and through group participations, and the way that group psychology functioned. He was particularly concerned with the reduction of intellectual thought among group members when they lose their capacity to think individually in a sophisticated manner, and give up their intellect to the general will of the group. Freud took two different analyses of this into account—Gustave Le Bon's and William McDougall's. The latter suggested that reduction of intellect in group activity could be overcome by assigning individual tasks within the group so that the group itself is not simply thinking collectively. If they are thinking collectively, then each individual feels less of a responsibility to use his or her own intellect to its full capacity, especially given that there are differential intellectual levels in any one group. If they are thinking to the best of their ability, they are not thinking *as a group,* but may be competing within it or being educated within it; this sets up different levels, thus causing the group to be differentiated, and potentially thus causing it to break down because of the development of a *critical agency.*

The Loss of a Developmental Ideal:
Mourning and Melancholia

For Freud, the development of the modern group creates, it follows, a reduction of individual intellect for the sake of the group. This runs counter to a developmental model in which the modern nation-state was, in Freud's era, the apotheosis of the group. Freud had hoped for the advancement of modern man toward pacifism in "Why War?" (1933) and "On Transience" (1915), suggesting that people could hope for adequate mourning and thus the restoration of beauty. The threat of transience gives it "scarcity value," goes Freud's argument. In war, the values of the beauty of the world are lost. If mourning is not completed, then beauty will not be restored; but if it is, there will again be admiration for the world and civilization. But there is no faith in that advancement in Freud's writings, and it was already a thwarted ideal in *Why War?* Reading *Totem and Taboo* together with *Group Psychology,* the ambivalent feelings that are formalized by primitive man into taboo and mourning rituals become symptomatic of an inability to complete the work of mourning and an inability to be part of a group in the modern context. Freud, however, may explicitly tell a different story. "Just as primitive man survives potentially in every individual, so the primal horde may arise once more out of any random collection; in so far as men are habitually under the sway of group formation, we recognize in it the survival of the primal horde."[56] "The hypnotist awakens in the subject a portion of his archaic heritage which had also made him compliant towards his parents and which had experienced an individual re-animation in his relation to his father."[57] The function served by ambivalence in the modern context causes quite a different structure to the group than ritualized feelings of ambivalence into taboo. For Freud, ambivalence was conceptualized either, following Darwin, as conflict, or as repressed, ultimately causing disturbances, pathological mourning, or melancholia.

Lucille Ritvo has suggested that as early as 1895 in the *Studies on Hysteria,* "Freud looked upon the symptoms of his patients as the result of a conflict between an unacceptable wish or thought and the ideational mass or ego." Ritvo saw this as an offshoot of basic Darwinian thought, claiming that "Lamarck's evolutionary theory seen as 'innate tendency to evolve' and 'volition' did not, like Darwin's 'struggle for existence,' stress conflict. The idea of conflict is omnipresent in Freud's work and remained basic to his thinking throughout his life."[58] In Freud's later writing, most notably

"The Ego and the Id," this conflict between the unacceptable wish and the ideational mass becomes the conflict between ego and superego. Finally differentiated from the ego-ideal if not very clearly so, the superego is theorized as having a more regulatory function than the ego-ideal, who represents more what the subject would like to be than what she feels she is expected to be. Within the ego, conflict functions slightly differently, as does ambivalence. Trauma, and the memory of it, causes a splitting whereby the ego is separated into "separate psychical groups" that need to be bound together through psychical working out.[59]

This early concept of psychical working out is later described, in "On Narcissism," as a damming up of libido to protect the singularity of the ego. In "Mourning and Melancholia," the idea of working out or through is accompanied by a loss of concern with the world that is demonstrative of a retreat inwards of libidinal energy. This retreat confirms to the mourner that he or she lives. Memories associated with the dead person have to be retrieved and *killed off*, being relegated to a place in the history of the individual rather than intruding on the present. The threat of death that is often associated with the guilt of remaining alive is thus *worked through* in mourning, and much of the quite narcissistic work that needs to be carried out involves "a devotion to mourning," but simultaneously, a "reality testing" that confirms the loss even in the face of a desire to cling to the illusion that the dead still live.[60] Pathological mourning occurs, however, when some ambivalence has existed in relation to the person or thing that is now lost. "The conflict due to ambivalence"[61] causes the subject to feel responsible for the death.

In melancholia, it is unclear what the subject has lost, because the ego has identified with the lost object through a process of inversion. Freud's example, in "Mourning and Melancholia," involved a widow who reproached herself for being incapable when she was in actuality criticizing traits of her dead husband. In melancholia, "dissatisfaction with the ego on moral grounds is the most outstanding feature." The patient has experienced "a loss in regard to his ego." This causes the existence of the *plaint* or a kind of lament.

The abandoned object was "swallowed whole" into the melancholic self. Freud described the complaints by the melancholic as a critical agency separate from the idea of the ego itself. Self-regard is totally lost: "part of the ego sets itself over against the other."[62] Self-criticism originated for Freud in the conscience. The conflict between the ego and the loved person has turned "into a cleavage between the critical activity of the ego and the ego as altered by identification."[63]

Occasionally, melancholia changes into mania, "a state which is the opposite of it in its symptoms."[64] Mania, a kind of psychosis characterized by elation and acceleration of both physical and mental activity, is in some ways the flip side of the depression associated with melancholia. But there is a failure in mania of reality-testing.[65] When one is mourning, one does the work of expending energy that dissipates an attachment to a love-object. Because of feelings of ambivalence toward the love-object in melancholia, however, the work of dissipation becomes much more complicated.[66] The same kind of reality testing is also not possible, because it is unclear to that melancholic what has been lost;[67] the ideal could be something as abstract as a nation.[68] There is thus some "withdrawal from consciousness," as a number of different repressed thoughts and actions are at work in the process of melancholia. "The accumulation of cathexis which is at first bound and then, after the work of melancholia is finished, becomes free and makes mania possible must be linked with regression of the libido to narcissism. The conflict within the ego, which melancholia substitutes for the struggle over the object, must act like a painful wound which calls for an extraordinarily high anticathexis."[69] The regression to an earlier stage then disengages any *conscience* that has been functioning to maintain the ego in civilized society through complying with its norms and shaping its own desires accordingly. Mania occurs at that moment of regression because there is no conscience functioning and there is a proliferation of libido cathected toward the ego. Mania in this sense arises out of a conflict between the sexual instinct and the ego-instinct—or instinct for self-preservation.

Freud acknowledged that his theories concerning mourning, melancholia, and mania were unresolved. But he returned to them in *Group Psychology*. It is here that Freud assesses differences between the primal horde and the modern group. Whereas ambivalence was located in the simultaneously sacred and profane taboo or in the rituals of religion in the cultures Freud discussed in *Totem and Taboo*, it is now internalized into a splitting which has to be sutured in the narcissistic work of binding if it is not to become pathological, melancholic, or manic.

Ambivalence was not unconscious in the totemic clan or the primitive religious groups described by Tylor or Frazer. The process of mourning is similarly not unconscious, even though the temporary self-absorption afforded by the process of the work of mourning may seem very similar to a pathological state. However, when there is ambivalence toward the lost object, there does not remain in modern society any ritualized way of channeling it other than into the pathological behavior witnessed in melancholia and in mania. An early ambivalence thus becomes pathologized, and interestingly confused by Freud with similar symptoms of ambiguous feelings, uncanny or confused feelings that could be symptoms of a repressed heritage of the primal horde's slaying of the father.[70]

The totemic clan was held together by the formalization of ambivalence into totem and taboo. The modern group, however, in Freud's logic, is thus threatened by feelings of ambivalence. The split between ego and ego-ideal gave rise to group cohesion around a shared ego-ideal that was cathected onto a leader. But when this is considered in relation to melancholia and mania, if the leader, who is in the place of the ego-ideal, fails to live up to that ideal, a critical agency may be employed that causes self-criticism in the case of melancholia when the "ego-ideal might be temporarily resolved into [the] ego."[71] In the case of mania, "the ego and ego-ideal have fused together so that the person, in a mood of triumph and self-satisfaction, disturbed by no self-criticism, can enjoy the abolition of his inhibitions, his feelings of consideration for others, and his self-reproaches."[72] Importantly, this mania gives rise to rebellion. Both mania and melancholia cause a redirection of libidinal energy away from the group leader and members onto the self or manic activity.

The conflict that in Darwin or in Freud would in theory give rise to the survival of the fittest actually may be responsible for its dissolution, since "civilization's" social contract did not adequately account for ambivalence. The terms of melancholia and mania, as well of course of narcissism, give us the information about the psychology of the ego perhaps more than group psychology. But Freud's emphasis was to move away from the idea of a Jungian collective consciousness, or other interpretation of a group mind supplied by Le Bon and McDougall. Where once social models dealt with conflict, ambiguity, and disturbance through the use of totem and taboo, in the archaeological model of the unconscious, uncanniness, déjà vu, and ambiguity arise, all of which result in temporary destabilization, causing one to feel simultaneously at home and not at home when a once buried memory interferes with consciousness and temporarily disturbs the stratified model of the psyche.

Past memory traces and perhaps a heritage of the species now exists under the influence of modern civilization and its incipient restrictions on desire through repression. But what was specific to Freud's concerns, and what he suspected had always been necessary, was an analysis that did not reduce the group to a singular mind, but understood group psychology as a collection of individual psychologies working together and creating unique dynamics. Thus group trauma or a national unconscious cannot be discussed without considering how and why that may be temporarily created. And although libidinal energy is crucial for the binding of a group, and, narcissistically, for a person, there can be no simple analogy of the person and the group, because the very dynamics of ego to group are fundamental to an understanding of the latter; and also the former.

Freud contrasted the modern artificial group with the primal horde because of the nature of civilization's repressions and the multitude of groups, artificial and real, to which one belongs. Repressions cause the very existence of an ego-ideal, for in Freud's views, instinct and civilization run counter to each others' aims. Whether this is caused by education, by the natural development of an "organic repression," or by both varies in Freud's work. In *Three Essays on the Theory of Sexuality* (1905) he wrote, "One gets an impression from civilized children that the construction of these dams is a product of education, and no doubt education has much to do with it. But in reality this development is organically determined and fixed by heredity, and it can occasionally occur without any help at all from education."[73] Following his 1923 theorization of the superego in *The Ego and the Id,* however, the external forces relating to a child's early understanding of the world in which he or she lives as well as the effect that world has on her seem to take more of an active role in psychoanalysis, both Freudian and otherwise.

In *Civilisation and Its Discontents* Freud could continue the work started in earlier essays like "'Civilised' Sexual Morality and Modern Nervous Illness" (1908) and clarified in *Totem and Taboo,* in which he suggested a more genealogical approach. "The single comparison between taboo and obsessional neurosis is enough to enable us to gather the nature of the relation between the different forms of neurosis and cultural institutions, and to see how the study of the psychology of the neuroses is important for an understanding for the growth of civilisation."[74] *Civilisation and Its Discontents* marked an explicit move from individual to social concerns. While the previous books and articles discussed in this chapter had obviously concerned social makeup of *primitive culture* or the psychology of the group, the *civilized* individual who was the potential psychoanalytic patient was of primary interest, set against those anthropological cultures of the nineteenth century. While those individuals were being created in contemporary Europe in opposition to or in progression from the *primitive colonies,* there was, until *Civilisation and Its Discontents,* no sustained study of the culture as a whole that individuated, nationalized, and defined it as civilized.

Civilization and the Oceanic Feeling

At the beginning of *Civilisation and Its Discontents,* Freud set up the modern ego against something named the *oceanic feeling.* The term was derived from Romain Rolland, who on reading Freud's text on religion, *The Future of an Illusion,* had corresponded with him calling for a broader understanding of feelings afforded by religious experience. Rolland's 1927 letter reflects insight from his work on the Indian mystics Vivekananda and Ramakrishna, as well as Mahatma Gandhi. His interest in India had started in the 1890s at the Ecole Normale Supérieure, where he had read the works of the orientalist Eugène Burnouf. Burnouf had introduced Europe to the Zend language, worked extensively on the Indian Parsi community, and had translated from Sanskrit into French and published in both languages the *Bhâgavata Purana.*

But it was not until World War I that Rolland turned his scholarly focus to India in an attempt to explain Hindu mysticism to Europe. Horrified by the ravages of war,[75] he turned to India to try to create a more synthetic, if romanticized, worldview that was free from conflict. While he had some reservations about Ramakrishna's singular vision and devotion to the eternal,[76] he was more enthusiastic about Vivekananda, Ramakrishna's disciple who was responsible for setting up the Ramakrishna order. Vivekananda, for Rolland, was not only a spiritual leader who thought spirituality to be at the heart of Indian society; he was also concerned with the poverty of India, and saw a remedy for this in Western science. Rolland admired this greatly, and saw within it a theory of synthesis that characterized for him India's spirituality, indeed, its oceanic nature. According to Rolland's biographer William Thomas Starr, "he refused to admit two divisions of humanity based on geographical factors."[77] In a letter to D. K. Roy, Rolland spoke of the unity of mankind, seeing Aryan kinship as a telling factor in this: "Now I am a Frenchman of France born in the heart of France, in a family which has been nurtured on the soil for centuries. When I was barely twenty I had no knowledge of the religions and philosophy of India. —I believe therefore that there is some direct family affinity between an Aryan of the Occident and an Aryan of the Orient. —And I am convinced . . . that it was I who descended . . . the slopes of the Himalayas along with those victorious Aryans. I have their blue blood flowing in my veins."[78] Of Mahatma Gandhi he spoke with admiration of a man who

> makes no compromise to admit having been in the wrong. . . . Literally "ill with the multitude that adores him," he distrusts majorities and fears "mobocracy" and the unbridled passions of the populace. He feels at ease only in a minority, and is happiest when, in meditative solitude, he can listen to the "still small voice" within.
>
> This is the man who has stirred three hundred million people to revolt, who has shaken the foundations of the British Empire, and who has introduced into human politics the strongest religious impetus of the last two hundred years.[79]

Rolland's despair at World War I caused him to regret the loss of spirituality in the West, but interestingly, led him to see the spiritual not as an alternative to political or modern life, but rather as something that exists alongside it. Whatever our misgivings about Aryan mythologies now, more than a half century after World War II, Rolland, in the aftermath of World War I, was looking for a cohesive vision of the world without conflict.

In his study of Gandhi, the psychoanalyst Erik Erikson claimed that Freud was chiding Rolland for his exposition of the "oceanic feeling."[80] But Freud's own sense of despair about the state of "civilisation" in 1929/30 would suggest rather an incapacity to believe, and also a vision of conflict outweighing cohesion, which led him to believe that modern man, rather than seeking happiness, seemed to pursue unhappiness as well. This is made all the more clear when considering the work of Erikson's student Sudhir Kakar, on Ramakrishna in *The Analyst and the Mystic,* which throws into doubt Freud's skepticism about the oceanic feeling, although Kakar still sees the mystic's experiences in terms of a regression: "The mystical regression is akin to that of the analysand, an absorbing and at times painful process at the service of psychic transformation. It differs from most analyses in that the regression is deeper."[81] Kakar goes on to explain that the more relational analysts like Winnicott and Kohut are more suitable for mystical analysis than Freud, although, like Freud, he considered the oceanic feeling as a regression to primary narcissism.[82]

But it was exactly the progressive argument that Freud needed to employ in *Civilisation and Its Discontents* to express his despair, which at the end of his life came to a head with *Moses and Monotheism*. Earlier in his career, in 1914, when boasting the widespread applicability of psychoanalysis, Freud had written of the English neurologist Berkeley-Hill's analysis "of Mohammedan Indians," which revealed "that the aetiology of their neuroses was no different from what we find in our European patients."[83] But at this point, as such critics as Ashis Nandy[84] or Kalpana Seshadri-Crooks[85] have demonstrated, the institutional existence and extensive correspondence between the Indian Psychoanalytic Association (founded in 1922) with Freud did not influence a counter-model for psychoanalysis, but rather local adaptations within a larger ethnopsychological framework.

While Freud's own writings and his own ambiguous relationship to nationalism and the state may have allowed for a reading of him "invisible to those too close to him culturally," his writings were never more than ambiguous on the topic of civilization. As Nandy has said, he could be read by the highly colonialist psychoanalyst Berkeley-Hill in India in a manner that would see him as a "radical critic of the savage," or by the first Indian analyst Grindrasekhar Bose as "a subverter of the imperial structures of thought that had turned the south into a dumping ground for dead and moribund categories of the Victorian era."[86]

But Freud's conjecture in *Civilisation and Its Discontents* that civilization led man away from the family into larger groups,[87] and that woman runs counter to civilization,[88] is set against the romanticization of the primitive by Europeans, as well as such colonial obsessions as cleanliness and soap. Anne McClintock's "Soft-Soaping Empire"[89] has made us all aware of the colonial obsession with Pears soap, and reading Freud's "we are not surprised by the idea of setting up the use of soap as an actual yardstick of civilization"[90] thus appropriately appears to express the coexistence of state civilization and colonialism.

Given the emphasis in Freud's own late work on the destructiveness of civilization, it hardly comes as a surprise when Gananath Obeyesekere writes of Freud's earlier topography found in *The Interpretation of Dreams* to be more appropriate to the South Asian context.[91] The aggressiveness, even violence, of the superego in the second topological phase of Freud's thinking in, for example, *The Ego and the Id*, he claims, is too focused on a Judeo-Protestant consciousness. Concentrating on the distinctions between symptom and symbol, he contends that the boundary-building strictures of the superego are not relevant in the South Asian context, which leaves us once again with something like the oceanic feeling— symptom is translated into symbol. Seshadri-Crooks's observation that Obeyesekere is able to account neither for the origin nor for the recurrence of the symbols because he rejects the second topology is pertinent here, for translation from symptom to symbol occurs only with these processes. However, both Nandy's and Obeyesekere's contention, in quite different contexts, that psychoanalysis is not a science but rather "a historical and theoretical discipline"[92] allows us to understand why the second topology is inadequate to the task of mystical analysis. Like Bose, Obeyesekere and Nandy want to leave aside the "arrogant social evolutionism"[93] that runs through Freud's work, and counter it with a reading of Freud that ignores the progressivist framework and sees the utility of the distinctions between a European colonialist and nationalist psyche and a Hindu or Buddhist mystical one.[94]

But if the first topography is adequate to the anthropological analysis of South Asia, Freud, in a phylogenetic framework, would have had no surprises. Nandy's political question and Seshadri-Crooks's political concern lead us to another, as does Obeyesekere's observations on anthropological intersubjectivities. Nandy asks whether the colonialist analysts Berkeley-Hill and Daly were "merely tropical extensions of the arrogant international, 'universal' culture of knowledge of which psychoanalysis was trying to be a part," or were "adapting to the stress induced by the colonial situation with the help of existing psychoanalytic categories."[95] Seshadri-Crooks questions whether Freud's interpretation of the religious (understood largely as monotheistic) framework can account for the polytheistic context of Hinduism. Obeyesekere calls for consciousness of the transferential relationship between informant and ethnographer, in a move that situates him in opposition to Foucault, who considered transference as the defining feature of psychoanalysis and that which distinguished it from ethnography.[96]

Georges Devereux, extolling the universal applicability of psychoanalysis, described it as "the most penetrating set of conclusions ever drawn from the intensive study of a single social class, living at a certain point of history, in a distinctive cultural milieu, which is not even remotely duplicated in intensity or exhaustiveness by the very best existing ethnographic reports."[97] But what these critics demonstrate is both a failure of universalism and simultaneously a relevance of the second topology. Critics like Seshadri-Crooks have demonstrated both the provincialism of psychoanalysis and its broad applicability in the interpellated colonial context. Conflict, as Freud understood it, could be related to out of the framework of World War I, Jewish oppression, and psychic or biological phenomena in which the fittest would survive. The aggression of the superego, understood as the power of this natural science, created, as Deleuze and Guattari would later tell us, Oedipus everywhere. The complexities of local uses of psychoanalysis and reformulations of it, as well as an acknowledgment of the "spread" of the pathological, certainly offer a persuasive argument for psychoanalysis. But Deleuze and Guattari need not be read as counter to this argument for the usefulness of psychoanalysis when they claim in *Anti-Oedipus* that psychoanalysis has performed a colonization of the psyche.

Freud's progressivist model, seen not as evolution but as a history in which those whom he understood to be savages really did *await treatment*, finally both reveals the inadequacy of the oppositional and evolutionary framework in which one is superior to another and shows us the very working of the superego, which interpellates at the expense of an *oceanic feeling*.

Freud's concept of self was clearly one that was created as a national self conceived as civilized. The pathologies he described were ones he perceived to be particularly modern problems that emerged with "civilisation." "Curing" those pathologies (in a structurally parallel manner to reforming in the anthropological material) meant confirming the values of civilization, something that was at times difficult for Freud. But the illnesses he saw emerging in modern individuals and groups like the nation-state were ones in which remainders of ambivalences went unaccounted for in cultural institutions, giving rise to such illnesses as melancholia, characterized as it is by critical agency.

COLONIAL RESCRIPTINGS

3. War, Decolonization, Psychoanalysis

There is a very tenuous "analytic" link between a philosophical conception and the concrete political attitude of someone who is appealing to it; the "best" theories do not constitute a very effective protection against disastrous political choices; certain great themes such as "humanism" can be used to any end whatever. . . . Among the French philosophers who participated in the Resistance during the war . . . none of the philosophers of engagement—Sartre, Simone de Beauvoir, Merleau-Ponty . . . did a thing.—Michel Foucault, "Politics and Ethics: An Interview"

Freud died in 1939 in London, having escaped from Nazi Vienna. The story of psychoanalysis and colonialism resumes four years later in 1943, when Sartre published his philosophical treatise on consciousness, *Being and Nothingness*. In 1945–48 he wrote both *Anti-Semite and Jew* and "Black Orpheus," texts that would become extremely influential for the negritude movement and for theorists such as Frantz Fanon and Octave Mannoni, who were to analyze the colonial mind and who were influenced by psychiatry, psychology, and psychoanalysis alike. In the later part of the chapter, other influences on the negritude movement, particularly in its early pre–World War II years that preceded Sartre's interventions, will be discussed. The journals *Légitime Défense*, *Étudiant Noir*, and *Tropiques* bear testimony not only to the influence of surrealist interest in psychoanalysis but also to other uses of psychoanalysis neither wholly Freudian nor existential.

The previous two chapters analyzed psychoanalysis through provincializing it, that is, through understanding it as a product of a time when nationalism was being theorized, when the self was understood increasingly as a national self, and when nations were being formed and formulated in tandem with the expansion of colonial interests. Through the narratives of colonial disciplines like archaeology and anthropology, Freud theorized his notions of the individual, the group, and the process of unconscious formation. And he elaborated these through theories of the repression of feelings unacceptable to *civilization*. But the understanding of psychoanalysis as a discipline of its time and location, turn-of-the-century middle-class Vienna, is only a part of this project. The view that psychoanalysis was at origin a colonialist discipline like archaeology and anthropology does not explain adequately why it has persisted, or indeed why it was used by theorists of decolonization. Critical anthropologists such as Dipesh Chakrabarty have called for the parochialization of European Enlightenment narratives so as to understand them both contextually and ethnographically. Understanding psychoanalysis as a theory of nationalism allows us to see it as an exemplary document of the modern European moment that gave rise to narratives of nationhood and selfhood that are today so much a part of internal imaginaries that colonials and postcolonials alike *cannot not* think of selfhood entirely independently of psychoanalysis. *Provincialization* also allows us to understand how European literary and disciplinary movements were constituted through the colonial relation rendering psychoanalysis not only a Western discipline or an ethnography of the West, but also importantly a national colonialist formation of the East/West North/South encounter.

The focus of this chapter is the historical moment of Nazism in Austria from which Freud was fashioning the field that was being persecuted as the Jewish science: psychoanalysis. In France, intellectuals during World War II struggled with how to act politically and how the self was to be conceived ontologically so as to allow for action. An ambivalent France was occupied, and one had to choose whether to join the resistance or not. After the war, the issue shifted to support of the de-occupation of France's colonial outposts.

Freud's notion of selfhood began to change as he neared the Second World War. Sartre's position takes an opposing trajectory to Freud's and leads to a notion of *consolidated being,* in contrast to Freud's notion of "splitting." But Sartre's contribution to ontology obviously cannot be reduced to a causal relation with its foundation in the postwar period. He was, like Lacan, greatly influenced by Kojève's lectures on Hegel. Before the war, Sartre, following Freud (as did Lacan in "The Mirror Stage" the same year, 1936), was to write *The Transcendence of the Ego,* which acknowledged the split in self in a way that was not merely echoing the dialectical split of Descartes's "I think therefore I am" but something much greater than that. It was a continuation of Rimbaud's "Je est un autre" (I is another/ I is someone else).[1] Later, in *Being and Nothingness,* he formulated the concept of the *autrui,* which would also bear some resemblance to Lacan's early concept of the Other.

But for Sartre, the dialectical form demanded that in order to establish responsibility—a theme increasingly urgent after the war—the unconscious could not be fetishized, and it could not hold within it the buried secret of an event in the subject's life that would be causally linked to events and feelings in the future. Sartre's notion of being was substantially different from Freudian models, and eventually would be taken up by him to talk about the subjects that are of concern in this book: racism, anti-Semitism, and, most important, colonialism. The postwar years saw increased rights awarded to many peoples from both British and French colonies, increased unrest within the colonies, and independence won by many. Both a sense of horror in response to the dehumanization of Jews during World War II and the recognition by many in the colonies that they would never be given full rights as citizens, even though they were expected to die for the mother-country, led to more of a sense of urgency both in decolonization movements and in the political implications and responsibilities of various theoretical models that remain with us today.

Existential Psychoanalysis: The Ontology of Political Commitment

In postwar France many theorists of decolonization followed in Sartre's footsteps. Some coupled their praise with at times quite harsh critique, like Fanon; others saw him as importantly offering a model of decolonization. There is, in the writings of the period in the French context, a change in response to Sartre. Fanon in *Black Skin, White Masks* (1952) remains quite critical of Sartre's work on negritude even as he displays an interest in *Anti-Semite and Jew.* But as he composed his swan song that would become the revolutionary bible for many a liberation movement, he asked Sartre to introduce the more overtly existentialist *Wretched of the Earth* (1961). Negritude poets Aimé Césaire and Léopold Sédar Senghor, highly influenced by surrealism and surrealist endorsement of psychoanalysis for political ends in the early years preceding the war, would in 1948 have Sartre write the preface to *L'Anthologie de la nouvelle poésie nègre et malgache,* and in 1947 Sartre would be invited by Léon Gontran Damas to write an article in the first issue of *Présence Africaine.* Albert Memmi, whose autobiographical novel *The Pillar of Salt* (1955) is a text quite different from the later and more famous *The Colonizer and the Colonized* (1965), had Sartre preface the latter. The political stakes of the moment demanded, for Sartre and the theorists of decolonization alike, that subjectivity come to the fore in consolidating a theory and practice of political commitment. Freudian, and on occasion Jungian and Lacanian, psychoanalysis for a time satisfied the need for theories of subjectivity for many of the theorists of decolonization. But Sartre's ontology, developed out of a sense of despair at political commitment that seemed to be justified through the unconscious, eventually became the more influential in decolonization struggles.

Sartre's ontology was, in spite of the fact that it decried the irresponsibility of the theory of the unconscious, named by him *existential psychoanalysis.* His work situated psychoanalysis in the philosophical realm of the psychological. Sartre did not psychoanalyze political situations. When he worked on politics, psychoanalysis functioned for him to consolidate his notion of the subject. He placed even his contextually based analyses on an ontological framework. While this may have had ethical implications, he asserted that his work was an ontology rather than an ethics. Sartre saw the attempt to achieve authenticity and freedom as a necessary endeavor to move from fragmentation to consistency. Alignment between consciousness and actions could eventually allow for a transcendence of violence, or, as he would say in the posthumously published *Notebooks for an Ethics,* "In terms of psychoanalysis, one could say that violence is the refusal of being born. It is also the refusal to go from the parts to the whole."[2] Whereas his contemporary Lacan saw the gestalt of the individual as a misrecognition, Sartre saw it to be a necessary, if illusionary, thing to strive for in order that one could act responsibly on the journey to freedom for oneself and others.

But in what way can Sartre's ontology be called psychoanalytic? If the unconscious is taken to be one of the primary terms of psychoanalysis, and its central contribution to be the analysis of the relationship between unconscious and conscious states in individuals and in cultures, perhaps it is incorrect to call Sartre's work psychoanalytic at all. And yet in *Being and Nothingness* Sartre has a chapter on *existential psychoanalysis,* and in the revised 1949 publication of "The Mirror Stage," Lacan, affirming the Freudian heritage that retains the unconscious at its core, situated himself in opposition to a simplistic description of what he also begrudgingly referred to as existential psychoanalysis:

> [Existential] philosophy grasps negativity only within the limits of a self-sufficiency of consciousness, which, as one of its premises, links to the *méconnaissances* that constitute the ego, the illusion of autonomy to which it entrusts itself. This flight of fancy, for all that it draws, to an unusual extent, on borrowings from psychoanalytic experience, culminates in the pretension of providing an existential psychoanalysis.
>
> At the culmination of a society to refuse to recognize that it has any function other than a utilitarian one, and in the anxiety of the individual confronting the "concentrational" form of the social bond that seems to arise to crown this effort, existentialism must be judged by the explanations it gives of the subjective impasses that have indeed resulted from it; a freedom that is never more authentic than when it is within the walls of a prison; a demand for commitment, expressing the impotence of a pure consciousness to master any situation; a voyeuristic—sadistic—idealization of the sexual relation; a personality that realizes itself only in suicide; a consciousness of the other than [*sic*] can be satisfied only by Hegelian murder.[3]

Lacan correctly noted the centrality of the term *commitment* in Sartre's philosophy, and identified a crucial difference between the two: not the much talked about Lacanian split subjectivity, but rather the location of negativity. Lacan also criticized the apparent autonomy of the Sartrean subject, but it is the dialectical murder, or *aggressivity* toward the Other, that is at the crux of the difference between Lacanian and Sartrean notions of the self. It led eventually to a different sense of the status of the Other in politics and in ethics.

We will return to this issue, but first it seems necessary to identify what Sartre meant by an *existential psychoanalysis* and how he differentiated it from what he called *empirical psychoanalysis,* that is, Freudian psychoanalysis. Why would Sartre's existential model become so influential for French decolonization and what influence does it have on those theories today? Psychoanalysis for Sartre was a historicist technology of the individual. It was not something mysterious, and it was not something that sought out the mysterious. It was far from an exploration of a *dark continent,* or, for that matter, the discoveries of sources of rivers or lakes in Freud's language concerning repression, female sexuality, and the unconscious. For Sartre,

> the *goal* of psychoanalysis is to *decipher* the empirical behavior patterns of man; that is to bring out in the open the revelations which each one of them contains and to fix them conceptually.
>
> Its *point of departure* is *experience;* its pillar of support is the fundamental, pre-ontological comprehension which man has of the human person. . . . Here as elsewhere, truth is not encountered by chance; it does not belong to a domain where one must seek it without ever having any presentiment of its location, as one can go to look for the source of the Nile or the Niger. It belongs *a priori* to human comprehension and the essential task is an hermeneutic; that is, a deciphering, a determination, and a conceptualization.[4]

While Freud's scientific descriptions of the unconscious could be advanced as necessarily empiricist, his prose, rich with archaeological metaphor and the language of exploration, was a far cry from Sartre's. Sartre very explicitly defined psychoanalysis in opposition to language associated with mystery and the inaccessible and unacknowledged parts of self. Even as the language of exploration has a recognizable teleology, Sartre's own language shrouds Africa in alliterative mystery—Niger or Nile, the French colonial territories of West Africa or Egypt—it hardly matters for the colonial representation of the unknown. But Freud very definitely saw his work as a part of that discourse of exploration; Sartre's opposition, which reinscribed colonial exploration as mysterious, saw psychoanalysis as quite distinct from that.

His distinction between empirical and existential psychoanalysis formalized the conscious agency that performs the technology, either as analyst or as analysand. There is no part of psychoanalysis, then, that is beyond a hermeneutic, and Sartre maintained a fundamental distinction between psychoanalysis and diagnostic, more directly curative psychology. The material of analysis may be unknown to the patient, then. But the analyst is explicitly not a colonial explorer or an archaeologist, but rather a philosopher, a scientist, and a responsible figure who is not seduced by the mysterious ambiguity of the unknown. Rather, the analyst is keen to decipher it in order that actions undertaken will be responsibly, and perhaps unforgivingly, chosen and conducted. In *Notebooks for an Ethics,* written in 1947–48, he spoke of psychoanalysis and historical materialism thus:

> Typical and modern idea of *hermeneutics:* the explanation must be hidden. Violence has to be done to man to find it. No doubt chasing after Pan has always presupposed a bird hidden in the bush that needs to be flushed out. But it is only by analogy that one speaks of resistance. Instead the object to be found was *buried.* Whereas the modern idea (which is applicable only to the sciences of man) implies the idea of negative forces that must be conquered, intent as they are on keeping their secret. . . .
>
> . . . . In both cases [psychoanalysis and historical materialism] it is a question of practical methods aimed at changing the world more than at knowing about it. Analysis is a method aimed at a cure: historical materialism is just an empty word if it is not to be found in and through the class struggle.
>
> In both cases these kinds of pragmatism are at the same time forms of skepticism—they fail to ground truth. Therefore to found themselves. Question: what is the structure of our society that provokes the appearance of this emphasis on hermeneutics?
>
> Failure.[5]

Sartre proposes, then, the psychoanalytic in a manner quite in contrast to Freud. Whereas psychoanalysis appears to work within a model of "typical hermeneutics," Sartre seems to suggest its more modern character. Psychoanalysis, rather than failing to find an end, seems to have one that is quite clearly proposed: it is aimed at a cure; negative forces must be captured because they conceal secrets, and closure to the analysis can thus be sought. This form of scientism, for Sartre, stands in contrast to the endorsement of the mysterious, the unconscious, and the speculative. Failure to achieve this end is what fuels a hermeneutic rather than endorsing a process of analysis. Yet, he suggests, psychoanalysis is also a failure to ground truth.

But this curative model of psychoanalysis stands in contrast to Sartre's analysis when he distinguishes between psychoanalysis and psychology.

The necessity of proclaiming an *end* stems from the importance of commitment, which, he proposes, is elided if we cannot posit the subject as at least potentially free. This, of course, is what Lacan finds most profoundly objectionable in Sartre's work, because choice for Lacan will always be complicated by the workings of desire.

Lacan's characterization of Sartre's existential analysis as sanctifying Hegelian murder will be returned to shortly, for Sartre's own distinction seems more nuanced than Lacan allows for. Sartre, after all, in doing away with the unconscious, is not assuming blind faith in the autonomous ego. In fact, his similarities to early Lacan in regard to the constitution of the subject are more profound than his differences. The decentralization of the autonomy of the "I" in psychoanalysis is usually at least partly attributed to the existence of the unconscious. Sartre, however, locates it elsewhere: "Empirical psychoanalysis in fact is based on the hypothesis of the existence of an unconscious psyche, which on principle escapes the intuition of the subject. Existential psychoanalysis rejects the hypothesis of the unconscious; it makes the psychic act co-extensive with consciousness. But if the fundamental project is fully experienced by the subject and hence wholly conscious, that certainly does not mean that it must by the same token be *known* by him; quite the contrary."[6]

Read through the lens of postcoloniality, the colonial project in Sartre's understanding of psychoanalysis did not allow for an exploration into the Other and into the primitive unconscious of the (Western) self, but was actually a conscious choice to know the unknown that had come into the consciousness of the West (and eventually to exploit it under the guise of exploration). Sartre cast a shadow over the notion of the unconscious, as any act that is performed was, for him, a part of consciousness even if its meaning is not fully known by the subject. For Sartre, the idea that one can decide to censor information from oneself already locates that decision and its subject matter within consciousness. For if the censoring mechanism itself is unconscious, then what is the distinction between the censor and the material censored? Sartre saw the benefit of the psychoanalytic model, as distinct from the psychological one, in the understanding of the present totality of the self in each act that demands accountability for one's act and responsibility for its outcome.

Both kinds of psychoanalysis consider all objectively discernible manifestations of "psychic life" as symbols maintaining symbolic relations to the fundamental, total structures which constitute the individual person. . . . Psychological investigations aim at reconstituting the life of the subject from birth to the moment of the cure; they utilize all the objective documentation which they can find: letters, witnesses, intimate diaries, "social" information of every kind. What they aim at restoring is less a pure psychic event than a twofold structure: the crucial event of infancy and the psychic crystallization around this event. Here again we have to do with a *situation*. Each "historical" fact from this point of view will be considered at once as a *factor* of the psychic evolution and as a *symbol* of that evolution. For it is nothing in itself. It operates only according to the way in which it is taken and this very manner of taking it expresses symbolically the internal disposition of the individual.

Empirical psychoanalysis and existential psychoanalysis both search within an existing situation for a fundamental attitude which cannot be expressed by simple, logical definitions because it is prior to all logic, and which requires reconstruction according to the laws of specific syntheses.[7]

The fundamental difference between the psychological and the psychoanalytic for Sartre, then, is a methodological one that suggests a different relationship to ontology. For the presence of the entire ego is evident in each action. Whereas the psychologist researches an entire picture, considering each action and feeling as a particle within it that belongs to a larger logic, Sartre saw each act essentially as an *acting out,* with the situated experiences of the analysand as a crucial part of his or her condition. This speaks a hermeneutic shift in notions of historicity. Each occurrence or situation is not just a factor of history that builds toward a larger picture of what happened or indeed of a Zeitgeist, but it is an encapsulation of that history—it expresses a *totality of being* that is prior to all logic only because it does not in itself offer a missing part to a larger structure; rather, it is that structure in a capsule. But whereas empirical psychoanalysis may see the cause of this *acting out* as originating in some unconscious factor or desire, Sartre would find it within consciousness—in fact, in the historical reality that makes up both the situation of man and consciousness. Not in knowledge, for if this consciousness is prior to logic, then it is also prior to conceptualization. But its source does not lie in the unconscious—unexplored territory or not. It is a synthesis of strands within consciousness that are as yet unconceptualized.

In this regard, Sartre is not really very different from Plato in his understanding of knowledge as conceptualization, but he is significantly different in his understanding of an intrinsic split, and in what Simone de Beauvoir would term the ambiguity in subjectivity that calls for a choice in both ontological freedom and regard for the ontological freedom of another.

Freedom, Aggression, and the Other: Sartre vs. Lacan

In postcolonial studies, as in feminist studies, the category of the "Other" has been central to the analytical frameworks that have formed in these fields. How woman is positioned as the Other of man was the central concern of Simone de Beauvoir's *The Second Sex*. How the "Orient" was constituted as the Other of Europe was the theme of Edward Said's *Orientalism*. The relationship of the Self to the Other, of the constitution of the Self through the Other, and of the aggression between the Self and the Other are as much philosophical as political questions. In what follows, Sartre's conception of Self and Other is shown to be distinct from other paradigms that referred to themselves in the terminology of psychoanalysis. This will begin to clarify how and why Sartre's form of existential psychoanalysis became influential in the politics of decolonization, and perhaps how and why the politics of decolonization often failed to address questions around sexual difference.

In 1936, in *The Transcendence of the Ego,* Sartre wrote of the meaning of the "I" and how it is constituted in consciousness: "Is the *I* that we encounter in our consciousness made possible by the synthetic unity of our representations, or is it the *I* which in fact unites the representations to each other. . . . The *I* is the ego as the unity of actions. The *me* is the ego as the unity of states and of qualities. The distinction that one makes between these two aspects of one and the same reality seems to us simply functional, not to say grammatical."[8] The undervaluing of the functional and the grammatical as something simple and of negligible significance will mark a break with Lacanian distinctions between the "I" and the "me." But the synthetic nature of selfhood, and indeed the split between the consciousness that projects and the "I" that is synthesized certainly bears some resemblance to the Lacanian mirror stage initially formulated in the same year. Lacan followed Henri Wallon's *psychological* mirror test of 1931, in which he observed the behavior of chimpanzees as they saw themselves reflected in a mirror, and compared it to a six-month-old child's.

The chimpanzee quickly understands the reflection to be an image and loses interest, but the child's interest persists. Wallon, although interested in psychoanalysis, did not hold much faith in the concept of the unconscious,[9] whereas Lacan saw the mirror stage in terms of the unconscious location of the origin of self-awareness, and later aggressivity toward the self image. The split in consciousness for Lacan comes as the child views its image in the mirror and recognizes it as himself but experiences feelings of ambivalence, or aggressivity in Lacan's terms, toward it. It appears complete, whereas the child experiences him or herself as fragmented. The child is filled at once with admiration for the completeness of the self image and feelings of inadequacy.

The autonomous ego so vehemently rejected as a concept by Lacan is a product of the *misrecognition* (*méconnaissance*) of the image of corporeal wholeness reified as psychic wholeness or autonomy. The split that characterizes that misrecognition establishes feelings of aggressivity, and later, in Lacan's *Seminar IV* (1956–57), the mirror stage is not just a historical occurrence in the life of any child, but is actually constitutive of the relationship of aggressivity toward one's own body image — "The mirror stage is far from a mere phenomenon which occurs in the development of the child. It illustrates the conflictual nature of the dual relationship."[10] This dual relationship is in the realm of the subject and an imaginary signifier denoting its gestalt. While this coincides with another factor — that is, the entry into language and the Symbolic — the ambivalence is located in the relationship with the image itself, and in order to resolve this fundamental tension of rivalry with that image, identification takes place, and the self is sutured with that image. The child never feels, however, as complete as it supposes others do around it. The apparent completeness of the mother, a misrecognition in itself, confirms the power of and entry into the Symbolic order, for it is through language that the adult can confirm wholeness on the child. The wholeness of the ego, then, remains a fundamental misrecognition, and so wholeness itself will never be ordained as a goal or cure for the Lacanian. Aggressivity exists in feelings of ambivalence toward the Other that the Symbolic, the big Other itself, confirms. Ambivalence and aggressivity are directed inward, and continue to be directed thus at all moments of identification.

The recognition of these feelings of aggressivity, and therefore the understanding of the gestalt as a misrecognition, is fundamental to Lacanian analysis. In Freud, this aggressivity could be understood in terms of feelings of ambivalence that sometimes arose as ambiguity, déjà vu, the discontents of civilization and the struggle for survival, or indeed uncanniness. They are ambivalent responses to the return of the repressed, and inevitably so if repression is understood as the censorship from conscious life. In the previous chapter, we saw how *ambivalence* was located for Freud in earlier civilizations as *taboo*—the simultaneously sacred and profane encapsulated the working through and reification of ambivalent feelings. In societies without a highly developed ritualistic means of accommodating taboo, these feelings become individualized and indeed individuated. These led to feelings of guilt in relation to ambivalence toward someone who has died, or to something like the creation of a fetish, which Sarah Kofman describes, following de Man, as where the notion of undecidability is foregrounded in Freud's work. For Kofman, the fetish is always a substitution for the undecidable, so "the penis substitute" is actually for Freud a fetishization of the penis itself. The child who creates the fetish looks at the woman with the terrifying undecidable question—*does she have one or not?* To which Freud answers—"No! Substitute something else!" Given the fetish's conceptual history in colonial transaction, which has been elaborated by William Pietz and Anne McClintock, it can be seen now as a figure not only of sexual substitution and ambivalence toward the immanent knowledge of castration, but also of the important nature of the materiality of language in the colonial encounter; for language is the manifestation of undecidability, the acting out of the ambivalence that has no totemic ritual to, as it were, exorcize it.[11]

In an age in which the creation of fetishes is generally deemed abnormal, one of the functions of analysis is to understand the significance of ambivalent feelings, toward an object, toward a person, toward a memory, and in the transferential situation of analysis, toward the analyst him- or herself. The transferential relationship in Freudian psychoanalysis is important for the analyst to witness firsthand the occurrence of a patient's symptom, and he or she can then understand what occurred that caused the patient to *act out* in this way. Having understood this, the analyst can then more fruitfully assist in the working through of the cause of the symptom. Given the internalization of conflict as ambivalence or ambiguity in Freud's understanding of both the symptom and the transferential process, the disturbance that is caused does not distinguish between ambiguity and ambivalence toward another. Thus the relationship to another remains on the level of the subject's own response. In

Lacanian terms, language, as the material form of undecidability, therefore bears the trace of the encounter with the Other experienced through the Symbolic. This is why the linguistic turn in literary, psychoanalytic, and anthropological theory—that is, the introduction of Saussure's linguistics in analysis—has become so crucial. For Lacan, language becomes its own material source for understanding subjects and their aggressivity toward Others; and perhaps, as we shall see in a later chapter, social contexts.

For Sartre, aggressivity is located elsewhere, and this is extremely important for his politicized ontology. Although the existence of the self is similarly confirmed through the gaze of the Other (and in this sense, "I is another"),[12] that Other is not located in the parental figure who is imagined by the subject to either be it (in the case of the mother) or have it (in the case of the father). Although early in Lacan's career his notion of the gaze seems to be the same as Sartre's, later it does not, characterizing their different concepts of Otherness and how they relate to the specular image. For Sartre, the gaze (le regard), that is, the act of looking, confirms to the subject that the Other is also a subject because seeing the other also gives to the subject the possibility of being seen by another.[13] In the process of seeing, then, a parallel is set up between the two subjects, one constituting the self, the other constituting the Other. However, the gaze is also an act of aggression because it is potentially sadistic in its motivation. It seeks to define the Other. The conflict that is a part of being-for-Others, which is being defined by the gaze of the Other, can be overcome by sadistically forbidding the Other to look back, thus confining the Other to masochism.

Lacan's notion of the gaze is similarly suggestive of a parallel in the early years. However, by the time he writes *The Four Fundamental Concepts of Psychoanalysis* (1964), it is precisely a lack of parallelism of the gaze that is at issue. The split between the eye and the gaze itself, which always takes place from a point from which one cannot be, is akin to the split of subjectivity for Lacan. Just as speech divides the Lacanian subject from him/herself into the speaker and the subject of enunciation, so does the look. The one that sees the other looking is not the same as the one who is seen. For Sartre, however, it is the same, for there is not an *unconscious gap* in split subjectivity, and the other does not become a replay of the spectral image in the mirror that causes aggressive feelings in the process of identification.

The split for Sartre is rather between consciousness, or negativity, and being. This is best elaborated in relation to Sartre's key terms of "being-in-itself" (*être-en-soi*), "being-for-itself" (*être-pour-soi*), and "being-for-Others" (*être-pour-autrui*). Being-in-itself denotes the state of existing without any reflection on that state. This state is in some ways the purest form of being because it exists without negativity and without consciousness of that state. This is a state driven entirely by inauthenticity. While Sartre claims that he is not providing an ethics, his language certainly betrays a value system, and this inauthenticity suggests passivity, a total lack of reflection or consciousness, and therefore, in Sartre's terms, an absolute lack of freedom.

Consciousness comes with being-for-itself. Consciousness, as I have described, is not *being;* it is defined as negativity, since it is only a relationship to being without which it does not exist. As negativity, it desires *to be,* although it cannot be. Consciousness is what brings *nothingness* into existence, as relationally it has caused being-in-itself to cease to be complete. Consciousness is, however, the only possible source of freedom for the subject, as it recognizes the subject's *facticity,* or the manner in which material circumstances affect and influence the subject phenomenologically. By being conscious of everything the subject does, and particularly by being astute about the *choices made* by the subject, it allows for authentic behavior, in that one can act in accordance with conscious choices authentically. If one consciously makes a decision to ignore choices, one is acting not in freedom but in *bad faith.*

But if *facticity* is transcended, then there is detachment from pure existence into being-for-Others. In this state, one ceases to be a subject, and similarly ceases to regard Others as subjects, but rather as objects, or as Others. The for-itself realizes that it has existed as a Self for the Other even if it is unavailable as an entire entity for itself. There is therefore no possibility of *unconscious* actions or thoughts in the Sartrean topography. Although consciousness is not the same as *knowledge,* it is necessary for the subsequent existence of knowledge; it is, however, nothingness and as such is not necessarily conceptual in its abilities.

Transference, Countertransference, and Responsibility

Given that there is no unconscious according to Sartre, one could well ask what the function of an analyst is. Sartre gives us a response to this.

We are not dealing with an unsolved riddle as the Freudians believe; all is there, luminous; reflection is in full possession of it, apprehends all. But this "mystery in broad daylight" is due to the fact that this possession is deprived of the means which would ordinarily permit *analysis* and *conceptualisation*. It grasps everything, all at once, without shading, without relief, without connections of grandeur—not because these shades, these values, these reliefs exist somewhere and are hidden from it, but rather because they must be established by another human attitude and because they can exist only *by means of* and *for* knowledge. Reflection, unable to serve as the basis for existential psychoanalysis, will be apprehended *from the point of view of the Other.* Consequently, the *object,* thus brought into light, will be articulated according to the structures of the transcended-transcendence; that is, its being will be the being-for-others even if the psychoanalyst and the subject of the psychoanalysis are actually the same person.[14]

The connoisseur's vocabulary betrays a sense of analyst as intellectual, and analyst as cultured art critic. The movement from reflection to knowledge is articulated as an appreciation of shading, that is, of the meaning of particular nuanced effects. But there is also the possibility of a self-psychoanalysis. The connoisseur may be both analyst and analysand. This being the case, what is it that happens to that other fundamental psychoanalytic category, transference? It is true, of course, that Freud himself performed a self-analysis. But Freud was developing his ideas of psychoanalysis at the time and found self-analysis ultimately to be inadequate; it could be preliminary at best, narcissistic at worse. His "Autobiographical Study," or Selbstdarstellung,[15] situated material about oneself—like a dream—as an artistic form. The self-analysis, then, becomes a project in literary criticism. Just as autobiography is a narrative arranged by someone about his or her self and is understood to be crafted—selective and in some ways fabricated—we may read our own lives in such a light. This is, of course, not without its difficulties, especially in relation to resistance.

Sartre's *psychobiographies* do not exactly fall within the same genre, for he is writing of someone else, but still out of materials by and about that person; in fact, what he considers unique to his form of existential psychoanalysis is that "the behavior studied by this psychoanalysis will include not only dreams, failures, obsessions, and neuroses, but also and especially the thoughts of waking life, successfully adjusted acts, style, etc. This psychoanalysis has not yet found its Freud. At most we can find the foreshadowing of it in certain particularly successfully biographies. We hope to be able to attempt elsewhere two examples in relation to Flaubert and Dostoevsky. But it matters little to us whether it now exists; the important thing is that it is possible."[16] The autobiography, and analysis of it, posits the necessity of objectivity while acknowledging the difficulty of that, something Sartre did not have to consider in relation to the psycho*biography,* except, perhaps, if he were considering the effects of his own unconscious on his writing, or indeed the consequences of *countertransference.* Although Freud initially considered the analysis of one's own dreams to be an important part of becoming an analyst,[17] as long as one is "not too abnormal,"[18] he considered that its usefulness was ultimately limited, for if this were not the case, "there would be no illness,"[19] since one would analyze the cause of a symptom before or shortly after it became one.

For Freud, then, self-analysis is ultimately limited because of the unconscious interference with one's own sense of self and resistance to some information or subjects. This is why transference is so central to the Freudian paradigm. Transference is the emotional response of the analysand toward the analyst, especially when the analysand reacts to the analyst in a manner explicable only in the terms of the analysis, and in terms of the characters featured in the memories being worked through. Something that the analyst says or does may spark a reaction in the analysand that is disproportionate to what was said, signaling that the analyst has approached a subject or a thing that is causing a symptom. This is very useful for an analyst because she or he can witness the occurrence of a symptom as well as be the object of the analysand's reaction. Countertransference, when the analyst's unconscious feelings are at work in response to the analysand, obviously has to be kept in check, and Freud sees this as an arena in which self-analysis is important. The trained ear should be alert to such responses by oneself.[20]

So for Sartre—and perhaps this has its roots in Freud's notions of autobiography and his numerous references to and analyses of literary texts—the psychoanalyst can bring the patient to a more nuanced reading of his or her life story that allows him or her to move from consciousness to knowledge—an appreciation of life's shading. While Sartre suggests that neither the analyst nor the analysand is in a position of privilege to analyze the patient, his doubts about self-analysis are similar to Freud's and are suggestive of the importance of the Other as interlocutor and the mutability of the self as a being-for-Others. He writes: "Both our psychoanalyses refuse to admit that the subject is in a privileged position to proceed in these inquiries concerning himself. They equally insist on a strictly objective method, using as documentary evidence the data of reflection as well as the testimony of others. Of course the subject can undertake a psychoanalytic investigation of himself. But in this case he must renounce at the outset all benefit stemming from his peculiar position and must question himself exactly as if he were someone else."[21] The analyst's function, whether in psychoanalysis or self-analysis, is not to determine where a complex lies, as Sartre claims Freudian analysis does, but rather to find the *original project* or *original choice* that determines the behaviors of the subject. The original project, having been developed through a choice early on by the for-itself, determines the actions of the subject from that time.

That choice is of course fundamental in Sartre, and it is what determines all actions and the *ambivalent* feelings that may precede them. Sartre prioritizes ontology over causation. "It is . . . by a *comparison* of the various empirical drives of a subject that we try to discover and disengage the fundamental project that is common to them all—and not by a simple summation or reconstruction of these tendencies; each drive or tendency is the entire person."[22] Perhaps the priority of one ontology over causation is inevitable, given that Sartre stops short of presenting a method of curative psychoanalysis, even though he points to a cure as psychoanalysis's ultimate function. Sartre has shifted his reading; earlier he would differ with this clinical assessment and claim that psychoanalysis is not so much diagnostic as it is hermeneutic. Here, he points toward the cure as an ultimate goal. Interestingly, he draws on a mirror image to portray a cathartic moment of recognition that bears more relation to the first and second stages of Freudian analysis—the *remembering* and the *repeating* in a transferential situation, rather than the *working through* that presumably Sartre misreads as a curative rather than an ongoing hermeneutic:

> Precisely because the goal of the inquiry must be to discover a *choice* rather than a *state*, the investigator must recall on every occasion that his object is not a datum buried in the darkness of the unconscious but a free, conscious determination—which is not even resident in consciousness, but which is one with this consciousness itself. Empirical psychoanalysis, to the extent that its method is better than its principles, is often in sight of an existential discovery, but it always stops part way. When it thus approaches the fundamental choice,

the resistance of the subject collapses when he *recognises* the image of himself in a mirror. The involuntary testimony of the subject is precious for the psychoanalyst; he sees there the sign that he has reached his goal; he can pass on from the investigation proper to the cure.[23]

The moment of recognition, similar to the moment of *nausea,* takes the place of the transferential *acting out* or *repeating* witnessed in the Freudian scenario. Sartre, who hasn't found his Freud, will not be looking into the darkness, but rather, into the light reflection of sameness—the mirror image.

The fundamental original project in Sartrean thought is crucial for a model of human responsibility, a denial of which is, for him, a pathologization of everything. In the *Notebooks for an Ethics* he writes:

> There is no sickness, delirium, amputation or lesion that is not existed from the inside as a *project.* It is absurd to say that fever causes delirium. Delirium is the way the sick person lives out his fever in projecting himself beyond it toward the world. Similarly, a dream is not produced by sleep, it is the sleeper's enterprise, the way he exists his sleep.
>
> If not existed as a surpassed instrument aimed at the real future— because it has become an unusable mass—the body gets surpassed toward the imaginary as a pure analogon. And the imaginary so projected is *my total project* (whence psychoanalysis), but it is so having undergone the modification of nonpositionality.[24]

If actions and feelings can be ascribed to an unconscious to which there is no access, then, according to Sartre, no one can be presumed accountable for anything. Even though Sartre does not publish his work on ethics (the *Notebooks* appeared posthumously), the ontological argument about *bad faith* in *Being and Nothingness* demonstrates how he conceives of the subject as an entity that must be responsible to itself in order that it may be responsible to Others, even in circumstances that seem horrifying and inescapable. Because consciousness, or being-for-itself, determines our actions through choices, subjects are free. In fact, subjects are, according to Sartre, condemned to be free. Nothing is done unconsciously: "There are no accidents in life; a community event which suddenly bursts forth and involves me in it does not come from the outside. If I am mobilized in war, this war is *my* war; it is in my image and I deserve it. I deserve it first because I could always get out of it by suicide or by desertion; these ultimate possibles are those which must always be present for us when there is a question of envisaging a situation. For lack of getting out of it, I have *chosen* it."[25]

The harshness of this claim is perhaps understandable in the postwar years, when Sartre felt some disgust for the lack of active participation in the French Resistance during World War II. But Sartre is perhaps rather harsh on some participants in the war—subjects like any other—namely the victims of the Holocaust, although of course he saw that the freedom to say "no"—severely curtailed in that situation—was part of human dignity, and anyone who caused another to be unable to say no was acting in sadistic fashion, and was therefore ultimately unfree in ontological terms. If subjects are indistinguishable from and indeed constituted by actions as they speak the totality of existence, then they "have the war [they] deserve"[26] because they have chosen not to die. Perhaps this is what Lacan means by the Hegelian murder. In Sartre's logic, if the world and our experiences of it are constituted by reasoned choices, then they are synonymous with reality. We exist through our actions, and depend on Others for recognizing our choices. If, however, the sense of us as Other places us in a situation that seems unbearable, we may fight for recognition and die in the process through suicide. If not, we choose to live in bad faith, that is, ignoring the consciousness that tells us we are making a choice against freedom.

Herbert Marcuse's criticism of Sartre, written in 1948, identified a lack of understanding of reification in Sartre's work. He claimed that Sartre always saw man as free even when in a condition of actual enslavement. He suggested that the desire for a philosophical theory of freedom ultimately could not account for reification, for example, how the Jew has a very different relation to freedom than the Nazi. In Marcuse's view, philosophy consistently failed in its responsibility toward subjects, and Sartre's emphasis on the freedom of the for-itself was both undialectical and uncommitted. In his postscript of 1965, Marcuse will retreat, admiring Sartre for his preface to Fanon's *Wretched of the Earth* and his declarations against colonial wars. This, he wrote, was finally evidence of how "philosophy becomes politics because no philosophical concept can be thought out and developed without incorporating within itself the inhumanity that is today organized by the rulers and accepted by the ruled."[27] This raises a number of questions. Is the psychoanalytic ontology of the *engagé* intellectual flawed and compensated for by Sartre the man? Or is it possible that Sartre developed a form of psychoanalytically informed philosophy that could produce a level of political and ethical commitment in its practitioners?

The difficulty of Sartre's harsh philosophy comes to a head in *Anti-Semite and Jew,* in which the antagonism and fight for recognition that follows from the Hegelian master-slave dialectic is brought to a sensitive and topical issue. Fanon, in *Black Skin, White Masks,* was to take this text up for scrutiny and criticism as he was Sartre's "Black Orpheus." Sartre's growing interest in the movements for decolonization and the situation of blacks in America. As Sartre never published his work on ethics, which included a work on the situation of blacks in the United States and the justification for violence, it is difficult to analyze the philosophical stake in actual rather than philosophically abstract "politics." The sketches for a treatise on ethics, a work published posthumously, never satisfied him philosophically.

That writing about World War II would spawn more on decolonization is not surprising. Movements for decolonization, particularly in those colonies in which massive resources had been drawn upon for the Free France Movement, were in some cases initiated by activities of the colonized during World War II, and in others extended. The service with which the colonized had supplied France during the war gave credence, in some people's eyes, to the idea of independent nation-states. Sartre's work was important in this regard, for writing on World War II in similar philosophical terms to writing on France's colonies placed France in a position in which it was potentially culpable, once more, for systematic genocide. What is interesting to us in terms of psychoanalysis is how the existential ontological model was employed by those fighting for decolonization, and how Sartre's introductions to many of the important texts of the period from 1945 to 1962 served the function of a literary psychoanalysis.

Primitivism, Surrealism, and Negritude

Ann Stoler has suggested that French intellectuals failed to come up with an adequate analysis of race and decolonization in the postwar years. "Many loudly supported France's colonized populations during the Algerian war. While Albert Memmi, Frantz Fanon and Jean-Paul Sartre were among those who explicitly addressed colonial racism, they did not prompt a general theoretical engagement with racism nor a confrontation with the racial underpinnings of French society itself. The concept of class and the sorts of social transformations to which capitalism gave rise remained foundational in critical social and political theory; race and racial theory was not."[28] With this assessment of Sartre in mind, as well as the prefaces he wrote for Memmi, Fanon, and Senghor, I turn now to Sartre's writing on the issue of race.

Many who were eventually influenced by Sartre's brand of existential psychoanalysis also wrote well before World War II and exerted their own influence on the next generation. For example, Aimé Césaire's neologism — *negritude* — preceded World War II and Senghor and he had used the term in discussion four or five years before it appeared in *Cahiers d'un retour au pays natal* in 1938/39. In the interwar years, and through the Second World War, Suzanne and Aimé Césaire's journal *Tropiques* offered an ongoing critique of the Vichy regime, and formed a psychoanalysis of political resistance that responded to what they called "colonial trauma."[29] The journal offered an interpretation of psychoanalysis quite distinct from Marxist surrealism and existentialism (to which it is often reduced). Suzanne Césaire, Aimé Césaire, and René Ménil posed questions concerning how to address the specificities of colonialism through both psychoanalysis and politics. They came up with responses that foreshadowed many of the arguments in the works of people like Fanon and Memmi on desire, on colonial affect, and on what Octave Mannoni referred to as "the colonial situation," responses, indeed, that provide an alternative context for understanding their work, which is frequently assessed in existential and Lacanian terms.

Memmi and Fanon wrote within the context of negritude, and both implicitly and explicitly drew from this body of work. Indeed, Fanon was educated by Aimé Césaire in the French lycée in Martinique, giving him a more critical education than the lycée's policy of creating *évolués* children may have otherwise provided him. He later campaigned for Césaire when he ran for the position of parliamentary delegate on the Communist ticket. Although he would later become more overtly critical of both negritude and Césaire's politics, the influence of *Tropiques* on Fanon is very clear, not least because of its interest in formulating a psychoanalysis suitable for social critique. In contrast to Stoler, I would suggest that an incisive theoretical engagement with colonial racism began in that journal and that this was not subordinate to a class analysis.

Lilyan Kesteloot documented some time ago, as did Sartre, how

Tropiques followed in the path of more radical predecessors. In *Légitime Dé-fense*, writers like Étienne Léro proposed that the colonies produce poetry that would shed the conventions of assimilationist, academic nineteenth-century French poetry in favor of a poetry influenced by Marx, Rim-baud, Freud, and Breton. *L'Étudiant Noir* had been established by Césaire and Senghor in Paris as an earlier journal of negritude.[30] The stronghold of Freud on the imagination of at least early Martiniquan poetry was drafted in conjunction with Lenin's Third International and Breton's sur-realism, which was in turn heavily influenced by Trotsky's Fourth Inter-national, Freudian psychoanalysis, and primitivism. In fact, the manifesto "Art and Revolution," in which Breton and Diego Rivera wrote of the inextricable interrelatedness of (surrealist) art and (communist) revolu-tion was, Breton revealed, actually coauthored with Trotsky at the time of Breton's visit to him in 1938. For my purposes, the primary interest lies in their psychoanalytic justification for tying together the individual and the political burdens restricting the "emancipation of man"[31] through the Freudian concept of *sublimation:* the repression of early polymorphous libido and redirection of that energy into something more socially valu-able like work. Sublimation, they contended, "tries to restore the broken equilibrium between the integral 'ego' and the outside elements it re-jects. . . . The need for emancipation felt by the individual spirit has only to follow its natural course to be led to mingle its stream with this prime-val necessity—the need for emancipation of man."[32] Art was to be both an expression of the artists' psyche and of practical revolution, an idea that followed Trotsky's own views about art, and how Communists should be open to the teachings of Freud.[33]

Sartre's condemnation of Breton in *What Is Literature?* is interesting to read in this light, given also that Breton would write an introduction to Césaire's work and publish it in *Tropiques* some nine years before Senghor would request Sartre to introduce the *Anthologie d'une nouvelle poésie nègre et malgache.* While Sartre acknowledged Césaire's surrealism, he extolled its radical departure from surrealism rather than surrealism's radical char-acteristics themselves, which had been praised unashamedly by writers associated with negritude. Sartre wrote of Césaire: "Surrealism, Euro-pean poetic movement, is stolen from the Europeans by a black man who turns it against them and assigns it a rigorously prescribed function."[34] With Breton, and even to some extent with Etienne Léro, Sartre saw a surrealism that was simply formal and viewed the surrealist's adoption of psychoanalysis as a departure from the stoic ethics he thought should be condemned. His condemnation of psychoanalysis as an escape from responsibility is brought to bear in *What Is Literature?* on a rejection of poetry that draws attention to the language of the poem rather than that which it, in its most communicative form, designates. The surrealist rendering of language as materiality was, for Sartre, an escape from a real world that could more transparently be represented in prose. Justifications of poetry, he suggested, are akin to those of psychoanalysis: both are an escape from responsibility.

Sartre also saw the surrealist adoption of psychoanalysis as a bourgeois rejection of subjectivity and objectivity. He ridiculed the idea of a radical surrealist agenda that could destroy the structure of the object and thus the conceptual parameters that structure it. The breakdown of the artistic object effectively did nothing, Sartre claimed, for with dynamite and with war, both the artist and the art object about destruction would, of course, be destroyed. "It is always by *creating,* that is, by adding paintings and books to already published books, that it destroys. . . . He ends up doing a lot of painting and writing but he never actually destroys anything. . . . [O]ne must save oneself without breaking anything—or by a symbolic breaking—wash oneself of the original contamination without giving up the advantages of one's position. . . . The surrealists, more ambitious than their fathers, count on the radical and metaphysical destruction."[35] This evasion of the real stems, in Sartre's reading, from the adoption of the kind of psychoanalysis that has led to a watered down Marxism—the situating of subjectivity and objectivity within the same realm—since "the first thing to be done is to eliminate the conventional distinctions between conscious and unconscious life, between dream and waking."[36]

This evasion of the *real* in the name of destruction of bourgeois consciousness signifies to Sartre one of the fundamental characteristics of psychoanalysis. The surrealist project seems to be one of bad faith, with the art object remaining intact ultimately as a simple representation of the real though it does not actually bear on the real. He thus sees the destruction as encompassing a false notion of destruction, negativity, and nothingness. "Each [work] . . . is a project for annihilating the rest by annihilating itself along with it, Nothingness glitters on its surface, a Nothingness which is only the endless fluttering of contradictions. And the *esprit* which the surrealists wish to attain on the ruins of subjectivity, this *esprit* of which it is not possible to have an inkling . . . is neither Hegelian Negativity, nor hypostatized Negation, nor even Nothingness, though it bears a likeness to it; it would be more correct to call it the *Impossible.*"[37]

This condemnation extended to the surrealist embrace of communism. For Sartre, the appearance of a renewed common interest between the intellectual and the proletariat, "which was the good fortune of the authors of the eighteenth century," was not the same for the writer in 1947. "The surrealist is very little concerned with the dictatorship of the proletariat and sees in the Revolution, as pure violence, the absolute end, whereas the end that communism proposes to itself is the taking of power."[38] The lack of proletarian readers of surrealism lent further evidence of the falsity. Sartre saw surrealist support of both Trotsky and the Fourth International as the inevitable support of failed nay-sayers, who, he thought, would always seek out the "Impossible" in failed politics. Simone de Beauvoir adopted a similar position toward the surrealists and to Breton. In her *Ethics of Ambiguity,* she speaks of surrealist negation as a travesty, an ethic or a church of its own with Breton as its pope.[39]

By way of contrast, Sartre situated the negritude movement as having a different relationship to negativity—unsurprisingly much like his own—and saw it following a Hegelian dialectic far more logically. He referred to it as an "anti-racist racism,"[40] a term that has been largely rejected as appropriately descriptive by negritude scholars. This reading of negritude as something quite different from surrealism both as a literary movement and as a political movement need not, however, foreshadow the early investments of negritude in surrealism, and particularly the psychoanalytic side of it, or surrealism in negritude that extended the interest in African art. Without a doubt, the intellectual and political investments of the two movements were different. Lilyan Kesteloot has suggested that "in contrast to the French surrealists, it was not their *own* mental structures or their *own* society they were combating, but a foreign establishment and its detested social order because it was both conqueror and oppressor."[41] But the influence of surrealism and particularly of psychoanalysis led to a theory of a repressed society that should draw on unconscious forces to resist oppression. The libido of the people, suppressed as it is repressed, needed to be rediscovered in order to resist the force of assimilation so dominant in French colonial policy.

Some, like Fanon, would have altered Kesteloot's assessment. According to him, the oppression of a people resulted in a repression and conforming of mental structures that go on to cause either psychological problems or behaviors that are understood that way. For Fanon, repression was not working for the benefit of a healthy ego, or indeed a homogeneous society. Rather, repression was working toward a differential treatment of colonized peoples who were at once taught to assimilate in colonialist schools and simultaneously were excluded from the society that French education would offer a European French person, or more precisely, a European French man.[42] What seems important here, however, is the fact that surrealist anticolonial support as well as coalition with Trotsky's anticolonialism did share some ground with surrealist primitivism, which was inspired by Freud's anthropological and archaeological interest in the "primitive mind" as structured in "unconcealment." The primitivists wanted to be interpellated by the art object of the imagined naive primitive in order to break down unhappiness in "civilization." They hoped to tap into the primitive within themselves as if to escape the violence and strife of worlding. This was a rupture of a class-based aesthetic of advancement and the Kantian European aesthetic.

For the surrealists, the breakdown went beyond the aesthetic realm into the more overtly political. In 1925, following the publication of the "First Surrealist Manifesto," André Breton and his associates openly sympathized with Moroccan insurgents as France engaged in a minor war against these anticolonial rebels.[43] They embraced the challenge of Aimé Césaire's negritude, which disturbed through insurgent metonymy the purity of that most fetishized of things, the French language, and famously, in 1960, the surrealists drafted the "Declaration Concerning the Right of Insubordination in the Algerian War," which came to be known as the "Manifesto of the 121." And so even though the relationship to Europe's imagined "other" was problematic, the revolutionary desire to intervene in politics reflected a simultaneous attempt to both reveal and encourage a transculturation that blew apart a more fetishized and politically regressive distinction between the West and the Rest.

Freud's own interest in primitive art and archaeology cannot, of course, go without a mention here; neither can Breton's similar fascination with primitive artifacts.[44] Freud's office contained various archaeological finds, small artifacts as well as reproductions of pieces like the famous "Gradiva." Breton and André Masson would allude to that same "Gradiva" in their collection of poems, articles, and drawings, *Martinique charmeuse des serpents,* collected following their 1941 visit to Martinique when they met

Aimé Césaire. Freud's own reading of Schliemann caused him to think of the exploration of the unconscious in terms of an archaeological dig, and his own memories of his father led to the "disturbance of memory" on the acropolis initiated by the sight of the ravaged temple. Breton and Masson's feminizing of Martinique primitivized the land as if Gradiva had stepped on it, confusing the archaeological (Pompeii) with the mythical (Eden) and the anthropological, even as they wrote of the troubled waters of Martinique under Vichy rule during World War II and denounced the colonial system that governed Martinique:

> and always in the sun the gate of the *porteuses*
> It is the foot of Gradiva—
> Yes the soil is truly touched—the earth is pressed.[45]

In fact it was the materialization of the past in terms of the "primitive" that demonstrated not only Freud's own vexed relationship to colonial expansion, and his own desire for a naive past, but also perhaps Breton's. Freud himself in many ways was not only an inspiration for primitivist artists, but is in many ways the quintessential primitivist artist himself. His whole conceptualization of the modern subject was one in which a relationship with an unconscious was played out methodologically and materially in terms of a relationship with the past, a more naive moment, and a sense of radical rupture from that moment.

The poets of negritude were extremely interested in these ideas of primitivism. They shared the surrealists' knowledge of artifacts from antiquity and from an Africa they no longer knew: one that they could imagine existed prior to colonialism. They read, and republished, works by Frobenius like extracts from *Histoire de la civilisation,* and also published Breton's preface to Césaire's *Cahiers d'un retour au pays natal,* which spoke of Césaire as an essentially black poet—*un grand poète noir* who was "such a pure black."[46] But, among others, Suzanne Césaire had written of the limitations of a surrealist framework, suggesting that while it had brought possibilities, it was up to the negritude writers to find their own means of writing about their situation. In an article that foregrounded many of the ideas later pursued by Fanon in *Black Skin, White Masks,* Suzanne Césaire wrote of the mimicry of the *évolué* Martiniquan, suggesting that, like the hysteric who does not recognize that their illness consists of imitating illnesses, the Martiniquan does not realize that he does not know his barely existent "real nature." While surrealism and its sources legitimized an interest in Africa, Suzanne Césaire stressed that she was not advocating a return or a resurrection of an African past. Whereas Breton's poetry recalled a Gradiva in Martinique, Aimé Césaire's *Cahiers d'un retour* is in no way a return of the repressed, or, indeed, the suppressed.

The contrast between the European surrealists and the negritude poets is set up in a visual and poetic duet between Césaire and Picasso. The joint project, *Corps Perdu*[47] (Lost Body), which contained drawings by Picasso and a poem in ten sections by Césaire, begins with a section titled "Mot" (Word). The section was illustrated with a black mask by Picasso announcing the primitivist strain in the artist, but offset by the words of the black poet, and more particularly, a contemplation of the word *nègre*. The illustration following the poem is of a black man in profile. He is designated a poet with a laurel wreath, and, almost as if there has been movement from the black mask to the black skin beneath it, a face seems to emerge, carrying the shadow of another beneath it—a *corps perdu*, a spectral presence—announced through the barely visible process behind the illustration.[48] The shadow of the word *nègre* is also presented to us— what has it come to mean? What traces does it carry within it?

> vibrate
> vibrate you very essence of the dark
> the word nigger
> sprung fully armed from the howling
> of a poisonous flower
> the word nigger
> loaded with roaming bandits
> with screaming mothers
> crying children
> the word nigger
> a sizzling of flesh and horny matter
> burning, acrid
> the word nigger
> like the sun bleeding from its claw
> onto the sidewalks of clouds
> the word nigger
> like the last laugh calved by innocence.[49]

The duet between poet and painter draws attention to the multivalenced meaning of what it means to be black, and what it means to be interpellated by the image of the black for Picasso and Césaire in manners quite different from each other. The *corps perdu* seems for Picasso to be consistently located in animal and plant life throughout the text; and yet for Césaire, both the alienation of the black man and some hope for regeneration are communicated, as well as an irretrievable if romanticized loss. The loss is of an ideal of Africa, of an ideal of assimilation, and indeed of the spectral shadowy presence that suggests the loss of loss itself.

Suzanne Césaire wrote of the direction the Martiniquan needed to take in "Malaise d'une civilisation" as not a return to an African past that they have learned to know and respect, but rather taking control of the formidable mass of energy that was trapped within the Africans of Martinique. In an argument similar to that of Marcuse's in *One Dimensional Man,* Césaire suggested that the current manner of political and cultural organization limited the black Martiniquan, who was alienated from himself and repressed. This, she wrote, created a state of "pseudo-civilization,"[50] a kind of mimicry of loss. In a similar vein, Aimé Césaire wrote of the "trauma" of colonialism, of which poetry bore the trace. "Victim of the Colonial trauma and in search of a new equilibrium, the black man has not yet finished liberating himself. All the dreams, all the desires, all the accumulated rancor, all the formless and repressed hopes of a century of colonialist domination, all that needed to come out and when it comes out and expresses itself and squirts bloodily carrying along without distinction the conscious and the unconscious, lived experience and prophecy, that is called poetry."[51]

The political function of the poetry lay, then, in the affect of colonial trauma. For Césaire as well as some of the other poets, it was necessary to articulate some theory of a collective, as the poetry was conceived in terms of a large and fairly abstract group—black people who had gone through something both concrete and vague—"colonial trauma." The search for an underlying and unadulterated collective unconscious untouched by the colonialist offense is drawn upon here; the collective unconscious is in effect like the primitive, and yet, once again, it is not easily or perhaps even usefully accessed, even though the imagery of that collective unconscious seems, for both Césaire and Senghor, to find its source in "primordial images, which—encrusted in the collective unconscious—are universal, as the language of dreams proves, identical for all people above and beyond the diversity of languages and modes of existence."[52]

But, while Césaire, in "Poésie et Connaissance" (Poetry and Knowl-edge, 1944), wrote of Jung as an inspiration, Césaire's concept of a col-lective unconscious seemed quite different from that proffered by Jung (which Fanon referred to as a "frightening postulate"),[53] because it does not in anyway explain the psychic and mythological condition of peoples. Rather, it seems to draw from what René Ménil, writing in *Tropiques* in 1941, saw as the relationship between psychoanalysis and ethnography: "that they luminously reveal that the behaviour both of individuals and of peoples cannot be explained by the reasons they consciously give for their actions."[54] This stands in stark contrast to Sartre's own reading of the usefulness of psychoanalysis. Seeking inspiration from writers of the Harlem Renaissance and sharing a pan-African political agenda, negri-tude, the experience of being black needed some theorization, but the experience was, of course, by no means uniform. Césaire was also inter-ested in Freud's work, but the import of theories of primitivism that had so eagerly been adopted by surrealists for him did not give sufficient idea of political distinction: the primitive and the child were too frequently conflated in a slippage by the surrealists between *art naïf* and primitive art, leaving the modern-day "primitive" to be understood, patronizingly, as a child.

Although Freud was interested in group psychology, he never theo-rized anything like a collective unconscious even when he demonstrated a shared libidinal investment in an ego-ideal, as in *Group Psychology and the Analysis of the Ego*. Jung, by contrast, drew on mythological sources to explain the functioning of a collective unconscious. While Césaire defi-nitely drew from the idea of a collective unconscious, it was not limited to archetypes or the mythological. It drew on a collective history of a people, not necessarily experienced directly, but nonetheless held within the psyche of a historically reified group—black people who had been the trauma victims of colonialism. The mythical, then, was conceived as being always interpolated with the historical, making it at once particular and singular, material and messianic. Jung, for example, speaking of the grow-ing Nazi movement, saw this not as a manifestation of group psychology in which individuals became invested in an ego-ideal, or even shared in a collective unconscious of historical pressures; rather, he suggested that "private life, private aetiologies and private neuroses have become almost a fiction in the world today. The man of the past who lived in a world of archaic 'représentations collectives' has risen again."[55]

There is no doubt that Césaire's collective unconscious drew upon the mythological and the anthropological, but it was also very much constituted as a historical formation. He was without a doubt fascinated by the anthropological and mythological sources that the surrealists drew upon, but it is unlikely that Césaire had read Jung at the time of writing "Poésie et Connaissance," and he probably drew more from the anthropologist Maurice Delafosse when he spoke of a Jungian collective unconscious.[56] But whether Césaire's concept was Jungian or not, and whether his anthropological interest in Africa was similar to that of the surrealists, his sense of outrage at historical traumas of colonialism made him unable to romanticize the black, even as the enigma of the dark continent of Africa was displaced into the Freudian dark continent, read literally as the black woman. Unlike Breton's tendency to idealize a pure black in *L'Anthologie de l'humour noir* and in the introduction to *Cahiers d'un retour,* Césaire conceived the collective unconscious as a repository of historical occurrences that continued to haunt. For Césaire, "the black," conceived as collective, was as alienated from his past as was a worker; but the problem of colonialism was also not simply that of capitalism.

Sartre understood the collective differently, positing in the place of a collective unconscious in the poetry of negritude, a collective memory. Breton saw Césaire as offering a "revivifying breath, able to create new confidence"[57] in the French language, as if in himself a primitive libido was returning. He also expressed astonishment that this revitalization should come from a Martiniquan.[58] By contrast, in Sartre, the negritude poets were presented as capable of giving us "Negro poetry in the French language [that] is, in our times, the sole great revolutionary poetry."[59] For Sartre, the poets did not "wallow" in the newly found black soul, nor luxuriate in the French language; rather, they were engaged in a philosophical and political reflection: "The negro who vindicates his negritude in a revolutionary movement places himself, then and there, upon the terrain of Reflection, whether he wishes to rediscover in himself certain objective traits growing out of African civilisations, or hopes to find the black Essence in the wells of his soul. Thus subjectivity, the rapport of himself with himself, source of all poetry, which the worker has been compelled to reject, appears again."[60] In an earlier piece, he stressed that the French ("we") should

> be careful not to see these creations of the human spirit as homage done to French culture. It's a completely different thing. Culture is

a tool; don't think they've chosen ours. If the English instead of the French had occupied Senegal, the Senegalese would have adopted English. The truth is that the blacks are trying to get in touch with one another through an alien cultural world that others have imposed upon them. They have to retailor this ready-made suit of clothing. Everything, even the syntax, hampers and restricts them, and yet they have learned to make use of even this tool's shortcomings. An alien language lives inside them and robs them of their thought. But inwardly they turn against this theft, they master inwardly this European chitchat, and finally, by letting the language betray them, they put their stamp on it.[61]

Sartre saw the poets not as revitalizing through a return of the repressed. In contrast to the surrealist confusion of the anthropological and archaeological inherited from Freud, the negritude poets demonstrated as alienation from language something that Sartre saw as constitutive of the reflection necessary for ontological freedom. The black man was not simply being-for-Others in masochistic fashion, but returning the gaze, gaining ontological freedom and also giving that possibility to the white man who was trapped into not seeing his language. Read through the light of a short essay on "the oppression of blacks in the United States," an appendix to the posthumously published *Notebooks for an Ethics,* this reflection was for Sartre essential in understanding the phenomenology of the oppressor.

In that essay, Sartre suggested that because slavery was institutionally condoned rather than "para-institutional" like capitalism, the law functioned to relieve the oppressor's conscience. In effect, the oppressors would be questioning the status of the law were they to question the ethics of slavery, and as the "third and fourth generation of oppressors did not have behind it any truly painful memory of violence,"[62] slavery was normalized, as was colonialism. "Thus," wrote Sartre, "oppression does not reveal itself at first to the oppressor. It is covered over. He does not envisage it cynically as a factual state of affairs, rather, fact and right are inextricably intermingled."[63] It would take, then, the returned gaze of the black to jolt the oppressor out of his complacency, cause him to see his languages and institutions, and thus commit him to come to a new form of consciousness. The oppressor may not recognize himself when he is condemned as oppressor: "The oppression comes to you from the outside. You are constituted as an oppressor by the oppressed and this happens when you are most at home in your conscience. . . . [Y]ou do not recognise yourself in the portrait they make of you."[64]

For Sartre, the slave was similarly in a different position from the proletariat, something that reflected interestingly on Hegel's master-slave dialectic:

> In reality, Hegel saw just one side of the slave: his labor. And his whole theory is wrong, or rather it applies to the proletarian, not to the slave. The proletarian does not have to please, he has relations only with things. The slave (at least the domestic and urban slave) has relations with things and with masters. And he has to please, he acts to please. For doing so he is repaid, he avoids punishment. Thus his smile is both real and willed. He is protected in that he does not have to emerge into Nothingness through his transcendence. And he had to put on this lightheartedness to cheer up his master. . . . [T]he slave is offered a limited transcendence. Limited by the Other's freedom. The slave is a slave by right. If he has a good master and he takes up this inauthentic ethics he is happy, or he can be so. Nor does it matter that he often was so, let us say rather that it was woman and the slave who invented the search for a form of happiness that is the peaceful enjoyment of a justification within a closed universe.[65]

But when Sartre wrote thus, he was clearly suggesting that the master had profoundly limited the mental apparatus of the slave, who was condemned to justify his existence through that of another. The slave is thus unable to move toward freedom because his value is assessed in terms of denying that very transcendence.

While Sartre's analysis grappled with historical processes and events through taking what Marcuse called an "ontological shortcut,"[66] Césaire's notion of the historical was very definitely tied to the collective rather than individual. In "Poésie et Connaissance," he praised poetry in a contrasting manner to Sartre in *What Is Literature?* Whereas Sartre condemned the self-indulgence of a poetic language that complacently drew attention away from the *real*, Césaire says, "La France mourait de prose" (France was dying of prose).[67] Situating scientism as one of the causes for a depletion of man's ways of knowing, Césaire followed a different path than did Sartre, who saw technology and prose as necessary tools for the proletarian revolution. Césaire's condemnation of scientism, and thus prose, as "*pauvre* et *famélique*" (impoverished and prosaic)[68] situated the depletion of knowledge as both historical and antihumanist on a broader scale. While he wrote of man as animal, vegetable, mineral, and the universe, he offered Baudelaire's moment as one in which poetry came to revitalize France:

1850. — La revanche de Dionysus sur Apollon.
1850. — Le grand saut dans le vide poétique.[69]

[1850. — The revenge of Dionysus on Apollo.
1850. — The great leap into the void of poetry.]

The mythological, psychological, and historical came together for Césaire; the anthropological and the psychoanalytic could not be as easily separated for him as they were for the surrealists, because they very definitely had historically and politically grounded disciplinary borders. Anthropological subjects were not only *primitives,* however that term was conceived; neither was psychoanalysis merely a hermeneutic for the West. Colonial trauma called both disciplines together, as Ménil had suggested in 1941, and poetry was the expression of this. Perhaps, in Sartrean terms, it was this historical and newly felt trauma that differentiated the fourth-generation oppressor from the fourth-generation colonized person. The primitive was not simply the source of "precivilization" drives; and the resource of blackness was not perceived as an essential source, for that in principle was shared universally. The writers of *Tropiques* conceived the collective of blacks as sharing a consciousness that came from political and historical commonalities derived from the fact of being black. That these had psychical implications was a given. "The latest anthropological discoveries finally offer man access to man. . . . But the impulses that define our activity's frame do not appear to consciousness in all their furious nakedness. Physical and social prohibitions force them to veil themselves. This is why they are not normally visible to the mind's eye except in the form of a *vivid drama.* . . . Any poem at all expresses human destiny more fundamentally than all the political treatises in the world."[70]

The constitution of the poetic image as the drama of a situation gave meaning to a materiality of language that carried the trace of colonial relations. While these images broke through boundaries between disciplines and peoples to "regenerate" the language of the French for Breton, they situated for the negritude poet a more specific notion of poetic language as the material affect (though not simply a symptom paraphrased or explained in a political treatise) of colonial trauma. Language itself became constitutive of politics and vice versa, rather than simply being the vehicle of its expression as Sartre envisaged in *What Is Literature?* The black man had been reified, a process that Marcuse said Sartre could not recognize, and out of that reification came a use of language that, as Senghor wrote, conceived the image as ideogram.

While Senghor's notion of the ideogram, and thus of African surrealism, was different from Césaire's, the materiality of language was still crucial to him. In his essay "Speech and Image: An African Tradition of the Surreal," he suggested that European surrealism was *empirical* rather than mystical and metaphysical. Contrasting his surrealism with that of Breton, who suggested that surrealist empirical analogy was the stuff of surrealism and did not presuppose "beyond the visible world, an invisible world striving to manifest itself," Senghor nonetheless assumed a collective mystical unconscious, which he suggested has concrete basis in a variety of African languages that contrast, in notions of the abstract and the concrete, with Indo-European ones.[71] While Césaire at times assumed a precolonial pan-Africanism, it did not follow this form of mysticism. It seemed, in effect, to be more empirically based, as did Ménil's concept of the psychological causes of the *"drame imagé."* Not only in the overtly political works like *Discourse on Colonialism* but even in his earliest works of poetry, like *Cahiers d'un retour au pays natal,* Césaire did not simply suggest that negritude grew from the soil ("Takes root in the ardent flesh of the soil / it breaks through the opaque prostration with its upright conscience") in order to establish a sort of essential being. Rather, he constantly showed that the soil and land itself and its inhabitants could not be thought outside the horrors of colonialism. The soil, the land, along with its inhabitants, had suffered the consequences of worlding:

> So much blood in my memory! In my memory are lagoons. They
>   are covered with death's-heads
> They are not covered with water lilies.
> In my memory are lagoons. No women's loincloths spread out on
>   their shores.
> My memory is encircled with blood. My memory has a belt of
>   corpses!
> And machine gun fire of rum barrels brilliantly sprinkling
> our ignominious revolts, amorous glances swooning from having
>   swigged too much ferocious freedom.[72]

Thus, contrary to what Ann Stoler has suggested, there is a cogent race analysis that emerged from the French decolonization movements that was not identical to, nor a simple off-shoot of, a class analysis, even as it shared something in common with the work of Marcuse, some of which would seem to draw on a race analysis rather than vice versa. Marcuse's words in *One Dimensional Man* elaborated on the importance of language to social critique, and the necessity of psychoanalyzing that language in words that echo much in *Tropiques*. In fact, Marcuse's language is haunted by the same ghosts even as he thematized those very specters:

> The redefinition of thought which helps to coordinate mental operations with those in social reality aims at a therapy. Thought is on the level with reality when it is cured from transgression beyond a conceptual framework which is either purely axiomatic (logic, mathematics) or coextensive with the established universe of discourse and behavior. Thus, linguistic analysis claims to cure thought and speech from confusing metaphysical notions—from "ghosts" of a less mature and less scientific past which still haunt the mind although they neither designate nor explain. The emphasis is on the therapeutic function of philosophical analysis—correction of abnormal behavior in thought and speech, removal of obscurities, illusions, and oddities, or at least their exposure.[73]

Psychoanalysis was being used by Césaire and his fellow writers at *Tropiques* in a manner different from that of both Sartre and the surrealists, because of the way the black man had been reified. This reification, which Marcuse suggested Sartre was unable to theorize, was what marked the materiality of poetic language as the substance of ongoing trauma. This process held something in common with the reification of the proletariat, but was by no means identical to it. While for the surrealists the proletariat could be a source of regeneration, as were psychoanalytically conceived primitives, no such confusion of the anthropological and the archaeological would be possible for them. Rather, the coming together of the psychoanalytic, the ethnographic, and the politico-historical was inevitable; and it was through the medium of poetry, or language as trauma, that this would emerge:

> Negritude . . . is a concrete rather than an abstract coming to consciousness. . . . We lived in an atmosphere of rejection, and we developed an inferiority complex. I have always thought that the black man was searching for his identity. And it has seemed to me that if what we want is to establish this identity, then we must have a con-

crete consciousness of what we are—that is, of the first fact of our lives: that we are black; that we were black and have a history, a history that contains certain cultural elements of great value; and that negroes were not, as you put it, born yesterday, because there have been beautiful and important black civilizations.[74]

History is understood by the negritude poets as something almost inaccessible. In the context of Martinique, René Ménil had written, in an essay he titled "Psychanalyse de l'histoire," that colonization had fragmented Martiniquans and their history. No understanding of Martiniquan history was possible without performing an analysis, that is, a psychoanalysis, of it. The social pressures of Martinique had, he suggested, produced a distorted history that was possible to understand only through an analysis of its language. He wrote: "A concrete psychology, descriptive of the consciousness of real Martiniquais, that gave a synoptic table of condensations, repressions, frustrations, nervous ailments that we work on, will allow us to understand and to explain the nature and dispersion of historical visions described by our historians."[75] The materiality of language as well as that which it, in its most instrumental usage, apparently represented, was designated as bearing the traces of colonial trauma, which could be understood as such through psychoanalysis.

Psychoanalysis was clearly not something to be simply rejected by the 1930s–1960s generation of French decolonizers, and neither was it fully rejected by Sartre. As Albert Memmi asked in his 1965 preface to his 1957 publication *The Colonizer and the Colonized*: "Does psychoanalysis win out over Marxism? Does all depend on the individual or on society? . . . Psychoanalysis or Marxism must not, under the pretext of having discovered the source or one of the main sources of human conduct, preempt all experience, all feeling, all suffering, all the byways of human behavior, and call them profit motive or Oedipus complex."[76] For the actors in the theater of colonialism, whether Prospero or Caliban, what is evident is a situated analysis. When psychoanalysis was employed, it was not to analyze the individual mind so much as to understand the situation of colonialism much in the vein of what Sartre saw as the great tragedies, specifically those that do not psychologize but stage a "situation [as] . . . an appeal." The situation "surrounds us, offering us solutions which it's up to us to choose . . . which present alternatives one of which leads to death. Thus freedom is revealed in its highest degree, since it agrees to lose itself in order to be able to affirm itself."[77]

The Prefaces of Decolonization: "Black Orpheus"

Sartre's prefaces to the texts of decolonization invited the white man to read texts of protest by black men. In that sense they were addressed to the oppressor, the phenomenology of whom Sartre was particularly interested. In all the prefaces to the texts of decolonization—Senghor's *L'Anthologie de la nouvelle poésie nègre et malgache,* Fanon's *The Wretched of the Earth,* Memmi's *Portrait du colonisé* and *Portrait du colonisateur*—Sartre claims that the works were written with a specifically black audience in mind.[78] Thus he stands as a kind of liaison, and his preface to *L'Anthologie de la nouvelle poésie nègre et malgache,* titled "Black Orpheus," became extremely influential in writing circles in both France and elsewhere, and a journal of African literature borrowed its title ten years later.[79] Sartre attempted to explain the importance of the anthology and the negritude movement more generally, explaining, in the wake of *What Is Literature?,* how he could endorse this poetry as a form of anti-prose. While this needed explanation for the white audience (by Sartre, in prose) and while Sartre's language certainly reflected much of the sentiment expressed within the terminology of the poetry, the preface was harshly criticized by Fanon for its characterization of negritude as a temporary phase in the development of black people's consciousness and as a negativity.

While Sartre was adamant that the poetry of negritude was not surrealist, there was very definitely a degree of romanticization of a primitive collective black consciousness, which drew from Senghor more than other poets in the volume. Sartre conceived of psychoanalysis as a science that was not about exploration of the mysterious, but in "Black Orpheus," he presented such an exploration. Scientism and prose were for the worker who was alienated through the mechanisms of technology; the black man, on the other hand, had been robbed of what it meant to be black. In a reaffirmation of the stereotype of black man as phallus, an image that Sartre's prose shared with some of the poetry in the volume, it became quite clear that the black man sought a feminized, mysterious Africa that consistently eluded his gaze. But negritude was also androgyny:

> For our black poets . . . being comes from non-being as a rising phallus. Creation is an enormous and perpetual coition; the world is flesh and son of the flesh. On the sea and in the sky, on the rocks, in the wind, the Negro rediscovers the velvetness of the human skin; he is

"flesh of the flesh of the world"; he is "porous to its every breath," to all its pollen. He is by turn the female of Nature and its male; and when he makes love with a woman of his race the sex act seems to him the celebration of the Mystery of being. This spermatic religion is like a tension of the soul balancing two complementary tendencies; the dynamic emotion of being a rising phallus, and that softer, more patient and more feminine of being a plant which grows. Thus negritude, in its most profound origin, is androgyny.[80]

While androgyny was the professed nature of negritude, clearly the imagery of the searching consciousness was masculine; and this is something that contrasted quite drastically with the images from Picasso two years later, in *Corps Perdu,* where both the masculine and the feminine were plants in turn penetrating and being penetrated. Césaire's black woman remained quite exotic, and she was a mutilated black, hacked into pieces. She would regenerate herself and her dismembered mate:

> Long ago oh rended one
> in bits and pieces She
> gathered her dismembered one
> and the fourteen pieces
> took their triumphant place in the rays of the sun
> Woman's body restituted island
> woman's body full freighted
> woman's body foam–born
> woman's body retrieved island[81]

In Sartre's prose, Africa, like Freud's dark continent, was feminized once again as the unknown. Read through the mythological language of a black Orpheus, Africa was Eurydice, barely remembered, in effect a *corps perdu* stolen away by Pluto, possibly raped by still another, and ultimately elusive and unconcealed: if Orpheus failed to regain his African Eurydice on Pluto's terms, she would disappear.

Although he picked up on the masculinism of much of the poetry, the framing mythology of the preface affirmed both a masculine bias and an essentialist vocabulary. Sartre's concept of negritude as a phase and a negativity suggested that blackness, like Jewishness in *Anti-Semite,* was produced in situations and in response to actors in those situations. He drew on a vocabulary that confirmed both a stereotype of the hypermasculinity of the black man and a kind of pan–African essential spirit such as could be found in Senghor's writing about essential African traits. Julio Finn has contended that the writers of negritude wrote poems about black women that differ drastically from those of Europeans producing protagonists who are catalysts of action rather than statues. It is, however, unclear whether either Senghor or Sartre were at all concerned about black women as actors in the coming anticolonial revolution, or whether they endorsed the racist view of the Negro as genital.[82]

Black woman's "tropicality" was exoticized, her flesh made plastic, her form made supine, much in the way Sartre had claimed the black man's had been in the European imagination. If black man returned the gaze of the white man, he certainly also gained a position of privilege to create an object at the same time. Rather than simply being "the rapport of himself with himself, source of all poetry, which the white worker has been compelled to reject,"[83] this rapport was constituted through positing woman as the Other, much in the vein of Baudelaire, of whom Sartre wrote shortly after.[84] Sartre's negativity, or nothingness, was the androgynous sexual encounter between the poet and a black woman, out of which was born the phallus.

Within Sartre's own language, as in that of the majority of the negritude poets, feminism was not conceived, nor indeed even the femininity of women. Read against our analysis of Freud's use of the imagery of the dark continent, this image of Africa, and its unconcealing of women, present an interesting twist. While colonialism seemed to be a blind spot in the theorization of psychoanalysis, the feminine was inconceivable in this work on decolonization, which was adopting a form of psychoanalysis to aid a political as well as a literary movement. White men may have felt ashamed when the gaze of the black man, in the terms of *Being and Nothingness,* caused them to acknowledge the black man's freedom, because they had sadistically viewed blacks as objects.[85] But black men, in their creation of poetry, left no room for women as subjects of that poetry. They were in effect acting out of sadism themselves, creating black women as objects. For Sartre, who viewed love as a fluctuation between sadism and masochism, this was probably an inevitable movement in the dialectic of freedom. However, the degree of solipsism evident in not acknowledging the gender dynamic did not posit a prioritization of freedoms with the ontological being the fundamental crux. Rather, it rendered the question of women's anticolonial subjectivity opaque at best, irrelevant at worst. The essence of man for Sartre was neither the subject that thought and made decisions about actions nor the being-in-itself in its existence, nor the being-for-Others that caused an understanding of self situated in facticity, and in a sado-masochistic framework.

The Prefaces of Decolonization: Fanon

Fanon, who was not much more informative when it came to the situation of colonized women until late in his career[86] (he wrote in *Black Skin, White Masks,* "I know nothing about" "the woman of color"),[87] was critical of negritude on a number of counts, although he endorsed much of what Césaire wrote, particularly in *Discourse on Colonialism.*[88] Fanon wrote of Antillean poets as white figures[89] who drew, mistakenly, on Jung's idea of the collective unconscious as a mythical and essential given. But nevertheless, he suggested drawing on Césaire, who interestingly defined negritude through a list of negatives ("My negritude is not a stone, its deafness hurled against the clamor of the day / my negritude is not a leukoma of dead liquid over the earth's dead eye / my negritude is neither tower nor cathedral . . .")[90] and who, as we have seen, understands poetry and its producers as existing in particular contexts. Césaire's pan-Africanism was a political rather than a Senghorian essential coming together of black peoples. Although Césaire did, in rather vague terms, proffer a pan-African precolonial relationship that had no empirical basis, his emphasis was on a defiance of "indefensible" Europe. This was not a way of creating a national culture, as Fanon would suggest in *The Wretched of the Earth,* but rather a defiance of the Europeanist bourgeois construct of the nation itself. From 1945 to 1956 Césaire ran on a communist ticket, and shared a communist internationalist agenda rather than one that endorsed nationalisms.[91]

Fanon criticized Sartre's "Black Orpheus" for his positing of blackness as nothingness. Kesteloot has suggested that this was a misapprehension of Sartre's philosophical terminology, but what was clear was that relational affect of consciousness, or the ambiguity of being-for-itself, was conceived as a preliminary to the proletarian struggle against capitalism. For Sartre it was a temporary state that was needed to exorcize a collective state of mind. Fanon's critique of negritude and Sartre's part within it was also implicitly a critique of Jung. Fanon suggested that a collective unconscious was acquired through persistent treatment of a group in a certain way over time, rather than a given. He also believed, contra Freud's explicit theories, that between ontogeny and phylogeny lies *sociogeny*, particularly for understanding the psyche of the Negro. His concept of a sociogeny was very similar to a Sartrean-situated analysis that asserted an authentic being rather than one that was a masochistic projection of the white man. Between the development of man and the evolution of the species lay sociological pressures: man was situated in ways that caused him to act according to overdeterminations. To be free, he would have to act with consciousness and against bad faith.

This was, in effect, the argument of Sartre's *Being and Nothingness*. Negativity is the relationship of consciousness to being because it does not exist as such; it is not lack in the Lacanian sense, and it does not imply that the being-in-itself does not have a history or indeed a facticity. There is no essence of being that can be explained for always, nor are there verifiable essential differences between groups of people that exist outside a particular situation. Rather, in consciousness we decide to act in particular ways even as we know that our acts will be understood by others differently from the manner in which we perceive them. We have to acknowledge their freedom, and can object only if it limits the freedom of others. In both *Anti-Semite and Jew* and in the preface to Memmi's *The Colonizer and the Colonized*, Sartre examined not simply individuals being-for-Others, but groups of people who become "those people" because designation as such by another causes conflict. On an individual basis, conflict arises if the presence of another causes one to adjust one's relationship to surroundings, to see oneself as the Other sees one, and therefore to renegotiate the ambiguity of the new object state with consciousness. When groups of people are designated in a particular way, "this object state is not a simple modification of his being which is parallel with that which I undergo, but the two object states come to me and to the Other in a global modification of the situation in which I am and in which the Other finds himself."[92]

Sartre's studies of Jews, anti-Semites, the colonizer, and the colonized took this form of understanding group identifications, and it shared much with Fanon's own critique. Sartre's position was more explicitly stated in his work on blacks in the United States, in which he sounded very much like the young Fanon: "The White represents the individual face of destiny for the Black, as well as his concrete obligations."[93] This acknowledged both how Manichaeanism was established, and also how solutions were conceived. This stood against Marcuse's assessment of Sartre as someone who did not understand the relationship between the individual and the group or the manner in which groups become reified. For Sartre, it was effectively through the gaze of a third person that one came to consciousness of both how one is seen and therefore with whom one shares a group—class consciousness, racial consciousness, ethnic consciousness. A collective consciousness was, then, a collective memory that caused certain assumptions. There was, of course, no individual or collective unconscious.

Fanon criticized Sartre for his characterization of negritude as negativity and as a phase, saying "black consciousness is immanent in its own eyes. I am not a potentiality of something, I am wholly what I am. I do not have to look for the universal. No probability has any place inside me. My Negro consciousness does not hold itself out as lack. It *is*. It is its own follower."[94] He responded in a similar manner to those who criticized *Anti-Semite and Jew*, a text that Fanon considered to be one of the finest he had read. For Sartre a collective identity could be perceived only in a situation, and any sense of the continuity of a people was a "historical community . . . basically *national* and *religious*. . . . They have in common the situation of a Jew, that is, they live in a community that takes them for Jews . . . it is the anti-Semite who *makes* the Jew."[95] Any sense of group identity comes from being overdetermined, and in any struggle for liberation, this would result in symptomatic liberation. Sartre wrote: "Manichaeanism is a defence mechanism. It's refusing to see collectives of men other than in terms of institutions."[96] And the Jew in France in the 1940s is determined partly by the precariousness of Israel's existence. For Sartre, acting as if the community had an essence and denying the existence of the Jew or one's Jewishness, or choosing something instead like hyper-rationality or a democratic French profile, are equally problematic. Neither took the situation into account. Similarly, the non-Jew who acts as if there were no difference between the French Jew and the French Catholic is acting inauthentically, because a difference had been established, albeit on a false basis. Any form of identification that was not situation-bound and situation-conscious was inauthentic.

Perhaps needless to say, Sartre's Jew is for the most part male. When he discusses a Jewish woman, she is figured first as a sexual partner who arouses disgust, which results in impotence in the anti-Semite upon the realization of her background,[97] or a Jewish prostitute who causes the Jew to vomit. When the Jew visits her, he is not simply disappointed to find a woman of his own race—as the French man apparently frequently did when visiting a brothel abroad. He also feels humiliated, seeing in her the degradation of Israel and Jews generally.[98] Just as Sartre's essay on blacks in America was basically about the ontology of the oppressor, so *Anti-Semite and Jew* was incidentally about Jews because of the importance of analyzing Jews when they were about to return to France. The book's subtitle, *An Exploration of the Etiology of Hate,* is its more fundamental theme.

Sartre's preface to *The Wretched of the Earth,* like "Black Orpheus," was addressed to the European. He introduced Fanon as someone with a new tone, not an *évolué* about whom the French could congratulate themselves, or a poet Europeans could endow with the Goncourt or a Nobel Prize for literature. Quite different from the negritude poets, Fanon's call was to other colonized peoples internationally to develop nationalist movements and cultures that would not simply mimic those of the European mother countries. The colonial power held nothing of interest for the colonized people, and that power was anyway declining. The "mother-country" had a sickness that he could analyze, but that he has no interest in curing. Sartre wrote of the new tone of this generation of colonized peoples. They were not shadows of Europe like their fathers were; they were indifferent to the Europeans. Fanon's analysis in *Black Skin, White Masks* of the colonial relation as being much like the European familial relation could be recalled here. No longer should colonized peoples be in that relationship, adopting pathologies of the West, like the Oedipus complex once inherited through the colonial relationship. Sartre, however, sought to change Europeans too through this analysis. Inviting them to read, he compelled them to feel shame. "As a European," he says, "I steal the enemy's book, and out of it I fashion a remedy for Europe. Make the most of it."[99] His task was to rehumanize Europeans who consistently acted in bad faith and who failed to recognize that they did so. They had thus lost their humanity.

The dehumanization of Europeans was exemplified for Sartre in their participation in hatred, oppression, and systematic annihilation. Sartre could not attribute this to an unconscious because he saw such a rationalization as a means of excusing oneself of responsibility, on the one hand, and pathologizing those victims of Europeans' bad faith on the other. However, the use of existential philosophy by black writers of the postwar period did not reject psychoanalysis, but rather reinvigorated it in a form that concretized.[100] It was not simply a Sartrean existential psychoanalysis. It redrafted a collective unconscious in a concrete, empirically based, and sociological form. And it collapsed a distinction between the strictly anthropological and the psychoanalytic.

The Prefaces of Decolonization: Memmi

Memmi's difference from Sartre, who greatly influenced his work, began with his emphasis on the experiential. For Memmi understood situations through experience rather than through *systems* of colonialism. He condemned colonialism through examples of dehumanized behavior. Memmi's work, in contrast to Sartre's *Anti-Semite and Jew,* consisted of what he called *portraits* of the colonizer and the colonized. He emphasized how their behaviors participated in the colonial system to sustain a Manichaean relationship. Even as each individual was responsible for what he did, his energies needed, in Sartre's view, to work against systemic oppressions that caused others to live without freedom. Memmi's position was not very different from this. However, he proposed a theory of individual behavior: the Nero complex. When Memmi began his "Portrait of the Colonizer" with the question "Does the colonial exist?" he was questioning Sartre and Fanon. Sartre's statement that it is the anti-Semite who *makes* the Jew"[101] was a sentiment that Fanon drew upon: "The black soul is a white man's artifact,"[102] and "The black man does not exist. Anymore than the white man." Memmi's response was that, structurally, the colonial is always the colonialist, and is defined through actions that oppress. Effectively, therefore, even the colonial with a heart of gold is a colonialist. There was therefore no such thing as the good or bad colonial, or even colonizers; rather the colonial system that produced colonizers fed the Nero complex that rendered them colonialist. As soon as they willingly accept this role, they become heavily invested in the system that privileges them above the colonized and, therefore, pits them against the colonized. The Nero complex is the complex of the usurper who first illegitimately accepts the role of colonizer, and ultimately inscribes this role into law. Only the colonizer who accepts the illegitimacy of his position can be rid of this complex; and the more resistance there is to his illegitimate role, the more tyrannical he will become.

Sartre's resistance to Memmi's psychologization of the situation is due to the apparent release of responsibility and the ensuing inevitability of the behavior of the colonialist. His own analysis understood the ontology of the oppressor as institutional. Marcuse's critique of Sartre, that he takes an "ontological shortcut" through the political is in some ways echoed here: Sartre saw Memmi as taking a psychological and situational shortcut, which can be accounted for once again in the notion of aggressivity. While Memmi presented a psychological determination for the oppressor's self, Sartre assigned a motive. The oppressor's passions, desires, and emotions were the cause of his acts, and these were freely constituted, given that split subjectivity is the resource for every man's potential freedom. Everyone who does not act against colonialism has made an active choice to follow self-seeking consequences with conscious motives.

The shackles of the Nero complex are, then, consciously motivated by self-interest. While only socialism, for Sartre, was a state in which man was not dominated by systems, everyone had the potential to free himself of these once he acknowledged his facticity and the weight of history. In Sartre there is a kind of distinction between ambiguity and ambivalence lost in the Freudian psychoanalytic work. Ambiguity is internal to the subject, involving the relationship of *being-for-itself* to *being-in-itself*. Ambivalence, on the other hand, involves conflict with another. While this has ontological implications, the distinctions are quite clear, allowing for an analysis of external pressures, or of sociogeny. This allowed for a concept of aggressivity that was based in political systems, which are importantly distinguished from the potential for ontological freedom. Political freedom and ontological freedom were thus related but ultimately separate entities. This distinction was reinforced in Sartre's work as he became more explicitly invested in condemning the system of capitalism. As man could be free in the political sense only after the establishment of socialism for Sartre, that system was the end point of any political analysis, and the basis of any ontological freedom. However, as will be discussed in another chapter, the starting point of any critical or political analysis will be responsibility to act toward the freedom of oneself and others.

While Foucault has suggested, in the context of discussing the difficult relationship between "Ethics" and "Politics," that none of the philosophers of engagement did anything during the resistance in World War II—something that could perhaps be agreed upon—it is not clear that this was because of a shortfall in the relationship between politics and philosophy, or, for our purposes, existential psychoanalysis. Surely Foucault would have to end up agreeing with Marcuse's reassessment of Sartre—that his philosophy ultimately caused him to act and think in a manner that was politically and philosophically contingent, and in a manner that shared common ground with both Foucault and with Marcuse. Whether or not this was partly because of the horror of the war and guilt concerning relative inactivity in the resistance, one can only speculate. However, a different relationship to national consciousness emerged for Sartre in response to World War II, as it did for the poets and actors of decolonization in the postwar period. Psychoanalysis entered into those debates, and became a crucial part of assessing how to act, how to conceive of self, and how to assess the individual's relationship to that large artificial group: the nation-state.

4. Colonial Melancholy

Pathology is considered as a means whereby the organism responds to, in other words adapts itself to, the conflict it is faced with, the disorder being at the same time a symptom and a cure. —Frantz Fanon, *The Wretched of the Earth*

Does psychoanalysis win out over Marxism? Does all depend on the individual or on society? . . . Psychoanalysis or Marxism must not, under the pretext of having discovered the source or one of the main sources of human conduct, preempt all experience, all feeling, all suffering, all the byways of human behavior, and call them profit motive or Oedipus complex. —Albert Memmi, "Preface," *The Colonizer and the Colonized*

The limitations of the "psychological" interpretation do not prevent us from making progress with the problem [of interracial conflict], from ridding it of its distorted or emotional elements. But no psycho-analyst, unless he himself is possessed of an optimism which resists all analysis, will assert that all the problems encountered in the actual world are due only to misunderstandings, strong emotions, illusions; or that once he is free of racist feelings, the white man will be able to greet the black man as his true brother. For as we know (indeed, all too well, although we are constantly expressing surprise at it) when the white man reaches that point, the black man will refuse to acknowledge him as his brother, and will not prove content with this humanist solution. It will seem to the black man that in order to reach this solution, the true terms of the problem have been, quite simply, bypassed. . . . Here what is in fact only the optimistic denial of the terms of the problem is presented as its solution. —Octave Mannoni, "The Decolonisation of Myself"

Each quotation that heads this chapter is a reflection on earlier work. Fanon's, from *The Wretched of the Earth* (1961), reflects back not only on his professional work in the Blida clinic of Algiers where he was a psychiatrist working with European and North African patients acting out colonial affect, but also on his youthful study *Black Skin, White Masks* (1952). Memmi's is a 1965 preface looking back to the 1957 *The Colonizer and Portrait of the Colonized*. Implicitly it can also be read as a comment on his first work, the autobiographical *Pillar of Salt* (1953). Mannoni's is from "The Decolonisation of Myself" (1966), an essay he was invited to write by the British journal *Race* to comment on the way in which his position had changed since writing on the psychology of colonialism in *Prospero and Caliban* (1950). Curiously, later works by these authors often "write off" the earlier findings as symptomatic of colonial affect. But it is precisely in reading that affect that the complex forms of repression, condensation, and displacement at work in the colonial encounter emerge. Mannoni, Fanon, and Memmi all engage with the psychical affect of colonialism.

Dislocation

For Octave Mannoni, the psychical affect of colonialism was akin to undergoing psychoanalysis:

> I spent twenty years in Madagascar, from 1925 to 1945, as an ethnologist and the director general of the information service. In 1947, I was trying to undergo analysis, and I chose Lacan's couch on the advice of the brother of Jacques Baron. At the first session, Lacan took my blood pressure. At the time, sessions lasted three quarters of an hour. He remained silent, but occasionally made some good interventions. He should be compared to Dali or Buñuel. He had the same ambition of becoming rich and famous. I had the impression that he was playing at being an analyst. Then the sessions began being less long. After an interruption, I began again in 1952. Everything had changed. There was a domestic. The sessions became shorter. Lacan didn't prevent me from undergoing psychoanalysis, but I wasn't interested in it since, in Madagascar, I had cured myself of an obsessional neurosis. I understood, moreover, why Rimbaud had cured himself in the desert. Dislocation can do the job of analysis. Being a white man among the blacks is like being an analyst among the whites.[1]

Reflecting back on his life, Octave Mannoni wrote that he cured himself of an obsessional neurosis in the French colony of Madagascar where he had been in the service of the French government for some thirty years. During that time, he occasionally returned to France for psychoanalytic sessions with Jacques Lacan. Mannoni claimed to have been "cured" by a form of countertransference with the black natives, and the increasingly absent Lacan therefore became less important to him, and to his analysis. However, in rejecting his teacher and his analyst, he effectively came to occupy his place, although it remains unclear why he should have ceased to be interested in psychoanalysis in 1952 rather than in 1947 if Madagascar was really the reason. The white among the blacks became synonymous with the analyst among white patients. And thus, both analyst and analysand (that is, both colonizer and colonized) gained psychical benefit from the relationship. Mannoni seems scarcely aware that this pertains even more so if the colonizer, like Lacan, is increasingly absent. Obviously, the inverse to this is not the case: the black man among whites was rarely the ethnological investigator; and, because of structural positioning, in the company of whites the black man would probably not find a psychoanalytic substitute; in fact, his difference would be pathologized, as would his behavior in response to the injustice of the colonial endeavor. One has to wonder what forms of disavowal are at work in Mannoni's statement. Through a network of openly identified substitutions, Mannoni identified, in this passage, the analyst as *non arrivé,* even as the analysis had been delivered through other means. One wonders then why Mannoni would go on to become a psychoanalyst.

This theme of dislocation has been one engaged since the beginning of this book. Dislocation from political affiliation led Freud to a different conceptualization of the ego. Freud positioned himself as Boabdil's messenger, who was killed because Boabdil chose to understand the bad news the messenger was carrying as *non arrivé.* Freud suggested that this form of disavowal constituted a conscious effort not to acknowledge what was consciously known: in Boabdil's case, that power had been lost. The news was not repressed, nor was it denied. Rather, disavowal of the situation was a conscious act that balanced knowledge with absence of that same knowledge. In his 1969 essay on Freud's theory of disavowal, Mannoni would gloss this process: "*Je sais bien, mais quand même*" (I know very well, but even so. . .).[2]

Freud's own melancholic response to the loss of national affiliation, and thus also of power, was eventually acted out in the form of a lament, that is, in a form of melancholia rather than one of disavowal. But this melancholic response emerged as affect in the theory of disavowal, and in "a whole series of more or less clearly pathological methods on the part of the ego"[3] that are attributed to a dislocation.

Primitivism drew on the idea of a dislocation to an earlier evolutionary moment, thus allowing for the id to express itself. And in a sense, this project as a whole—dislocating psychoanalysis and placing it in the context of nineteenth- and twentieth-century colonialism—has allowed for a different perspective on some of its assumptions and potentials for postcolonial critique and analysis. All three of our central figures in this chapter are displaced. Mannoni shuttled back and forth between Madagascar and France. Fanon went from Martinique to France and then on to Algeria, from where he was exiled at the end of his life. What Memmi called Fanon's "impossible life" was marked by an inability to come to terms with his home, Martinique. The process of sublimating the confusion into physical dislocation led to his very important political work in the decolonization of Africa. Memmi's dislocation from the Jewish Tunisian ghetto to hard labor camps during World War II and subsequently to France caused him to attribute great significance to the "portraits" of types and peoples, the complex lives and affiliations that emerge in the tonalities of representation. The theme of dislocation has been central to psychoanalysis on the most basic level: that of questioning the centeredness of the ego, the various psychical planes that constitute mental life, and the splitting in subjectivity as discussed by Freud and later emphasized by Lacan. Recently, some have suggested that the theme of dislocation makes psychoanalysis a particularly Jewish science, and the father of that science, Freud, a wandering Jew.[4] If this assessment of psychoanalysis is to be taken seriously, however, a related question arises immediately. *Dark Continents* has been concerned with historicizing psychoanalysis by displacing it from its institutional and political origins to its colonial outreach and this necessitates examining why the narrative of the wandering Jew occurs at different historical junctures. Freud's exile was not simply the exile of a Jew, but specifically a modern exile: Nazi aggression in the context of Europe in the world. The messianic story of Jewish exile is thus understood in terms of modern nation-statehood. The particular moment of exile of interest here necessitates putting the idea of the wandering Jew into the context of European nation-state formation through the imperial enterprise. If psychoanalysis figured so prominently in conceptual frameworks for analyzing colonialism and decolonization, it was perhaps because of the critical agency and melancholy emerging from Freud's changed theory of the subject and changed relation to the nation-state.

Colonial Psychiatry: Pseudomelancholy

Mannoni's *The Psychology of Colonialism* (renamed *Prospero and Caliban* in the 1964 edition) is one of the few texts of the period that attempted to understand the psychical workings of colonialism in both the colonizer and the colonized. Like Fanon, Mannoni would make generous use of literary texts rather than more empirical or anthropological evidence to sustain his argument, and like him also, he saw the necessity—eventually—of what he would call "decolonizing oneself."

Mannoni's aim in *Prospero and Caliban* was to change how colonialism was conceived in psychological and psychoanalytic circles. Freud (following Frazer, as Mannoni reminds us) and Jung had been interested in "primitive peoples" in order, in the case of Freud, to further understand the nature of the ego's relation to the id and the superego, and, in the case of Jung, to understand a "lost innocence." But they were not interested in colonialism per se, or, indeed, in the way in which the notion of primitivism was imbued with colonial consciousness. Mannoni sought to understand the peculiarly new psychical conflicts that emerged from the colonial situation. "I chose another method," he wrote, "laying greater stress, particularly at the beginning, on our position as white men in the context of the colonial situation."[5] Rightly, he saw colonialism giving rise to a unique configuration of desire, conflict, and, most importantly, dependency. In order to communicate the importance of colonialism in understanding Madagascar, it was important not to reify Malagasy difference, or to stress the particularity of local custom. Mannoni's emphasis was on encounter rather than clear-cut difference. His concept of dependency explained the encounter through overturning a basic assumption of both anticolonial politics and colonial psychology: the idea that the colonized felt inferior to the colonials. His assertion that it was colonizers who felt inferior was controversial even among intellectuals of decolonization.

Mannoni's concept of the dependency complex was drawn from many sources, including Freud, Jung, Adler, and Künkel; Shakespeare and Defoe; Lévy-Bruhl and a few anthropological sources. He drew very little from his "fieldwork," confining himself to describing dreams taken from essays written by students in French classes and impressions he gained from his time spent in Madagascar as a colonial officer from the late 1920s to the early 1950s.

His psychoanalytic theories were very preliminary in *Prospero and Caliban,* but were still very different from more conventional psychoanalytic literature on primitives because of the emphasis laid on the colonial situation. But Mannoni's work was also markedly different from the ethnopsychiatrists of the day. Interestingly, Fanon, at the end of *The Wretched of the Earth,* summarized much of this work in discussing Algerian violence during the revolution. Ironically, given the content of the work of colonial psychiatrists like Antoine Porot (an honorary professor and a psychiatrist at the Psychiatric Clinic at the University of Algiers) and J. C. Carothers, a doctor and a psychiatrist in the British Colonial Service in Central and East Africa, Fanon's tone was curiously far less critical of the psychiatric literature than of Mannoni's more psychoanalytically inflected work about Madagascar.[6] Both Porot and Carothers concentrated their analysis on violence among the Algerians and the Mau Mau respectively. Porot wrote the bulk of his work prior to the revolution in Algeria, and he paved the way for other discussions about violence, brutality, and what he would call "savagery." As Fanon also noted, Porot's thesis was not so much evolutionary as congenitally rationalized. Muslims, unlike Kabyles, he argued, were constitutionally violent, and prone to an odd form of melancholia, or what he called "pseudomelancholy," which caused them to kill rather than to turn to introspection and suicide, which were more common among melancholic Westerners. Porot was responsible, during the revolution, for advising on how to deal with questions of justice and the penal code for cases in which such psychiatric conditions were concerned. In spite of the fact that he did not seem to believe that evolutionary development could take place (whether Lamarckian or Darwinian), he suggested nonetheless that penal sanctions could educate the North African Muslim by exposing him to the value of and respect for human life.[7]

Carothers, whose work was initially commissioned by the British government and the World Health Organization, also focused on melancholia and depression. Just as Porot found in Algeria, Carothers found the sub-Saharan African less prone to introspective melancholia and depression than the European. Like Porot, and to some extent Mannoni, he could not imagine that rebellion and violence could be thought-out political protest in which the "moral responsibility" generally associated with introspection could be directed outward into organized action. When he reissued a revised version of *The African Mind in Health and Disease: A Study in Ethnopsychiatry* (1953) as *The Mind of Man in Africa* (1972; an uncommissioned work), Carothers reflected back on changes in diagnostic fashion after independence. Given that both he and Porot had underlined the increased sense of moral responsibility and introspection among melancholics, it is perhaps unsurprising that they found those in whose hands the *mission civilisatrice* lay to be more prone to depression. However, in the 1970s, Carothers, following R. H. Prince, would take into account what Mannoni, in 1950, had referred to as "the colonial situation." Here is how Carothers summarized his agreement with Prince about the political reasons for diagnostic changes:

(1) The Prestige Factor; whereby, due to a belief, deep-rooted in Europeans, that it is only responsible people with a well-developed conscience who are subject to depression, this diagnosis only became appropriate for Africa in the era of Independence; the observing psychiatrists of each period being influenced by the climate of opinion of their time.

(2) The concept of Masked Depression; whereby, in the earlier period people complaining of a variety of bodily ills but not of depression were not included under that heading.

(3) The Alteration in Observational Study; whereby depressive cases are likely to be admitted to the custodial type of mental hospital where most of the older observations were made, whereas recent observations have also been made in out-patient clinics, rural surveys, etc.

(4) A True Alteration in Disease Pattern; whereby severe depressives do in fact occur more frequently with Westernization.[8]

Carothers added that many patients were assessed after electric shock treatment, which masked symptoms of depression. Much of what Carothers concluded was that the colonial situation may have masked not only forms of diagnosis, but also the form of illness itself. Of course, given that Carothers was working on British colonial contexts, theories of such psychic mechanisms as assimilation would have taken on a very different form than in the French colonial context in which Porot, Mannoni,

Fanon, and Memmi worked. The policy of assimilation was quite different in Britain, and difference was prioritized as a concept over the creation of a population of *évolués*. But what is clear is that Mannoni's interest in psychoanalysis, however preliminary, allowed him to assess psychical disorders quite differently from his counterparts in the world of psychiatry. And we shall see later that even the idea of pseudomelancholy can be read psychoanalytically against the grain to understand the affect of coloniality.

Prospero and Caliban: Dependency, Assimilation, and Mimicry

Like Freud in *Totem and Taboo* and in *Civilization and Its Discontents,* Mannoni attributed the existence of different psychical states to variations in social structures. He understood the differences between group formation and the structure of personality, and the manner in which groups are newly formulated in the colonial situation. Emphasizing that " 'colonial problems' stem from conflicts within European civilization itself, and [that] the racialist reactions of the white man to the black are the product of elements already present in his psyche,"[9] he wondered how the "native" would adjust to the different group formation of the modern nation-state or nationalist consciousness. Concluding that the aim of decolonization movements was the creation of a cohesive sense of group unity arrived at in nationalism rather than independence itself, he argued that this could be understood only through a psychological explanation of group formation. The political call for independence was thus seen to be inadequate because of the contradictions, or maybe disavowals, it embodied.

> The historian, accustomed as he is to explaining great and complex events by relatively simple abstract causes, never hesitates to tackle the question of colonial nationalism, but the psychologist is shy of this delicate problem, for he feels obliged to decide either what is the exact place occupied in the personality by "national sentiment" or what personal feelings correspond, in the individual psyche, to the nationalism of the group, and lend it their support.
>
> The idea of a collective unconscious is hardly admissible, for it is really a contradiction in terms. The contradiction might perhaps be less glaring if we were to speak more loosely of a collective psyche. But we must not allow ourselves to be deceived by a metaphor; the

collective psyche can only be apprehended through individuals; at most it is the group aspect of the individual psyche.[10]

In saying this, Mannoni added—rather like Renan, who asked why people are willing to die for the nation—the question of what the psychical mechanisms are that cause men to face imprisonment in the name of liberty, to die for a better quality of life, or unite to protect individualism. The ideal, he suggested, is sacrificed over and over again in order that the concept of the Ideal be maintained.[11] To fail to understand the contradictory nature of the struggle was to fail to understand an important part of the constitution of the modern group, that is, of the nation-state. It is, in fact, to read the metaphor of the collective literally, that is, *to de-metaphorize* it. Mannoni was suggesting how the Malagasy in the colonial situation experienced changes in societal structures: from the *Fokon'olona* of the precolonial days, to colonial rule, and on to nationalist feeling for independence. In stressing the contradictory desire for nationalism, he construed dependency as an ambiguous desire for political independence. "Civilization," he wrote, had brought its own set of problems for those existing both prior to and within modern nation-states.

> The psychological phenomena which occur when two peoples at different stages of civilization meet and mingle can probably best be explained and understood as the reactions to each other as two differently-constructed personality types. Indeed, to talk of the interaction of personalities which may be considered typical of each group is to discuss the same problem with two different vocabularies from two different points of view, for the personality is simply the sum total of beliefs, habits, and propensities, organized and linked one to another, which go to make up the individual *as* a member of his group.[12]

While he insisted that he did not mean to infantalize the Malagasy, and differentiated himself thus from paternalistic colonialists,[13] Mannoni saw the Malagasy as existing within the same framework as early Europe. He agreed with Jung that "errors of perception in colonial matters may well be . . . the result of the projection onto the object of some defect which is probably attributable to the subject," but he criticized Jung's idealistic primitivism.[14] He envisaged evolutionary stages for man that tied in very exactly with historical periods. The first aligned primitive behavior with interdependence and egalitarianism; the second, brought about by feudalism, destroyed the egalitarian nature of primitives, leaving dependency in its place. With the onset of revolutionary republicanism, and, presumably, the third estate, came individualism and the ideal of egalitarianism, which led to a rejection of dependency. This in turn led to national inferiority complexes and the possibility of existential freedom. Those who suffered from inferiority complexes, like French colonials in Mannoni's assessment, sought out people to dominate, like the "primitive" and the feudal Malagasy. As such, the relationship between colonizer and colonized was not oppositional in Mannoni's work, even as it was relationally constituted. The relationship could be understood only through a third term: the colonial situation. Thus "the colonizers" and "the colonized" made sense as nouns only in a "colonial situation" that was historically and geographically specific. It is not therefore like the anti-Semite who makes the Jew in Sartre's terms; neither is it the extreme form of Negrophobic Manichaean thinking that Fanon attributes to Western civilization's rendition of the Jew as intellectual and the black as sexual animal.[15] Rather, according to Mannoni, "dependency and inferiority form an alternative; the one excludes the other."[16] Colonizers sought out dependents as they were overcompensating for their inferiority complexes; and the colonized welcomed the colonialists on whom they felt they could depend.

Of course, there are evidently many ways in which Mannoni's position has been and can be criticized. Some argued that he had made a metaleptical error in his description of dependency. While Mannoni claimed that it was a dependency complex that caused the Malagasy to seek out colonial rule, Fanon, for example, insisted that dependency emerged from the colonial relation and not vice versa, and Memmi characterized Mannoni's position as representing "the fundamental bias" in colonialist thinking.[17]

Maurice Bloch criticized Mannoni on anthropological grounds, faulting his neglect of local customs and context. In his analyses of dreams, for example, Mannoni placed little emphasis on the fact that these dreams were collected from essays written in French classes when students were asked to describe their dreams. This demonstrated a lack of understanding regarding the complexity of the use of French in the education system, the effects of the context of language teaching, or the psychical consequences of colonial education. This is in spite of the fact that he discussed changes in the education system that would make it more "useful" in bringing the Malagasy out of his feudal dependence and into democratic republican "inferiority."

Similarly, his chief example of colonial dependence was drawn from a description of his relationship to his tennis instructor. When the coach fell ill, Mannoni gave him some medicine. Expecting some indication of gratitude, Mannoni was surprised when the instructor reciprocated with further demands rather than an exchange as he expected. Mannoni read this as dependence, whereas Bloch reinterpreted the incident in the anthropological context of social hierarchy and gift exchange in Madagascar. Mannoni paid very little attention to preexisting cultural mores, although this was perhaps wrongly ascribed to his overall psychoanalytic framework by Bloch. For there seems to be no reason why one could not make a psychoanalytic argument concerning the psychical structures of people within different social formations without prioritizing an evolutionary framework of progress, or neglecting cultural specificities. Indeed, the psychoanalytic questions raised by Mannoni concerning the formation of groups and national consciousness were crucial, even as they were employed in *Prospero and Caliban* to rationalize the dependency complex, the origins of which were ill-conceived.

One of Mannoni's most interesting theorizations was of colonial mimicry, which he associated with forms of psychical assimilation and the assimilation policy that was in place in early French colonialism. The early phase of French colonialism was based on slavery; some colonies, like Martinique, did not gain independence, but remained after the eighteenth century. The policy of assimilation was different, and only partial, for the later colonies like Madagascar, and the different forms of colonial mimicry are associated with this.[18] Mannoni writes what can be read as an indicator of colonial agency in the later colonies, although he chooses not to interpret this as agency, but rather as a misreading on the part of the French colonials: "They accept everything in detail but refuse our civilization as a whole, and it is this attitude which gives Europeans the impression that the native is ready enough to mimic them but never succeeds in emulating them. . . . It may well be that it is just because we look for a too faithful copy that we tend to see the actual result as grotesque mimicry."[19] He attributed this mimicry to the encounter between different personality structures, and in this he preempts Homi Bhabha's work on the subject, and indeed Fanon's from fifty years ago. Whereas Bhabha contended that colonial mimicry emerged at a moment in which the colonized appeared to be *almost the same but not quite,* this did not pertain to the type of context Mannoni described, or cases in which assimilation did not occur to the same extent.[20] However problematic and indeed racist his understanding of the colonized Malagasy may have been, Mannoni recognized that the failure to assimilate historically and psychically led to particular and varied forms of performative resistance.

Mannoni differentiated between conservative and liberal colonials and colonizers, and among the Merina, the Malagasy, the *évolué,* and the less Europeanized; indeed his underlying principle of these psychological "types" governed the organization of the study; his theory of the dependency complex did, however, attribute cause to what appears to be the result of the colonial encounter. On the one hand, he paid attention to the magnitude of material exploitation that accompanied colonialism; on the other, he claimed to have only a limited interest in this. His position was different from the leftist, economistic anticolonialism of the time, even though he asserted his sympathies for it. He argued, therefore, against the Manichaean analysis of colonial rule in terms of master and slave, and thus also against an identity politics in which the adjective *colonial* was transformed into identifying nouns: *the colonizer* and *the colonized:*

> We must not, of course, underestimate the importance of economic relations, which is paramount; indeed, it is very likely that economic conditions will determine the whole future of the colonial peoples. And it cannot be denied that there have been and still are shocking abuses in this direction which have outraged public opinion. But they are not to be explained solely in terms of economic interest and exploitation. . . . The "colonial" is not looking for profit only; he is also greedy for certain other—psychological—satisfactions, and that is much more dangerous. Accurate observation of the facts would no doubt show us that he very often sacrifices profit for the sake of these satisfactions. . . . Why? . . . [I]n a colonial situation economics are colonial and it is the adjective, not the noun, which interests us.
>
> The colonial peoples have long been aware of the meaning of this adjective. They draw a clear distinction between the European proper and the colonial European; after all, they have had plenty of opportunity of watching the one turn into the other.[21]

What are named the colonizers and the colonized, that is, Europeans and the Malagasy, Mannoni claimed, are drawn together in ways that satisfy each of them, and this is because they are at different stages of societal formation in what he sees as the evolution of civilization. While they may have been drawn to each other for reasons of mutual need—for the allaying of feelings of inferiority on the part of the colonizer, and for dependency on the part of the colonized—they went through transformations in the "colonial situation," bringing about a third space, a third term, and a third imaginary that elsewhere Mannoni would call the Freudian "Other Scene."

The Other Scene: Literature and Psychoanalysis

Mannoni saw the third space emerging in the paradoxes and nonreferentiality of both the literary realm and physical displacement: Crusoe and Prospero thus are reinforced as prototypes. Thinking of Schreber, Cervantes, Drury, and again of Defoe, whom he discussed at great length in *Prospero and Caliban,* Mannoni wrote of the third space, or the Other Scene, thus: "Authors of chivalric novels (like Defoe, but also Drury!) transport us to another place of the real world, or another moment in history, that which had constituted the other scene through naive realist means, that could, besides, be completely opposed to realism in literature."[22] But while the Other Scene is something that slips between nonreferentiality, the unconscious, colonial space, folly, and uncanniness, Mannoni does not make all these third spaces, or other scenes, equivalent, but rather grounds them in particular contexts.

Many of Mannoni's psychoanalytic arguments are conveyed through both critical and appreciative readings of literary texts, and in this he shares a great deal with Freud, Fanon, and Memmi: Fanon discussing Mayotte Capécia's novels or Breton's comments on Césaire; Mannoni drawing on Shakespeare's *The Tempest* or Defoe's *Robinson Crusoe,* and writing his own *Lettres personelles;*[23] Memmi writing *The Pillar of Salt, Strangers,* and many other novels, in addition to his "portraits" of the colonizer, the colonized, the Arab, and the Jew; Freud suggesting in his *Autobiographical Study* that psychoanalysis was created out of mythologies and literature like *Oedipus Rex* or *Hamlet* rather than medical discourse.

Implicitly, and, in Mannoni's case explicitly, the literary is associated with the psychoanalytic "Other Scene," which allows insight into a *real* social problem through understanding the work of dreams, madness, and creative—particularly literary—production. The "Other Scene" is a concept Freud draws from G. T. Fechner.[24] He employs the term to discuss the status of the dream and the work that the dream does. The dream cannot be seen simply as expression of a desire or a wish, but needs to be understood as work. The work of the dream is conducted in a spatially distinct scene that exists alongside a consciousness made up of unconscious drives and repressions, and a preconscious repository of the means of signification, images and associations not repressed but not at the forefront of conscious thought. "Dreamwork" is the manifestation of the unconscious in the signifiers, or the language, of the preconscious. It does not transparently communicate unconscious wishes to consciousness, but functions rather on a different psychical plane.

Each image in the Other Scene will need analytical work to decipher the dreamwork that typically condenses images together to forge new meanings, or displaces an idea from one signifier onto another. This work is done through analyzing the processes of condensation and displacement, and it recognizes the rebus, or puzzle set forth in the dream, as a laconic expression of unconscious drives. Creative work is, in Freud's analysis, akin to the work of dreams, and psychoanalysis is thus a fitting instrument for its interpretation. But more than this, psychoanalysis itself is a hermeneutic built of such mythological ground, and is thus a form of the literary itself. It thus functions as the interpreter of dreams and creativity, and the marker of the difficulty, if not impossibility, of performing that task of pure transliteration of stylistic particularity and the crafting of signifiers that would suggest a total understanding of the Other Scene. And so the dream, or the creative product like a literary text, is not a "pure" form of psychological or political insight. Nor is explicit literary content devoid of political import (even as the distinction between form and content breaks down in this formulation of language as structure, and structure as meaning).

For Lacan, and hence also for Mannoni, the Other Scene became synonymous with the Other, or the Symbolic. For Freud, the image or the word in dream content or in an artifact became a laconic expression that was part of a rebus to be deciphered. For Lacan, this meant that signifiers became arbitrary repositories of meaning that at times, for equally arbitrary reasons, are imbued with fixed meanings. While meaning is largely dependent on relations between words, and the manner in which displacement (or metonymy in Lacan's language) and condensation (or metaphor) take place, there are times when signifiers drop beneath the bar of signification, appearing then to attain fixed meanings. The arbitrariness of the sign provokes, in Mannoni's terms, "a fearful remission" because meaning as fixed through law is undermined. The simultaneously referential and nonreferential nature of the sign, and thus of our understanding of reality, causes the literary text—like the dream, the double entendre, and speech—to give us insight into psychical affect because it carries within it the expression of unconscious drives and therefore informs us equally of them and of their means of expression.

Mannoni insisted that this insight into the Other Scene constitutes a necessary understanding of the political, for it is composed through the manner in which all people, and not only the deluded, form their realities. This is not to say that Mannoni thought all social problems could be solved by psychoanalysis, literary criticism, or theory, or indeed that anyone could be disabused of fantasies in any simple fashion. That idea was deemed universalizing and was also phantasmatic given psychoanalysis's own literariness.[25] Neither psychoanalysis nor literature offers a metalanguage of the functioning of the unconscious. Like Memmi and Fanon, Mannoni understood, by 1966, that some problems need to be solved through political and economic changes. But alone, these will be insufficient as a solution for social unrest or inequities, or indeed for the particular problems of coloniality and decolonization.

Mannoni's contribution is extremely pertinent if the colonialist assumptions that make up his worldview as it stood in 1950 are extracted —in other words, as Ashis Nandy would say, without its "arrogant social evolutionism."[26] To some extent, his later prefaces and "The Decolonisation of Myself" ask us to read his earlier work exactly in this light, and thus to understand as problematic the title given to the second edition: *Prospero and Caliban*. For if Mannoni was keen that differentiations and variations be understood, particularly in the work of colonized peoples in the colonial situation, the many facets of the ephemeral, and yet manacled, Ariel would have to be reconsidered. While Caliban turns against Prospero with the weapon of language that Prospero has given him (rather like Mannoni suggesting that the Malagasy want what the Europeans have, without wanting them as rulers),[27] Ariel is a more haunting figure who is too often left out of the political landscape. His ghostliness is constituted by his negative capability as much as his incarceration. Alongside that of Prospero and Caliban are the "unreal" relationships sustained in the colonial encounter.

Mannoni read the play as Shakespeare's dream, and thus as access to his unconscious. He also read it as a later reworking of *Hamlet. The Tempest,* he wrote, "repeats, in order to resolve it, the Hamlet situation."[28] *Hamlet*'s unresolved nature will be discussed later. But what Mannoni considers in this literary accessing of the colonial unconscious is lack of oppositionality: alongside Prospero the paternalist is Gonzalo the utopianist; and along with Caliban, submissive Ariel and Miranda waiting to come into their own. Wulf Sachs, writing in 1934, characterized Hamlet as the person Shakespeare would have been had he not written the play. Similarly, Mannoni considered Prospero to be an unsublimated Shakespeare. If Hamlet is what Shakespeare would have become early in his life, Prospero is the later representation of that figure.[29] Shakespeare's farewell to the stage is equally, then, a farewell to the colonies and the introduction of a different set of relations, somewhat idealistic, within them. It is almost as if the spaces of both writing and coloniality imposed their own limitations, and Shakespeare as Ariel, rather than as Prospero, were finally set free of the obligation to be a spirit of the imagination.

Fanon later adopted some of Mannoni's paradigms, most notably that the colonial situation was formed out of a unique encounter between peoples from Europe and those from the colonized countries, and that the specificities of those contexts determined how that colonial situation would be configured. But he also lost something of Mannoni's differentiation among colonial types as he became more closely associated with Sartre's more oppositional logic. For while, as I have said, Mannoni did not pay close attention to local customs, or to his own investment in a colonialist evolutionary framework, he did nonetheless draw distinctions between conservative and liberal colonials, and, perhaps more importantly for the context of today, differences between those who had assimilated partially and those who had not. Fanon, on the other hand, failed to do this, and so his colonized person as described in *Black Skin, White Masks* always appeared to be an *évolué*, unless that colonized person was a woman. Women in Fanon's terms were in need of exorcism because they did not adequately conform to his ideal of femininity, nor did they share anything with black men. He addressed Mayotte Capécia thus as he criticized her desire to be white, that is, her "lactification":

> May she add no more to the mass of her imbecilities.
> Depart in peace, mudslinging storyteller. . . . But remember that, beyond your 500 anemic pages, it will always be possible to regain the honorable road that leads to the heart.
> In spite of you.[30]

Mannoni's own gender politics was quite horrifying. The colonial who denies that torture and rape occurred against the colonized is deluded, even as he is right to acknowledge that the language of testimony cannot simply be read as referential evidence.[31] But he left some room for understanding the differences between Europeanized and non-Europeanized peoples, the specific complexes arising from relative degrees of assimilation, and the links between political and psychical assimilation. When he discussed sexual relations between Malagasy and European men and women, he was significantly less judgmental than Fanon, even though his views on all the players concerned may have been somewhat stereotypical. Malagasy women, he wrote, "correspond fairly closely to an archetype of the collective unconscious, like Friday or Ariel. . . . [T]he personality of the Malagasy woman is so little externalized that it acts like a mirror and reflects back to the European his own projections on to it. . . . If a man lives in the midst of his own projections without truly admitting the independent will and existence of other people, he loses his own will and his own independence, while the *ego* inflates as it becomes empty."[32] The peculiarity of the metalepsis is quite evident here. The Malagasy woman was blamed for the inflated ego of the European man, when perhaps the more appropriate response would have been Virginia Woolf's — that woman appears to exist, under a patriarchy, in order to reflect back man at twice his size — or, indeed, Irigaray's — that woman does not see an image of herself reflected in a mirror, but rather comprises the reflective material that makes up the mirror itself. She appears, however, to be a blank slate. Mannoni's own ego apparently became too inflated to understand how political mechanisms regulating interracial relationships created psychical ones. The white woman, rather like the black woman for Fanon, was deemed difficult to comment upon without individual analysis, although she was likened to the nouveaux riches in Europe, who overcompensated for their inferior status with racism. As in many commentaries on colonialism, women were seen as the most virulent racists, and thus the cause of colonial relations turning sour. The European in the colonial situation was thus transformed, leading, according to Mannoni, not to Malagasy racism against Europeans in general, but rather to a sense of the inferiority of Malagasy Europeans to those in Europe.[33]

"The Decolonisation of Myself": "Je sais bien, mais quand même"

In the 1966 essay "The Decolonisation of Myself," Mannoni retracted much of what he had said about the evolutionary model of societal maturity that attributed forms of dependency to certain social configurations. The essay cast an interesting light on the previous material by Mannoni because it highlighted the difficulties inherent both in universalist theories of the psyche and in particularist and situated arguments. Racial and sexual politics today confront the same sort of impasse of bringing together universalist and particularist arguments to counter social problems concerning racial, sexual, and class conflict. Mannoni revealed a psychoanalysis that challenged a developmental psychology dependent on cause and effect in favor of one that prioritized such notions as deferred action and affect. In this changed emphasis, he provided a way of breaking past this theoretical impasse.

The more reflective work constituted changes in both the politics and the methodologies of the three figures under analysis. The importance of balancing psychoanalysis and material analysis becomes clear, because while none of them asserts the universality of psychoanalysis, each considers that the *singularity* of affect is crucial for understanding coloniality. Simultaneously, each asserts that the *particularity* of context needs to be accounted for, with local political and economic changes brought about within them. This balancing of the singular and the particular (Mannoni), the psychoanalytic and the Marxist (Memmi), and the identical nature of the symptom and the cure (Fanon) assert positions embodying contradictions and incompatibilities. To the extent of the conscious exposition of this contradictory balancing, they are inassimilable to any established political or theoretical argument. Perhaps this is the nature of the affect of coloniality they all attempt to describe. In each of them, inassimilability to any position, whether it be one of liberal humanist universalism, evolutionary science, psychoanalysis, or Marxism, is articulated in terms of visuality, or what I will call *whiting out* (following Emily Apter) and *coloring in*.

Apter has observed how Mannoni analyzed his own form of *whiting out* in his essay on the Freudian notion of disavowal, "Je sais bien, mais quand même" (I know very well, but even so . . .). Mannoni distinguishes disavowal from repression, fetishism, and the splitting of the ego, in that it is a conscious repudiation. Mannoni describes a moment in which his receptionist, knowing that he was expecting a call from a black poet, misheard the name given to her on the telephone. Telling Mannoni that the poet had called, she was instructed by him to invite the person for a drink. When the caller arrived, he was not the poet but a white patient. Even though it was late, Mannoni realized that he had to treat the patient as he would normally, and asked him to recline on the couch for the session. The patient then said that he realized the offer of a drink was a psychoanalytic joke from doctor to patient, but came anyway. *Je sais bien, mais quand même.* Mannoni read this as a form of transferential metalepsis, in which the patient *knew* that Mannoni did not want to see the black poet, and thus *whited out* the visit by coming, thereby deciding to act as if a mistake had not been made. The white patient thus came instead of the unwanted black guest. A reading of Mannoni's own desire was aided by the transferential relationship, because he did not really want to see the poet. To this end, he actually did invite the patient, who *read his mind.* A desire to white out manifests itself through disavowal, as if to say: I know I was expecting the black poet, but I was happy to see the white patient, who, in this scenario, is the patient-without-color (not racially marked). Disavowal, the conscious repudiation of something simultaneously believed to be true, becomes the ground upon which the desire to see no color amounts to a form of universalism that equates it with the desire to see white. Apter sees this reflection on the nature of disavowal as a belated commentary on colonial racism, and colonial affect, as seen in *Prospero and Caliban* (which was published nineteen years earlier).

Through this idea of belatedness and disavowal as symptomatic of coloniality, and thus typical of colonial affect, Mannoni offered a critical language for coloniality. Or, as he would put it, "how the ghost of the former colonial subject haunts" constitutes an important understanding of colonial affect. For "ghostliness," in spite of its ephemeral nature, paradoxically grounds the "Other Scene," belatedly, because the manner in which colonial affect haunts, that is, the manner in which "disavowal" functions in the colonial context, constitutes an autocritique for the colonial. It also, interestingly, offers a way of understanding the differences between melancholia—understood as political and psychical inassimilability in the adjectival colonial situation—and disavowal—the conscious repudiation of something believed to be true, and the subsequent balancing of contradiction. These balancing contradictory positions are necessary for analyzing coloniality and its affect—Fanon employing Sartre and Lacan; Said bridging Gramsci and Foucault; the coming together of singularity and particularity; and Derrida's haunted aphorism that asks us to consider together two statements: that we always speak only one language; that we never speak only one language. These points of contact emerge as spectral echoes that send back to the colonizer a haunted and belated sense of the impossibility of assimilation (or melancholia), and a form of disavowal that balances paradox and apparent contradiction. The relative impossibility of assimilation will be a theme that runs through all three of these writers, and it will connect interestingly the themes of political assimilation and psychical assimilation, neither of which is worked through to completion. We find instead colonial mimicry, parody, and colonial affect.

Thinking of the concept of assimilation in slightly broader terms, an interesting Mannonian theory of the psychic structure of coloniality emerges. On the one hand, he discusses the impossibility of full political and social assimilation, which leads to mimicry. On the other hand, he writes somewhat idealistically of the lesser repression evident in the primitive or the feudal peoples of Madagascar that renders only the dead as adult: "Instead of protesting, like the European, that he is a man like his father, the Malagasy appears to claim that all men are children. He projects his own dependence on everyone else. The word for 'child' appears frequently in the names of Malagasy tribes, and ultimately it is only the dead who are to the Malagasy what adults are to European children."[34] "It would be no exaggeration to say that the dead and their images form the highest moral authority in the mind of the 'dependent' Malagasy, and that for him they play the part filled for the European by the moral conscience, reason, God, King, or party."[35] Thus he analyzes the Malagasy as having a wholly different relation to repression in terms of the superego, and this also translates for Mannoni as a lack of split in the ego: "The oriental 'face,'" he writes, "is different from the Jungian *persona* in being more firmly welded to the whole being. . . . The individual is held together by his collective shell, his social mask, much more than by his 'moral skeleton.'"[36] And so the difference in moral structure in turn is indicative of a more bounded sense of community, and a less individuated form of relation to moral pressure or death. "In ourselves, however, more important than this moral pantheon, this mythology of authorities, is the continuous, barely conscious debate in which the Ego negotiates with the Superego and the Ideal its chances of existence. It begins with a guilty desire or an agonizing longing to escape from autonomous authority by seeking refuge in some higher authority, and this flight has given our civilisation its distinctly evolutionary character. . . . Only the west has the courage to live out its myths."[37] And perhaps, by the same logic, only the West, paradoxically, has Boabdil's ability of disavowal, and of fetishism. For, as Freud says, when "throne and altar" are in danger, that is, when the most fetishized ideals of reason, God, king, or party, are in danger, the ensuing consequences are irrational.[38] Mannoni wrote, of course, right after the 1947 rebellion of Madagascar, when the repression of the Malagasy population led to the murder of so many. Burning the evidence and killing the messenger of political disquiet effectively demonstrates how France, and indeed how Mannoni in *Prospero and Caliban,* chose to hear the news as *non arrivé.*

In his later, more politically outspoken essay "The Decolonisation of Myself," he read the failure to analyze messages designed to destabilize those in power and sent by the politically disenfranchised, as denial rather than disavowal: "What is in fact only the optimistic denial of the terms of the problem is presented as its solution." That solution, indeed, is presented as liberal humanist universalism, something that Mannoni eventually understood as a form of *whiting out.*[39]

Mannoni's "colonial situation" is the adjectival expression for a situation in which change can satisfy neither the "dependent" colonized nor the colonial suffering from an inferiority complex (or indeed, from an obsessional neurosis, like Mannoni himself). The colonial situation coming undone, in fact, demonstrates how disavowal on the part of the colonial constitutes a form of whiting out that can later be seen as a denial. But Mannoni implicitly suggested a different psychical arrangement for the colonized, one that needs, once again, to be cleansed of its arrogant evolutionism. Mannoni presents the reader with a few versions of the colonized Malagasy: the Merina, the Malagasy proper, those who have assimilated more, those who have assimilated less. There is no one, however, who is quite like the colonizer, and in fact, this evolutionary breakdown is attributed to the failure to assimilate according to the model of the superego.

The different relationship to the dead as it is described may well be erroneous, and yet the apparently overdrawn differences between the colonizer and the colonized in this regard (that is, creating the noun out of the adjectival *colonial situation*) leads to the question of the psychical transformations undergone in the processes of colonial rule and of the attempt to assimilate. In other words, in mimicry. Indeed, the mimicry of the colonizer involves mimicking one who lives within the structure of the superego, that is, the internalized moral standard of the family and particularly the grandparents. Obeisance toward one's own dead demonstrates that mimicry is a result of the loss of assimilability, to either tribe or colonizer, and thus a melancholic critical response to it. In decolonization struggles, however, rather than openness to disavowal, there is a form of demetaphorization.

Demetaphorization, according to Abraham and Torok, is a symptom of melancholia. Melancholia, or the refusal to mourn, is a form of incorporation, that is, swallowing whole something that cannot be assimilated, or introjected. In such circumstances, what makes sense figuratively (that is, that a loss has been suffered, in this case the loss of both former affiliation to the group and impossibility of assimilation to the colonizer) and in terms of a process or an adjectival clause is understood and experienced literally. Thus the symptom of demetaphorization is also the cure, for the creation of the noun out of something that makes sense only adjectivally (creating the opposition "colonizer" and "colonized" out of the "colonial situation") leads once again to the question of how the political and psychical cures are connected. It seems clear that at the time of decolonization (if not still, even in the era of globalization) the political "cure" could be only national independence (or possibly, in the case of Martinique, given its proximity to the neocolonial power the United States, increased autonomy for the *département*). But national independence leads to its own psychical quandaries in the old European nation-states and differently in the "new" nation-states that constitute the postcolonies of Europe. Mannoni would recognize the bittersweet nature of independence for all concerned. "It seems . . . there is no alternative to the painful apprenticeship to freedom; that alone will solve all problems amid which both Malagasies and Europeans are floundering—it is a medicine which will cure them both. If it appears sweet to the one and bitter to the other, it is an illusion in both cases. The way will be much harder for the Malagasies than they imagine, while the Europeans have no idea of the extent to which a genuine and successful liberation of their subject peoples . . . would liberate them too."[40] These bittersweet psychical quandaries led to their own configuration of disavowal, because it is impossible to return to the political or psychical configuration[41] of a "before colonialism." Colonial disavowal functions as a form of melancholy for subjects of colonized states. The loss of metaphor, which is also the loss of figurative language, caused coloniality to become fixed in oppositional and nonmetaphorical nouns, as if the colonizer and the colonized were entirely and definitively oppositional categories.

Fanon and the "Historical and Material" Constitution of the Subject

Fanon understood the existence of colonial melancholy when he wrote with concern on the need for a national culture and the failure of the colonized bourgeoisie in his late work *The Wretched of the Earth.* While he saw that psychiatric and psychoanalytic work could help his patients only once political independence had been won, the difficulties of the postcolonial psyche clearly concerned him a great deal. It is this factor, perhaps, as Kobena Mercer has asserted, that has caused the massive critical attention to Fanon's early work *Black Skin, White Masks,* for that text, less clearly formulated and more contradictory than the later work, curiously appears more pertinent today as nation-states are losing their power to multinational conglomerates and to global capital. Fanon's rallying cry to arms in *The Wretched of the Earth,* the bible, so to speak, of third world nationalist movements, has itself more recently been displaced in favor of the early texts, a phenomenon also seen in feminist work on, for example, Simone de Beauvoir. So why go back fifty years at this point rather than to these writers' late work, which indicates a clearer and a different intellectual trajectory? Why go back to the end of the war, to the anticolonial struggles for independence, to the publication of de Beauvoir's *The Ethics of Ambiguity* or of Fanon's *Black Skin, White Masks?* Why is the moment of return the middle of the century, and what is it that has caused, in a way, a sense of delayed affect so the fifty years is marked less by a return than by a new experience—of displacing *The Second Sex* with *The Ethics of Ambiguity,* or *The Wretched of the Earth* with *Black Skin, White Masks;* of seeing a resurgence of Holocaust studies that has made trauma a fresh topic as well as a secondary affect; of marking the fiftieth anniversary of Indian independence and the partition of India and Pakistan, and moving beyond it. Much of the work on ethics fifty years ago revolved around major events—World War II, the wars of decolonization—that marked the end of an era and also created *events* that marked the end of certain eras. The texts I have referred to emerge in response to those events in order to consider what it means to be a politically and ethically strong subject at a moment when subjectivity had been threatened through forms of extraordinary violence and the threat of genocide. And there has been a return to them again now, marking, perhaps, the spectral nature of coloniality, coupled with the trauma surrounding World War II.

Kobena Mercer suggests that the reason for this lies in the "fading fortunes of the independent left."[42] Additionally, much of the left, while maintaining a critique of transnational capitalism, has also supported a critique of the nation-state in the postindependence era. While Fanon preempted some of these criticisms in *The Wretched of the Earth,* he was clearly writing in support of independent nation-states, and his emphasis was thus less psychoanalytical than the earlier work. Mercer reminds us that earlier generations, "at the height of the optimism of postwar social movements," ignored the early work. Indeed, this form of optimism turns into cynicism among contemporary left critics of postcolonial theory in the disparaging tones employed to discuss the endorsement of the early work. Cedric Robinson, for example, talks of the "petit-bourgeois stink" of *Black Skin, White Masks,* which has been peculiarly appropriated as the relevant text by Fanon in recent years, leaving behind the more important text of black Marxism. *The Wretched of the Earth* demonstrated a sophisticated "immersion in the revolutionary consciousness of the Algerian peasantry."[43] Stuart Hall has recently underlined the similarities between the early Fanon and the late, suggesting that the developmental trajectory underscored both by Mercer and Robinson from very different positions fails to recognize that Fanon was centrally concerned with colonial affect, whether he was talking of abstract desire between the inhabitants of Martinique in *Black Skin, White Masks,* the "North African Syndrome" in *Toward the African Revolution,* or "affective intellectual modifications" after torture in *The Wretched of the Earth.* As Françoise Vergès and Homi Bhabha have discussed, there is a different concept of personal history and social history in the works of Fanon that is always in tension, and, perhaps, never fully resolved. But the forward movement of history suggests that a new national man has to be created even as individuals are plagued by affective disorders brought about by events within the colonial situation.[44]

The new man, wrote Fanon, will have to be created in order to take forward a new form of national belonging. Neil Lazarus would call this national consciousness "nationalitarian" rather than simply nationalist.[45] Fanon's new man, and his new nation, will not simply through appropriation or imitation become what Europe is; rather, the specific histories and interaction with Europe and her modernity constituted through colonialism will engender a particular kind of new man. It is this new man that Fanon famously formulated in his rendition of Lacan's "mirror stage." He created out of that model not simply a black version of the colorless blueprint of the Lacanian theory of entry into language, nor simply a Sartrean existentialist dialectic of birth into a synthetic new man from the split of the dialectic. Reading the footnote that has constituted a large proportion of recent critical attention to Fanon, the following words from the end of *The Wretched of the Earth* need to be kept in mind to show how Fanon is quite a lot more than what Henry Louis Gates[46] has called the "black Lacan" that he has become in the hands of psychoanalytic theorists.

> Europe undertook the leadership of the world with ardor, cynicism, and violence. . . . Yet it is very true that we need a model, and that we want blueprints and examples. For many of us the European model is the most inspiring. . . . When I search for Man in the technique and the style of Europe, I see only a succession of negations of man, and an avalanche of murders. . . . So, comrades, let us not pay tribute to Europe by creating states, institutions, and societies which draw their inspiration from her.
>
> Humanity is waiting for something from us other than such an imitation, which would be almost an obscene caricature.
>
> If we wish to live up to our peoples' expectations, we must seek the response elsewhere than in Europe.[47]

This call for a different form of nation building is equally a call for a different understanding of the psychical structure of man. Fanon clearly had departed from Mannoni's view that the Malagasy wanted what the European had. For Fanon, it was necessary rather to create something quite different out of the nationalist blueprint offered by Europe. If that form of the nation-state were held up as an ideal, so would be exclusivist politics, racism, and homicidal tendencies. It is through psychoanalysis that this new form of the social and the individuated, however problematically, are connected by Fanon.[48]

And so the psychiatrist Fanon, lately recuperated as a Lacanian by such critics as Homi Bhabha, considers, in a long footnote that constitutes his most lengthy engagement with Lacan, how the Lacanian theorization of the mirror stage can be used for an analysis of the relationship between the black man and the white man. The footnote is interesting because it makes use of apparently contradictory concepts drawn simultaneously from Sartre and Lacan to understand the pressure of social context on the constitution and structure of the racially differentiated subject. Looking to Fanon's early *Black Skin, White Masks* is a marker of the times, for it is far less explicitly laying out a political agenda. Interestingly, however, it deals with the quandary of the colonial affect in a manner that makes it difficult to conceive of postcolonial critique without acknowledging the importance of psychical damage performed through colonialism, and the psychical work that goes into nation building. Fanon's footnote revolves around the male, but it brings up some important questions about psychoanalysis's relationship to historical and material questions that concern the status of the Other more broadly:

> It would indeed be interesting, on the basis of Lacan's theory of the *mirror period,* to investigate the extent to which the *imago* of his fellow built up in the young white at the usual age would undergo an imaginary aggression with the appearance of the Negro. When one has grasped the mechanism described by Lacan, one can have no further doubt that the real Other for the white man is and will continue to be the black man. And conversely. Only for the white man The Other is perceived on the level of the body image, absolutely as the not-self—that is, the unidentifiable, the unassimilable. For the black man, as we have shown, historical and economic realities come into the picture. . . . It is in white terms that one perceives one's fellows. People [French and Antillean] will say of someone, for instance, that he is "very black" . . . . One family in particular had an excellent reputation. . . . The father was given to walking up and down his balcony every evening at sunset; after a certain time of night, it was always said, he became invisible.[49]

Fanon, then, clearly establishes a differential for the psychical relationship to the gestalt in the black man and in the white; for the apparent universal has gone through a process of what Fanon, elsewhere in *Black Skin, White Masks,* will dub a process of lactification—that is, a process that can only work for white men at this historical juncture has been assumed to be applicable to all. It is for that reason, and perhaps for that reason only, that Fanon will become increasingly interested in *negritude,* and particularly, as Jock McCulloch has pointed out, in the political efficacy of reemerging in black culture (Césaire's "psyche of ascent") even though this may strategically essentialize blackness in a manner akin to the nativist trend in national culture that Fanon characterizes as the second stage of decolonization. While Fanon adds the words "And conversely" following his claim that "the real Other for the white man is and will continue to be the black man," the way in which this manifests itself is clearly different, for blackness is, for the white man, the most visible, and that which cannot be "whited out." For Emily Apter, the form of whiting out of body image that occurs for the black man as he looks into the mirror paves the way for an understanding of a form of "subjectivity beyond race."[50] This is effectuated, she claims, by a kind of historically escapist fantasy. While she acknowledges on the one hand Fanon's interpretation of this "loss of body image," this notion of historical escapism surely misses the point of Fanon's notion of whiting out, even though the spectral resonance of that idea appears frequently in current notions of racial morphing and drag as she discusses them.

Fanon's reading, after all, is about psychical violence and the forms of disavowal to which it gives rise. For Fanon, it is the *historical and economic* that characterize the manner in which the black man's psyche is constituted, and, implicitly, it is historical and economic privilege that causes the white man's psyche to be apparently free of such concerns even as the white man's absolute Other is the black man. Interestingly, in this visual rendition of psychical makeup, the *historical and economic* "come into the picture." They also, it seems, potentially "become invisible," to the white man. The figure made up by these conditions is said to fall out of the visual realm of the French and Antilleans alike, because of the associations with blackness for one, and the historical and economic effacement for another. Insofar as the mirror stage in Lacan's rendition coincides with the child's entry into language, and therefore with a grappling for control over the visual and linguistic realms, it does not so much doubt the existence of the imago in the mirror, but it is unsettled by that image; it recognizes itself as potentiality.

Françoise Vergès reminds readers that Fanon was working from the 1938 published essay by Lacan rather than the version from 1949 published in *Ecrits.*[51] The early version makes it even clearer that Lacan's notion of the other at this stage was rather binary, and closer to Sartre's than to the triangulation of vision in *The Four Fundamental Concepts of Psychoanalysis,* in which a look is not returned to the place from which one sees but actually to another; thus the look cannot confirm the wholeness of oneself, nor can it initiate, through conflict, an ontological shift. Rather, the subject remains split, watching *himself* being watched by another. But for Fanon, it is the white man who makes the black, and vice versa, just as Sartre's anti-Semite makes the Jew, and as de Beauvoir's woman is made the Other of man. But in this description of the black man walking to and fro on the balcony, his disappearance is always threatened, and can be rectified effectively only through a visual contrast — light that illuminates the blue of the black man against a darkened background.

The "And conversely" in connection with the black man's being the Other for the white man may suggest two different notions of the Other posited by Fanon at this early stage — perhaps even three: the oppositional Other who, like Sartre's Other, affronts the existence of the subject by entering into his visual realm, thus disturbing his sense of spatial relationship to things; the Other who is different; and the Other who comes to be irreducible and yet is created and sustained by the manner in which the *historical and economic* shape the perception of the *biological.* The dialectical structure of the argument, one that is in some ways consolidated in *The Wretched of the Earth,* insists on a parallel formation. But the threat of disappearance suggests something else: that the white man can refuse to look, that neither black nor white man may see the black man, however "respectable" he is, because both black and white look to construct the black man as the imaginary other in order to bind themselves as egos that rely on the absolute otherness of the black.

The black man looking, in this scenario, would, however, be very different structurally, from the white. And it is this sort of confused position that the Antillean holds, because his mirror imago *does not appear to have a color* that would oppositionally construct him. In this sense, that Other does not inscribe itself as *difference,* or dialectical opposition, but rather simply as Otherness, which is irreducible and is not, therefore, constitutive of oppositional subjectivity. And for Fanon, it is not a linguistic alterity but a historical and material pathology that leaves one lacking and always searching, inevitably in vain, for the signifiers we think will make one whole by returning the gaze oppositionally to fulfill one through love or through antagonism that confirms that wholeness. Alterity, thus, is a notion that lacks color not so much because of a Lacanian concept that does not conceive of Otherness as raced. Rather, the Other lacks color because of a violence done to the black man so that he too sees other black men through white eyes, i.e., sees them disappear at night. The Other as alterity rather than as opposition seems to be rather like this fading figure caught between *fort und da,* intimate yet exterior. While Lacanians would no doubt see Fanon's explanation of this form of Antillean *alterity* (caused by historical and material circumstances) as a dangerous confusion of absolute alterity (caused by linguistic lack) with racial difference that further deludes subjects that they can be whole, Fanon's reading allows for something slightly different. In *Black Skin, White Masks* he suggests, through this twist of both the Sartrean and the Lacanian, that this form of absolute alterity is distinguishable from and irreducible to difference, but is nonetheless historically and materially constituted.

For Fanon, the test case is a man, and this raises a question about the manner in which the *fort und da* game was described by Freud, and how it has been rescripted by Fanon outside the realm of sexual difference (quite surprising in psychoanalysis). It also seems to be downgraded as a concern by Fanon even though it is at the crux of Freudian and Lacanian psychoanalytic thinking and the way it conceives of woman as the ground upon which egos are sustained.

This resonates with another mirror here, the one in front of which the child stands as he plays the game of *fort und da* discussed by Freud in "Beyond the Pleasure Principle." While Freud initially formulates the repetition describing a game in which the child throws away and then retrieves a toy asserting *fort* (gone) and then *da* (there), in a footnote he also describes the child standing in front of the mirror, asserting *da* and then crouching so his reflection was gone, and so he becomes invisible to himself, saying *fort,* or rather uttering negativity as *o-o-o-o,* which Freud will interpret as an attempt by the child to say *fort.* The fact that the man was described as "being given to walking up and down his balcony every evening" as if awaiting the point of disappearance in the eyes of observers—French and Antillean, white and black alike—could also be seen as an attempt to control that potential loss, "making *himself* disappear," and thus moving into a realm of subjectivity that does not become invisible for reasons beyond his control, for example when the *historical and economic*—or darkness—come into the picture. The black man is visible through contrast with white—"like prunes in a bowl of milk," Fanon suggests, quoting a common Martiniquan saying. But when the difference in *his-*

torical and economic factors enters, the black man becomes invisible. These are factors as predictable in their effects as the sunset and the sunrise, that is, of the passing of time and the coextensiveness of any moment with its unfolding.

It is precisely this inevitability that causes the *historical and economic* to intrude upon the white man's self-image, and causes repetition to take on a somewhat psychotic dimension. "The Negro, because of his body, impedes the closing of a postural schema of the white man—at the point, naturally, at which the black man makes his entry into the phenomenal world of the white man. . . . What is important to us here is to show that with the Negro the cycle of the *biological* begins."[52] It is this statement that initiates Fanon's lengthy footnote on the mirror stage. And even though that footnote will acknowledge the "affective value, illusory like the image," the field in which this virtuality is played out is that of the black man's body, biologically, historically, and economically situated. And the psychic constitution of both black man and white, according to Fanon, develops through these relations, thus bringing them into subjectivity, shape, and visuality. What we have here, then, is an assertion of materiality and the manner in which this intrudes upon the idealism of the Lacanian apparently "color-free" model. How does that materiality come to bear on the Lacanian framework? And how is the Negro figured phenomenologically and differentially depending on who is doing the perceiving?

In some ways, this is precisely the question that initiates the study *Black Skin, White Masks*—how the black man perceives the white man and the white woman (but not the black woman, about whom Fanon famously says, "I know nothing about her"),[53] and how these figures' perceptions of each other relate in various combinations and permutations. But not only does it follow a Lacanian framework in the sense that it asks us to consider what constitutes the other differentially within the Symbolic; it also introduces terms into that Symbolic that bring pressure to the Lacanian framework, for the *economic, historical, and biological* are not simply symptoms of the psychical universe described in Lacan. They are not shaped and produced by subjectivity; rather, they are what causes subjectivity to be constituted in this way. Effectively, castration, as the primary trauma, and importantly as a gendered trauma, is displaced by something else: the economic, the historical, and the biological. While castration may perhaps figure as a structural factor in the constitution of subjectivity, it is given prime focus by Fanon neither in a more developmental Freudian model, nor in a more structural Lacanian psychical constitution. The mirror period for Fanon is clearly not simply something that refers back to or structurally constitutes a stage or phase that occurs around six months or upon the beginning of consciousness of language. In the example Fanon gives, it seems to occur at least every night as the sun goes down. And it happens for historical reasons, that is, in the unfolding of time rather than simply as a repetition.

Fanon, Pseudomelancholy, and Politics

When Fanon is read along with Mannoni, who positions himself more explicitly as an alternative to Lacan in the colonial context, we can see that both consider the psychical contingency of coloniality (that is, the adjectival colonial situation) to situate both notions of psychoanalytically conceived selves and the political conceptions of decolonization. It is this notion of the colonial situation that Fanon implicitly addressed in his important essay "The North African Syndrome."[54] Writing about the "pseudopathology" and the "morbidity" of the Algerian Arab, to whom he applies the term "pseudo-invalid," he considered the imprecise symptoms of the Arab when he comes to the hospital, and also the reasons for the French doctors' responses to these symptoms and the Arab patients. Patients, he wrote, often come to the hospital complaining of general pain, feeling ill, and commonly, the sense that they will soon die. Repeated encounters with the patients do not necessarily lead to further clarification of the symptoms, a factor that led Fanon, and some other doctors, to diagnose psychosomatic rather than physical lesion of some sort. His source was an authoritative article on psychosomatic disorders by Heinrich Meng, who distinguished "situational" from "somatic" diagnosis.[55] Fanon cites Dr. E. Stern's summary of Meng's theory. Stern is dismissive of the relevance of Meng's criteria for the Algerian Muslim, claiming (in a manner that characterized him as a caricature of the racist colonial physician) that the situational workplace is irrelevant because the North African does not work; his sex life is irrelevant because he is a violent rapist (and she is a prostitute); relations are irrelevant because he has no real relationships but only "bumps"; tension is irrelevant because he has no inner life or introspection. Fanon situated himself somewhat ambiguously. While criticizing colonial doctors who were plagued by the racist politics of the situation (he cites Dr. Mugniery on the sentimental premature awarding of some Algerians with French citizenship even though the *évolués* are basically primitive),[56] he implicitly offered different explanations. One was that the North African faked illness in order, for example, to be treated to a warm hospital bed when it was cold. Another was doctors' failure to interact appropriately with their patients, patronizingly addressing them in the familiar and disrespectful second person singular (*tutoyer*), thus introducing a hierarchical relationship between doctor and patient. And a third was that illnesses were psychosomatic functions of colonial affect, because of expatriation, torture, or cultural confusion.

In the "North African Syndrome" it is not always clear with whom Fanon identifies. Memmi points out that the personal pronouns in this essay suggest an identification with the French. This stands in contrast to the use of pronouns in *Black Skin, White Masks,* in which the "we" refers to Martiniquans, and in *The Wretched of the Earth,* in which Fanon appears to be reborn as an Algerian freedom fighter in the blueprint of the *moujahedine.*[57] But once again, as with the confusing suggestions in the footnote on Lacan, parallels could not easily be drawn, and "pseudo" illness could be interpreted differently depending on historical and economic reasons that determine any understanding of the biological. Pseudo-illness could be understood equally as one that is deliberately faked by the "pseudo-patient," or one, like a pseudopregnancy, that is psychosomatically experienced as real in spite of there being no physical basis for the symptoms. It could also be understood as an illness as yet unrecognized by the medical profession, in which generalized psychological pain is "demetaphorized" into metonymies of concretized locations.

Fanon associates the pseudo-illness of Arab morbidity with expatriation. If the Arab is a morbid figure, convinced (or claiming) that he is dying rather than presenting the doctor with a specific health complaint, Fanon diagnosed this generalized pain as a bona fide symptom. He looks to psychoanalysis to understand this morbidity: "Think of all those who lead a life without a future in their own country and who refuse fine positions abroad. What is the good of a fine position if it does not culminate in a family, in something that can be called home? Psychoanalytical science considers expatriation to be a morbid phenomenon. In which it is perfectly right."[58] Because the Arab will settle happily neither in France nor in Algeria, he is morbid. Having been "taught" to be French, Algerians are now resented for being in " 'our' country." Addressing the Frenchman,

Fanon adds, "You know perfectly well you rob him of something, that something for which not so long ago you were ready to give up everything, even your life."[59] If Fanon reminds the French that not so long ago, in World War II, it was they who were laying down their lives for national sovereignty and freedom, now he places them in the position of an occupying power in an unconditional condemnation. Arab morbidity is thus linked to a loss of both the French ideal and a sense of home.

Perhaps it would not be stretching the argument to link morbidity in the pseudo-illnesses of Algerian Arabs to the idea of a pseudomelancholy theorized by Porot in the psychiatric school of Algiers. This, after all, was the immediate intellectual context for Fanon's research as he puzzled through his own and other doctors' responses to pseudo-illnesses. And his own response to the doctors' racism and French national interests added to the complexity of his own position. For while he appears to begin to identify with Algerians at times in this piece, he is clearly not identifying himself as a Martiniquan, or even as one who is so évolué that he is closely identified with the very French doctors he criticizes. Pseudomelancholy, understood through this mournful morbidity, suggests indeed a different form of colonial melancholy linked very closely to national belonging. Pseudomelancholy was theorized by Porot in a manner that suggested the lesser moral fiber of the Algerian Muslim. Rather than experiencing a form of melancholy that was introverted and suicidal (he is like Mannoni here when discussing the Malagasy psyche as unlinked to anything like the superego), the Arab was homicidal. Melancholy linked to morbidity implied a response that was moral and political, with the extroverted homicidal response, which was coupled with an unaccounted for introverted morbidity, linked to the political and psychical quandaries that were a consequence of expatriation.

Freud's theorization of morbidity, disavowal, and expatriation elucidates this. Freud's disturbance of memory on the Acropolis, reported some years after the initial experience in the "Open Letter to Romain Rolland," was clearly centered on filial piety and national affiliation, with concerns about passports, legitimacy of citizenship, cultural roots, national rape, and criticism of the power of the state all being analyzed. The disturbance of memory causes a disturbance also in a continuous sense of national history documented through the glories of the state or indeed the empire.

As Mannoni reminded us in "Je sais bien, mais quand même," it is in the open letter that Freud also formulates more extensively the concept of disavowal, which will later contribute to the concept of the splitting of the ego as a mechanism of defense that he theorizes in exile from Nazi Vienna. If "The Disturbance of Memory" is a symptomatic and introverted response to increased insecurity for the Jewish Freud, "The Splitting of the Ego" is a more directly mournful, and morbid, response to expatriation and impending death in the face of real dangers to himself, his children, and the discipline of psychoanalysis he had created. If, as Emily Apter interestingly formulated, Mannoni theorized the French response to coloniality through disavowal, the conscious repudiation of an idea known to be true, the responses of other colonial doctors, like Porot and Carothers, can be read in this light. Deliberately misunderstanding political rebellion, protest, and indeed moral outrage at colonial oppression, and formulating a contorted concept of pseudomelancholy in its place, seems initially to be a form of disavowal that, in its most extreme forms, seems somewhat more like denial.

This form of melancholy, similar to that of "Westerners" losing a person or an idea, or experiencing expatriation, works slightly differently from the blueprint presented in the forms of psychoanalysis taken up by colonial psychiatry and psychology. In fact, this could be read as a deliberate and conscious escape from moral responsibility, "manifestly and abjectly disingenuous."[60] This is effectively the accusation leveled against them by Fanon in "The North African Syndrome."

Morbidity replaces disavowal among the expatriated Arab population of Algeria, and the melancholic moral responsibility is played out in the political field of injustice. Different national status and possibilities of affiliation give form to a different sense of self. This is not simply an existential rebirth out of the Sartrean split, that is, between a thesis and an antithesis experienced ontologically breaking way for a new man. Melancholic morbidity, rather, manifests itself through affect, and "self" criticism, where that "self" is itself uncertainly conceived out of an expatriated sense of home, origin, and source of birth.

Ethics Outside Europe and the Hexagon:
Lacan and Fanonian Melancholy

Morbidity and melancholy, then, grow out of vague symptoms of uncertain national affiliation. They also allow us to see that the more politically and explicitly anticolonial works of Mannoni, Fanon, and Memmi could be symptoms of melancholy. To some extent, these works are reifications of oppositions that emerge from the colonial situation, and are demetaphorizations of the very large and confusing affiliations spurned by the colonial situation, and the situational diagnoses it requires. And perhaps, as Memmi suggested, the symptom is politically necessary for a change to be effectuated, even though it may ignore some of the complications of doing so. For while the opposition between colonizer and colonized makes sense politically, it reduces the situation to its most simple binary, failing to account for the interrelations between those categories over the many years of colonial rule.

This is an old problem, one that has been among the fundamental questions psychoanalysis has posed to Marxist theory, and, more recently (in the last ten years or so), one that has entered the realm of cultural studies: the problem is one not only of chicken and egg (what came first, the psychical condition or the material and discursive — that is, the question that came up in relation to the metaleptical error in relation to Mannoni's dependency complex in *Prospero and Caliban*) but also one of how to understand one without the other. In terms of theoretical figures engaged in these questions, the two most frequently pitted against each other in recent debates are Michel Foucault and Jacques Lacan, and more recently Slavoj Žižek has reminded us that Althusser and Lacan must be contrasted in order for us to understand the full import for social analysis of Lacan's notion of the split subject. Lacanian work that calls itself political frequently pits itself against a Foucault-influenced cultural studies and the new historicism, both of which have been highly influential for postcolonial and feminist work concerned with colonialism and therefore with nationalism and postcoloniality. The dominant politics of these studies has prioritized the local, the contextual, and a combative prose that speaks the language of dissent. At the same time, it registers a significant difference from an oppositional revolutionary prose and political logic that could be associated with the three phases of decolonization mapped out by Fanon in his less psychoanalytically oriented work *The Wretched of the Earth*.

The language of postcolonial critique does not necessarily reject all forms of knowledge thought to be or to have contributed to colonialist thinking. For example, Marxist thought has had an enormous influence on theories of decolonization, neocolonialism, and postcoloniality, and Foucault has been greatly influential in current postcolonial scholarship. But both those bodies of thought in most variations have prioritized the historical in a manner that has been neglected in much psychoanalytically influenced writing. This is because psychoanalytic scholarship in the field of postcolonial studies has been dominated by Lacan and a conception of history that is not chronological and not causal. It is, then, with some trepidation that I suggest the positive effects that psychoanalysis has had on postcolonial feminist thought while simultaneously asserting the importance of the *historical, economic,* and even the *biological.* In other words, making use of Fanon's parochialization of the psychoanalytic allows for a way of thinking about psychical work endemic to the process of decolonization. It forces us to acknowledge the workings of psychical contingency without reducing the notion of contingency to space.

Contingency, understood psychoanalytically, has drawn most effectively from the Freudian notions of *Nachträglichkeit* and affect that posit a different notion of the temporal than that based on a causal and chronological flow. Contingency, then, is translated from context to subject, and it is constitutive of the emergence of subjects understood as citizens, or the black man who can control his visuality in the game, or obsessional practice, of *fort und da* as he walks from one end of the balcony to another. Contingency understood as affect does not so much destroy the relation between the social and collective, on the one hand, and the individual and singular on the other, but rather it potentially allows for an understanding of the process of individuation in social contexts.

Returning to the black man from the family of good repute walking back and forth along the balcony, fending off, perhaps, the inevitable moment of disappearance, there is a quite different dynamic from Freud's grandchild, who will not inevitably be confronted with an absent mother, unless absence is characteristic of all forms of loss. In that sense, the primary loss is the apparently inevitable moment at which a child begins to feel need, which signals a separation from the mother. But in Freud's example there is another absence that seems more obvious than that of the mother; one that is much more marked in its political implications than fear of losing the mother. The boy "masters" the threat of loss through his game of *fort und da.* "At the outset he was in a *passive* situation—he was overpowered by the experience; but, by repeating it, unpleasurable though it was, as a game, he took an *active* part. These efforts might be put down to an instinct for mastery that was acting independently of whether the memory was in itself pleasurable or not. . . . Throwing away the object so that it was "gone" might satisfy an impulse of the child's . . . to revenge himself on his mother."[61]

The boy assimilates the process of loss into the structure of his game, thereby assuring himself that he can control the fear of loss that the anxiety of separation from the "gone" mother has triggered in him. Freud's interpretation of the game as "revenge . . . on [the] mother" almost definitively ignores the *material* factors of the absences in the boy's life in favor of a kind of idealized model of castration—understood in this case as the loss of the mother's affection. It is true that the boy seems to fear the absence of his mother, but the greater absence in this situation is that of his father, who is at war and who is very definitely on the boy's mind. He would say "Go to the F(w)ont!" as he threw away the toy, and his father was "At the Front." The absence of the father during war must have been a common experience for all war children, but Freud does not seem to give this much attention. He seems to suggest that the fear of loss (in this case, of the mother) is akin to that of the fear of being wounded. The threat of this is always greater than the wound itself. But in the example of the mirror game, the mother had been away for several hours, only to be greeted upon her return with the utterance "baby-o-o-o-o!"—as if the child was threatening the mother with his own disappearance rather than warding off the threat of losing the mother. In the game, the child would, Freud says, "hail [the toy's] reappearance" as he drew it back to him. In the mirror game, he, in a sense, hails his mother's return (and thus *hails her as mother*) with the threat of his own absence—a threat, of course, that equally threatens the mother's status and subjectivity *as mother*. Here, then, the boy child puts the mother on a string. He threatens her in his game rather more than she threatens him, even though she is perceived as a threat because she may disappear. So while the black man moves back and forth himself in a rather self-contained fashion, the woman as mother cannot perform the game, because, perhaps, she is always already marked as absence in relation to her boy child who develops his ego against the backdrop of his mother.

Fanon's example of the disappearing black who is perceived as invisible first by whites and then consequently, according to Fanon, by blacks, raises a number of important issues that relate to the status of the material and the manner in which it shares in the constitution of subjectivity. Just as the mother is threatened by the (boy) child's game, and thus has her subjectivity threatened by something beyond her control, the black man, attempting to attain some agency over what will apparently inevitably occur because his circumstances make him invisible in spite of his good reputation, eventually disappears in the eyes of both white and black. In the eyes of others, subjectivity disappears. This is, of course, different from the threat to one's own subjectivity by the imago in the mirror, because it is suggestive of the mechanisms that constitute the mirror itself. It is not something transparent, or something through which assurance of existence can be guaranteed in a familiar "mirror" pose. Rather, it is akin to the *historical,* the *economic,* and notions of the *biological* that go into the constitution of image making. It potentially restores, in fact, the shock of the gestalt when we see it for the first time (as when the child first looks in the mirror), or when catching a glimpse of oneself in a mirror unexpectedly.

This may leave one with the experience of worrying strangeness (an uncanny ambiguity), which is both recognition of oneself and its lack. It is the experience of oneself *as other,* if the mirror is considered as a simple medium of reflection. But if the *historical* and the *economic* cause the *biological* to be rendered masklike, the mirror is constitutive of the self, since it is a mask that renders not uncanniness so much as ambivalence. Perhaps the white can be reflected back to him. But the black man is reminded of his intrinsic otherness every time he looks in the mirror, knowing that his face may disappear because it does not refract light. The mirror understood thus is rather like the lens of a camera that sees and is seen as a different entity from the photographer, emitting and inviting a gaze that is different from that of the subject photographer. The mirror as a means through which the subject gains or loses subjectivity introduces it as a separate element between viewer and viewed, a relationship akin to the later Lacan rather than the early formulation of the correlation between viewing and subjectivity. It replaces the centrality of images to the Symbolic formulation of oneself as "I" with that of the relationship between the Real and the Symbolic. The Real could be conceived as the inaccessible fragments of a mirror, discursive networks established through mirror makers, or actors in civil and political society that together constitute a reflection of an "I." In that sense, an absolute Other would be constituted in the material of the mirror, which becomes the invisible matter upon which subjectivity can be constituted. That Other could occasionally be glimpsed, as it is repeatedly consigned to material fragmentation and alienation from the projected image made possible through the lens of a camera, but ultimately consigned to invisibility.

Understood thus, the mirror as a reflective tool, or the artistic as representation of something knowable, would be challenged. One would no longer think of looking into a mirror in order to find a true reflection; nor would one exactly be looking at the mirror in the manner in which one looks at a picture, or through it as one would a window. Rather, there would be an oscillation between seeing the mirror as at once lens and image maker, understanding oneself both as constituted and in a conflictual relationship to that constituted imago. This would be acting in accordance with desire, moving back and forth between one's constitution and the manner in which it is crafted. There would be a movement between the Ideal, as visible, and invisibility, existing on the threshold between them, a threshold that causes an oscillation as between the sweetness of honey and the bitterness of mustard, or on the threshold of a pleasure principle that is regulated by the death drive—an ideal tainted and yet made real and satisfying by its local manifestation.

Lacan begins his series of lectures on ethics with a curious episode on the subject of honey, informing us that what he is trying to give his interlocutors that day is "the honey of my reflections."[62] And he ends the *Ethics* with the image of swallowing books. In the final chapter, he refers to the book of Revelations as if to explain this. Looking to Revelations, the bitter-sweetness is associated with the idea of swallowing books.

> 8. And the voice which I heard from heaven spake unto me again, and said, Go and take the little book which is open in the hand of the angel which standeth upon the sea and upon the earth.
> 9. And I went unto the angel, and said unto him, Give me the little book. And he said unto me, Take it, and eat it up; and it shall make thy belly bitter, but it shall be in thy mouth sweet as honey.
> 10. And I took the little book out of the angel's hand, and ate it up; and it was in my mouth sweet as honey: and as soon as I had eaten it, my belly was bitter.
> 11. And he said unto me, Thou must prophesy again before many peoples, and nations, and tongues, and kings. (Revelations 10: 8–11)

At the beginning of his series of lectures, Lacan says that he wishes to bring us, his audience, honey. And apparently we will all know the experience of eating honey in bed in the morning. *We* contain honey, like mustard and the rest of *our* harvest, in pots; *hexagon pots* he stresses. And so France, as the hexagon, is introduced into this curious beginning situating both the speaker as well as a presumed audience. It is the plentiful harvest contained in pots that seems to be likened to desire that we attempt to contain in tight political boundaries. These boundaries supply a sense of pleasure in community as well as defining the contours of acceptable pleasure even though desire exceeds those borders. The pleasure of that national community is always tainted by a desire for and of (*de*) the Other—that which lives beyond the hexagon, that which causes, in fact, the hexagon to be so stringently defined in a geometrical ego formation. "We no longer imagine that the hexagons in which we tend to store our harvest have a natural relationship to the structure of the world."[63] Like honey, desire is continuous and overflowing. We attempt to contain it in pots, but it always exceeds those pots, and thus the pot of honey itself always conjures up a certain bitterness (like mustard). While the hexagon is binding, it collects desire together in a manner that is a fiction of community, not a "natural relationship to the structure of the world," in which the hexagon could be said to shape the honey as if still in the honeycomb. It is this fiction, which Lacan will call the Symbolic, that at once binds the ego (and perhaps the nation) and sets the limits of pleasure and shapes the unconscious (which exceeds the borders set up by the Symbolic). What exceeds the Symbolic can, however, be understood only in the Symbolic's terms; its fictitiousness in and of itself does not stop it from being important. Rather it defines what is crucial to what exceeds its limits. The hexagon is a catachresis that demonstrates both the establishment of hegemony in mainland France and the exclusion of the colonies from that geometrical metropolis in spite of their apparent status as overseas territories and departments of France.

The book and the word are purveyors of the trace of the Symbolic's fictionality. They are the trace of the unconscious in which the desire that exceeds the fictional pleasure intrudes in the language of the Symbolic. They have to be swallowed so that the nation may exist—more precisely, a model of the nation-state that holds within it both a Christian idealist model of proselytization (the gospel of St. John) and a Kantian model of the beautiful. For Lacan, Kant's aesthetic holds within it the (inevitably failed) attempt to bring together the noumenal and the phenomenal other than in a flash or a brief moment. The inevitability of that failure is exactly what sustains the fiction as a fiction, and what allows for an ethics developed not from a universal law but from a universal catachresis made apparent as catachresis through linguistic traces that expose desire as it exceeds its limits. In other words, the ethics of psychoanalysis has to be derived from a theory of the aesthetic, where desire itself may be akin to the inaccessible sublime, but where the *ich* can be understood only as the relation (which is always bitter-sweet) between the noumenal and the phenomenal as we may see it in the beautiful.

Evidently, Lacan's metaphors make use of a theory of an idea of community when he actually attempts to make sense of the group. While it may be the case that in *Group Psychology and the Analysis of the Ego* Freud suggests that the group works best when it thinks as an individual, he does not metaphorize the group as a single subject, even though the individuals that constitute the group may share an ego-ideal. Yet *The Ethics* here suggests the need for a collective thinking, or more importantly, a collective belief that is like the swallowing of the book. The need is for a belief in the fiction and an imperative to enjoy, with a simultaneous acknowledgment of the importance of that very fictionality, hence Žižek's imperative "Enjoy your nation as yourself!" The imperative to enjoy, it seems, is the only possibility of acting ethically; and thus, in an age of relativism, the only political structure that for Žižek seems to carry moral weight is that of fanaticism, because it *appears* to embody a single-minded pleasure that is Other to the fragmented scattering of relativity found in the liberal state. If there is to be an effective counter to fanaticism, then the fiction of an Ideal imago must be maintained.

At the end of the *Ethics,* Lacan suggests an ethics quite distinct from a politics that would work within the realm of the national, without attending to the structure of desire that both maintains and threatens its borders. Politics, it seems, attends to the symptom as affect without recognizing it as affect or considering it within a larger structural model. It will therefore inevitably be blinded by its own symptomaticity.

Structure is not seen in Lacan to be akin to a metaphysics of the physics of the geometrical *ich* or the hexagon. Rather, it is a recognition of the bitterness in the belly that inevitably structurally accompanies the sweetness in the mouth. That modernity positions us all in a certain relationship to desire and constitutes desire in a particular fashion is a very general point that causes the loss of nuance in any particular argument, and thus a potential reduction of the postcolonial to the postmodern. It may also cause us to forget that the Martiniquan black man walking up and down the balcony has a very problematic relation to the hexagon of which he is politically a part, even though he is evidently not included in the geographical contours of the geometrical rendition. The black man, speaking the language of the hexagon and yet outside its boundaries, will surely have a death drive that manifests itself quite differently from that of one within. Different community consciousnesses, not necessarily uniform in their differences, will emerge from the repression of Martiniquans by mainland France. The fictionality of the nation-state has consequences that make it impossible to enjoy the group, that is, the inhabitants of the hexagon. The Martiniquan supposedly belongs, because of a shared language — French — to that group. But what is therefore revealed is not only the duplicity of that pleasure as it may exist for the inhabitants of the hexagon in varying degrees, but also its exclusive fantasy structure that demonstrates the warlike nature of the history. The threat of the black man's disappearance is not the only reminder of the bitterness in the belly that marks the unboundedness of desire. Visibility itself is a threat because the shape of the Antillean is not that of the hexagon, and blackness is not understood as being reflective in the manner that whiteness is.

There is clearly a difference between a manifestation of social antagonism and one of psychic antagonism, even though these bear structural similarities. The psychically split subject has a propensity for sociality because completion, wholeness, or the loss of antagonism can be based solely on a subject's fantasy and *reflects* directly or askew a fundamental split afforded by modernity. Collapsing the social to the psychical lacks a fundamental distinction between ambivalence and ambiguity (often manifested as memory and history). Both are understood as simple antagonism without attention to the internal and external valences and affects that some understanding of the *function of the meta-* (or maybe, in Fanon's terms, the function of alterity as opposed to difference) may supply. For without these distinctions, the ethical is inevitably pursued only in terms of the subject as an ethical responsibility to oneself; and a social antagonism is implicitly always *caused* by the psychic antagonism because it is reduced to the psychical work of fantasy formation. In short, Lacan leaves us with a kind of solipsism that is highly problematic in social analysis, and it inevitably loses sight of the degree of antagonism, the placing of the subject in relation to Others, and a limit to the manner in which we may conceive of freedoms, oppressions, and ambiguities in contexts.

That initial split in the Lacanian subject could be understood as the metanarrative of modernity and nationalism. Fanon's notion of alterity makes use of the structural analysis of Lacan, understanding it in his terms of Antillean pathology. This alterity could be dangerous if reduced to revolutionary struggle and oppositional self-definition because of the principle of the honey and mustard, which both seek something beyond the national model of the hexagon. If Lacan saw the ethical imperative of psychoanalysis as speaking in accordance with one's desire, i.e., acknowledging the guilt that reveals the excess of desire as it flows from the hexagon, then that naturalized hexagon of modernity may be constituted in the colonies according to different structural parameters that bring to light the historical and the material. Freud and Lacan suggested that the analyst should not be cheered by the discovery of a *real event*. Any event, for them, has to be understood as linguistically constituted, as the event itself is lost. However, speech can be understood in its psychical and social constitutiveness through considering the relation between a perceived event and its constitution. Otherwise, as in Lacan's own language, history is reduced to its individuated rendition, and the archive exists only as memory, however vicariously that memory may be conceived, or however haunted one may be by the phantoms it encrypts.

Fanon's footnote on the Lacanian mirror stage leads to reconfiguration that demonstrates how he was less a Lacanian than a Sartrean. Effectively, the mirror stage marks the colonial figure as constituted through the mirror-as-camera where its lens renders the biological *historically* and *economically* situated. As such, the modern becomes something quite different in the colonies than in the colonial metropole. The psychoanalytic ambiguities of the mirror stage are, in a sense, then, the flip side of the colonial machinery that renders the colonized subject split, and visible only when reflecting a certain form of light. The modern colonized subject has, then, a different ontological makeup than that of the colonizer rendered through the relationship of looking, and not seeing oneself as a mask, but rather, one's gestalt as a mask, and one's mask as a self.

Žižek; or Swallowing *The Ethics of Psychoanalysis*

Fanon's rendition of the mirror stage poses the question of the locality of the psyche and of politics, and also distinctions between the modern and the postmodern. For Slavoj Žižek, this distinction is rather loosely conceived; this is most striking in his article "A Leftist Plea for Eurocentrism." Consider Žižek's *post-communist plea* in light of the fact that communism and Marxism do still exist elsewhere in the world—through parts of Africa and India, for example. This reveals how the notion of the universal-modern-Other that Žižek posits against that of globalization-difference-other is one that is particularly constituted in national-colonial contexts, i.e., European powers, like France in 1789, consolidating their ideas of the modern in the colonizing modern nation-state. Resistance to that colonization, which may be read retroactively, as Homi Bhabha pointed out in his discussion of the distinction between the postmodern and the postcolonial, begs the question of whether a resistant form of the modern is misread, or more accurately, ignored by Žižek as the global postmodern, and whether that misreading demands a different notion of the other because of the *weight of history*. Žižek writes of the confusion of the distinction between *universalism* and *globalization*. He distinguishes between global late capitalism's imperial features and the common notion of humanity suggested by human rights discourse. On the other hand, these must be distinguished from universalist desires such as those created by the demands of the Third Estate in revolutionary France, which give to all of us the possibility of representation, and therefore of political agency. Without this possibility—and he takes his cue from Etienne Balibar's *La crainte des masses* here—senseless and spectacular violence will ensue.[64]

Interestingly, Žižek takes as an example the African American single unemployed lesbian mother, as displaying a form of violence that appears excessive and irrational. The reason for this is that there is no belief in the possibility of attaining representation, largely because the liberal debunking of the universal in favor of the local and particular has eroded the very idea that political representation is possible or desirable. For Žižek, desire for representation is crucial, because it posits the "Truth-Event irreducible to (and unaccountable in the terms of) the Order of Being."[65] In this scenario, the *Order-of-Being* is on the side of difference, and the *Truth-Event* is more on the side of the Other, where the individuated subject's desire is precisely what affords the possibility of group formation and realpolitik.

The strength of Žižek's argument is the emphasis on a politics that retains faith in the possibility of representation. He is critical of politics that seeks redress for victimization from those who appear to have caused it, or who come from the same social groups as those people. However, while the dismal alternative according to Žižek has been the proliferation of identities claiming difference in postmodern times, it would appear that there are other forms of the European legacy that need to be addressed, namely the bedrock upon which it was built. That is not simply to say that redress is valid; I will leave that question aside for now. Rather it is to pose the question of how those universals have been parochialized in the colonies that inherited them from the European legacy, the maintenance for which Žižek pleads. It seems that in many of those contexts the European legacy has been maintained with violence that begs the question of the locality of the proselytizing spirit of *swallowing the book*—or faithfully swallowing the spirit of the *first text:* the Bible; *the second text:* the *Communist Manifesto;* or indeed the *third text: The Wretched of the Earth.* Žižek's swallowing of Lacan's *Ethics,* and the Christian idealism it holds within it, gives the postcolonial rather more than the bitterness in the belly and the sweetness in the mouth of inhabitants of the *hexagon.* For while his adoption of Balibar's centralizing of "the unconditional demand for freedom" exposes the necessity of a form of order, his own sense of his task is quite horrifying in its historical and referential homologies: "Is then our task not exactly homologous to that of Christianity: to undermine the global empire of capital, not by asserting particular identities, but through the assertion of a new universality?"[66] Not exactly homologous, surely. Žižek warns that the proliferation of identities based on *ressentiment* continually confuses Otherness with other people, and that this will result in fanaticism. And fanaticism, a kind of radical evil that Žižek in a sense seems to admire in that it retains an *ethical* argument rather than a *political* one (however political that ethics may be), needed to be countered with an alternative, and tempered, universalist ethics.

Fanon's interest in nationalism interestingly gives a way of understanding that alternative universalism. "National consciousness, which is not nationalism, is the only thing that will give us an international dimension."[67] Universalism gets grounded as internationalism. The "fight for democracy against the oppression of mankind will slowly leave the confusion of neo-liberal universalism to emerge, sometimes laboriously, as a claim to nationhood."[68] Similarly, the death drive that informs Lacan's concept of ethics is grounded as morbidity, which I have extended to a concept of colonial melancholy.

Melancholy, conceptualized through the symptom of demetaphorization, could be understood as the anesthetization of man's varied desire.

Swallowing the book of *The Wretched of the Earth,* the moral position of the paradoxical call to arms (the willingness to die for freedom) is revealed in politics. Understanding the swallowing as an incorporation, however, uncovers the excesses and confusions of *Black Skin, White Masks* have not been entirely put to rest by the oppositional discourse of melancholic revolutionary politics, which amounts to understanding the unconscious as a repository of energies suppressed by the colonial regime.[69]

Lacan writes that "the important thing is not knowing whether man is good or bad in the beginning; the important thing is what will transpire once the book has been eaten."[70] The future thus holds desire ("anesthetized, put to sleep by moralists, domesticated by educators, betrayed by the academics . . . taken refuge . . . repressed")[71] not simply as understood in structural terms, but also as the affect created by swallowing whole the blueprint of national liberation, and not assimilating it psychically. The tempered response to national liberation, uneasily accepting it as a goal of universalism and democracy, and seeing it as a source of liberation and the cause of European violence, causes a melancholic response to the national idea. While Lacan may see the notion of cause as the source of an impoverished concept of ethics in the service of goods (thus anesthetizing desire), he also situates this impoverished notion of cause "throughout this historical period."[72] Throughout the period of European nation-states, the structures of desire have been different for colonized and uncolonized peoples, set against each other in demetaphorized opposition even as they were mutually constituted as modern subjects. What the future holds for Lacan is, perhaps, a whited out notion of political context, in which the death drive and the Other are without color. Fanon's new man, and Freud's split ego, are mechanisms of defense as much as affects of melancholia—the loss of the ideal of national affiliation. For Fanon, as perhaps with Freud, the future needs more closely to be understood as something that emerges from the present and the past, something that is historically situated if not always causally linked.

Memmi on Fanon: Identifying a Melancholic

In his essay "The Impossible Life of Frantz Fanon," Albert Memmi presented Fanon as a tragic hero who persistently failed to understand the importance of the "lived experience" of his own childhood, and therefore what it meant to affiliate himself with a people. In spite of the fact that Fanon devoted a chapter of *Black Skin, White Masks* to the "Lived Experience of the Black" (L'expérience vécue du Noir), in Memmi's estimation, Fanon failed to understand the importance of "portraiture" in his life, that is, the way in which he was seen, and also the manner in which he understood how the particularities of his early life would result in certain affective conditions. Through Memmi's reading, Fanon appears as a colonial melancholic, deliberately ignoring his own contradictions and his own confused sense of national and regional affiliation to Martinique, and the France to which Martinique belongs, in order to be reborn as an African, militantly struggling against France and other European colonial powers.[73]

Fanon's symptoms, identified by Memmi, could interestingly be read as forms of demetaphorized morbidity and melancholy. The symptoms that demonstrate confusion around affiliation, or the failures, as Memmi calls them, of Fanon that led him away from self-examination, could be read as a type of demetaphorization that led him into revolutionary struggle. If Mannoni considered the nouns that developed out of the colonial situation to be misguided in their Manichaean establishment of absolute difference, Memmi sought an understanding of why the nouns came into existence and dominated the revolutionary moment in which colonies fought the powers under whose rule they existed. Fanon's melancholia led him to understand that revolutionary violence, however problematic and symptomatic, was the only possible recourse to national independence.

In Memmi's view, analysis of "portraits" offered a means of understanding these phenomena. In his books *Portrait of the Colonizer Preceded by the Portrait of the Colonized* (published as *The Colonizer and the Colonized*) and *Portrait of a Jew*, as well as in his essay "Frantz Fanon and the Notion of Deficiency,"[74] the portrait is both the mythology attached to the noun, and an examination of the lived experiences constituted through this mythology, and defiant of it: "The accusation [of laziness] disturbs him and worries him even more because he admires and fears his powerful accuser. 'Is he not partially right?' he mutters. 'Are we not all a little guilty after all? Lazy, because we have so many idlers? Timid, because we let ourselves be oppressed?' Willfully created and spread by the colonizer, this mythical and degrading portrait ends up being accepted and lived with to a certain extent by the colonized. It thus acquires a certain amount of reality and contributes to the true portrait of the colonized."[75] In a manner that stands in stark contrast to the "fashionable notion . . . of 'dependency complex'" theorized by Mannoni, Memmi stated that the colonial situation created situations in which the colonized internalized various mythologies about himself, and thus effectively became dependent. The mythology thus became a part of "the true portrait" for economic as well as psychical reasons.

Memmi distinguished himself from Sartre on exactly this point on a number of occasions: the importance of the objective conditions imposed on one through the oppressive Other permanently changed the way in which one was treated, not simply perceived.[76] In "Negritude and Jewishness," Memmi implicitly took Sartre to task for understanding negritude as negativity. Speaking of the similarities between Judaism and an essence of negritude, on the one hand, and Jewry and "Negrity" on the other, he explained that "Negrity does not correspond to a racial community, but to a community of *condition,* which is a condition of oppression, under the mythical pretext of race."[77] Sartre did not account for this adequately in Memmi's eyes, and this inattentiveness to the experience of perception and the material conditions that accompanied it constituted Memmi's major critique of Sartre and of Fanon's understanding of his own life. While he suggested that Fanon was ambiguous on the notion of an internalized and lived experience of the mythological portrait, Memmi insisted that his own notion of colonial privilege was first economic, but also "psychological and cultural," understood through an examination of the lived experience.[78]

It is this criticism of political strategies for overcoming oppression and domination that remains with Memmi throughout his book *Dominated Man.* For Memmi, the portrait was constituted as much through historical identity as conceptions, mythological or not, of that identity. Hence, in *The Colonizer and the Colonized* Memmi showed how the mythological Manichaean divisions between two types are reified in a manner that fails to account for their mutual imbrication in a shared colonial drama. While clearly Memmi was well aware of the power differentials and contrasting material comforts of colonized and colonizing peoples, he was also cognizant of the internal relations and the importance of particular differences.

While one could argue that Fanon also emphasized the psychological and the cultural, there are certainly moments in which he failed to engage his own lived experience. For Memmi, this was most apparent in his failure to analyze his own life, and the affiliations he chose. This led Fanon to be concerned with the future, and Memmi's criticism of Fanon interestingly focuses on his messianism. Calling him a prophet of the third world, Memmi suggested that Fanon was unable to come to terms with his own past, and specifically his regional and particular location. He traced the changing use of the personal pronoun in Fanon's work, as it designates a sense of belonging or alienation, of community or isolation. Four failures of belonging and allegiance characterized Fanon's legacy. Three of these revolved around a lack of judgment surrounding a sense of self, or the importance of portraiture as Memmi conceived it. Fanon first thought himself a Frenchman, and realized his mistake in this only once he went to Paris. Peter Geismar's biography, which Memmi reviewed in 1971, suggested that even racism in the French army was initially attributed by Fanon to the Vichy regime rather than to French colonial attitudes, an impression he would maintain at least until he first went to Algiers to fight in the Free France movement, which would eventually rid France of the occupying power with which Vichy had collaborated.[79]

Fanon's second mistake was to leave behind Martinique and Aimé Césaire, whom he had admired so profoundly. This rejection of negritude was, in Memmi's eyes, a rejection of his own existence, and a pan-Africanism that began with self-examination. Choosing Algeria over Martinique gave him a way of identifying with a revolutionary consciousness that he did not see in his native Martinique. Memmi cites one of Fanon's Martiniquan compatriots speaking of a conversation with Fanon in Tunisia: "When I met him in Tunis in 1958, he greeted me coldly. Well are you still politicking in the West Indies and Guiana? One of these days, France will give you a kick in the ass that will force you to seize your independence. You will owe it to Algeria, our Algeria that will turn out to have been the whore of the French colonial empire."[80] Presumably the economically minded "whore" would seek reparations for her usage, in Fanon's terms, while the differently feminized, and uxorious Martinique would remain in a bad marriage and continue to be abused. Memmi's emphasis, however, is on Fanon's inability to come to terms with his own past, even though at times he appears to perform an outright rejection of it.

Fanon's third failure was, for Memmi, his universalist pan-Africanism, which once again neglected to attend to particularity. Having claimed a commonality with Algerian peoples, Fanon failed to explore the particularities of their lives, or indeed to examine the consequences of Algeria's brand of revolutionary violence for a black Christian like himself in the future of an independent Muslim Algerian nation-state. Of course, Fanon died before he would have to encounter the problems of an independent Algeria, which would come into its own the year following his death. For Memmi the psychologist who knew Fanon as a practicing psychiatrist, his lack of attention to identity was astonishing.[81] He remarked on not only Fanon's lack of self-exploration, but also his inattention to learning Arabic, even though he showed some consciousness of the difficulty it posed in the doctor-patient hierarchy. "Language is never simply a tool . . . it is a reservoir of a people's soul. Fanon was often mistaken in his view of Algeria. He openly admitted this on several occasions."[82] Memmi ultimately suggested that Fanon moved too swiftly into abstractions of political oppression without attending to detail. An exploration of the difficult details of the personal was crucial in understanding not only the nature of oppression, but also the effective and ineffective mechanisms for instrumenting change. Memmi rejected universalist messianism, which he saw as typical of Marxist movements in particular but also typical of most other discourses around oppression:

> What can an individual do on discovering that he cannot step outside his singularity, not erase it in the minds of others to the point of being adopted by them? The next step is to deny to the utmost of all singularities, all those accursed differences which stand in the way of communion between men and prevent one from being simply human among other humans. All individuals are then blended into the universal and the universal is declared to be the only reality, the only ethic. . . . [D]uring the last stage of his life, Fanon decided on the universalist solution. . . . He needed a mediator. This was the role of Africa.[83]

Memmi began by chiding Fanon for not going back to Martinique, where a form of pan-African negritude was in place. He insisted that negritude sought out a shared cultural memory absent from Fanon's messianism, which invented from nowhere an inspiring new third-world man[84] akin to Marx's belief in the "universalist messianism of the proletariat."[85] Memmi saw Fanon's messianism as one that failed to account for how the revolutionary ethic emerged. In fact, it was this failure to see the difference between singularity and his particularity that caused Memmi to dismiss Fanon's inspiring quality as messianism rather than more complexly messianic: that is, taking account of the haunting that overshadows any hope of future redemption.

The lived condition of being black, that is, Memmi's idea of "negrity," took into account the shared cultural memory popularized through "negritude" without confusing this portraiture and mythology with an essence of being that was not dependent on the colonial situation. Fanon's version of pan-Africanism involved a similar secularization of the mystique of negritude with Africa as mediator. But it did not account for the colonial past that had partially formed the systems of dependence and revolution which inevitably defined the future nation-states of Africa.

For Memmi, an unexamined past was a denial of interiority that would in time have disastrous consequences for the future of the new nation-states and lead to a lack of critical attention to the colonial formation of the nation-state structure. Memmi's way of making sense of the past, and particularly his own past, was through the genre of autobiographical fiction. He distinguished this from autobiography in the context of writing about Simone de Beauvoir's work in the chapter of *Dominated Man* titled "A Tyrant's Plea," in which Memmi identified himself as being "on the wrong side of the fence; in talking about women, I observe with embarrassment and a touch of malice, that this time I am to be counted among the oppressors."[86] In an essay that rehearsed many familiar criticisms of Simone de Beauvoir—that she failed to explore adequately her own pain, relationships, and loves, and in particular that her thoughts on motherhood appeared to deny the essence of femininity (as Memmi understood it)—Memmi suggested that one opens oneself up to such criticism in autobiographical writing. "The publication of an autobiography is probably always a bad move on the part of a writer. If he is wholeheartedly honest, he exposes himself irrevocably; without the comfortable disguise of fiction he cannot escape swift condemnation. If, with a different kind of honesty, he warns us that he is not telling us the whole truth, he will immediately be suspected of hiding the most important elements, and then be contemptuously rejected. Why announce an autobiography if one intends to omit what is most significant?"[87]

Memmi criticizes de Beauvoir for her Hegelian neglect of what he understood as the feminine in her attempt to rid women of their "femininity" and to eschew any acknowledgment of failure to be independent. This femininity involved, for Memmi, a shared dependence between a couple that re-creates the relationship of dependence between a child and a parental figure, particularly a mother. While he acknowledged that culturally women's dependence appeared to emerge from being dominated by men, he insisted that mutual dependence was necessary, and allowed Man to become a social being. He applauded de Beauvoir's attempt at self-revelation, but read into her work an affective manifestation of concealment. He insisted that her relationship to Sartre, far from being the success she claimed because of her emotional and economic independence, actually hurt her deeply. The autobiography failed to document this, but rather overcompensated for the failure. This was effectively an affective manifestation more suitable to the fictional work than to that of memoir or autobiography, for autobiography, according to Memmi, calls for the whole truth, not a dissociation of emotion, as would be appropriate for a more literary, and psychoanalytic, assessment.

In order to avoid such criticism for his own part, Memmi explored his own lived experience through semiautobiographical fiction. *The Pillar of Salt,* for example, was an examination of what it meant to be a Jew during Tunisian decolonization; later works also engaged the Six-Day War, which confirmed that Jews' relation to the Tunisian state was problematic. In *The Colonizer and the Colonized,* he drew from his own experiences to consider how the position of the Jew complicated the overdetermined roles of the Manichaean division between colonizer and colonized, with all the class and ethnic variations that came into play, as well as the complicated history of assimilation itself.

In semi-autobiographical fiction, the contradictions of belonging, alienation, and disappointment, indeed of melancholia, could be thematized without being resolved and could present the aporetical affiliations without seeming to present political betrayals. The impassable and contradictory feeling of being both colonizer and colonized could be shown through the emotional and linguistic conflicts experienced by a young man without casting doubt on his commitment to national independence. It could also show how a tempered response to national independence and the logic of revolutionary structure emerged out of an examination of lived experience.

In *The Pillar of Salt,* Memmi conducted this examination through the figure of Benillouche, and the main text exists within parentheses, the substance of the bracket being quite literally an examination. The occasion for writing, as revealed in the frame narrative, was a philosophy exam that would allow him to teach in the French university system. Much postcolonial fiction and nonfiction describes the colonial education system which provided access to the metropolitan center and academic "transcendence" of shameful colonized origins of a class of *évolués*.[88] Benillouche ultimately refuses the examination (an apparently irrelevant essay on the influence of Condillac on John Stuart Mill), interestingly in contradistinction to Memmi himself, who took the exam and eventually taught philosophy in universities in both Tunis and Paris.[89] But the semiautobiographical work allowed for an exploration of the difficulty of accountability without condemnation. While *The Colonizer and the Colonized* ultimately saw the revolutionary struggles for independence that caused colonizer to be pitted against colonized as a necessary messianic revolutionary moment, the autobiographical novel communicated the constant and aporetical shortcomings of such a venture.

Benillouche's thoughts on language use at different stages in his life are testimony to this. Asked as a young boy in school to discuss Alfred de Vigny's work, he was carried away with his enthusiasm for the subject and, deciding to speak without notes, slipped into slang. His teacher responded thus: "Your report has been most odd. I can add very little to what you've said about Vigny. But, in order to speak without notes, which in itself should merit approval, you've allowed yourself to slip into the language of the street urchin."[90] The French conveys more directly perhaps the class condemnation of the appropriate style of academic investigation and the importance of erasing any difference in language use from that of the metropolitan center; Benillouche is condemned for using the language of the *concierge*. His response, quite predictably, was one of shame. Reflecting on the moment, he narrates: "In effect, the language I spoke was an amalgam, a dreadful mixture of literary or even precious expressions and of idioms translated word for word from our dialect, of schoolboy slang and of my own more or less successful inventions. I tried, for instance, to find names for certain sounds which had not yet, so far as I knew, been identified either in French or in our local dialect; or I attempted to create in French those verbs that existed only in dialect. My language was thus as wild and turbulent as I was; it had none of the quality of a clear and placid stream."[91]

This form of *métissage*[92] makes Memmi *not quite* the colonizer, not quite Jewish (his father being Italian-Jewish, his mother being Tunisian-Berber), not quite Tunisian (he is not fully accepted into the ranks by his friends and has won a scholarship to a privileged colonial school in spite of his poverty), and not quite French (he is poor, and identified as a Jew rather than a Frenchman when, along with all Jews in North Africa, he loses his French nationality during the years of the Vichy regime). It becomes clear, however, through the course of the novel that at different moments his material conditions would be determined by how he was seen from the exterior. Thus, for example, although he was not technically a Jew (matrilineal descent being the determining one in Judaism) he found himself, during the desert war, under Nazi threat in a forced-labor prison camp, from which he escaped.

It was in that camp that Benillouche discovered that the language of the street urchin was no longer his, and that in effect it existed now only in spectral form, as "an obscure and obsolete part" of himself:

> I think in French, and my interior monologues had for a long time been in French. When it happens that I speak to myself in dialect, I always have the strange impression, not so much of using a foreign language, as of hearing an obscure and obsolete part of myself, so forgotten that it is no longer native to me. I do not feel this strangeness when speaking to others, it is rather like playing on a musical instrument. But I did not know enough words of Judeo-Arabic to convey my whole meaning to them. I can express myself well enough in Arabic for concrete everyday purposes, but I have always used French in social and intellectual exchanges and the expression of ideas. I would have liked to speak at length to the men [in the forced-labor camp] and, above all, convey to them certain things under the very noses of the guards. For that, certain subtleties which only French allowed me were necessary, but unfortunately their knowledge of French was deficient. In the last resort, I decided to attempt the experiment in French, although I realized how much closer I would have been to them and how much more intimate had I spoken their own tongue.[93]

The echo of this passage, now an "obscure and obsolete part" of him, documents the ambivalent relationship to assimilation while simultaneously presenting a picture of successful assimilation. In other words, it is precisely the inassimilable that the literary text allows for, because the affective obscure and obsolete remain in a manner that calls much more for attention to the process of loss than to the successful transcendence of failure or immanence, or indeed the accomplishment of authenticity that Memmi suggests autobiographical writing claims.

If the desire for assimilation was an inevitable lie of colonial rhetoric as Memmi stated in *The Colonizer and the Colonized*[94] (the logic of assimilation being to erase difference; the logic of colonialism being to maintain it), the belated realization of the impossibility of assimilation emerged as affect in the other scene, or the literary text. While Memmi's criticism of de Beauvoir failed to account for both her theorizations of an ethics of ambiguity and the affective conditions that haunt some of her writings, he recognized the important lasting affect of lived experience as something that cannot and should not be transcended, but rather should cause one to maintain a critical agency in relation to the possibilities of the future. This is extremely pertinent for understanding some of the problems of postcolonial states today, and for understanding the inadequately critical response to the colonial structure of the nation-state that emerged from the former colonies, as well as the demetaphorized structure of revolutionary struggle.

In the first essay of *Dominated Man,* Memmi contrasted the revolutionary politics of James Baldwin and Malcolm X. He criticized Malcolm X, although he understood him to be in some ways an inevitable creator of myth. Memmi wrote of the unrecognizable form of Islam in the universe of "black angels and white devils," and described the Nation of Islam as "a new Messianic religion."[95] Identifying with Baldwin, who was for him "the intellectual, sincere and emotional . . . [who] has grasped the fact that the moderates are by now in the wrong,"[96] he emphasizes the "rhythm" of revolt, and the apparent impossibility, but simultaneous necessity, of consistently maintaining an idea of justice. The colonizer and the colonized were bound together through the pathological logic of the colonial situation, which created the terms as dialectically opposed even as the situation gave rise to many contradictory positions—Memmi's, of course, being a good example of this. Memmi claimed that the colonizer had a Nero complex, usurping the role of ruler while constantly being aware of the injustice of doing so. While it may have been the case that, for example, leftist colonizers existed alongside well-meaning but exploitative assimilationists (though they often left the colony, and Memmi never really explores the metropolitan colonizer), a mythical portrait (a demetaphorized version of the colonial situation into oppositional beings rather than oppositional politics) will inevitably ensue that establishes absolute difference. The black man and the white man in the United States were in a similar situation, wrote Memmi in 1965. The logic of racist revolt (as with colonial revolt) functioned within the logic of racism in Malcolm X's moment. It is not that Memmi advocated a liberal response to colonialism or racism that would ultimately be compliant with, and would benefit from, the continuation of establishment exploitation. Rather, Memmi explored how attention to the mutual imbrication of the colonizer and the colonized would allow for a future that worked outside the logic of colonialism. And this would involve a critical relationship to the desire for an independent nation-state built on the model of the colonizing power—that is, built within the logic of exclusiveness and the possibility of expatriation. Memmi ended the section on the "Portrait of the Colonized" with words drawn from the legal discourse of witnessing, medical discourse of the cure, Marxist terminology of alienation, and Fanonian concepts of decolonization: "In order to witness the colonized's complete cure, his alienation must completely cease. We must await the complete disappearance of colonization—including the period of revolt."[97]

If melancholic morbidity gave rise to the rhythm of political struggle in Fanon's assessment, this for Memmi was symptomatically lacking in an exploration of lived experience that demanded a critical relationship to new nations as much as to colonial rule. Fanon too criticized the national bourgeoisie of postcolonial nation-states for being incapable of establishing an adequate national culture. He too called for a fourth phase of decolonization that moved beyond a relation to the colonizer. However, if Fanon's rhythm of prophetic decolonization consisted of a first phase of imitation of the colonizer, a second of nativism, a third of revolt, and a fourth of a future as yet unimaginable, Memmi's rhythm called for an attention not to the prophetic but to the past, to ambivalence and to the "obscure and obsolete." If the future could be just, therefore, it involved for Memmi a critical agency toward decolonization movements themselves born of the specter of the inassimilable. They were born of a melancholic critical agency emerging from inassimilable specters, obscure and obsolete, that may hold the source of a future justice. Memmi ended his essay "The Paths of Revolt" with: "Later perhaps there will be a return to Baldwin's way of thinking, to a greater lucidity in self-examination and in the understanding of one's own people and of others. Meanwhile, once he has entered the fray, the revolutionary can hardly be expected to judge himself justly, when he has been so unjustly crushed and humiliated, so that his retaliation must transcend all justice."[98] While Memmi did not draw a simple parallel between the white racist and the black revolutionary (clearly, he wrote, the black man is oppressed and to the advantage of the white man),[99] he was extremely wary of the logic of mythological identification that continued the segregation of peoples into groups which suffered the interior oppression of the lie of assimilating to a norm. It was this that led Memmi to plea with the left to reclaim a refashioned form of universalism, and to critique nationalism even while it may have supported nation-states:

> Nationalism is at present the standard to which many nations (whether colonized or not, in point of fact) rally in their fight for freedom; it is for this reason that it is something genuine and constructive. To reject it is mere abstract intellectualization: the negation of what is real. But, if we accept nationalism without argument and without reflection, we are again disqualifying ourselves. We must judge it and make up our minds about its errors and about the various manifestations which give it a bad name and in the end do it harm, or, more simply, do harm to the lives of other groups of people.[100]

Memmi: Portraiture, Lament, and the Double Lesson of Freud

In Memmi's essay on Freud that prefaced David Bakan's book *Freud and the Jewish Mystical Tradition,* it becomes clear that psychoanalysis is not only a mechanism for allowing us to understand the "obscure and obsolete" from our pasts, but also represented for Memmi a hermeneutic (Jewish in its constitution) for consolidating communities into new nation-states. To this end, Memmi wrote that Freud, in *Moses and Monotheism,* "devotes himself to a methodical questioning of Jewishness in its double aspect: a denunciatory analysis of the aggression of others, and a reasoned revolt against the traditions of his people."[101] Memmi's claim differed from that of David Bakan, who argued that psychoanalysis grew out of the Cabalah tradition and shared, with its heretical offshoots, a mystical tradition. Rather than seeking out the origins of psychoanalysis in tradition, Memmi sought them in Freud's experience of anti-Semitism and his subsequent sense of how to create a modern Jewish identity. For Freud, this would have to allow for a group identification between Jews that did not hark back to the type of tradition he abhorred. While he believed it was overstating the case to say that Freudianism was a "laic transformation of the Jewish mystique,"[102] Memmi suggested that the "interior revolt against Jewry" that was "a revolt against Judaism"[103] was a way of seeing oneself as Jewish, but simultaneously in opposition to Jewish orthodoxy.

The portrait of Freud that Memmi gives us is of a child and an old man living through horrifying mythologies of anti-Semitism that at once caused a rejection of Judaism coupled with a sad reality of the persecution of Jews. Freud's recognition, rather like Benillouche's, was that he was nonetheless part of Jewry. Memmi analyzed Freud's *Moses and Monotheism* in this light, insisting on the import of Freud's identification of the centrality of mythology in group identity:

> Freud, with great shrewdness, understood something that historians did not: that Moses is, above all, a myth, by which I mean that his physiognomy and his behavior as they are imagined are far more important than his actual physiognomy and behavior. For this fictitious character was created by a whole people who express themselves through him. . . . [T]he book . . . sets out to destroy an allegory. . . . Moses personifies Jewish tradition and law, everything that binds the Jew from within.
>
> With the desire to liberate the Jew from this interior oppression, Freud methodically attacks the Jew's most prestigious collective dream: the myth of Moses. For myths are the waking dreams of humanity, and Moses is the collective myth of the Jews. We are dealing with a psychoanalytical procedure, admittedly applied to a whole group of people, but there is an extension in its meaning: to become a man one must kill one's father. To liberate the Jews one must kill Moses.[104]

Memmi interspersed these comments with what he referred to as Freud's mistake: his attempt to discredit Moses through unreliable historians who led to the wrong question — that of his ability to authenticate his claim (a problem not unrelated to that of Memmi's criticisms of autobiography). He suggested at the same time, however, that Freud was in no real need of the work of historians, as his mythological discrediting worked sufficiently without it. And yet the manner of this "merciless dismantling of Judaism"[105] perhaps demonstrates how the mythological, in the modern period, relies on an idea of archival documentation. Freud's killing of the father was, then, dependent on the mechanisms of truth building that underlie modern belief. If Laius had to be killed mythologically so that Oedipus could come into his own, so Moses had to be killed historically for the laic Jew to come into being. But if Laius's death continued to overshadow Oedipus's life, so the remainder of Jewish oppression continued to bind the modern Jewish community. Living as a secular Jew involved the archival remainder, more than the guilt perhaps, of killing the father in order to understand the future to come.

Memmi's reading of Freud bears some resemblance to that other North African Jew's reading of Freud as he discussed another book that contemplated psychoanalysis as a Jewish science, Yosef Hayim Yerushalmi's *Freud's Moses*.[106] Rather like Memmi's attention to the lived experience, with all its variations, ambivalences, and ambiguities often obscure and obsolete, Derrida posits the performative:

> It is a question of this performative to come whose archive no longer has any relation to the record of what is, to the record of the presence of what is or will have been *actually* present. I call this *messianic,* and I distinguish it radically from all messianism.
>
>   . . . . Yerushalmi had deployed the question of the future or the immortality of Oedipus. And what he had held in opposition to Freud, finally, is an experience of the future or of hopefulness which seems to him to be at once irreducible to oedipal repetition and irreducibly, *uniquely, exclusively Jewish, proper* to "Jewishness" if not to "Judaism."[107]

The performative to come is perhaps a melancholic remainder of the inassimilable that maintains a critical agency toward the mythologies working within the logic of the colonial situation. Memmi rejected Judaism, "the whole of the teachings, beliefs and institutions of the Jews," in favor of understanding how "Jewishness," "the fact and manner of being a Jew; all the objective, sociological, psychological and biological characteristics which make a Jew" led to becoming a member of "Jewry," or "a group of Jewish persons,"[108] and perhaps to a Zionism he supported—a position, he asserted, that did not contradict in any way his commitment toward third world nations.[109] He compared this unmythological manner of being Jewish to the situation of blacks thus: "negrity" would be akin to Jewry and would refer to black groups; "negroism" would be akin to Judaism and would be the mythological "traditional and cultural values of the black peoples"; and "negritude," like Jewishness, would be "reserved for the manner of feeling oneself to be a black man, by belonging to a particular group of men and by adherence to its values."[110] If mythology is associated with Judaism and negroism for Memmi, it also leads to unexamined messianism in the form of new religions or unexamined faith in nation-state formation. Within this logic, the "messianic" as understood by Derrida could be akin to the possibility of Jewishness rather than Judaism—that is, an examination of the manner in which past inassimilable experiences constitute phantoms or specters, and manifest themselves as melancholic affect and a form of critical agency for the future to come. The messianic, in the age of the colonial nation-state, is quite different from religious messianism, then. And if psychoanalysis is a Jewish science, it is as much a science that emerges from the colonial situation and the modern nation-state.

It is in that messianic future, as Memmi and perhaps Derrida conceived it, that justice, theorized as the spectral through psychoanalysis, may come. In the next chapter I turn to this concept of justice in order to consider the difficulties of and the hope for transnational feminism, given the weight of colonial history and the enormity of the specter that overshadows relations across national borders.

HAUNTING AND THE FUTURE

5. The Ethical Ambiguities of Transnational Feminism

You do not die from being born, nor from having lived, nor from old age. You die from *something*. The knowledge that because of her age my mother's life must soon come to an end did not lessen the horrible surprise: she had sarcoma. Cancer, thrombosis, pneumonia: it is as violent and unforeseen as an engine stopping in the middle of the sky. My mother encouraged one to be optimistic when, crippled with arthritis and dying, she asserted the infinite value of each instant; but her vain tenaciousness also ripped and tore the reassuring curtain of everyday triviality. There is no such thing as a natural death: nothing that happens to a man is ever natural, since his presence calls the world into question. All men must die: but for every man his death is an accident and, even if he knows it and consents to it, an unjustifiable violation. — Simone de Beauvoir, *A Very Easy Death*

One of our contradictions was that we denied the unconscious. — Simone de Beauvoir, *The Prime of Life*

Making friendly gestures toward Simone de Beauvoir means pursuing the theoretical and practical work of social justice she carried on in her own way, not blocking the horizon of liberation she opened up for many women and men. . . . Her vision of that horizon was certainly in part inspired by her long, and often solitary, walks in the *garrigue,* in the wilds. Her enjoyment and her accounts of her walks seem to me to be the one of her messages that we must not forget. — Luce Irigaray, "Equal or Different"

Luce Irigaray's reflection on her relation to Simone de Beauvoir on the occasion of de Beauvoir's death in 1986 was a personalized positioning in relation to her "big-sister figure." For most of us, however, the "death" of Simone de Beauvoir takes on a different sort of guise—one that is not personalized (given that there was no contentious relationship, as characterizes most relations between younger and older sister, or mother and daughter) but remains nonetheless associated with a profound sense of (often nostalgic) loss concerning the state of modern feminism. While there are active feminist movements all over the world, it is frequently the case that one finds oneself, in an era of "postfeminism," grieving for a feminism more ethical, more political, and more accountable. In Europe and in the United States one is overshadowed by an image of the dead mother of modern feminism. This melancholic relation to Simone de Beauvoir, rather like the melancholic relation that has emerged in remembering Frantz Fanon in the arena of decolonization struggles, calls for a return to the early texts of these political writers in order to sense what discrepancies haunted their own incitements to political activism. If *The Wretched of the Earth* is haunted by *Black Skin, White Masks, The Second Sex* is haunted by the text de Beauvoir considered to be at once the worst thing she ever wrote, as well as that which caused her to write *The Second Sex*. I refer to her frequently ignored book *The Ethics of Ambiguity.*

I have cited Fanon and de Beauvoir together, as I find myself repeatedly returning to their work to think about questions of transnational feminism. While I begin with a work that precedes the overtly political texts like *The Wretched of the Earth* and *The Second Sex,* I do not want to prioritize the ethical questions that surround the complexity of colonial subjectivity at the expense of the manifesto of decolonization. Nor do I want to prioritize the dialectic of ambiguity over the historical and material devaluation of women. Rather, I want to consider how a psychoanalytically conceived spectral overshadowing, or what I would like to call *an ethics of lament,* is created through the attempt to balance the two (often lamenting the possibility of doing so), and to consider the validity of doing that balancing in philosophical and practical terms in the context of transnational feminism.

The strengths of transnational feminism in the last decade have also been weaknesses. Feminism has split not only between activism and theory, but also into particular feminisms that struggle with the perceived inadequacies of a feminist universalism. At the same time, the splitting of feminism has allowed for a comprehensive study of local contexts and their feminist agendas and causes. The accusation of ethnocentrism that feminism in the West faced in the eighties and earlier has become a central part of the discussion of local contexts, while how to "do" feminism (both within the academy and in practice) has been the focus of feminist ethics. But this has had more than one effect on transnational feminism. On the one hand, conflict within feminism and between women has become part of the agenda to be addressed. It has also at times resulted in paralysis, or a rather self-satisfied navel gazing on the part of some who agonize about how to be ethical when it comes to dealing with gender politics outside of one's own context. The fracturing that seems inevitable to transnational feminism also threatens feminist international coalitions.

How to address ethics has thus become a crucial part of feminism within and outside the academy. But the term itself has fractured. No longer does the word *ethics* have solely an idealist connotation; in its daily use, the production of which owes a great deal to feminism, *ethics* connotes local and grounded codes of behavior. In the workplace, *workplace ethics* is discussed; in the hospital, *medical ethics;* increasingly, the term has been tied to a litigious context that revolves around what is admissible or inadmissible behavior in the eyes of the *law* and how one judges one's own and others' personal behavior. The local rescripting of ethics has removed it from the realm of *justice* and in some instances placed it firmly within the realm of the *law;* while in others it has conflated the ethical with the *political,* because it is thought, probably correctly, that politics should attempt to be ethical.

But in the realm of ethics, not only has there been a shift from *justice* to *law,* but also from responsibility to another person, to responsibility to a set of rules. Transnational feminism has allowed us to perceive the centrality of this different relation to rules. This perception has initiated a fracturing. Difference has been reified to such an extent that separate ethical universes have been produced, with the only overarching imperative being that one does not comment on another context. An ethical response, then, often amounts to a nonresponse. Chandra Mohanty has called on us to understand the *complex relationality* between women transnationally; all too often this recognition results in paralyzing feelings of guilt by those who structurally and economically benefit from the impoverishment of others, and resentment on the part of the neocolonized. This frequently makes the respectful coalition called for by many feminists, from Spivak to Mohanty, Lugones, and Spelman, seem impossible.

Given this situation, an ethical response that results in inactivity and the reification of difference is ambiguous and, more often than not, politically inefficacious. From fear of an overarching ethnocentric universalism of the claim of justice, a new concern arises for feminism. How does one respond to another, and how does one address conflict with an end in sight that allows for transnational feminist action and scholarship?[1]

The particularization of ethics into codes and laws has moved ethics from the realm of justice to that of law, as I have said. If we consider a series of relationships: justice/ethics; ethics/politics; justice/law; law/ethics—what emerges is two different concepts of justice and ethics: one is somewhat messianic, the other more pragmatic. Thinking the two together requires juggling two different concepts of the Other: the singular and the particular. But in the context of transnational feminism (and perhaps, feminism more generally) it is necessary to maintain both the messianic concept alongside a more pragmatic one, juggling the apparently contradictory understandings of the Other as singular and as particular. What amounts to a contradictory position does not, however, leave us at an impasse but, rather, allows a way of dealing with the inadequacies of each concept of ethics and the justice for which it ostensibly aims. Feminism has favored necessarily a pragmatic understanding of law and politics that addresses particular and immediate concerns, inequalities and violence directed toward women. Messianic concepts of justice often appear to address nothing at all in concrete terms except as a possible consequence of a more generalized relationship to the philosophical concept of justice, or to a "God." However, the pragmatic concept of ethics as a form of social justice in the realm of transnational feminism consistently fails to account for the legacies of colonialism and empire that haunt it, particularly of course in instances when first-world feminism acts upon the third world. Like international law, and often in conjunction with it, transnational feminist activism from the first world often fails to account for the colonial legacy. This manifests itself in patronizing and ill-informed gestures (for example, urgent but sensationalist struggles against female genital mutilation) and hasty assumptions of sameness (for example, the claim that the globalization of sweatshops is universally exploitative without taking into account local conditions and international relations). Similarly, on the part of feminist activists from formerly colonized countries, any gesture from nonlocal feminists is frequently viewed with rightful suspicion; and colonialism is designated as the cause of the problem, as if colonialism itself were transparent or knowable in its entirety, and able to be designated as a particular event.

Paradoxically, the breakdown of a singular ethics also threatens the breakdown of transnational feminism, not because of any breakdown of boundaries national or otherwise but because of a fetishization of the local at the expense of coalition. When it becomes difficult to respond to another because of the inevitable inadequacy of that gesture, one can't help but think that the rendering of ethics as the litigious and the local fails to consider the boundaries that the feminist movement in particular has called into question: the personal and the political; the individual and the collective; the private and the public; the event and the everyday; the inside and the outside; the psychical and the social; the ethical and the political. The emphasis on particularized ethics has made us all anonymous and concerned primarily with our own behavior rather than with the repercussions of that behavior for another. Deciding how responsibility can be most useful raises the question of whether the concept of an ethics as *useful* is flawed in and of itself. Transnational feminism is haunted by this puzzle concerning the relationship between the messianic and the pragmatic, and how to understand the relationship of ethics to politics, law, justice, and the ontology of the Other as much as that of the self.

It may be the case that responding most usefully to another's needs means effectively bringing them into the eyes of the law, thus understanding justice as restitution or reparation. This necessary concept of justice assumes that both wrongdoing and its righting take place at a particular moment in a historical event. Clearly, crime and wrongdoing, on one level, have to be assessed in terms of what can be referenced and evidenced. But that which remains beyond the boundaries of a particular event cannot easily be accounted for in terms of restitution or in terms of rights awarded. This is the problem with the very important work performed by liberal feminism. It too often endorses the status quo by giving some women the right to reap its benefits.

Let us hypothesize for the moment a concept of justice that would reach beyond the litigious realm of rights, restitution, and reparation. I will posit feminism as the gift to another of something that may be impossible to give—that is, the uncertain possibility of justice that precedes any particular law even as it actualizes the possibility of justice. If we were to think of a feminist ethics, it would probably include such a wishful impossibility: that of the gift to women of the possibility of justice where that gift itself is a kind of impossibility and is based on no concept of granting, exchange, or patronage.

In the context of transnational feminism, the concept of a gift may well set off alarm bells, because it has been associated, for good reason, with a colonialist and patronizing gesture. What I want to explore, however, is why ethics needs to be restored to feminist discourse and practice so as to maintain a distinction from politics. It is only with categories as abstract as those of *justice* that feminist transnational politics can take place. This is, of course, an extremely thorny area considering the colonial legacies of juridical systems, the institutionalized (and frequently well-meaning) racism and sexism that mark its history, and the violence attendant in so many forms of law that cross national borders today. The call for justice is difficult to claim when its *manifestation-as-law,* effectively the only manner in which it can make itself manifest, has worked in the opposite direction more often than not in the history of international gendered oppression. This has introduced ambivalence about a desire for an idealized and universal concept of justice that has frequently worked against the oppressed and the disenfranchised. Both transnational feminism and the discourse of human rights and international law that it frequently references are haunted by the specter of colonialism. This specter, like Derrida's when he speaks of specters of Marx, is historical even if it is not dated, and casts a shadow over any imagined community.[2] In this sense postcolonial nations and international relations are haunted by colonialism; thus, when thinking of such things as phantom public spheres, to use Bruce Robbins's phrase, they appear as not simply imagined or lacking any concrete existence but as carrying secrets and traumas from the past in the language and affect of the community as made up of psychical entities.[3] This affect could haunt through generations, thus suggesting the manner in which ideological tenacities are psychically inflected, carried through a people, and extended through generations. History, in that formulation, exists in psychical affect differently from in memory and separately from the archive, even as both memory and archive are constitutive of the workings of affect. Occurrences in the past, whether everyday or major events, would thus manifest themselves in terms of the everyday as affect.[4]

Any inroad into a discussion of the *future* of transnational feminism has to find a way of accounting for such spectral overshadowing, without surrendering to the ghost. For what remains of a crime, once reparation is awarded? What remains once a right has been secured? What can be felt or done in the name of culture and of rights that dispels something that cannot be accounted for by a verdict, or indeed by the kind of reparation we may hear of on a group level—for example, after a war, or in instances when the only reparation offered is independence itself, as in colonialism? When we think of writing in the time of or in the aftermath of war, we may think of a restoration of women's sovereignty when that has been threatened both directly and metonymically in relation to a state or a people. And when we think of the everyday, rather than simply those major historical events that dominate our understanding of history, we could think of difficulties of such things as reproductive technologies, domestic violence, rape, the politics of aid, economic and cultural exploitation, or the possibility of coalition. In the feminist realm, ethics and politics for the most part have been conceived together. Now, once again we may not want to reduce ethics to politics.

The specter that cannot be accounted for by the pragmatic notion of justice and ethics raises questions of the unaccountable and the nonreferential. If justice and ethics are the spectral remainder of law and pragmatics, they are not simply impossible to achieve. Rather, they constitute *the impossible*.[5] The distinction between the two is crucial for transnational feminism, which cannot escape the specter. If the ethical (understood as the nonreferential and unaccountable responsibility toward oneself and toward another) is simply impossible, then its relation to the political seems potentially irrelevant. However, if it is understood as *the impossible*, the mutually constitutive nature of the two is made apparent as experience of the necessity for and inadequacy of the law.

If questions of ethics arise most prominently in relation to a *historical event* that may or may not be the same as a *traumatic event* when the need of, for example, international intervention may be required, this leaves us potentially with little sense of how, and whether, to respond to everyday occurrences. The everyday is the category that feminism has always maintained to be central to feminists' struggle against hegemonic exploitation. An ethics formed in relation to events may not embrace the difficulties of the everyday. Conversely, an ethics of the everyday may not be adequate for *tragic* historical events involving women and all those feminized as weak and tragic victims.

In order to tackle these questions, and to see why transnational feminism should be the locus for conceptualizing an ethics that deals with the event and the everyday, we first need to address what we mean by transnational feminism. Feminist interaction across national borders does not exist simply because of globalization; rather it exists because of the *idea* that women internationally are materially oppressed *because they are women*. This oppression does not usually manifest itself in the same ways, nor does it preclude the possibility that women have a complex relation to each other. Women may structurally and economically disadvantage one another, and may not have anything in common simply on the basis of being women. Following the deconstruction of the sex/gender distinction in 1990s feminism, identifying something called *women* is itself problematic; the category itself holds no stable meaning, and the material figuring of women varies.[6] Talking of *women's issues* also becomes problematic, because while we may want to say that, for example, low income relative to men in the same context, reproductive technology, and rape affect women, we would also have to acknowledge that this pertains in varying degrees. It seems that the *possibility* of being put in the same position because of gender is what calls for some kind of unity; but this possibility of exploitation produces a prostration before the narrative of exploitation, and the attempt to move from that position to one in which the said exploitations may be dealt with *justly*. Let's for a moment, then, suggest that feminism is constituted through two unknowable categories—justice and women. *Justice* for *women* internationally and through transnational coalition is what we aim for in feminism. We seek justice in the context of a traumatic and/or historical *event,* in terms of the everyday—and in terms of how this everyday is partially structured through the affect of an event. Acknowledging the abstraction of the terms *justice* and *woman* places feminist coalition in both the psychical and the material realms simultaneously, for the idea that we have to maintain the possibility of justice for women involves a psychical investment in that idea, and not simply a strategic aim.

Writing at the turn of this century to consider the possibilities for a future ethics of feminism, and considering what the question of ethics has to do with that of temporality and politics, calls for a reflection back fifty years to another major ethical quandary faced by intellectuals who considered themselves engaged. European powers were losing their colonies and struggling with the fact of a new form of genocide seen in World War II. The question of how to address France's inactivity in the Resistance during the occupation of the country, and then how to move on from that ignoble period to address issues of the day haunts the texts of

France's midcentury intellectuals in a manner that resonates with today's quandary concerning what we could call the *ambiguity of ethics* and its troublesome relationship to politics and ontology.

Ethics, Ontology, and Ambiguity

Simone de Beauvoir attempted to tackle how ethics and politics could be brought together in a manner that accounted for man's "tragic ambiguity": his knowledge that he and his fellow human beings are building toward death, which intrudes upon and shapes the experience of the present. The first page of her *Ethics of Ambiguity* immediately deals with the notion of death, the "tragic ambiguity" of man's condition, and his subsequent inability to access truth because of the temporal unfolding unto death that dominates his relationship with both himself and others, and with the events that surround him.[7] She writes therefore of the relationship between temporality and the event in relation to ethical and political quandaries. World War II had signaled a massive ethical quandary about war and genocide that continued to maintain a hold on intellectual life. What was distinctive about much of *Ethics of Ambiguity* was its determination to respond to occurrences that seemed like everyday wrongdoings rather than only to great events like wars. Great events, after all, are often temporalized retrospectively, leaving aside the ongoing inequalities upon which they are built.

So let us return to the time in which de Beauvoir wrote her ethics, and see whether credence can be given to the concept of *justice for women* as the aim of feminism internationally. In the story of ethics, at least in an ethics that has been associated with political engagement such as feminism or nation-building, we conventionally consider ethical behavior to include another person at least indirectly if not directly. It usually involves an ability to respond to another person or a people after analysis and decisions that clarify any ambivalent feeling toward a given situation, and any ambiguity in its terms or meaning. While ethics is certainly about an assessment of a person's actions, it has usually considered these in relation to an idea of the *good* and, at least since Benthamite utilitarian thought, the *usefulness* of that good, or how that good has come to bear on the greatest number of people. In fact, we can assess this largely by the happiness or pleasure with which the good, ethical behavior has been received. But many have argued that this concept of ethics assumes a relationship to others only, rather than also to an understanding of a structure of ethical ontology.

Sartre, in contrast to de Beauvoir, believed that his model of engaged ontology could not be a model of ethics. He considered *Being and Nothingness* to constitute an ontology rather than an ethics, because the drive to resist "bad faith" originates not as a result of the relative happiness of others, but rather because of the effect the presence of an other has on one's own ontological structure.[8] The ethical concern is translated into a model of *engaged* ontology, but when Sartre attempted to derive an ethics from the general model of an engaged psychoanalytically informed philosophical position, he found it to be inadequate and did not publish the work that we know now as the fragments that make up the *Notebooks for an Ethics.*[9] It was as if he implicitly agreed with his Marxist critics, for example Marcuse, who claimed that the philosophical concept of freedom, as Sartre employed it, was a solipsistic retreat into the ontological from the arena of the political, and that the political, with which Sartre attempted to engage, was inadequately addressed by the concept of freedom.[10]

By contrast to the existential dilemmas concerning the relationship between ontology, ethics, and politics, Lacan claims in Seminar XI that his psychoanalytic framework is ethical rather than ontological, a claim that resituates the psychoanalytic firmly in the realm of philosophy and that disclaims the centrality of a theory of being within psychoanalytic thought. While various theories of being emerge from the Lacanian corpus, the "master" himself presents that being as implicated within a larger ethical framework that causes a certain figuring of guilt, antagonism, and pleasure within the subject. So a kind of reversal of expectations has occurred here: Sartre, the philosopher of freedom, has apparently rejected the possibility of allying political engagement with an ethics, while Lacan, an analyst of the psyche whom we may expect to give a theory of being, offers an ethics rather than an ontology. Sartre rejected an "engaged ethics" at least in part because of the concept of the universal it implies that does not concur with his understanding of writing for one's own time and responding with some sense of immediacy.[11] Following neither liberal teleologists such as Bentham, concerned with ends and our duty to meet them, nor deontologists such as Kant, who proffered ethics as actions we are obliged to conduct prior to local value being assigned to them, Sartre saw his concept of freedom as an ongoing ontological conflict that we have to resolve creatively in order to act toward authenticity. If we make a choice that is counter to bad faith, we work toward the freedom of ourselves and everybody else because there is a contradiction inherent in the idea that one can work toward another's freedom in a way that works against one's own. If ambiguity is resolved in a choice, then this will result in acting in a manner that works toward one's own freedom and that of others.

Lacan, on the other hand, follows Freud's ethical dilemma from *Civilization and Its Discontents*.[12] Is the ethical function of the analyst to encourage a libertarianism that runs counter to the repressions of modern civilization, which contribute to the development of neuroses, or alternately, work in the service of civilization and the goods it values? Lacan's extension of the dilemma is not, however, articulated so much in terms of the work ethic suitable for psychoanalysis as in the structure of the ethical question itself. Neither of Freud's responses is satisfactory, and both work within the logic of servicing certain ideas of what is good. According to Lacan, this idea of the "good" is premised upon the concept of happiness and therefore fails to account for desire that is unconscious and does not function as if it were possible to find satisfaction and happiness. Lacan's maxim "have you acted in accordance with your desire?" thus commands that complexities of desire are acknowledged so that *es* can become *ich*. The analyst's function is about getting the patient to understand the discrepancy between actions and desires often manifested in guilt, a discrepancy that reveals the duplicity of such concepts as happiness.[13] While feminism—and, I would argue—particularly postcolonial feminism, has been concerned with political and representational inequality, the turn in the 1990s toward Lacanian psychoanalysis has centered on his theory of desire with the claim that it offers a means of analyzing the social that is politically efficacious. Interestingly, in Lacanian-influenced social commentary, one of the most significant departures from most models of thought that claim to be politically pertinent is not only the rejection of the imperative of the good and of happiness, but also the historical rationalizations for emerging factors in people's lives.

It is in historical work that we have seen a feminist counter to the Lacanian model. Much of the historical work has been influenced by Foucault, with some, notably Judith Butler, bringing Lacan and Foucault to bear on each other.[14] But the work of feminist Foucauldians, and particularly new historicists, has challenged both an ethics of ahistorical desire they see in Lacanian-influenced work and the ontological obsessions of an ethics in the realm of philosophy. If the ethical imperative of learning had, at one point, been "Know Thyself," it now seems to be "contextualize." The fall of the transcendental spatial relation and a sovereign good to the particular context and its relative moral and political stakes has effectively meant a philosophical turn from abstractions and universals that dominate Enlightenment thought to a genealogical and contextual critique that often operates in the name of oppressed peoples whose lives cannot be analyzed in the terms of universal categories. Thus the contextual is offered as a counter to what is understood as the universalist—a predetermined and ideological response to a political context or to a text that emerges from the very epistemologies (and perhaps the very group) that is considered to have caused the initial oppression. Specific and contextual assessments, understood thus, make for the possibility of an ethics that becomes redefined as politically responsible behavior, disconnected from absolutes and able to analyze and propose political processes and responses to the aesthetic.

The question posed by Lacanian psychoanalytic theorists of the social, for example Žižek, Copjec, and Salecl, raises questions about this, and ostensibly raises them from the left.[15] They ask if there is any way to understand ethics as linked to the aesthetic and democracy that is not about the radical contingency of space, cause and effect, and historical sequence. They question how the notion of contingency can be reconfigured so as to offer a way of understanding a located subjectivity. The argument against *historicism* in Lacanian social and cultural critique draws from a problematization of both the temporality of affect arising from events on people's lives and the structural lack in the subject. The emphasis on "cause" in political critique, Lacanians contend, assumes an unfolding of events that have a sequential logic. This rejection is precisely why it is difficult to conceive of how a social analysis that is politicized—such as that of the scholarship on postcoloniality or feminism, or, for our purposes, postcolonial transnational feminism—can make use of Lacanian psychoanalysis that prioritizes a structural trauma of the subject in modernity rather than a trauma in the history of the individual. Lacanians like Žižek contend that the notion of cause and an attention to the real understood as the material is faulty because we have no access to the real even though it is a part of us. It is also, crucially, exterior to us in the manner in which the exterior is simultaneously interior; it thus follows the structure of a hole in a doughnut.

This issue of access to the real, understood in terms of this hole, is linked to the persuasive dismissal of historicism in Copjec's work also. In *Read My Desire,* she critiques the "notion of an existence without predicate, or, to put it differently, of a surplus existence that cannot be caught up in the positivity of the social."[16] While the "positive unconscious"[17] of the episteme in the early Foucault did not reject psychoanalysis, the later Foucault rejects both psychoanalysis and much semiotics; Copjec, echoing the May 1968 criticism of structuralism among Parisian students, speaks of "structures marching in the streets," but she is criticizing Foucault's post-1968 genealogical studies rather than the pre-1968 structuralism. She rejects what she sees as a reduction of society to relations of power and knowledge and takes him to task for the apparent immanence of this power—that it circulates among subjects rather than being an oppressive external force. She concludes, "We are calling historicist the reduction of society to its indwelling network of relations of power and knowledge,"[18] and offers, as a counter, that "some notion of transcendence is plainly needed if one is to avoid the reduction of social space to the relations that fill it."[19] This is a fault, according to Copjec, that can be found as much in contemporary cultural studies and historicist political critique, and she sees Foucault as the source of many of these problems. The social space cannot be understood, she contends, via Foucault unless we are going to reject subjectivity as a serious component of that space, for such a nonpsychoanalytic model would be inadequate to the task of assessing how those subjects that come to constitute social space are also constituted by it. Such a delicate balance needs to be maintained if the relationship between social context and psychical affect is to be grasped. This puzzle seems to be, from very different directions, the central problem of both psychoanalysis—how is the superego or even the ego-ideal constituted in any way that would explain the socialization of groups— and Marxism—why does the individual agree to, and even defend, his or her role in a civil society that is exploitative of its members. One obvious factor is power, which is why Foucault's *genealogical* nontrajectory is so persuasive; and another is Althusser's *interpellation,* which reappears, for example, in Fanon's moment of recognition on the occasion of a hailing: "Look! A Negro!"[20]

If the most consistent employment of Lacan in the postcolonial context is by Homi Bhabha, it is in Bhabha's use of the notion of affect that Lacanian psychoanalysis is most persuasive. Bhabha centralizes the distinction between postmodernism and postcolonialism, a distinction that, quite astonishingly, gets lost when resistance to political conflict is reduced to a psychical function of the modern, losing its historical particularity even as it argues for singularity. Foregrounding the concept of *Nachträglichkeit,* Bhabha reminds us that affects frequently associated with the postmodern today—such as the instability of master discourses, unstable identities, and coexistent temporal multiplicities—can be seen not only now at the moment of decolonization or postcoloniality but also at earlier moments of the North-South colonial encounters manifested as what he calls a time-lag. European modernity's constitution through the colonial enterprise, however, may mark a colonial form of identity that we can retroactively read as a resistance to colonial rule. Yet, it is only in a deferred manner that we can understand this form of affect in terms of resistance. The function of reading this resistance today is, I would argue, to mark it as a discrepant modern rather than as the postmodern. These moments of iteration may be understood as affect in terms of postcoloniality, but spatially they can be understood as constitutive of modernity's geographical split, the impossibility of the consistency of its European narrative even as power without hegemony was established.

Bhabha differentiates himself from Derrida and de Man through opposing the "foreign interstitial" with the "metonymic fragmentation of the 'original.'"[21] Taking his cue from Benjamin, Bhabha's challenge is that of foreign cultural translation's dislocation of the original, rather than an excess or an interruption caused by the structure of metonymy. But we could bring the two concepts together very usefully as a notion of affect as a concept that acknowledges the catachresis of the origin of a trauma and that leaves its trace on the individual. This allows for a reading of historical and political processes as instruments of violence on groups—racism, sexism, colonialism, slavery—rather than seeking an absolute origin that may posit, for example, ethnic violence as always rooted in the same psychical structure of lack; or, on the other hand, trauma as originating in a singular historical event that sidelines the everyday. Even though some may suggest that with the end of the cold war and with the advancement of globalization we move politically from the law of the father to the regime of the brother, postcolonial *Nachträglichkeit* may well throw a spanner in the works of such reduction of the historical to the leveling of trauma and its ahistorical postmodern aftereffects and affects. The existence of different forms of globalization, of its interpretation, and of the destructive nature of the end of the cold war for much of the third world reasserts the validity of the historical, the political, and specifically *modern* forms of trauma in many postcolonial contexts. Assertion and critique of the centrality of national contexts and modern processes continue, even as MTV and CNN are on urban elite's TVs, CD ROMS are in their PCs, and Nikes are on their feet. Increasingly, however, women cannot identify with men in this critique, for where it is initiated from anticolonial nationalisms, women's continued lack of representational possibilities has caused a disidentification following the desire for but also the loss of the ideal of national independence.

The structural figuring of subjectivity in Lacan, which is quite different from that of Freud, creates a different status for the historical and therefore a different relationship between the subject and society, as well as a different notion of how the subject is socially and politically constituted. If Freud, in *Group Psychology and the Analysis of the Ego,* attempted to understand how people became involved in group psychologies and what appears to be collective thinking around an ego-ideal, and in *The Ego and the Id* introduced the concept of the regulatory superego, he was attempting to understand the mechanisms of identification and disidentification. His broad anthropological sweeps in *Totem and Taboo,* as well as all the work on explaining traumas, certainly problematizes temporality through the concept of Nachträglichkeit. It does not, however, give up cause in favor of effect, thereby implicitly arguing that a structural castration constitutes the fundamental antagonism of the subject.[22] In Lacan, it is not so clear how to conceive of historical occurrences that appear to cause and be caused by particular psychical traumas and identifications, in spite of the fact that Lacanians insist on *singularity* and *contingency.* While the structural split or antagonism seems to be intrinsic to the subject in Lacan's corpus, and therefore attains the status of a universal condition, it is not clear where there is very much room for understanding how the particular, with all its historical permutations, exists alongside this universal. Although the universal does not necessarily trivialize the particular, it certainly seems to in much Lacanian thought with its constant prostration in front of the big Other and its careless rendition of historical events or interpretations of them. Copjec and Žižek have suggested that the written law of interactions between people based on a Benthamite principle of the greatest good for the greatest number assumes that law to be an external phenomenon about which one may feel ambivalent but by whose rules one is required to live within a state. For Lacanian psychoanalysis, however, those laws are internalized, through interpellation, as the big Other and contain within the subject what Žižek calls a *supplement* that we recognize as *desire*.[23] So Lacan's ethical question is "Have you acted in accordance with your desire?" And is later reformulated as *l'éthique du bien dire*—have you spoken in accordance with your desire?[24] Feelings of guilt and of this disjuncture between desire and action often culminate in a sense of ambiguity or uncanniness that raises questions about political efficacy and responsibility—indeed, the ethics of an individuated ambiguity as a central model for a social theory.

Ethnocentrism/Universalism

In his essay "A Leftist Plea for Eurocentrism," discussed briefly in the previous chapter, Slavoj Žižek makes a plea that, one could say, clearly does not need to be made, for, as we know, Eurocentrism is alive and well both as a lens of scholarly activity and as the form of politics with which Žižek equates it. He laments the passing of communism and the self-generating nature of capitalism into a *postmodern* economy of credit; far from being in a period that precedes the fall of capitalism in an evolutionary sense, we are rather in "the domain of appearance."[25] He is quick to distinguish between this notion of *appearance* as "symbolic fiction," which exists in the realm of the Symbolic, and *simulacra,* as the "retreat of symbolic efficiency." This blurs the distinction between real and imaginary in a manner that cannot address the value, in sociopolitical terms, of the *symbolic efficiency* of the fiction as fantasy structure. If, however, we read Žižek through the lens of coloniality, reversing the conventional direction of theorizing the third world, he appears to be Eurocentric in somewhat different terms that locate him firmly in the first and (formerly) second world. For his vision of modernity and politics as developed in the West (from Ancient Greece through to the French Revolution and beyond) fails to understand the development of the modern in Europe in relational terms—that is, as being built on and constituted by colonial exploits that continue to haunt.

Žižek has reminded us of the centrality of psychical work in political formations. Reading him in the context of coloniality, we may see, however, that causality has to remain, even as it may be posited as an uncertain *event*. Even though the event may not have a singular identity and cannot be reduced to a particular occurrence, it equally cannot be reduced to the primary scene of linguistics. This has a leveling effect that simply renders more or less anything traumatic in the same degree. In the appeal to universalism, what is at stake is the historicized production of psychical conditions, as well as the question of whether the international *postmodernity* in which different identities proliferate is postmodern at all. Returning to Bhabha, we could think of affects that resemble the postmodern but carry the historical weight of colonialism in a manner that renders them both modern and politically resistant to colonialist proselytizing. The notion of the Truth-Event may well be in place as resistant to the current globalization, but from quite different quarters and with quite different means compared to those proffered by Žižek. These different colonial repercussions are products of the *epistemic violence* (to use Gayatri Spivak's formulation) of the European legacy, but are far from Eurocentrist in their formulation.[26]

And this brings us back to our initial concerns about the problems that have plagued feminism in the 1990s. The dispersal of energies into *differences* within the feminist movement has accompanied the problematization of the term *woman*. Part of the motivation for this was the colonialist moves of some feminists in the first world who presumed to speak *for* women elsewhere. Another involved the racist exclusions of the feminist movement, with its prioritization of white middle-class women's issues and its rendering of others' issues as irrelevant. Of course, what has been decried since then is the loss of the women's movement and an era of postfeminism that seems to proclaim the end of feminism for no other reason than that it fails to deal with how political collectivities can cohere in an age of difference. In addition, the deconstruction of the term *woman* has caused us to wonder what our common term may be, now that we have acknowledged that there are few common causes. The term *woman* has begun to occupy a position in the political realm akin to the term *black* in British minority politics in the 1970s. And like that term, it has eroded as a political term of collectivity in the post–Thatcher-Reagan years, in which specific ethnic differences have sought recognition and distinction from each other, both as an argument for adequate representation and as a desire to distinguish one group from another. The multicultural hybridity celebrated as national liberalism or as postcolonial cosmopolitanism often conceals within it conflict and racism within minority cultures, and also within feminist movements.

If ethnocentrism as Eurocentrism is actually about a relation to the concept of the universal, then it is worth considering how that universal can exist without being Eurocentric. If it is true that, as Fredric Jameson puts it, "the so-called advanced countries are sinking into full postmodernity,"[27] it is worth thinking through what temporal issues are at stake when we consider whether the postcolonial puts pressure on the concept of the postmodern. In this sense, the postcolonial modern is called upon to put pressure on its post- as it were and, perhaps to emphasize the affect as well as the material of the historical and economic. This effectively maintains the trace of the critical political distinction between justice and law, as well as between the archive and memory. For even if we would want to contend that a desire to form certain memories and histories causes some documents to be deemed relevant or irrelevant, and thus to be archived or destroyed, the reduction of archive to memory fails to account for reading against the grain, or indeed an incorporation (or introjection) of that material in the colonies with very different consequences.

Feminism and the Relation to Another

Simone de Beauvoir's feminist argument in *The Second Sex* actively takes issue with ideologies that perpetuate the positing of woman as man's Other, denying the sameness of woman's ethical ability. We could say that de Beauvoir, in her attempt to analyze how this seems to occur internationally, repeats some of that otherizing herself—of Tunisian women, for example, who cannot move in and out of their cavernous existence, unlike Tunisian men, and incidentally, unlike herself figured, as it were, as the philosopher-king.[28] While her argument is based on sameness and identification, she wavers into positing a difference as well, and this is necessary for her very complex notion of freedom and liberation, which is quite distinct from Sartre's. It is not only in her work on Djamila Boupacha, the young woman tortured during the Algerian war of independence, that we see how her concept of ethical behavior in the face of violence emerges. Certainly, it is encapsulated there some thirteen years after *The Second Sex*. But de Beauvoir's early text, *The Ethics of Ambiguity*, like Fanon's early writing in *Black Skin, White Masks*, presents us with models quite different from the ones they claim to build upon. If Fanon effectively rewrote Lacan's mirror stage for the colonial context when he situated suffering as the Other in the realm of historical events, economic circumstances, and biological phenomenological asymmetries, de Beauvoir rewrites Sartre's concept of freedom and gives us at least two versions. For while de Beauvoir appears to be challenging the critique of Sartre's *Being and Nothingness* as solipsistic, she actually refashions that text and situates an ambiguity and desire in the notion of freedom—for there are, she suggests, multiple freedoms, ontological and political. Sartre conceives the freedom of other people as threat to the ontology of the subject, even though it is also the source of the subject's recognition of *his* own being-for-Others. It propels one into the ambiguity of existence that is the tension between being-in-itself and being-for-itself. The arrival of another person, and, most importantly, the look of that other person, is an aggression, and this is why, as Sartre puts it in *Huis Clos,* hell is other people. As Debra Bergoffen persuasively demonstrates, the key distinction between Sartre and de Beauvoir in this regard is the notion of pleasure;[29] and, I would add, the notion of each person's ontological existence in ambiguity as a kind of liberation. As de Beauvoir writes, "To will man free is to will there to *be* being, it is to will the disclosure of being in the joy of existence; in order for the idea of liberation to have a concrete meaning, the joy of existence must be asserted in each one, at every instant."[30]

The idea of liberation itself, the acknowledgment that the Other is also a self, commands that one asserts the necessity of each person's freedom. Both in *The Ethics of Ambiguity* and in her work on the Djamila Boupacha case, de Beauvoir asserts the coexistence of horror to the self—the Other ceases to be a self if individuals are not thought to be important, and, of course, vice versa.[31] There is, she suggests in the early text, a kind of horror to the fact that we can look at photographs of concentration camps and be immune, or that, in the context of Algeria (and she says this in 1948) "colonists appease their conscience by the contempt in which they held the Arabs who were crushed with misery: the more miserable the latter were, the more contemptible they seemed, so much so that there was never room for any remorse."[32] But acknowledging the sameness of the Other, that is, that the Other is a self, also paradoxically allows one to see that the Other is actually different, and has its own history that propels it into desiring a future in which political freedom for oneself and others can be worked for alongside ontological freedom.

The possibility of such a coalition has been taken up by feminists for some time now. Irigaray's engagement with Levinas, for example, stresses the threshold between people as constitutive of a necessary call that allows both for understanding and its impossibility.[33] Coalition establishes a border between subjects even as it highlights the differences between them. Much feminist literature has resulted in the refashioning of genres so as to draw attention to the importance of similar forms of mediation between women—the highly debated *testimonio* of Rigoberta Menchú, the epistolary style of Mariama Ba's *So Long a Letter,* the second-person narration of Assia Djebar's *Sister to Scheherazade,* and, in a slightly different relationship, that of the translator-editor and writer in Spivak's translation of Mahasweta Devi's *Imaginary Maps.*[34] Each of these texts examines this relationship of coalition between women on the level of particulars and offers, in very different ways, what Irigaray examines as the centrality of mediation, which is both a hinge between subjects and between the philosophical and the political—indeed, an acknowledgment of the particulars of difference. Difference, however, is understood as allowing for the positing of an ethics of mediation.

In some ways this solves the Levinasian problem; while in his concept and in the manner in which it has been taken up by Drucilla Cornell the importance of the call of the Other is always an irreducible and ongoing presence to the self, that Other is necessarily figured rather vaguely and always seems to be the same in its abstraction. We are presented in de Beauvoir with an ethics of coalition that recognizes not only a sense of acting usefully or acting in accordance with one's desire. Rather, the ethics of coalition that exists on a day-to-day level as well as on the level of a traumatic event allows for an acknowledgment of one's pleasure and pain in acting in a certain way, and the desire that propels it, based as it is in historical and economic circumstances that lead to a notion of the future as potentially free. "An ethics of ambiguity," de Beauvoir says, "will be one which will refuse to deny *a priori* that separate existants can, at the same time, be bound to each other, that their individual freedoms can forge laws valid for all."[35] In this formulation, the Other remains Other, even as unity is proffered.

The quandary of relating to another in the context of transnational feminism is assisted by this idea of the universal, however, only inasmuch as it acknowledges the differences between the two types of freedom—the political and the ontological. Transnational relationships must acknowledge the differences between, on the one hand, the ambiguity of subjectivities and, on the other hand, political ambivalences with others that frequently cause conflict. I would add to de Beauvoir something she clearly rejects, the psychical affect carried by the subject who attempts to will being, or, we could say, will completion or will justice even as that is known to be of value as *will* rather than as *being*—and involves understanding of the psychical weight of history and that history itself.

If we think, for example, of de Beauvoir's work during the Algerian war of independence to assist Djamila Boupacha and Gisèle Halimi in seeking legal representation, her gesture is made as much toward Boupacha as toward the nation she comes from, for France, she says, is suffering from a cancer of the imagination. She is also, and we can see this from her autobiographical writings, doing the work for herself, to mark a difference from Sartre and to move out of his shadow; she therefore, to some extent, receives pleasure from this pain. (In a class I taught on those texts, this pleasure was taboo, as if we have an ethical responsibility to suffer for others because they suffer, a fact that seems to me to be a form of vicarious suffering that must cause some pleasure in order to be so eagerly endorsed.) But de Beauvoir's, and Halimi's, immediate problem was to get a fair trial for Boupacha even as they were confronted with the legal system itself colluding with the torture and abuse of those whom it was supposed to protect. De Beauvoir focused on the goal of legal representation to communicate that a war was going on and that torture occurred because Boupacha was deemed to be a *terrorist* allegedly performing acts of war before it was acknowledged that a war was going on. The ethical quandary for de Beauvoir was to communicate Boupacha's suffering, which would at once allow Boupacha to be politically represented and also to publicize her pain. Maintaining a faith in legal systems that were simultaneously the instruments of Boupacha's violation necessitated demanding a national recognition that war was enacted for the armchair colonialist. But perhaps today the quandaries are different, because even though de Beauvoir called the Algerian struggle a war in 1948, in effect making everyday struggle into war, when she wrote of Djamila Boupacha, it *was* during a war, and when she wrote of Algeria in *The Ethics of Ambiguity,* she wrote of the horrors of complacency about national wrongdoings—passivity in World War II, and not acknowledging the exploitation of Algerians.[36]

Today, however, in the period of postcolonialism, different ethical quandaries exist because of the psychical as well as the political quandaries of colonial legacies. Whether we think of such problems as developing laws in the United States to regulate clitoridectomy, or whether we are considering international human rights laws, the colonial legacy is still very much in place, on both a psychical and political level. For the colonialist gesture of outlawing clitoridectomy is a very modern commitment that became frequently associated with nationalist movements, making the outlawing of it all the more problematic because of nativist resurgence of the practice. A practice deemed reprehensible by so many women internationally can nonetheless not be dealt with outside the acknowledgment of a prior juridical failure on the part of colonizers, and a contemporary ethical failure on the part of well-meaning but badly informed feminists.[37] On the other hand, letting it alone is similarly problematic, because the issue is international and has been debated in transnational contexts. Relativism returns us to the problem with which we began and leads to a breakdown of the possibility of coalition both in everyday terms and also in moments of crisis. An ethics that bases itself on a theory of desire is a problem; it is solipsistic because desire for subjective wholeness ultimately falls into a kind of idealism. This is why Fanon, in *The Wretched of the Earth,* will ultimately turn to the political realm, even though he saw it as causing psychical damage.[38] Equally, an ethics that does not account for desire as justice is not taking into account the workings and parochializations of colonial and postcolonial modernity. The fantasy of justice and the fantasy of freedom are not simply a type of release of desire that constitutes the collective free will. Rather, they concern understanding demand in relation to need and desire—a desire that cannot be satisfied and perhaps then propels us toward the future but also allows us to see the dynamic between psychic and political contingency in the present. A psychic contingency in the present embodies within it the persistence of history, or, as Spivakian deconstruction would have it, "the impossibility of a full undoing,"[39] not simply as fantasy or as memory but also as archive distinct from memory. Colonialism and the ethical quandaries to which it has given rise for transnational feminism always reinscribes the postcolonial in the transnational. This is not simply replacing globalization with universalization; rather, it is asserting that transnational feminism is always dealing with the thorny area of postcolonialism and that any ethics is always built upon a universal renegotiated locally. For feminist practice, and for feminist scholarship, this has meant underscoring the political and psychical affect of colonialism and the modernity of postcolonialism.

The spectral nature of postcolonial modernity means that an incorporation of forms of law, of languages, and of systemic inequalities into colonized countries did not amount to an introjection, or a full psychic assimilation. This incorporation of Eurocentrism and of historical abuses in the form of individuated violence was common to colonial spheres. While clearly de Beauvoir does not engage the important contribution of psychoanalysis to a concept of ethics, her model of an ethics of ambiguity nonetheless leaves room for the necessary coupling of the historical and the psychical in any work that involves international or transnational relations in the postcolonial era. (Perhaps, ultimately, this is expressed most clearly by de Beauvoir in the most personal of realms, in relation to the death of the mother, the inevitable but "unjustifiable violation.") Unfortunately, Lacan, particularly in the manner in which he is employed by Žižek when Žižek makes a leftist plea for Eurocentrism, is also inadequate to the task. If the question that haunts the quintessential text on spectrality, *Hamlet,* demonstrates the impossibility of identity and complete interpellation ("Who's there?"), it is because, while wrongs may have been done, they cannot necessarily be attributed to one occurrence that we can deem to be from the affect of events that unfurl. But clearly, something has occurred to Hamlet that sets off a traumatized psychical state that extends beyond a structural problem. Bringing the notion of spectrality as affect (and as haunting) to any critique and politics that concerns formerly colonized countries validates neither a relativism nor a simple criticism; rather it demonstrates the weight of history as an ethical and psychical structure, an epistemic violence, a melancholia, a phantom or an "unjustifiable violation."

While transnational scholarship has often idealized the moment of the loss of boundaries, feminist transnational scholarship and practice, I would suggest, cannot and does not endorse this. For while globalization has initiated to some degree the breakdown of national boundaries, it also maintains neocolonial economics, and often colonialist relations, when it comes to such issues as, for example, nuclear arms, pharmaceuticals, or ecology. But while postcolonial feminists have frequently resisted interference from people who threaten to repeat colonial gestures, anticolonial nationalism has clearly been brought under critical scrutiny. I would suggest that even as modern political and national boundaries persist, it is imperative for women to be vigilant, not only with a critical eye toward colonialism but also with one toward nationalism. The largely masculinist nationalisms that emerged out of the former colonies frequently, as we know, put women's issues on the back burner, even in contexts of apparent progressive thought, as in Algeria—a country that, as we know, has failed to be the avant-garde third-world nation it once promised to be, one where corruption would not occur, and where women would not be second-class citizens. The psychical affect caused by this loss of an ideal on the part of women, I would suggest, has brought about a sense of despair, a form of melancholia.

Women carry with them incorporated traumas swallowed whole, traumas that manifest themselves as continuing symptoms and traces where the anticolonial struggle is still so new and relevant. Political failures have brought about a disidentification with the nation that failed to represent women. It is this disidentification, or the melancholic recognition of the suffering of another as one's own "unjustifiable violation" that, I would suggest, allows for coalitions between women internationally where a concept of *justice* is forged in the full knowledge of the thorniness of the specters of colonial relations and local abuses of women.

6. Hamlet in the Colonial Archive

Hamlet . . . is the central drama of modern literature. What gave Shakespeare the power to send it expanding through the centuries was that in Hamlet he had isolated and pinned down the psychological streak which characterised the communal change from the medieval world to the world of free individualisation. . . . This colossal change in the organisation of social function was the very basis of individual personality. But from the start it was inseparable from a tension between individual freedom and social responsibility. To the extent that any modern man thought at all, he was subject to this tension. And it was nowhere greater than in the man for whom freedom of thought and speculation became a specialised function—the intellectual . . . [T]he two tendencies were balanced in a tension that finally destroyed him but created an imperishable drama, a great recording of a model stage in the development of civilisation.

. . . [F]or Hamlet the process of thought is his conception of action. And modern scholarship has done an inestimable service in putting the idea that a tragic character must have some flaw in his character into a fitting subordinate place in Aristotle's thought. The habit of thought was no flaw in Hamlet's character. It was his character. If it was a flaw, it was a flaw in the whole construction of civilisation from the sixteenth century onward. And inevitably, with this polarisation of action and thought in social function and personality, there developed in the men of thought a sense of isolation, of impotence, of melancholy, because you wandered through eternity, you voyaged in strange seas of thought, alone, that is to say, with an ever growing consciousness of the divorce between the boundless exhilaration of thought and its divorce from reality. All who read the original

thinkers felt it. Hamlet felt this. The intellectual was an organic part of rationalist society and Hamlet is the organic intellectual. That is why the character
endures. . . . The creative work of Shakespeare, the portrayal of the new individuality, was destined to blow sky-high his [own] commonplace conceptions of
contemporary government and politics; not government and politics in general,
but the kind of government and the kind of politics he knew. —C. L. R. James,
"Notes on *Hamlet*"

In the *Interpretation of Dreams* Freud wrote an extensive footnote on *Hamlet* in which he castigated Goethe for misleading generations of critics and
readers of the play. Goethe saw Hamlet's failings as those of an intellectual who thought too much ("sicklied o'er with the pale cast of thought")
and was therefore unable to act. But Hamlet, Freud emphasized, was perfectly capable of acting; for example, he murdered Polonius. The only
action he hesitated to perform was the murder of Claudius, and Freud
attributed this (perhaps rather predictably) to the Oedipus complex. For
Freud, Claudius showed "him the repressed wishes of his own childhood
realized. Thus the loathing which should [have driven] him on to revenge." Claudius was "replaced in him by self-reproaches, by scruples of
conscience, that remind him that he himself is literally no better than the
sinner whom he is to punish."[1] Hamlet's inner conflict arises, according
to Freud, because he could not do what Claudius could. This is not thematized overtly by Shakespeare, as it was by Sophocles, because of the
increased repression of oedipal desires that took place with the advance
of "civilization." Freud wrote:

> The changed treatment of the same material reveals the whole dif-
> ference in the mental life of these two widely separated epochs of
> civilisation: the secular advance of repression in the emotional life of
> mankind. In the *Oedipus* the child's wishful phantasy that underlies
> it is brought into the open and realized as it would be in a dream.
> In *Hamlet* it remains repressed; and—just as in the case of a neuro-
> sis—we only learn of its existence from its inhibiting consequences.
> Strangely enough, the overwhelming effect produced by the mod-
> ern tragedy has turned out to be compatible with the fact that people
> have remained completely in the dark as to the hero's character.[2]

Ernest Jones, taking off from Freud, emphasized that Hamlet is "torn and
tortured in an insoluble inner conflict."[3] Psychologizing Hamlet's every

move, Jones found it fitting that "the greatest work of the world-poet should have had to do with the deepest problem and the intensest conflict that have occupied the mind of man since the beginning of time—the revolt of youth and of the impulse of love against the restraint imposed by the jealous elder."[4] Taking the route of psychologizing the character, he did not question the advance of repression over centuries. Given the prominence of Jones's reading, and its expansion of Freud's musings in his footnote, this emphasis on changes in the manifestation of the Oedipus complex has been inadequately explored.

Wulf Sachs, who will be the focus of this chapter, was a Lithuanian Zionist who worked in South Africa and was responsible (with Fritz Perls) for establishing the South African branch of the International Association of Psychoanalysis. He had trained all over Europe, and this wandering Jew settled eventually in South Africa to escape an increasingly anti-Semitic Europe. He wrote both on "Hamletism" in general, in his overview of psychoanalysis, *Psychoanalysis: Its Meaning and Practical Application*,[5] and in the "literary form of psychoanalytic biography,"[6] in *Black Hamlet*, his biography of a South African native doctor. Sachs's initial study of psychoanalysis was based on Jones's "masterly analysis"[7] of Hamlet, to which he added by drawing on faulty biographical information about Shakespeare, to which Freud also alluded: Shakespeare's son Hamnet (whom Sachs calls Hamlet and whose name Freud reads as "identical to Hamlet")[8] had died shortly before the play was written, and, wrote Sachs, incorrectly, his father passed away just a year before the first performance of the play. Reading the play as a necessary sublimation, Sachs saw Hamlet as "what Shakespeare might have been if he had not written the play. The fantastic creation is a sublimated solution to the internal conflict. Not only Hamlet but also the other characters are symbols and introjections thrown out from Shakespeare's mind. By writing the play, Shakespeare symbolically satisfied the demands of his superego and the impulses of the id. Hamlet, if he had existed in reality, would have had to repeat the fate of Hamlet in the play, who killed people round him and then killed himself. Shakespeare escaped by writing the play."[9]

Sachs invoked the concept of paternal trauma as informing the writing of the play, and the repetition of Hamnet/Hamlet's proper name. Writing of paternal trauma at the loss of a child, Cathy Caruth has suggested that the belatedness and inassimilability of trauma are apparent in the transmission of words. She commented on Lacan's reading of Freud's study in the *Interpretation of Dreams* of a father's trauma at surviving the death of his child, whom he was dreaming about in a fire. In hearing the child cry out in the dream, the father awoke to find the child dead with a burning candle on the body. The trauma arose from failing to save the child. But also because the father failed to witness the child's death, since the father's dream, in a sense, necessitated his presence to keep the child alive in dreamlike fashion. Caruth comments on the words that awaken the father, and how they are repeated by Freud numerous times, and then by Lacan (and, we could add, now by Caruth). If trauma is understood as living in the repetition of words that cannot be assimilated (the child's awakening call), then the materiality of that language constituted a form of ethical remembrance intrinsic to the structure of trauma. For while Juliet Mitchell has reminded us that the work of psychoanalysis is to allay the symptoms of trauma rather than the original (often irretrievable) trauma itself (clearly, the fact of the child's death and the father's shock at his survival apparently at the expense of his child's cannot be changed), in Caruth's reading, an ethics of memory can be attributed to the father's traumatic response. The language of the child that is repeated through generations conveys the chiasmic displacement inherent within a trauma of witnessing: one carries another's trauma in language (whether this be the projected suffering of the child dying, or the belated sense of trauma at an event that did not appear to be traumatic at the time of its occurrence). The father, through displacement, becomes the ghost through his traumatic survival.[10]

Like Sachs, James Joyce speculated on the displaced effect of Shakespeare's bereavement. Stephen Dedalus poses the question, "What is a ghost?," and thereby speculates whether Hamlet's ghost *is actually* Shakespeare, the player, "who played the part of the spectre."[11] A chiasmic substitution has taken place, whereby Shakespeare creates and plays a ghost partly because of the experience of the death of his child. The actor who plays the ghost, if he indeed was Shakespeare the author, carries the words of a dead father to a living son, thereby creating a play about filial piety. What interests Joyce's character most is the repetition of the story itself, indeed, the continual performance of spectrality that keeps the child Hamnet suspended between life and death, in what Stephen refers to as *limbo patrum,* the limbo of the fathers. "Is it possible that that player Shakespeare, a ghost by absence, and in the vesture of Denmark, a ghost by death, speaking his own words to his own son's name (had Hamnet Shakespeare lived he would have been prince Hamlet's twin) is it possible, I want to know, or probable that he did not draw or foresee the logical conclusion of those premises: you are the dispossessed son: I am the murdered father: your mother is the guilty queen. Ann Shakespeare, born Hathaway?"[12] In the novel, then, Joyce presents Stephen Dedalus reading Hamnet, who, *were he to have lived, would have been* Hamlet's twin, his uncanny double, who was made uncanny because he was dead. Hamnet appears to live on as that which cannot be written about Hamlet, indeed as Hamnet's incommensurability with Hamlet. If it is the dead child who lives on in the play, it appears that Shakespeare's trauma is here performed, both as Shakespeare the player in conversation with his son's uncanny double in a nightmarish scenario, and in terms of trauma itself being carried in the play's language.

As Stephen Dedalus posed the question about Shakespeare's dead son and the acting (out) of *Hamlet* by Shakespeare, it is exactly the transgenerational haunting of the play that peeks his curiosity. But while both Dedalus and Caruth begin their musings on the unassimilable through stories of individuated trauma, Dedalus will relate such haunting to places. In doing so, he does not simply analogize the temporal and the spatial, or indeed the individual and the group, but the space of the metalepsis is questioned through the image of a colonizing and a colonized metropolis. "What is a ghost? Stephen said with tingling energy. One who has faded into impalpability through death, through absence, through change of manners. Elizabethan London lay as far from Stratford as corrupt Paris lies from virgin Dublin. Who is the ghost from *limbo patrum,* returning to the world that has forgotten him? Who is King Hamlet?" Besides the fact that a number of different critical positions are represented in the responses to the question, what is interesting is that the modern-day intellectual, Stephen, is in some ways puzzled by the same question as his intellectual forebear, Hamlet himself. We could, in fact, conjecture that intellectuals are haunted by the question of what or how to identify ghosts, that is, to demarcate the spectral. For Stephen, the questions alight upon places, and we could ask how *limbo patrum* relates to Paris or Dublin, and—particularly in the context of a metropolitan colony like Ireland—what it means to be haunted in the space in between a colonizer and a colonized. Stephen's questions ask us to pose others about the efficacy of speaking of something as deliberately vague as the spectral in the context of cultural politics, and what it may mean to say that *specters* (as opposed to the colonial legacy) *are haunting the world—specters of colonialism,* specters that belong to the future as much as to the past.[13]

What the current interest in the spectral demands, largely because of the sustained interest in a play that continues to haunt not only Western audiences but those around the world, is a reading of the ghost as the protagonist. We could attend to Nicolas Abraham's plea to understand the ghost who continues to haunt us, to question whether he tells the truth, and ultimately, to put him to rest.[14] While this tribute to the ghost has broader implications for social critique,[15] I want to address it in particular in relation to colonialism. To this end, I will discuss Wulf Sachs's study of John Chavafambira, *Black Hamlet,* and pose, among other questions, that of whether Sachs himself could be understood as sublimating a murderous urge in authoring this text, as he says Shakespeare was. This involves reading the analyst's text for countertransference, making him, momentarily, into the psychoanalytic subject — perhaps rather indiscreetly, in view of Russell's question in *Ulysses:* what use "this prying into the family life of a great man"?[16] If Sachs considered *Hamlet* a sublimation of paternal trauma, what conflict did Sachs escape by writing *Black Hamlet?* What haunts him? What "inner conflict" is he working through? With what form of mourning, or filial piety, did he contend as he wrote *Black Hamlet?*

If *Hamlet* reconfigured *Oedipus* in a repressive vein, it also placed a story of mourning, melancholia, and filial piety at the very heart of it, and at the heart of intellectual endeavor more broadly. The journal of the International Psychoanalytic Association criticized Sachs for failing to understand the transference and countertransference between himself and John Chavafambira, and clearly Sachs's Zionism led him to desire for Chavafambira some degree of nationalist politics.[17] This, indeed, was a phenomenon he had analyzed himself in *Psychoanalysis: Its Meaning and Practical Application:* the Jews "who are fighters for someone else's national or racial rights."[18] Through a reading of *Black Hamlet* I will consider the role of the spectral in thinking about the postcolonial intellectual, and more specifically, the question of whether there is a differing psychical structure in the traditional and in the organic intellectual in gendered postcoloniality.

Black Hamlet is Sachs's first-person narrative about his extended relationship with a native doctor, to whom he gave the pseudonym John Chavafambira. Chavafambira was from Rhodesia, and Sachs first encountered him in Johannesburg, South Africa. The narrative describes how Sachs met Chavafambira, the manner in which Sachs viewed the relationship as reciprocal, and the pseudopsychoanalytic relationship they had. In the first part of the book, Sachs described how Chavafambira, on the couch, told Sachs of his arrival in South Africa, and of his encounter with a witch (who haunts the remainder of Sachs's narrative). Chavafambira also told of his childhood and the police violence he encountered. The bulk of the narrative involves Sachs relating discussions about events that took place during the period of their friendship. It ends with the two returning for a short period to Chavafambira's family at a time when Chavafambira realized that he could no longer relate to his group. It also relates the growth of Chavafambira's nationalist consciousness, and Sachs's own investment in this. The narrative also tells the story of Maggie, Chavafambira's wife, who, because of her ill health, was the occasion for the meeting of Chavafambira and Sachs, who thought he could treat her for pain in her lame leg. The "nagging Maggie," as she is referred to, while relegated to the sidelines of the narrative, is central to it. *Black Hamlet* also bears witness to detribalization, urban modernization, and the social upheaval these processes create. Sachs consistently rationalizes this colonial violence by depoliticizing it while reading it as symptomatic of a Hamletism without context. Not acknowledging it directly, Sachs nonetheless indicates the political tensions at work. Keeping in mind the Gramscian distinction between the organic and the traditional intellectual and C. L. R. James's characterization of Prince Hamlet as an organic intellectual, can we draw a sharp distinction between the interests of a psychoanalyst, Wulf Sachs, a "traditional intellectual," and his analysand, Chavafambira, a black native doctor, an "organic intellectual"? Is there a structural psychical difference between the two that would mark a distinction between traditional and organic in the colonial context? If the traditional intellectual began with a sense of liberal disinterestedness, what would he become as a result of the structure of a dispersed hegemony in which his own political disempowerment had been the cause of his arrival in South Africa? The condensation of the black man and Hamlet together in a psychoanalytic framework throws the "civilized" and "primitive" distinction into doubt.[19]

Black Hamlet and Anthropology

In their illuminating writings on *Black Hamlet,* both Saul Dubow and Jacqueline Rose address how Sachs wanted to prove to the International Psychoanalytic Association that the structure of neurosis was uniform internationally. For readers today, the impetus to impose a psychoanalytic framework developed in the West, as well as a canonical Shake-spearean psychologization, seems simply racist in its assimilationist impulse. Sachs sought the contrary effect, with all the shortcomings that such a humanitarian response entails.[20] Whereas Freud drew some distinctions between the primitive mind and modern consciousness (and, in relation to Hamlet, the "two widely separated epochs of civilisation"), Sachs ignored differences between communities with different and conflictual social structures, and between tribal and familial groups, and what Freud called "artificial groups" like churches and armies:

> It was not long before I made what was to me a startling discovery.
>
> I discovered that the manifestations of insanity, in its form, content, origin, and causation, are identical in both natives and Europeans. There is, perhaps, a slight difference in the nature of the delusions and complexes of the native as compared with those of the European; but the difference is no greater than that found in comparing the insane Englishman with the mentally deranged Frenchman or German.
>
> This discovery made me inquisitive to know if the working fundamental principles of the mind in its normal state were not also the same. . . . [I]t was difficult to find a native who would be willing to become the object of a deep and protracted psycho-analytical study.[21]

Sachs acknowledged that inner conflicts arose because of detribalization and Westernization in South Africa, changes that affected the mental states of its inhabitants,[22] and yet he does not discuss these conflicts directly as formative of "Hamletism"; rather they are seen as effects of it. Even though he introduces the discussion of "Hamletism" immediately following that of the inner conflict caused by the political situation and the subsequent conflicting value systems that ensue, he does not take the leap that seems implicitly pertinent. Rather, he chooses to write of Chavafambira's conflict with his father and uncle/stepfather, a conflict that draws him closer to Prince Hamlet. Rose argues that Sachs saw the radical destabilizing work of the unconscious. "If fantasy moves across the racial line," she writes, "it is not only the ego's self-possession that flounders; such mobility also gives the lie to the doctrinal and symptomatic rigidity of racial difference doing its deadly work above ground."[23]

The shift, however, is by no means insignificant, and represents the introduction of a different form of anthropological framework in psychoanalysis. If Freud was sympathetic to armchair anthropologists like Tylor and Frazer, Sachs represents a more lively interest in Bronislaw Malinowski's anthropology, and in particular in the Malinowskian study that Ellen Hellmann, who introduced him to John Chavafambira, did of Rooiyard, the urban slum in which Chavafambira lived for some time.

Malinowski, in *Sex and Repression in Savage Society*,[24] argued against the universality of the Oedipus complex, in a move that ran counter to Sachs's desire to prove psychoanalysis's universal applicability. Shifting the emphasis from sexuality to power, Malinowski contended that in societies in which the figure of authority is not the father but someone else, children demonstrate few ambiguous feelings toward their fathers. His analysis was drawn from Trobriand Islanders in New Guinea. Malinowski did not simply argue against psychoanalysis, and he took seriously its frameworks and its challenge. But he departed from Frazer's model of anthropology. Malinowski conducted very specific studies of how cultures went through changes, thereby understanding "primitive" or "savage" societies as far more dynamic than did Frazer, Tylor, or indeed Freud. Positioning himself as the new wave of anthropology (even though he was a contemporary of Frazer's and of Freud's), he maintained the importance of specificity, organic unity, and an understanding of dynamic change.[25] Ernest Gellner wrote of his arrival on the anthropological scene in Frazerian terms: "As the paradigmatic anthropologist, Frazer was killed and replaced by Malinowski during the interwar period."[26] So, if Frazer haunted Malinowski in his staging of filial piety to his contemporary, Sachs's filial piety toward Freud also gave rise to questions of how to make use of a psychoanalysis based on social organization, belief, material circumstances, and language.

Ellen Hellmann, who was both a Malinowskian and someone to whom Malinowski referred in his work on cultural change, studied Rooiyard to understand two phenomena that were causing anxiety to British colonials: detribalization and Westernization. Saul Dubow and Megan Vaughan have written of the "deculturation thesis," which suggested to colonials "that African psychopathology resulted from an inability to cope with the breakdown of tribal restraints and from the strains imposed by the demands of western education and cultural values."[27] But Hellmann's work on detribalization and Westernization represented a very different agenda, one that criticized the economic oppression of South

African blacks. She was also bold and canny concerning the reasons for European concern about detribalization:

> Urban residence, which brings with it a multiplicity of contacts with Natives of numerous tribes, widens the horizon of the Native who, in tribal life, is inclined to be insular in outlook. Oppression by the European has given the Native a greater unity in common suffering. Urban contacts—forcing upon him the realization that though Natives of other tribes may differ, they yet share many habits and customs, desires and ambitions with him—are tending to make of him a Bantu citizen and not merely a tribesman with tribal loyalties. Much is spoken of the dawning of a Bantu national consciousness. White South Africa is intimidated by the threat this emerging "nation" directs at its own security. But common persecution, common suffering and a disillusionment shared by most, if not all, Natives have not yet brought about a triumphant national awakening, sweeping away all petty definitions. Instead, it is my belief, this widening of perspective and increase of knowledge has created a Native with divided loyalties. He feels his unity with the Bantu people as a whole; but he has not emancipated himself from feelings of tribal superiority which has caused each tribe in turn to call itself "The People." These divided loyalties—*the outcome of an unresolved inner conflict*—manifest themselves in diverse and often contradictory ways.[28]

The nature of this unresolved "inner conflict" is not disclosed; Hellmann acknowledged Sachs, she cited Freud at times,[29] and, of course, she would have read *Black Hamlet,* which had been published a decade before. But it seems like a rather odd statement for the Malinowskian— that the divided loyalties are the outcome of the inner conflict rather than the other way round. Even Freud himself, after all, attributed the inner conflict to increased repression due to the advances of society and the impositions of education systems. But Hellmann approaches from the other direction, as if the inner conflict precedes detribalization and Westernization. These phenomena were not identical for Hellmann, and neither were the consequences. "Natives," Hellmann wrote, employing the reifying uppercase "N" rather than the descriptive "n," were not simply without tribe or Westernized but something quite different from the two. They had what she called a "composite culture," wherein a "new whole is created which differs from the mere sum-total of its constituents."

Hellmann's emphasis on the preexistence of the inner conflict was like Sachs's. Sachs insisted that the mental life of natives is the same as people, especially men, from the West—without attributing any of these similarities, as Freud would do, to changes in the structure of society. Hellmann insisted that native culture was not being "submerged by European culture." "If the European policy were one of absorption," she wrote, "results might be very different. But the European policy of using the labour of the Native and of creating out of the Native populace a market for the consumption of the products of European industry, while at the same time increasing political and economic bars and restricting mobility and other freedoms so that the Native is not drawn into the full circle of European life, has had the effect of revolutionising Native economic life while affecting other facets to a far lesser extent."[30] Her critical position necessitates a humanitarian premise—or perhaps more accurately, a liberal humanist perspective—that forbids the exploitation of other humans capable of and susceptible to the same form of mental life as their counterparts in Europe. And in a sense this precludes any possibility of particular mental states emerging from the context she is at pains to describe precisely. She is thus closer to Sachs than to Malinowski himself. Dilemmas that arise may well be different depending on context, but at the core they are the result of the same inner conflict, which itself is not reconfigured by them, and is not constituted by them. It is an irreducible given, and a liminal point that characterizes the human as a species.

Hellmann's work opened itself to the kind of critique that has now become quite familiar: that in this (well-meaning) assumption that the human is ultimately the same in mental structure, with contexts creating only slight variations, she presents a very particular concept of the human and of personhood, which is then generalized. This concept of personhood is also assumed to be the baseline for humanitarian concern, and indeed, of rights in any political economy. For Hellmann, this allows her to criticize, through her anthropological system, the treatment of blacks in South Africa, and in particular those in the urban slum-yard Rooiyard. Fanon writes in *The Wretched of the Earth* that "pathology is considered as a means whereby the organism responds to, in other words adapts itself to, the conflict it is faced with, the disorder being at the same time a symptom and a cure."[31] For him, as for Hellmann perhaps, the symptom of anger toward exploitation is simultaneously the only available recourse to cure, bringing together the pathological and the political.

But even in the work of a humanitarian political theorist like Gramsci, there are those who exist outside that civil society in which rights should be granted to its members. While it may well be the case that by the time one "knows" the subaltern, his or her history may be over *as subaltern,* it is possible that before these figures enter civil society, the structure of their lives may be very different, including the basic structure of their mental lives: the degree to which people are repressed, the familial structure of the ego itself, or indeed, the existence or the structure of the unconscious. While we, in civil society, could not, by definition, as Spivak has been at pains to explain, define the structure of a subaltern consciousness, let alone an unconscious, we would have to entertain the possibility of its completely differential structure, or even its nonexistence. We would also have to entertain the possibility of a very different relationship to the dead, to mourning, and to ghosts. If we can think of John Chavafambira as a figure emerging from a subaltern group, such anthropological questions as those concerning the structure of mourning in a changing society would cause us to consider this Hamlet as an organic intellectual whose relationship to ghosts affects his relationship to the social and the political environment enormously. And it is through this relationship that we can begin to consider why mourning is such a crucial process in understanding state politics, discourses of resistance, and critical nationalism.[32]

Black Hamlet, Melancholia, and the Intellectual

Returning to Sachs, we can ask, then, what it means that he saw *Hamlet* as a necessary sublimation for Shakespeare, and then, just a few years after writing this, posed implicitly the same questions about himself— what *inner conflict,* and what extraordinary mourning, was Sachs working through when he wrote *Black Hamlet,* a text that, in a manner of speaking, takes on the psychoanalysis of an individual, but is also a novel of sorts, an intellectual odyssey on the part of its author, and a political awakening. Sachs's choice of Hamlet as a theoretical framework for discussing John Chavafambira makes us consider his own "Hamletism" as much as Chavafambira's himself. It also casts the Shakespearean play in a different light, which exists alongside the one foregrounded here. It is not just a play about the tortured soul of an intellectual, but it is also a political play, riven with conflicts internal and external.

When reading the play in the context of this book on psychoanalysis, feminism, and colonialism, we are reminded once again of the question posed by Memmi, the North African Jewish writer: must the analyst of colonialism choose between a social analytic framework, like Marxism, and one that centers on the structure of individuation, like psychoanalysis? Judging by the later version of *Black Hamlet,* the 1947 *Black Anger,*[33] we may be tempted to read the trajectory of Sachs's career as suggesting that social analysis has to be privileged over psychical analysis. Psychological conflicts are attributed more directly to exploitation than to "inner conflicts" (much as the trajectory of Fanon's career also indicates). And yet when *Hamlet* and *Black Hamlet* are read in the manner suggested by Nicolas Abraham's "The Phantom of Hamlet, or the Sixth Act," in which the political maneuverings of the secretive ghost are foregrounded (and perhaps, after Joyce, the ghost as author), the spectral quality of the relationship between the social and psychical once again becomes important—perhaps, even takes primacy. Hamlet's status as "organic intellectual" seen in this light arises from the (rather modern) conflict between private and public, and the different ways in which these are constituted in civil and political society in various locations around the world.[34] It puts at the center of our analysis an apparently contradictory concept (for our day) in which memory has become personalized and psychologized: that of collective memory.[35]

The private and public also relate to other oppositions when we consider the organic intellectual, such as the shift from subaltern space to that of civil society—a shift that takes place in temporal rather than spatial terms, one of Stephen Dedalus's *limbo patrum.* For the "emerged subaltern," and sometimes the "organic intellectual," are retrospective figures; the history of the subaltern can be written only after it is completed and once the figures or insurgencies involved are over; the organic intellectual is "of the people" and yet always interacting with civil and political society as a whole, and therefore negotiating between the two, looking back to the state of "the people" and forward to the state in which she or he wishes them to arrive: one of representation, and one of justice; one in which the instruments of civil society can be called upon for protection. Living with an eye to the future (as perhaps we all do), the organic intellectual is yet haunted by the past of "the people" she or he seeks to represent, and this haunting is constituted partly by the realization that those very instruments of civil society fought for are, by definition, inadequate to the task of this representation. At best, the subaltern past can be only partially assimilated to those instruments of representation.

The work of establishing the existence of the subaltern is thus retrospective, and defined through its elusiveness. It is also defined by the way in which it haunts the archive. It is conceived as prior to civil society, and in that sense is rather like use value in that it is a back formation. It is also thus conceived as being from a prior social formation (as Gramsci says of the "traditional intellectual"). Not only is this a structural topology rather than an archaeological topography, but there is a melancholic rather than a nostalgic relation to it because it is not nostalgia for being the subaltern, and it is not exactly simply the uncanny understood as the sense of simultaneously being at home and not at home.[36] It is rather the loss of something irretrievable but unidentifiable in the current state of entering into civil society. It is available to the historian as silence, as gap, as discontinuity, or as *aporia*. Very often it is marked by violence in the shape of spontaneous insurgency and its quelling. The entry into civil society is marked, always, by an epistemic violence.

It is symptoms of this form of violence that Chavafambira, the doctor, tries to understand when he visits the asylum where Sachs worked. He meets many inmates who had been brought there from prison, and, as a result, is thrown into something of a depression himself, for he feels that he is unable to help. "He genuinely suffered for and desired to help all these unfortunates, to find out the cause and perpetrator of the poisoning. But they seemed utterly self-absorbed and showed no interest in him, he complained to me. It appeased him to hear from me that such patients behaved in the same manner to everyone; there was no external stimulus to which they reacted; it was as if they had lost all contact with the world; they lived, indeed, in a different land."[37] In *limbo patrum* perhaps. But this form of psychosis is something entirely new, and shocking, to Chavafambira. He related to Sachs an interchange between two of the inmates:

> In a corner next to the enclosure for violent, dangerous patients, a group of men were talking of the riches of which they had been robbed. "I am chief; I have many, many wives and cattle. But my brother has taken my women and keeps me here with these dirty kaffirs," a middle-aged man said in a sly, irritated voice.
>
> "You liar," an elderly Bushman retorted promptly, speaking in Afrikaans. "I am King George, and I know all the chiefs. You are not a chief! You are mad! If you don't keep quiet, I will give an order to have you hanged. You see all these people?" he went on, addressing the group. "They are my soldiers, my policeman. They will do

whatever I tell them." He ended his threatening tirade with a shrill cackle of laughter.

John found himself at a loss. Was the old Bushman, his face hatched and cross-hatched with wrinkles, really mad, or just playing the fool?[38]

Rather like the players in *Hamlet,* Lear's exchange with the fool in *King Lear,* and indeed, the mock trial in that play, the insight afforded by this spectacle to the larger plot is crucial. For it shows the psychic affect of colonialism on the inmates, and it demonstrates that there is a fine line, as Freud showed us, between sanity and insanity in evidence here, which Chavafambira notes himself. The difficult question of psychoanalysis is also the difficult question of epistemic violence — is this (unavoidable) entry into a different episteme of civilization one that produces insanity, and can it be counteracted politically? Is the political response always a symptomatic one that misses the necessity of conflict, which exists as a result of Hamletism or oedipal desires? Does it always work within the logic of secular nationalism or the reigning political economy, to give a solution that is political — like decolonization, the awarding of rights, indeed, like sovereignty itself, which, because of its symptomaticity, somewhat misses the point? It would seem so from Sachs's rendition, for just as political criticism seems believable in a number of the stories of the inmates, as they begin "to intone [their] lamentation,"[39] something intervenes to mark it with insanity. But can this mean that the political response can simply be abandoned — that claiming sovereignty and a ceasing of exploitation is irrelevant? Or does it rather have to be the starting point of any psychical investigation that acknowledges the violence of the very machinations of the institution, the "cure," and the new form of spectral presence that occurs? For as Derrida reminds us, the specter is somewhat different from the spirit, for it is marked by flesh:

> As soon as one no longer distinguishes spirit from specter, the former assumes a body, it incarnates itself, as spirit, in the specter. Or rather, as Marx himself spells out . . . the specter is a paradoxical incorporation, the becoming-body, a certain phenomenal and carnal form of the spirit. It becomes, rather, some "thing" that remains difficult to name: neither soul nor body, and both one and the other. For it is flesh and phenomenality that give to the spirit its spectral apparition, but which disappear right away in the apparition, in the very

coming of the *revenant* or the return of the specter. There is something disappeared, departed in the apparition itself as reapparition of the departed.[40]

In that sense it appears both human and not, sane and insane, political and messianic, fiction and history—politically possible and simultaneously marked by the impossibility of the political gesture.

If the words of the inmates are consistently referring back to the political structure, to the break with the tribes, to the accusation that the militant detribalized (and in that sense the figure who threatens to challenge the status quo politically) are being confined as prisoner, then we know that "the whole procedure of the court was entirely foreign";[41] we also know that there seems to be some grain of reality, or truth, perhaps of flesh in what they say. If Sachs is consistently unsure of whether Chavafambira is telling the truth or spinning a yarn, it is the fabric of that telling that is of interest to us, because it bears the imperfections of a story not wholly assimilated or introjected into the laws of history telling, but rather, paradoxically incorporated, swallowed whole. At first he seems quite sympathetic to this: "It was difficult to discern truth from fiction in this romantic story. But for the understanding of John, and to John's future life, it mattered little if the greater part of the story were fictitious. A psychological reality . . . an event which we imagine to have happened, emotions which we believe we have experienced—influence our minds and our lives as much as actual facts."[42] But then later, this storytelling clearly causes some frustration to Sachs: "There were . . . difficulties in reconstructing his past, for John was frequently carried away by his fantasies and often, more perhaps than the average European, inaccurate and careless in recalling his memories. I would ask him: 'Do natives tell lies easily? Are they the same with their own people?' and his reply was invariably: 'When you don't want to hurt, you tell a lie, but I don't mean anything wrong. Or when you are afraid of people. We don't like the white people. . . . I don't care what I say to a white man if only I won't be punished.' "[43] Small wonder that Chavafambira wishes to retain some secrets! And interestingly, while Sachs will immediately offer a defense of the manner in which psychoanalysis reconstructs the past through a few disparate facts—those consciously given, those consciously withheld, and those surmised through "hints and indirect material"[44]—he does not really think through the reasons for withholding information.[45] It is information, however, that relates to the past and the uneasy relationship to it caused by different forms of colonial impact—not anything as vague as becoming "Westernized" (as becoming, as Homi Bhabha puts it, "almost the same but not quite, almost the same but not white"),[46] but of having an uneasy relationship to the past out of which one has emerged, and to the uneasy relationship to the phantom of that past, which exists into the future with an eye toward it. If Chavafambira's phantom is the woman at the beginning, she is quite distinct from a spirit, or *midzimu,* and his relationship to her is fraught with carnal ambiguity. The interaction with Sachs, while not wholly violent, is emblematic of something else: the movement away from the tribe, of detribalization, of Judeo-Christianity, which causes an uneasy relationship to the past as there is an attempt to assimilate it to the present and to the future.

We could identify that epistemic violence as a kind of trauma linked to mourning, because it is marked by an entry that carries the subaltern forward, but leaves something behind that cannot be defined as consciousness as such. For the identification of the subaltern involves not only reading a text against the grain in the Benjaminian sense, reading empty time and messianic time together.[47] It also necessitates an open-endedness, a reading for ambiguity, and an alertness to not only the spirit of the subaltern (a "consciousness" as such) but also the phantoms that haunt the subaltern (perhaps made up of the exclusions that have shaped this spectral existence) and that may be carried into civil society.

Both the subaltern and the organic intellectual are, then, marked by a loss that creates a particular relationship to temporality, and that is produced by the form of assimilation to, and identification with, a group. While Gramsci writes of "subaltern classes," he simultaneously says that the subaltern has no class consciousness, is not part of a group that defines itself *as group,* and is identified as such only retrospectively. As former subalterns enter civil society, or as representation for them is negotiated by the "organic intellectual," they carry something of the past with them. Is it the "spirit" of subalternity, or of the past more generally, that remains even as one becomes assimilated to civil society? (And in that sense, is it rather like the "spirit" of Marxism that Derrida says has always been with deconstruction?) And does this spirit suggest a kind of assimilation of it into the present, in the form of an introjection, or a psychic assimilation of that which is lost? Or is it rather something less comfortable than an assimilation (which implies, along with assimilation, a dilution of the distinctiveness and separateness from the past)? The violent epistemic and physical entry into colonial civil society cannot be assimilated. This is because the construct of the civil society was conceived in European nation-states in the colonial period. Given the promise of autonomy, assimilation, or even of independence, the impossibility of the psychic assimilation of the past into the present creates a critical response to the present because of the way in which the past haunts it.

This structure of haunting is akin to incorporation rather than to introjection.[48] An incorporation involves not only the impossibility of mourning, and thus of a full psychic assimilation or introjection; it also involves a refusal of mourning, taking, as Abraham and Torok put it, the metaphor of introjection literally, as if one had full control over the process of mourning itself, of consciously withholding information, and laying it to rest in the archive. But this refusal to mourn, rather like melancholia, involves an impossibility of mourning, a refusal of and an inability to mourn what has passed. In the context of the newly grouped subaltern, or the newly constituted counter-hegemony, or indeed, of the newly independent nation-state, the difference of the haunted figure from the structure of the free citizen causes a recognition of being radically separate. The new citizen is both happy and unhappy to leave behind the unrepresented existence, one that both can and cannot be sketched out in the newly constituted civil society.

Both in *Rooiyard* and in *Black Hamlet,* this melancholia is rationalized psychoanalytically, and assumes a uniform notion of the subject to do this. Hellmann and Sachs therefore read violence and the response to it as symptomatic not of the political context but of a Hamletism that appears to be without context. Neither do Hellmann and Sachs theorize their own relation to their material, even if they do describe many of the difficulties attendant in their work.[49] Again and again, we hear that they were both treated with great suspicion by the inhabitants of Rooiyard. For example, the illegal activity of beer selling in Rooiyard had been largely ignored by the police until Hellmann and Sachs began their anthropological and psychoanalytic investigations; now they were challenged not only for such things as the suspected ritualistic murder of twins, but also for their bootlegging activities. Not only were they suspected of allegiance with the police, informing them of activities in the slum-yard, but their very method of questioning was challenged, and even by Chavafambira. And so the apparently sympathetic work appeared as interrogation raising questions about the relationship between state control and both psychoanalytical and anthropological investigation.[50] The assault of questions is likened to the aggression of the colonial endeavor in general, and to the police in particular. Having described Chavafambira's confusion concerning the relation of the psychoanalytic and anthropological endeavors to colonial violence, Sachs responds thus:

> I knew him to be involved in severe inner conflict and understood this hatred and bitterness towards me and all white people, though he himself said nothing. Consequently I did my utmost to encourage him to express his hostility, to talk out his feelings with regard to the white people in general, the detectives and the anthropologist and myself in particular. Occasionally I almost succeeded, for he would be on the verge of allowing his aggression to come out, of saying what he felt; but the affection, the respect, the confidence that he had felt in the past, which had carried him beyond his own fear, had weakened so that all my tricks of persuasion failed. He remained obstinately silent, or answered in monosyllables. The old relationship, based on admiration and confidence, and the desire to please, had not been restored.
>
> While the internal conflict in him was unabated, his present situation became, without my help, impossible for him to comprehend. Doubts, uncertainties, conflicting thoughts and desires, were, like the nagging Maggie, continuously with him. I decided that I must interfere and break down his resistance.[51]

Aggression toward white people is analyzed as psychoanalytical resistance, as a "nagging wife," and as the affect arising from internal conflict attributed to "Hamletism,"[52] which Sachs attributes to Chavafambira's relationship to his father and uncle/stepfather: "John's tragedy, at first glance, may seem far beneath Hamlet's, and one is justified in ridiculing at the start any comparison between John the witch doctor and Hamlet the Danish prince."[53] What does not occur to Sachs is another paternalistic relationship within which Chavafambira is imbricated, and another form of haunting that may cause him to be politically crippled: the loss of tribe and the ambiguous desire for, and impossibility of, Westernization. The detective, the anthropologist, the archaeologist, and the psychoanalyst are all then identified as being part of the same epistemic structure, one of aggressively solving a mystery, taking us back to the dark continent, and leaving a question hanging over it—what happens if you are the dark continent? What happens if you are the "problem of femininity" like the crippled Maggie, or the spectral figure who haunts John Chavafambira throughout *Black Hamlet*?

Detribalization, a thesis explored by the anthropologist Ellen Hellmann, is introduced into Sachs's narrative from the outset. Chavafambira told of how he left his kraal in Rhodesia for the Union of South Africa because "he wished to cut himself adrift from his ancestors, and above all from Charlie, his uncle and present father, who was so greedy and selfish."[54] Rather like Oedipus, who attempts to leave potential conflict in the home, apparently observing filial piety yet walking into its transgression, Chavafambira found himself on a hot, dusty road, with no shadow or guide to protect him, and found there a suffering man on the side of the road. This good Samaritan, and the son of a famous witch doctor, offered his services even though he had not been formally initiated. At these crossroads he had to choose between following the path of Charlie, his uncle/stepfather, and indeed of his own father, who had told him explicitly not to practice medicine until he was older, saying "for the young to learn; for the mature to practice";[55] or alternatively, to follow the path of the good Samaritan, the alien father. (For in religious terms, we could read Christianity as the stepfather who has dislodged the father, now commanding a new respect. In fact, John himself conjectures that the confusion of religion caused by the introduction of Christianity into tribal cultures may have been the cause of the man's suffering—"Perhaps they prayed to the wrong god, maybe they are Christians and they forgot their dead people.")[56] Having initially chosen the latter, he subsequently felt cheated by the old man; his recovery was so quick, and followed by such an astonishing demand—to save the people in his kraal from drought and the illnesses that accompanied it, and "to smell out the culprit"[57] who had caused the drought to occur. Once again he has to make a choice before he can "solve the riddle."

In other words, while it may well be the case that the internal conflicts experienced by John (or perhaps anyone else) may not be reducible to the external ones (for example, a politicized group of South African blacks in conflict with an oppressive European colonial presence), there are certain conflicting paradigms that may constitute different forms of haunting, and alterations in forms of mourning, the meaning of spirits, and the relationship to the dead or to the uncanny. Seeing the internal conflict as identical to the external may well be a symptomatic response to reading a situation or a text, but the affect caused by that external conflict must surely be taken more seriously than the shortsightedness suggested by the term *symptomaticity.*

What concerns Chavafambira, and what will continue to concern him for the larger part of Sachs's narrative, is that he will become "bewitched" by the same vague illness afflicting the kraal. The illness takes the shape of a woman from his own tribe, the Manyika. She claims, confidentially, responsibility for the sickness, and she also warns John that he must go: " 'The people here,' she whispered in Manyika, 'are the old witch-doctors. They have sworn to kill you. They are jealous of you.' "[58] In a dream, the spirit of his father has come to him, telling him he is too young to perform the rituals, and too hot-blooded to avoid the attraction of women, who may lead him onto a path that causes impurities in his treatment.

This situation could have occurred only in this moment of detribalization. What has been left behind is not simply the spirit of the tribe, as embodied in the father; rather the tribe is displaced onto the figure of a Manyika witch. This woman appears as if a phantom, the like of whom we do not meet again until almost the end of the book, when Chavafambira returns to his tribe with Sachs, and mistakenly becomes involved with someone of his own *mutupo,* an action that amounts to something like incest. "The same ritual animal as the man's relegates the woman to the position of sister or mother. To marry her is to be guilty of incest. Yet he had never asked the *mutupo,* he realized, hardly crediting his own senses. And I remembered, as he related this to me, that he had also omitted to ask the *murowi* in the bewitched kraal the same question. [H]e knew . . . he could arrange matters by the sacrifice of oxen and goats. But he would remain the laughing stock: the *nganga* who went to towns and became so civilized that he had been intimate with a girl without asking her *mutupo.*"[59]

A story of incest thus encircles the text, and it is a story that is not so much one of betrayal of the father as one of detribalization, a betrayal of affiliation rather than of filiation, one that marks the distinction between the tribal and the secular modern. The structure of the book (and therefore of Sachs's narrativization of Chavafambira's life) suggests the centrality of this incest story, which is not a Frazerian betrayal of the father in any simple sense. It is not simply the father who appears as the internalized disciplinary phantom that he is for the Western psychoanalyst, like the high priest at Nemi in the beginning of *The Golden Bough* who is slain by this transgression. In fact, as witch doctor, or *nganga*, Chavafambira jealously performs such a "trick" on Mdlawini, his patient and his wife's lover, attempting to turn him into the fearful Hamlet, haunted through Chavafambira himself. Suspecting Mdlawini of sleeping with his wife, Maggie, Chavafambira appears to divine this. Mdlawini, terrified, finds himself in a scenario much like Hamlet's in Gertrude's bedroom when Polonius is slain behind the arras: "Suddenly he awoke with a jerk. He had felt a touch. His hand instinctively closed over the assegai. The blood hung in his ears. His straining eyes made out a blur in the doorway—a vague, white, moving shape."[60] The trick is something he regrets, as the instruments of the law aggressively descend upon Mdlawini. For himself, the "superego," in this case the disciplinary resource of the parents, is not exactly internalized in the way that one may expect; Sachs attributes this to his infantile nature:

> In this direction he remained an infant throughout life. Usually, during the psychological development, an identification with the parents takes place: that is, a part of the parents becomes internalized in the mind of the individual, in the fashion of an unconscious moulding, with the result that the internalized characteristics become an integral part of the individual. People talk and act, like and dislike, in common with their parents' ideals and tastes without themselves being aware of it. In John's case it was different. Father and mother, though dead, remained accessible to him whenever he was in need of them. They were as omniscient as God, but in a concrete and tangible form. The *midzimu* even lived in their former huts in the kraal according to John's conception.[61]

Clearly, this is a very different relationship to parents, dead or alive, than that we see with Hamlet, or indeed in Hamletism. For Hamlet, the appearance of the ghost itself is shocking, and, as Derrida has noted, an essentially blind submission to his secret is demanded, and an obedience that will result in justice, as the ghost claims. For Chavafambira, the appearance of the ghost of the father, and indeed the spirit of the mother (who is still alive) is comforting; their identities are not in doubt, and they do not perturb at all. The one who perturbs is elsewhere, rather, in the shape of the woman.

For Marie-Cécile and Edmund Ortigues, it is this difference concerning parental death that exposes the limits of therapeutic psychoanalysis developed in Europe. The attitude toward ancestral spirits associated with cultural ritual in West Africa is clearly very different from individuated loss associated with the mythical Oedipus, or the lines of filiation Freud associates with the Oedipus complex in the shape of parents and the superego. Following E. R. Dodds,[62] the Ortigues speculate about a civilization of shame and a civilization of guilt. Shame exists in front of others, and emerges in cultures in which collective myth becomes the standard to live by. By contrast, the guilty have internalized the superego and the individual phantasm associated with it.[63] Given that relations between people within the familial context (mother/child, mother/father, father/child) are always mediated by a "juridical fiction" (une fiction juridique),[64] the cultural and collective myths, whether they be of community relations to the dead or of individuated mourning, need to be figured into concepts of filiation. This juridical fiction, which they call the phallus following Jacques Lacan, inevitably changes the iterations of the participants, whether they are analysts or analysands. In the case of West Africa, they claim, laws manifested as collective myths thematize incest taboo, phallic symbols, and the omnipotence of the father. What may be encrypted within the language of Europe constitutes the very language of the group in West Africa. It is therefore not individuated repressed material, but collective myth; hence the iterations of a "Black Oedipus" will be different from Oedipus. The Ortigues are struck by the commonality between what occurs in the European clinical setting and what they found in the one they improvised in West Africa. In both contexts, the foreclosure of the paternal Symbolic imposes itself on the individual. Parting explicitly from Malinowski's questioning of the universality of the Oedipus complex in, for example, matrilineal groups, they express a common understanding of the primary process, that is, the rejection of the affect associated with the implementation of the Law of the Father. What is encrypted in this foreclosure is the relation to the mother, who becomes lost-as-mother only to be resurrected as what is desirable for Lacanianism: the phallus.

We could, however, read the primal foreclosure as something that begins to break down at the moment of assimilation, producing a phantom as a reminder of the failure to assimilate. We will understand this phantom as something that emerges in response to encrypted matter when the individual is unable to assimilate fully something that shares the encrypted secret. "The term hantise, translated here as 'haunting,' also has the common sense of an obsession, a constant fear, a fixed idea, or a nagging memory. We will continue to translate it simply with the gerund 'haunting' so as to maintain a clearer link with the ghostly in general."[65] So says Derrida's translator. Sachs's claim that Chavafambira's internal conflict is ever present—rather like his wife, the "nagging Maggie"—is borne out when Chavafambira's phantoms keep manifesting themselves as women. Ellen Hellmann noted that detribalization takes place among men much more rapidly than among women. The inassimilable, or that which cannot be represented by the organic intellectual remaining from the subaltern, is encrypted for men such as Chavafambira in the language of civil society as that which cannot be expressed. Effectively, the accelerated pace of detribalization and the ritual fear of incest that persists from that older formation returns as a nagging presence of the feminine spectral.

But this is a somewhat reductive rationalization of a larger issue, one, perhaps, that demonstrates a form of symptomatic demetaphorization itself. "Demetaphorization" is a psychoanalytic concept elaborated by Nicolas Abraham and Maria Torok that carries important insights for the literary critic and particularly for postcolonial studies. For I am arguing here that the presence of the phantom, that is, the existence of material secrets caused through incorporation rather than introjection that can be carried through generations, has consequences for reading against the grain, reading politically, and for reading for difference in the colonial archive.

But perhaps we are overstepping ourselves here, for this enigmatic notion of the phantom currently seems to signify nothing distinct from its own mysteriousness, indeed, from its own lack of distinction or demarcation. This, in fact, is why the Derridean reading of the "specters of Marx" has caused so much angst among Marxists. For politically speaking, while the idea of a conspiracy, a secret, or a simple base structure that can be identified as determining the superstructure is a rather crude and reductive reading of the tenets of Marxism (and indeed of political literary criticism that finds its roots in that body of work), some possibility of demarcation of the specter, and indeed of the cause of the affect of a phantom, needs to be present. For the phantom, after all, is a symptom, and is the signifier of something, even, some of us would argue, in the world of global postmodern capital. While critics such as Slavoj Žižek, and, differently, Francis Fukuyama have insisted, quite persuasively, that Marx's third volume of *Capital* speaks of the end of history as capital generating itself and its own meanings in a frenzy of baseless self-generation, some would like to intervene into this meaningless doomsday scenario with demarcation and signification.[66] To that end, let's inquire as to the psychoanalytic meaning of two terms: the phantom or specter, and the secret, and see how they relate to the concept of demetaphorization I have introduced here. For the concept of the specter, apparently signifying nothing but its own incommensurability, has recently been used rather loosely, and rather indiscriminately, thereby losing the pertinence of its formation.

Black Hamlet and Hauntology

What is a phantom? What is a secret? A phantom constitutes a trans-generationally transmitted signifier of repression. It originates in a trauma or a repressed secret that has not been introjected, but rather, has been incorporated—swallowed whole rather than psychically assimilated. The repression is thus not something that can be worked through at all, whereas what has been introjected has been fully worked through. We know that Freud did not make use of these distinctions, which Abraham and Torok drew from Ferenczi, partly because the idea of a "working through" that can be completed once the source of the repression has been "uncovered" functioned in an archaeological and curative framework that was not Freud's. But what Abraham and Torok do give us, which is not available in the Freudian scenario, is the idea of a transgenerational repression, one that can be passed down particularly through familial lines, so one can, in a sense, be in possession of (and therefore possessed by rather than in ownership of) someone else's repression. This could then emerge as a phantom, that is, as a signifier of this secret or repression, at a given moment in which circumstances create the occasion for the phantom to emerge as symptom and as signifier in the use of words, in performative acts, and in the creation of narratives.

Abraham and Torok elaborate these terms in discussing mourning and melancholia; or, as they put it, mourning *or* melancholia. In other words, rather than seeing oedipality as the crux of psychical development, they see mourning and the attendant mechanisms of introjection and incorporation as central to development. Taking these insights into account, and also remembering Freud's (and later Derrida's) doubts about the distinctions between the terms *incorporation* and *introjection*—also seeing psychoanalysis as a hermeneutic rather than as a curative discipline—we can consider how a shift from the private familial context for the phantom to a public and ideological one may be useful for a discussion of postcoloniality, and perhaps for nationalism more broadly. This involves not only a shift from the medieval (feudal) familial framework to a communal (nation-state) context, but also from a model of filiation to one of affiliation; in this new model phantoms could be transmitted through an artificial group rather than through a bloodline. This involves neither seeing the psychical as offering an analogy for the nation, nor seeing the nation as psychologeme. Rather, it involves understanding the mechanism of affiliation to a nation (or to any artificial group) as being a markedly different phenomenon creating quite specific forms of haunting, narrative, sites of memory (Pierre Nora's *lieux de mémoire*), and psychical affect. Attaining an identity through affiliation, or even something understood as "an accident of birth," rather than through birth or blood involves both conscious and unconscious choices between groups and the actions and archives formed by them. Thus, while understanding such things as archives of collective memory makes sense on one level, on another it does not at all, because the very structures of affiliation make the idea of collective memory an affect of demetaphorization at best, and a problematic reduction of the historical to the autobiographical at worst.[67]

In introducing *Black Hamlet* into a trajectory that seems to move from Oedipus/Black Oedipus to Hamlet/Black Hamlet, I am not seeking to make *Black Hamlet* a test case of postcoloniality. What *Black Hamlet* does point to, however, is the distinction between filiation and affiliation, and the development of artificial groups in which ego-ideals on occasion replace fathers as liminal points of group characterization, and create their own set of psychical quandaries. If Chavafambira is torn between two fathers, they are not, after all, simply his biological father and his uncle/stepfather. They are more relevantly understood as Tembu, his nationalist friend, and Sachs, his "analyst," both of whom are metonymies for an emerging Bantu national consciousness and European modernization respectively. These "fathers" are set into an uncanny perspective by the figure of the woman who appears, in spectral form, to represent the effect that detribalization has on everyday life.

In a sense, then, we return full circle, to the moment when Freud, seated on the Acropolis, has an uncanny feeling of déjà vu that causes a quandary of national belonging. Except the late emerging nation-state does not arouse feelings of uncanny nostalgia so much as uncertainty, despair, and even melancholia: the failure to introject the loss of something. The trajectory set forth by Freud moves from parricide at Nemi, to Oedipal unconscious betrayal, to mourning and doubt concerning filial piety in *Hamlet*. In *Black Hamlet* we encounter melancholia as the failure to introject, which effectively causes a critical relationship to that which is lost and that which one attempts to assimilate psychically. In this instance, this amounts to the tribe, and to the new (and unavailable) ideal of national citizenship. It is such a dynamic of different artificial groups that causes this telescoping effect in which nothing can function independently of the critical and often uneasy relationship into which it is thrown by the encounter with another.[68]

So how do these different forms of the specter hang together—the psychoanalytic phantom, Hamlet's father, and the Derridean distinction from Abraham and Torok? And why may this be a useful concept, combined thus, for understanding the relevance of psychoanalysis in coloniality and postcoloniality? Haunting seems, in each case, to signify something else, but seems to be in excess of whatever can be defined as the root cause of a repression, or of an affect understood nonpsychoanalytically. The work of the detective as analyst, and indeed of the anthropologist as police worker and archaeologist as definer, all present an apparently reductive counter to the specter, and seem, therefore, to be demetaphorizing affects. If this is the case, however, we would have to conclude that any reading or analysis that attributed a particular and direct political cause, or uncovered, through demystification, a truth that lay beyond the apparent state of things, was a demetaphorized, if necessary, symptom. But does symptomaticity itself make an analysis less valuable, because it acknowledges some attenuated link with a secret, a repression, or a history that leads to unpredictable and unforeseen affects. These are not necessarily linked causally to that which has preceded them, nor are they simply oedipal responses to the Big Other. Rather, they are particular historical configurations of the psychical.[69] In Torok's terms, this form of analysis could be understood as *preservative repression*. The drives associated with an object cannot be assimilated, and a secret or a phantom is thus formed embodied in the guilty concealment of incorporation. It is a fantasy because what becomes evident is the impossibility of assimilation. The secret emerges in language. It is the refusal to mourn. It is a *demetaphorization* of introjection that causes the drives to be read literally, encrypted, we could say, as the literalness of the patronymic. Reading without trope, or understanding tropes literally, is as much a critique of political criticism as it is an analysis of incorporation:

> Introducing all or part of a love object or a thing into one's body, possessing, expelling or alternately acquiring, keeping, losing it— here are varieties of fantasies indicating, in the typical forms of possession or feigned dispossession, a basic intrapsychic situation: the situation created by the reality of a loss sustained by the psyche. If accepted and worked through, the loss would require major readjustment. But the fantasy of incorporation merely simulates profound psychic transformation through magic; it does so by implementing literally something that has only figurative meaning. So in order not to have to "swallow" a loss, we fantasize swallowing (or having swallowed) that which has been lost, as if it were some kind of thing. Two interrelated procedures constitute the magic of incorporation: *demetaphorization* (taking literally what is meant figuratively) and *objectivation* (pretending that the suffering is not an injury to the subject but instead a loss sustained by the love object). The magical "cure" by incorporation exempts the subject from the painful process of reorganization.[70]

The literal implementation of something figural, and something that is constituted figuratively, adds a curious twist on concepts of imagined communities, phantom public spheres, and archives.[71] For even if those technologies of sociality are phantomlike, they may, in fact, rather like the ghost of Hamlet, cover up something else: another form of spectral presence. In other words, reading the phantom as the end point of critical analysis does not allow us to think through what may have produced it while simultaneously acknowledging the problem of the reduction of phantom-production to a singular cause. Indeed, the reductionism of such a gesture could be understood as *objectivation* itself, the attribution to another of the suffering one has experienced oneself. One could think, as an example of such a scenario, of what Walter Benn Michaels rather patronizingly refers to as "forgotten histories."[72] If, for example, Afrocentrists write a history that appears to both distort and create a sense of continuity that is doubtful, one could either accept these narratives that create a sense of imagined community literally, understanding the continuity as something that could be positivistically affirmed, or in terms of their imaginative importance. Criticizing Afrocentrism for historical inaccuracy equally plays into the same logic (and this is Michaels's failing) and is a failure to understand its imaginative importance. It also claims a position of superiority for an alternative narrative of continuity (usually of liberal democracy) that fails to account for the exclusion that has existed historically and the consequent repressions, suppressions, and affect to which it has given rise, like, indeed, objectivation. This is the "traditional intellectual" mourning—remembering to forget while acting as if there is no interest in doing this.[73] We could level against both positions a certain degree of demetaphorization, for there is a drive to read literally what only makes sense figuratively (even if the facts presented could themselves be verified or refuted). Similarly, it is hardly sufficient to read the community or the nation as imagined; this is similar to simply acknowledging the existence of ghosts, say, in the Hamlet scenario (which are subtended by familial, oedipal relations), or the imagined community of nation (subtended by the state) without any reference to content or to the creation of "communities" or "ghosts" by the circumstances that undergird them. The idea that attention to content is necessarily reductive is one of the faults of psychoanalysis of recent times. Understanding particularities of the language of demetaphorization locates the repression and the haunting with some degree of local specificity.

This specificity is in greatest evidence for Abraham and Torok when they create the concept of the psychoanalytic cryptonomy in *The Wolf Man's Magic Word,* but even in a text like "The Phantom of Hamlet" a careful (if somewhat astonishing) scripting of the sixth act gives away what Hamlet's ghost was attempting to hide: "The phantom's lies are still to be revealed—/ Since falsehood is fraught and oppressed with guilt, / While truth endures light, fruitful, and untainted." Fortinbras bids Horatio, the intellectual, to reveal the secret behind the confusion wrought by the phantom. Horatio responds:

> My mind is slow. At last I understand.
> Our truths derive from the bungles of the ghost.
> Adverse to his son, he sold the Union
> To Norway. Why? You'll ask. The wise will know:
> To hide his shame over unlawful gains.
> Others, better advised, say other things:
> The Queen and Claudius conspired to slay

The traitor King. The inner circle delights
In bedroom scenes: Polonius, ready
To rape the Queen, was surprised by Hamlet,
Who killed him. Those in the know will rejoin . . .
Must I go on?[74]

It is the very specificities of the content of the verse that seem somewhat conjectural, surprising, and, in some ways, missing the point of literariness; and it is perhaps the poverty of the theory that attempts a definition rather than a gesture toward the possibilities encoded in the figure of the ghost. Here, those possibilities are given a proper name, through which everything else is apparently explained: the ghost of Hamlet. The ghost as metonymy for Hamlet's own confusion should not thus simply become synecdoche for national struggle, because making it into metonymy fails to account for its ghostliness; for our own investment in the very structures that make him a ghost; and for our own inability (in Freud's terms) to work through fully, or in Derrida's terms, following Abraham and Torok, to fully distinguish between introjection and incorporation. If Abraham supposes we can be exorcized, Freud and Derrida insist that we cannot be rid of ghosts, for the traces of them will always be before us. The answer, of course, has to be conceived, but it cannot be made representative.

What I'm suggesting here, though, is not only that there is a time lag in postcoloniality as Homi Bhabha has suggested, but also that there is a haunting at once more singular and more particular than the concept of the time lag permits. If we understand *Hamlet* as a text that continues to haunt "us," it is not simply because it is the literary text that has produced probably more criticism than any other in the English language, and not simply because as a core component of the literary canon it has been absorbed internationally through forms of colonial education. It has also gained a kind of mythical status, perhaps because of the way it haunts in areas irrevocably changed by modernity, and has, rather like Greek tragedy, become rewritten with local and particular stresses, linguistic contexts, and sexual politics. As Ania Loomba has very persuasively shown, it is an oversight to read any form of resistance as a further instrument of containment. Loomba demonstrates how Mizo renditions of *Hamlet* constitute a radical reshaping of the play, a restructuring of it as indigenous, a making it anew. It is neither nostalgically looking back, nor slavishly aping an older and alien form. The Mizo *Hamlet* is certainly doing far more than the overblown claims routinely made for every "new production" of Shakespeare today under new directorship.[75] It appears rather as a rescripting haunted by the past but in a melancholic rather than a prostrating manner—one which shows us that we cannot unlearn the plays of the canon, neither can we simply replay them as if they were our own, nor claim absolute difference, newness, and a shaking off of the past. (And I say "we" and "our" advisedly here, for in some sense, the past is a "foreign country" for all of us who live in nation-states, and "remembering" is for us as much a piecing together of something we claim as our own—the so-called "collective memory" of the archive.)

The past haunts the present, but does not offer a way of rationalizing exactly how and why nation-states act in the way they do, or, indeed, produce the literary texts they do. Numerous "rewritings" of *Hamlet* demonstrate this, whether in the various performances of *Hamlet* in India's state of Mizoram (some of which can be seen in Pankaj Buthalia's documentary *When Hamlet Goes to Mizoram*) or in Mrinal Sen's masterpiece, *Genesis,* a film that deals directly with questions of beginnings, of hauntings, of exploitation, of sexual politics, of transnational capital, and of temporality. The affect of haunting is to demonstrate the epistemic violence of the mechanisms through which the primary text "arrived," the incorporation of those texts that could never quite be assimilated, and also the refashioning of those texts in the very particular forms of haunting that emerged. Form, genre, prosody, and language thus become crucial mechanisms through which political criticism could be conducted, for it is there that the shape of the trace, or of the imprint, can be gauged. Reading for content only, and reading for overt politics only, works, in fact, entirely within the logic of melancholia. Such is a necessary reading, certainly, but one that also needs to understand how affect is incommensurable if the psychical workings of the inhabitants of states can be gauged.

I am suggesting here that melancholia brings to critique a form of critical agency initiated by the inassimilability, indeed the *incorporation,* of certain losses or ideals. This critical agency is unavailable to the mourner who *introjects* losses, and is therefore not haunted, and does not, therefore, appear to be interested. Critical agency, Freud says, is linked to a concept crucial for the understanding of the group: the ego-ideal. As we have seen in the discussion on Freud and anthropology, the ego-ideal is an agency or personality that is a combination of narcissism (ego-cathexis—

idealization of the ego) and identification with the parents, their substitutes, or their collective values; entry into civil society would be *at the cost* of an epistemic violence of the ego-ideal, becoming, as it were, grouped and assimilated. If introjection, as Abraham and Torok conceive of it, is part of the stuff of the everyday, a critical agency would arise only when introjection did not take place: that is, when an incorporation, leading to a haunting, would exist in its place. Freud says that melancholia involves a critical agency that amounts to self-beratement, that is, an incorporation understood through the norm of introjection: as the *failure* to mourn adequately, and thus a failure of oedipalization. In "On Narcissism," Freud speaks of a special psychical agency that is formed when sublimation does not take place:

> The formation of an ego ideal is often confused with the sublimation of instinct, to the detriment of our understanding of the facts. A man who has exchanged his narcissism for homage to a high ego ideal has not necessarily on that account succeeded in sublimating his libidinal instincts. It is true that the ego ideal demands such sublimation, but it cannot enforce it; sublimation remains a special process which may be prompted by the ideal but the execution of which is entirely independent of any such prompting. . . . It would not surprise us if we were to find a special psychical agency which performs the task of seeing that narcissistic satisfaction from the ego ideal is ensured and which, with this end in view, constantly watches the actual ego and measures it by that ideal. If such an agency does exist, we cannot possibly come upon it as a *discovery*—we can only *recognize* it. . . . It will certainly be of interest to us if evidence of the activity of this critically observing agency—which becomes heightened into conscience and philosophic introspection—can be found in other fields as well.[76]

As we know, critical agency is also a concept we meet the next year, in 1915, in "Mourning and Melancholia." Melancholia thus appears to be a failure to sublimate that links sublimation to psychic assimilation, and thus the failure to fully assimilate to a new group—to civil society on the part of the subaltern, or indeed, to a concept of the nation-state conceived in a manner that originally excluded its new member. This latter form of melancholia would apply to postcolonials who in the formation of national consciousness would be unable to fully accept the ego-ideal as a form based on European nation-statehood. This was a form that almost without exception informed the local nationalism and had been built on the basis of excluding those in the colonies, and by differentiating its subjects or citizens from the inhabitants of their colonies. What was lost would thus be both prior formations that would have to be discarded (like tribe) for the sake of identification (or affiliation) with the new group, and, because of uneasy assimilation to the new group, the ideal of nation-statehood itself. Critical agency, or melancholic postcoloniality, would thus give rise to critical nationalism, to haunting, and at times to demetaphorization. If Hamlet had been haunted by his corrupt father who had sold out one nation for another, then Black Hamlet was haunted by the ghosts of detribalization and the confusion of whether, and what, to sublimate. Haunting arose from the falsity of a choice between two fathers: the father or the stepfather—the nationalist or the colonial doctor. But neither can put the ghosts to rest, largely because both the symptom and the cure, as Fanon may say, are uniform: the haunting is a form of a critical relationship to nationalism, a failure, in fact, to assimilate anywhere, given the affect of epistemic violence. Haunting is, however, quite precise in its makeup, individuated and specific to certain contexts. One could, to some extent, say the structure of haunting would be similar in any group entering into a liberal democracy that was based on their exclusion: women entering into full citizenship in postcolonial contexts, or indeed otherwise, could similarly experience melancholic haunting.

In the later edition of *Black Hamlet* entitled *Black Anger*, Sachs describes his analysis of Maggie, undertaken at John's request to help him stop her from nagging. Sachs tells us, "I had long wanted to explore the inner workings of this simple woman's mind."[77] We hear little of Maggie, however, and what we do hear about is her distaste for sex, her antipathy toward men, her jealousy of Sachs's relationship with her husband, and her fear of the reproach of the spirits if she describes her dreams to Sachs, spirits who have been displaced by their move out of the kraal, by, in other words, detribalization. Sachs is dismissive of her concerns, speaks of them as gossip, and ignores her message concerning the coded signs of ghosts:

> "Why do you want *me* to talk to *me*?" she asked, baffled. She refused to tell me her dreams, saying, "What I see in my sleep, I tell no one. My dead people will be cross."

She went on to say, "I'm asleep, I'm like dead . . . and the *midzimu* come to talk to you then. And if they are too busy to come, they send a message by a snake, a horse, or some other animal. Sometimes, they let you know they are with you through other signs. . . . Bad and silly people forget their dreams. And so they don't know what's going to happen to them; then they come to John and he, through his bones and horns, speaks for them with their *midzimu*. John can talk with dead people any time."[78]

Drawing an implicit parallel between Sachs's work and Chavafambira's work as a native doctor, Maggie also identifies a difference: the reading of spirits and their signs is contrasted to the professional reading of symptoms of repression. Patients either go to the analyst to come to terms with themselves, or go to the native doctor, to read the messages from the spirits that they fail to interpret themselves. Failure to read signs from dreams leads to visits to the doctor, who reads the spirits manifesting themselves in other things (when their busy schedules do not allow for visitations in dreams). They are read not as bodily symptoms but as external manifestations of messages unrecognized that could be understood as much by the doctor as by oneself at an earlier stage. Here, of course, is a far more communal understanding of ghosts, and a conception of doctor-as-psychic that exists alongside the interpreter of the patient's words. But it is also a moment in the text of *Black Anger* that sheds light on *Black Hamlet;* we see that the function of psychoanalyst was never very distinct from that of witch doctor, and that the political circumstances that lead to nation-state formation also lead to particular forms of neurosis. The change from the communal thus resulted in the change to the necessity for a psychoanalysis: where "individual freedom and social responsibility" seem to be in tension. The psychoanalyst, however, fails to understand the nature of his own anger, and the nature of aggression more generally, ascribing it to a general sense that anger must out.

Chavafambira, on the other hand, is rather more like Hamlet, seeing both the dilemma of a choice between two fathers and the dilemma of a choice between filiation and affiliation, with all the narratives of belonging and ownership that can be found in those conceptualizations of the private and the public, the interior and the exterior, and the individual and the group. And it is Maggie who draws our attention to the similarities and differences between the traditional and the organic in this regard. In that sense, Maggie's words (and I do not mean to infantalize here) are rather like the words of the dying child in Caruth's reading of Freud's analysis of the language of trauma: they invoke the ethics of trauma that is attendant in colonies, and they attain, in that sense, a ghostlike quality.

Like Jacqueline Rose in her reading of the study, I do not wish to simply associate woman with truth here, so much as to try to listen to the signs that haunt this text, and therefore to evince the difficulties attendant in the humanist assumption that equality has to be argued in the name of sameness. For radical breaks have been created by colonialism as much as they have by nation-state formation, and in the colonial archive both the symptom of and the cure for the erasure of the failure of representation can be read in terms of the ongoing failure of psychical assimilation of the ego-ideal in the nation-state. For if identification itself is haunted by the notion that the structure of the state maintains the structure of exclusion that existed in the colonizing nations, then disidentification will almost inevitably follow.

If colonialism, as Ranajit Guha has persuasively argued, was constituted by rule without hegemony, nationalism (and through this, the civilizing mission) had to be constituted through hegemony, and the assimilation of that idea of colonial rule.[79] Anger generated by the lie of colonialism—that it afforded colonized peoples the same rights as colonials—was dismissed by psychoanalysis as the inevitable and necessary venting of the energies associated with hatred. If that hatred could be seen to be generated by nation-state formation, then we would have to conclude that uniformity exists across the board in modern peoples. But if it is differentiated by the nation-state's formal relationship to colonial rule, then we would have to conclude that a different psychical apparatus, one of melancholic critical agency leading to hatred, haunts the new nations, because of an attempt to sustain a hegemonic acceptance of the very form that failed to be hegemonic but, rather, was enforced from above.

This psychical difference would surely cause a difference between the traditional intellectual, understood as one emerging from hegemonic cultures, and organic intellectuals, who would necessarily emerge from a civil society with whom they had an uneasy relationship because hegemony did not exist. The attempt to create hegemony is precisely the affront from which disappointment emerged; we see this in Fanon's realization that he would always be treated with contempt in the French army he defended, in Derrida's or Cixous's surprise at French nationality being stripped from Algerian Jews in World War II, in Chavafambira's urge to escape when he was accused of a rape crime he did not commit. When the symptom and the cure—hatred and resistance—are identical, the impossibility of political assimilation, that is, the lack of necessity for the colonizer to create hegemony because of such an overwhelming power, informs the failure of psychic assimilation. The loss of an ideal, that is, of the ideal of representation within the nation-state, makes for an incorporation of the ideal, but a failure to introject. In turn, what is created is a critical agency, and a critical relation to the ideal of the nation-state.

Before ending, I would like to say a brief word about Maggie's mother. When she recognizes that her daughter is in danger of losing John, the mother intervenes and thereby organizes the possibility of future nagging. The position of the lame and apparently unattractive Maggie is secured by her mother in a rather shocking manner—she arranges it that John sleeps with Maggie's younger and more attractive sister. Her complicity with John's betrayal actually secures the relationship with Maggie, and allows all the women in the family to have a strong hold over him for as long as they wish. In fact, rather than functioning as the exchangeable goods in a masculinist tribe, the mother expresses a form of social organization that damages that form of sociality. (In Shakespeare's play, of course, not only does Ophelia end up mad and dead, but she also does not have a mother to counteract the masculine forms of exchange of Polonius, Laius, and indeed, Hamlet himself.)[80]

Let me return briefly to Abraham and Torok and the concept of the phantom. In his "sixth act of *Hamlet*," Abraham writes, as we have seen, a healing act. Contending that King Hamlet's ghost is the protagonist of the play, and appears only when his secret is in danger of being revealed, he suggests that the ghost does not tell his son, Prince Hamlet, the whole truth. Abraham presents Horatio as the intellectual who listens to the encryptions within the play. He finally understands that the king had sold the Danish union to Norway, and that he had done this out of guilt because he had taken Norway unlawfully. It was true that Claudius and Gertrude had killed him, but it was because he was a traitor. What King Hamlet had not realized, however, was that Polonius had conspired to bring about these levels of betrayals between Fortinbras of Norway and Hamlet of Denmark. Polonius's action is attributed to the political situation in Poland rather than simply individual fault: he has responsibility, but the cause is much broader than individual malice. And Horatio's discovery purges Denmark of its pollution.

On one level, such an interpretation seems rather bizarre, because it puts the phantom to rest, mourned for what seems like rather spurious reasons. But Abraham's interpretation shifts the psychoanalytic from character analysis to the political order governing the whole play. It shows, indeed, how melancholic supplements cause damage to the dominant framework, not just by offering a counter to it, but by interrupting in parergonal fashion. What is anecdotally and theoretically striking in the example of Maggie is her lack of exemplarity. Her generalized form of pseudo-illness and her nagging insistence on her own erasure—in the movement from communal to individual, from tribe to detribalization, and from melancholia to mourning—are constitutive of a haunting remainder that is at once the call for and the undoing of injustice.

If Sachs read Shakespeare's *Hamlet* as a play about filial piety that paid "tribute to father and son," we could read Sachs's *Black Hamlet* as a book about the traditional intellectual's piety in the face of the native informant existing within an ideal of modern hegemony. The traditional intellectual's apparent *disinterestedness* is testimony to the hegemony of the ideal of liberal democracy—that the failures of the past can be mourned and assimilated. Interest, in the shape of resistance, hatred, or anger, could thus be seen as a mark of melancholia, the failure to fully introject.

The ideal of Arnoldian disinterestedness is demonstrated in Eliot's "No! I am not Prince Hamlet. . . ." If Prufrock could be only a Polonius rather than the impassioned Hamlet (irrationally impassioned according to Eliot, for there is no objective correlative to mark the source of his anguish), he will, of course, potentially be killed by Hamlet, apparently for no reason. Though if we were to take Abraham's reading of the phantom seriously, we could understand the apparently harmless Polonius as a corrupt national politician, and a rapist. It is clearly ridiculous to conclude simply thus, that Polonius's lack of distinction is a metalepsis of the ideal of disinterestedness. But the introduction of Abraham's reading of Polonius allows us to consider how texts can be reread for what haunts them in a manner that allows for a critical response.

What marks Sachs's response to *Black Hamlet*, as I have been insisting, is his liberal humanism and his insistence on sameness. While he begins his study of Chavafambira in this *purely academic* frame, by the time he writes *Black Anger*, a text he believes to be more overtly political than *Black Hamlet*, he clearly feels anger and frustration on Chavafambira's behalf, an anger shared by Hellmann as evidenced in her criticism of the failure to assimilate "Natives" economically. Sachs interestingly creates a chiasmic displacement in his second edition title: *Black Anger*. His own growing anger is attributed to Chavafambira (who appears to have shared the same degree of anger when *Black Hamlet* was composed). Sachs's anger concerning the treatment of Chavafambira by the authorities could thus be read rather in the manner that Sachs read *Hamlet* itself. He writes his own anger out through the form of literary biography, and begins to work it through; in that sense, it is rather like the sublimation he attributes to the grieving Shakespeare. What we see is a working through of the assault on liberal democracy sublimated into writing as moral outrage. But just as Caruth saw an ethics of trauma evident in another's writing, that is, in the gaps, silences, and hauntings, we see that there is something that remains of a trauma that can be mourned by the traditional intellectual, but can be only lamented melancholically in the trace of inassimilability, that is, in the phantom, which we perceive in Chavafambira, and indeed, in Maggie and the other women in the text.

The refusal to assimilate brings the affect of the subaltern into the archive, an affect that can be recognized only psychoanalytically. If the archive appears by some to be a national monument and thus a collective memory, it can also be a home for the unhomely and unbeautiful: the phantoms from *limbo patrum*.

Coda: The Lament

Derrida's dedication in *Spectres of Marx* interestingly explores the problems of the "representative" in the context of mourning. It is a dedication that reads more like a lament, and goes to the South African communist antiapartheid activist Chris Hani, who had been killed just prior to the publication. As in "Apartheid: Racism's Last Word," Derrida sees apartheid as an exemplary form of racism, a metonymy that holds much in common with all other forms of racism, which find their extreme incarnation in that political system. While it is exemplary, it is also singular in Derrida's logic. His dedication is a musing on the move from metonymy to synecdoche, and then on to singularity, and thus, for the purposes of our discussion of the South African study *Black Hamlet,* a useful marker of postcolonial melancholic analysis that shows us once again how *the time is out of joint:*

> One name for another, a part for the whole: the historic violence of Apartheid can always be treated as a metonymy. In its past as well as in its present. By diverse paths (condensation, displacement, expression, or representation), one can always decipher through its singularity so many other kinds of violence going on in the world. At once part, cause, effect, example, what is happening there *translates* what *takes place* here, always here, wherever one is and wherever one looks, closest to home. Infinite responsibility, therefore, no rest allowed for any form of good conscience.

But one should never speak of the assassination of a man as a figure, not even as exemplary figure in the logic of an emblem, a rhetoric of the flag or of martyrdom. A man's life, as unique as his death, will always be more than a paradigm and something other than a symbol. And this is precisely what a proper name should always name.[1]

So in this logic of the lament—where Hani's greatness (as well as the magnitude of apartheid) becomes metonymic of all assassinations, and then the synecdoche of it—the singularity and the difference of Hani is what remains: "A man's life, as unique as his death." But this word "unique" begs questions; on the one hand, it would appear to signify singularity, that is, his incommensurability and unexchangeability; on the other, it would appear to suggest his particularity, or the commensurable (and exchangeable details of his life) that mark him as a character. The two appear to exist together in this citation, part spirit, part flesh. While particularity by itself could be exemplary, it is its meshing with singularity that marks lament; pure singularity would make lament meaningless. But it is also singularity that causes lament to be a function of melancholia rather than simply of mourning. Its singularity, however, in order to be marked with ghostliness, has to involve the flesh of particularity. Seeing melancholia as all flesh, and all particularity, is, however, a symptom of melancholia itself—one we have analyzed as demetaphorization—the literalizing of something that is experienced concretely but involves structures of melancholia born of the incommensurable.

While the organic intellectual was in a sense born in Hamlet's moment, when the communal and the individual world came together and when changes in the structure of society (Freud's secular advance of civilization) had caused a change in relations of filiation, the ghost, whether the greedy ghost who sold out one country for another as Abraham would have it, or the wronged ghost, who was usurped by his adulterous brother—part particular flesh of the past and part the structure of the trace—also began to cast its shadow over filiation and affiliation alike. Such a logic of haunting, mourning, and melancholia as a part of the structure of the everyday rather than as particularly one of the loss or death of a person, thing, or idea suggests a notion of temporality, historicity, and development that has implications for the understanding of postcolonial temporality of the nation.

Understanding temporality in postcolonial nationhood means taking account of the differences between mourning and melancholia, and how these concepts relate to those of the organic and traditional intellectuals. Understanding use value and the subaltern as back formations that always inform our understanding of exchange or of civil society, is necessary but insufficient, rather like marking subalternity or use value as liminal points on a framework or border, or the Lacanian Real. Such a reading alone would take anything substantive out of the back formation, make it a purely speculative factor, and create it as a structural origin of symptoms, something that would be as reductionist as claiming that Marx invented the symptom. Melancholia, however, more than mourning—and allowing for identification of the unassimilable past—leaves the mark of both subalternity and the difficulty of entry into civil society.

Rather like Benjamin in *The Origin of German Tragic Drama,* Derrida in "Archive Fever" speaks of the archive as a kind of aporia; it is both collective memory and the origin of memory—the point at which memory ceases is where the archive begins to perform its function. In other words, the existence of the archive appears to find its origin in aporetic form, as a monument of, and a memorial to, collective memory. In the case of the national archive, its existence is testimony to the will of the nation, or, in Renan's terms, the daily plebiscite that wills the nation into existence: remembering to forget, or assimilating psychically, the events that threaten to unsettle the official national narrative housed in the archive. Memorialization thus assists in assimilation because of the apparent introjection of traumatic events that highlight conflict and betrayal. But they become archived precisely at the moment when they fail to exist in memory, that is, when they must appear to be accounted for in the national narrative. The creation of a collective memory is thus an instrument of laying to rest, or of not needing to remember, remembering to forget. The archive appears, then, to be the locus of the spirit of the nation, and is accounted for as memory in order that its existence is willed, that is, that each anonymous individual who constitutes the national body is invested in its existence, and refers to it as the safe house of the national narrative.[2]

The archive, of course, holds in it other forms of knowledge, however, and it is perhaps through reading its silences and its hauntings that the nationalist blind spots of nations can begin to have critical relationship toward those narratives. The ghosts, the material aspect that problematizes the rather romantically conceived spirit of the nation, in a sense demand a more critical response to the narratives of nationalism. What cannot be mourned thus gives rise to a critical agency that we could call the melancholic postcoloniality that characterizes *limbo patrum*.

Such a claim is clearly massive, and represents a departure from the quite specific studies that have characterized this book: Freud's interest in archaeology and anthropology and their relationship to nationalism; the use of psychoanalysis by members of the negritude movement in Martinique and the particular form of existential psychoanalysis employed by Sartre to discuss issues of colonialism and race more broadly; the differences between the early and late works of Fanon, Mannoni, and Memmi in Martinique, Algeria, Madagascar, and Tunisia; the parochialism of uses of Lacanian psychoanalysis to discuss issues of nationalism and the ethics of psychoanalysis in discussions of contemporary transnational feminism; and Hamlet in the colonial context. Clearly, I have made claims from the first chapter of the book to the last about melancholia and nationalism, and the importance of the critical response. To call this special psychical agency that arises from melancholia "postcolonial" is in a sense to falsely reify something called the "postcolonial" and the "colonial" and is to ignore the empirical fact that some of the fiercest forms of nationalism today are located in the formerly colonized third world. On the one hand, specificity has been the calling of the project; on the other is the claim — one that does not distinguish between the different forms of colonialism in various historical periods and in distinct contexts — that all these affect people of different class backgrounds and different genders. And perhaps the claim is symptomatic, in that it embodies a demetaphorization that highlights something that can be understood only figuratively: the broad and somewhat dubious category of the postcolonial and postcoloniality. But my own interest in doing this perhaps highlights something else: that the inheritance of certain forms of nation-statehood in postcolonial contexts draws attention to a larger flaw in nationalist discourse more broadly, one that is frequently treated with apparent disinterest in the first world in spite of losses, traumas, and betrayals that have thrown the purity of the concept of nation-state into question. Such an idea, in a sense, takes us back to where we began, with the manner in which the study of the relationship between psychoanalysis, colonialism, and feminism sheds light not only on psychoanalysis outside its most usual province, but also on its most local context. While I have highlighted the critical nature of postcoloniality in this regard, it is to make a claim about nationalism more broadly, the role of the archive, and the *limbo patrum,* which, in its very specific formations, haunts all of us who live under the shadow of the nation-state.

Notes

Preface

The epigraph is taken from Luce Irigaray, *Speculum of the Other Woman,* trans. Gillian C. Gill (Ithaca, N.Y.: Cornell University Press, 1985), 365.

1   Louis Althusser, *For Marx* (London: Verso, 1996), 114. (*Pour Marx* [Paris: François Maspero, 1965], 113–14.)

2   Althusser, "To My English Readers," in *For Marx,* 13.

3   Ibid., 14.

4   Aimé Césaire, "Liminaire," *Présence Africaine* 57 (1966): 97; Fredric Jameson, *The Political Unconscious* (Ithaca, N.Y.: Cornell University Press, 1982).

5   "The notion of historical trauma represents . . . an attempt to conceptualize how history sometimes manages to *interrupt* or even *deconstitute* what a society assumes to be its master narratives and immanent Necessity—to undo our imaginary relation to the symbolic order, as well as to the other elements within the social formation with which that order is imbricated." Kaja Silverman, *Male Subjectivity at the Margins* (London: Routledge, 1992), 55.

Introduction: Worlding Psychoanalysis

1   Jacques Derrida, "Geopsychoanalysis," in *The Psychoanalysis of Race,* ed. Christopher Lane (New York: Columbia University Press, 1998), 66.

2   Ibid., 87.

3   The statement by Daniel Widlöcher can be found on the website of the IPA at http://www.ipa.org.uk/Durban-memo.htm, and the full report by the attending committee, written by Dr. Afaf Mahfouz, can be found at http://www.ipa.org.uk/Durban.htm.

4   Martin Heidegger, "The Origin of the Work of Art," in *Basic Writings,* ed. David Farrell Krell (New York: Harper and Row, 1977), 185.

5 Martin Heidegger, "The Thing," in *Poetry, Language, Thought,* trans. Albert Hofstadter (New York: Perennial Classics, 2001), 177.

6 Gayatri Chakravorty Spivak, *A Critique of Postcolonial Reason* (Cambridge, Mass.: Harvard University Press, 1999), 211–13. Also see Elizabeth Grosz and Gayatri Chakravorty Spivak, "Criticism, Feminism, and the Institution: An Interview with Gayatri Chakravorty Spivak," *Thesis Eleven* 10/11 (1984/1985): 175–87. For her characterization of her reading of Heidegger as a vulgarization, see Spivak, "Three Women's Texts and a Critique of Imperialism," *Critical Inquiry* 12 (Autumn 1985): 260 n.1.

7 Gayatri Chakravorty Spivak's notions of "worlding" can be found in *In Other Worlds: Essays in Cultural Politics* (New York: Methuen, 1987).

8 Carl Schorske, *Fin-de-Siècle Vienna: Politics and Culture* (New York: Knopf, 1980), 183.

9 Ibid., 186.

10 Ibid., 203.

11 Tom Nairn, *The Break-Up of Britain: Crisis and Neo-nationalism* (London: NLB, 1977), 359.

12 Robert Young's *Postcolonialisms* (Oxford: Blackwell, 2001) gives a wonderful genealogy of the relationship between the communist internationals and decolonization movements.

13 Edward Said, *Culture and Imperialism* (New York: Vintage, 1994), 66.

14 See, for example, Gauri Vishwanathan's *Masks of Conquest* (New York: Columbia University Press, 1989); Sara Suleri's *The Rhetoric of British India* (Chicago: Chicago University Press, 1992); Antony Anghie's "Finding the Peripheries," *Harvard International Law Journal* 40, no. 1 (Winter 1999): 1–80; Dipesh Chakrabarty, "Postcoloniality and the Artifice of History: Who Speaks for 'Indian' Pasts?" *Representations* 37 (Winter 1992): 1–24; James Clifford, *The Predicament of Culture* (Cambridge, Mass.: Harvard University Press, 1988); James Clifford and George Marcus, *Writing Culture* (Berkeley: University of California Press, 1986).

15 Chakrabarty, "Postcoloniality and the Artifice of History," 24.

16 Mary Ann Doane, *Femmes Fatales* (London: Routledge, 1991), 211.

17 Partha Chatterjee, *The Nation and Its Fragments: Colonial and Postcolonial Histories* (Princeton: Princeton University Press, 1993); Benedict Anderson, *Imagined Communities: Reflections on the Origin and Spread of Nationalism* (London: Verso Books, 1983).

18 Ernest Renan, "What Is a Nation?" (1882), in *Nation and Narration,* ed. Homi K. Bhabha (New York: Routledge, 1990), 8–22.

19 Pierre Nora, "Preface to the English Language Edition," *Realms of Memory* (New York: Columbia University Press, 1996), 1:xxiv.

20 Pierre Nora, "Between Memory and History," in *Realms of Memory,* 1:20.

21 Lawrence Kritzman, "Foreword: In Remembrance of Things French," in *Realms of Memory,* ed. Nora, xiii.

22 Richard Werbner, ed., *Memory and the Postcolony: African Anthropology and the Critique of Power* (London: Zed Books, 1998), 2–3.

23 Jacques Derrida has written on the peculiar trend in asking forgiveness for the unforgivable in *On Cosmopolitanism and Forgiveness,* trans. Mark Dooley and Michael Hughes (London: Routledge, 2001).

24 Shoshana Felman and Dori Laub, *Testimony* (London: Routledge, 1993).

25 Cathy Caruth, *Unclaimed Experience* (Baltimore, Md.: Johns Hopkins University Press, 1996).

26 Sudhir Kakar, *The Colors of Violence: Cultural Identities, Religion, and Conflict* (Chicago: University of Chicago Press, 1996); Vamik Volkan, "On Chosen Trauma," *Mind and Human Interaction* 3 (1991): 13.

27 For an excellent genealogy of the concept of trauma, and analysis of the problematic way in which it has been employed recently, see Ruth Leys, *Trauma: A Genealogy* (Chicago: University of Chicago Press, 2000).

28 Walter Benjamin, "The Storyteller," in *Illuminations,* trans. Harry Zohn (New York: Schocken Books, 1969), 87.

29 See Homi Bhabha, "DissemiNation," in *Nation and Narration,* ed. Homi Bhabha (London: Routledge, 1990), 291–322; " 'Race,' Time and the Revision of Modernity," in *The Location of Culture* (London: Routledge, 1994), 236–256.

30 C. L. R. James, "Notes on *Hamlet,*" in *The C. L. R. James Reader* (Oxford: Blackwell, 1992), 245.

31 Edward Said, *Orientalism* (London: Routledge and Kegan Paul, 1978); see also, for example, Ranajit Guha and Gayatri Spivak, eds., *Selected Subaltern Studies* (New York: Oxford University Press, 1988).

32 James, "Notes on *Hamlet,*" 244.

33 The most sustained of such spectral musings is Jacques Derrida's *Specters of Marx: The State of the Debt, the Work of Mourning, and the New International* (New York: Routledge, 1994), 6. (*Spectres de Marx* [Editions Galilée, 1993]).

34 David Lloyd and Paul Thomas, *Culture and the State* (London: Routledge, 1998), 1–30.

35 Sigmund Freud, *The Standard Edition of the Complete Psychological Works of Sigmund Freud,* 24 vols., trans. and ed. James Strachey (London: Hogarth Press and the Institute of Psychoanalysis, 1953–74) [hereafter referred to as *S.E.*]. "Mourning and Melancholia," *S.E.* 14:243.

36 It is this form of pathological mourning that Žižek discusses in "Melancholy and the Act." He is right to criticize those who claim that a form of melancholia is in place when someone seems to mourn permanently her lost past, lost culture, or some other loss that becomes constitutive of conceiving oneself as belonging to a melancholic group. However, my agreement with him extends only up to this point, as he insists that what is felt as lost is the constitutive lack in relation to the Lacanian Symbolic. I do not accept that all feelings of loss, whether the content of that loss is known or unknown, are merely reconfigurations of structural lack. See Slavoj Žižek, "Melancholy and the Act," *Critical Inquiry* 26, no. 4 (Summer 2000): 657–72.

37 Gayatri Chakravorty Spivak, "Echo," *New Literary History: A Journal of Theory and Interpretation* 24, no. 1 (Winter 1993): 17–43.

38 See Jacques Derrida, "*Fors:* The Anglish Words of Nicolas Abraham and Maria Torok," trans. Barbara Johnson, Foreword to Nicolas Abraham and Maria Torok, *The Wolfman's Magic Word: A Cryptonymy,* trans. Nicholas Rand (Minneapolis: University of Minnesota Press, 1983), xi–xlviii.

39 I am by no means the only person to make such a claim. See, in the context of

coloniality, Emily Apter, *Continental Drift: From National Characters to Virtual Subjects* (Chicago: University of Chicago Press, 1999), for an example of work making use of this idea.

40 Freud, "Letter 18," *S.E.* 1:188.

41 Frantz Fanon, *Black Skin, White Masks,* trans. Charles Lam Markmann (1952; New York: Grove Press 1967); *The Wretched of the Earth,* trans. Constance Farrington (New York: Grove Press, 1966).

42 Jean-Paul Sartre, *Black Orpheus,* trans. S. W. Allen (1948; Paris: Présence Africaine, 1976), 34–39.

43 Sartre, *What Is Literature?,* trans. David Fretchman (1945; Bristol: Methuen, 1967), 136–37.

44 See Fanon, *Black Skin, White Masks.*

1. Psychoanalysis and Archaeology

The epigraph is taken from Michel Foucault, *The Order of Things,* trans. A. Sheridan Smith (New York: Pantheon Books, 1970), 375.

1 Foucault, *The Order of Things,* 378.

2 Ibid., 378.

3 Ibid., 381.

4 Ibid., xi.

5 Ibid., xiii.

6 Sigmund Freud, *The Standard Edition of the Complete Psychological Works of Sigmund Freud,* 24 vols., trans. and ed. James Strachey (London: Hogarth Press and the Institute of Psychoanalysis, 1953–74) [hereafter referred to as *S.E.*]. See *S.E.* 2:8; *S.E.* 20:263–64.

7 Freud, "Construction in Analysis" (1937), *S.E.* 23:260.

8 Freud uses the Latin term *Agieren.* The French translators use *mise en acte.* It therefore appears that Foucault's *jouir* in *le savoir de l'homme joue* is not intended to reference the Freudian schema. See Freud, "Remembering, Repeating and Working Through," *S.E.* 11:151.

9 Judith Butler, *Gender Trouble* (London: Routledge, 1990).

10 Jacques Lacan, "Function and Field of Speech and Language," in *Ecrits,* trans. Alan Sheridan (New York: Norton, 1977), 48.

11 Ibid., 48.

12 Ibid., 49.

13 See Donald P. Spence, *The Freudian Metaphor* (New York: Norton, 1987); Lydia Flem, "L'Archéologie chez Freud," *L'Archaïque: Nouvelle Revue de Psychanalyse* 26 (Autumn 1982): 71–93. See also Donald Kuspit, "A Mighty Metaphor: The Analogy of Archaeology and Psychoanalysis," in *Sigmund Freud and Art,* ed. Lynn Gamwell and Richard Wells (London: Thames and Hudson, 1989), 133–51; Sabine Hake, "*Saxa Ioquuntur:* Freud's Archaeology of the Text," *boundary 2* 20, no. 1 (Spring 1993): 169–70.

14 Michael Rowlands, "The Politics of Identity in Archaeology," in *Social Construction of the Past: Representation as Power* (London: Routledge, 1994), 133. See also R. Robert-

son, "After Nostalgia: Wilful Nostalgia and Modernity," in *Theories of Modernity and Postmodernity,* ed. B. Turner (London: Sage, 1990), 31–45.

15 Sigmund Freud, *The Complete Letters of Sigmund Freud to Wilhelm Fliess,* trans. and ed. Jeffrey Mousaieff Masson (Cambridge, Mass.: Harvard University Press, 1985), 353.

16 Heinrich Schliemann, *Ilios: The City and Country of the Trojans* (London: John Murray, 1880), 1.

17 Freud, *The Complete Letters of Sigmund Freud to Wilhelm Fliess,* 353.

18 See Antonietta and Gérard Haddad, *Freud en Italie: Psychanalyse du voyage* (Paris: Editions Albin Michel S.A., 1995).

19 Sigmund Freud, *The Question of Lay Analysis S.E.* 20:212.

20 Donald Kuspit, "A Mighty Metaphor: The Analogy of Archaeology and Psychoanalysis," in *Sigmund Freud and Art,* ed. Lynn Gamwell and Richard Wells (London: Freud Museum, 1989), 134.

21 *S.E.* 7:12.

22 Sabine Hake, "*Saxa Ioquuntur:* Freud's Archaeology of the Text," *boundary 2* 20, no. 1 (Spring 1993): 169–70.

23 *S.E.* 4:15.

24 Kuspit, "Mighty Metaphor," 151.

25 Rowlands, "Politics of Identity in Archaeology," 130.

26 See Darius Ornston, "Strachey's Influence—A Preliminary Report," *International Journal of Psychoanalysis* 63 (1982), or his edited volume on translation problems regarding Freud, *Translating Freud* (New Haven: Yale University Press, 1992).

27 See Edmund Engelman, ed., *Bergasse 19: Sigmund Freud's Home and Office, Vienna 1938* (New York: Basic Books, 1976); Gamwell and Wells, eds., *Sigmund Freud and Art.* See also James Clifford, "Immigrant," in *Routes: Travel and Translation in the Late Twentieth Century* (Cambridge, Mass.: Harvard University Press, 1997), 279–97.

28 Sigmund Freud, *The Letters of Sigmund Freud,* ed. Ernst Freud (New York: Basic Books, 1975), 173. The letter is dated 19 October 1885. It is in his letter of 21 October that he addresses Martha as his "beloved treasure" (175).

29 Freud, *Letters,* 187. The letter is dated 3 December 1885.

30 See selections of Sir John Lubbock's writings in *Scientific Lectures,* 2d ed. (London: Macmillan, 1890).

31 The Jensen and Freud texts are published together as Wilhelm Jensen, *Gradiva: Delusion and Dream in Wilhelm Jensen's "Gradiva"* (Los Angeles: Sun and Moon, 1992).

32 Biographers such as Marjorie Braymer and Caroline Moorehead note a great deal of fabrication on the part of Schliemann. See Braymer, *The Walls of Windy Troy* (London: Victor Gollancz, 1962), and Caroline Moorehead, *The Lost Treasures of Troy* (London: Phoenix Giants, 1994).

33 Mary Jacobus speaks of this prioritization of the scientific over the literary in *Reading Woman: Essays in Feminist Criticism* (London: Methuen, 1988), 83–110.

34 Lynn and Gray Poole, *One Passion, Two Loves: The Schliemanns of Troy* (London: Victor Gollancz Ltd., 1967), 20, 36.

35 Schliemann, *Ilios,* 66.

36 Ibid., 66.

37 See Martin Bernal, *Black Athena: The Afroasiatic Roots of Classical Civilisation,* Volume 1: *The Fabrication of Ancient Greece, 1785–1985* (London: Free Association Books, 1987). One could say that Bernal is guilty of the same glamorization that he critiques in spite of the fact that his argument constructs itself around the Romantic erection of Ancient Greece. He replaces the idealized Greece with a similarly idealized Egypt. The argument does not disrupt the structure of the imperial attitude in itself. Although much valuable information is communicated, the attitude censured is simply deferred and eventually reinscribed. This does indisputably serve a political function, but one that does not really establish the way in which *knowledge about man is made possible* but rather the knowledge itself. For a fascinating account of both Schliemann's travels and the fate of the treasures, see Caroline Moorehead, *Lost and Found: The 9,000 Treasures of Troy—Heinrich Schliemann and the Gold That Got Away* (New York: Viking Penguin, 1996).

38 Grahame Clark, *Archaeology and Society* (London: Methuen, 1939), 196–98.

39 Sigmund Freud, "Über die weibliche Sexualität" (1931), in *Gesammelte Werke,* 14 vols. (London: Imago Publishing, 1948), 14:519.

40 Sigmund Freud, "Female Sexuality" (1931), *S.E.* 21:226.

41 Freud, "Medusa's Head" ([1922] published posthumously: 1940), *S.E.* 18:273–74.

42 See Peter L. Rudnytsky, *Freud and Oedipus* (New York: Columbia University Press, 1987), 348.

43 Sigmund Freud, "The Uncanny" (1919), *S.E.* 17:231.

44 Rita Ransohoff in *Bergasse 19,* ed. Engelman, 59. Also Ernest Jones, *The Life and Work of Sigmund Freud,* 3 vols. (New York: Basic Books, 1953–57), 2:14.

45 For an interesting account of literary inscriptions of women as the dark continent / woman as Africa, see Rebecca Stott, "The Dark Continent: Africa as Female Body in Haggard's Adventure Fiction," *Feminist Review* 32 (Summer 1989): 69–89; see also Peter Brantlinger, "The Genealogy of the Myth of the Dark Continent," *Critical Inquiry* 12, no. 1 (Autumn 1985): 166–203, reprinted in Peter Brantlinger, *Rule of Darkness: British Literature and Imperialism, 1830–1914* (Ithaca, N.Y.: Cornell University Press, 1988), 173–98; see also Bette London, "Reading Race and Gender in Conrad's Dark Continent," *Criticism: A Quarterly for Literature and the Arts* 31, no. 3 (Summer 1989): 235–52.

46 Anne McClintock, *Imperial Leather* (London: Routledge, 1995); Sander Gilman, "Black Bodies, White Bodies: Toward an Iconography of Female Sexuality in Late-Nineteenth-Century Art, Medicine, and Literature," *Critical Inquiry* 12, no. 1 (Autumn 1985): 204–42.

47 Sigmund Freud, "Die Frage der Laienanalyse" [The Question of Lay Analysis] (1926), *Gesammelte Werke,* 14:241.

48 Freud, "The Question of Lay Analysis," *S.E.* 20:212.

49 Henry Morton Stanley, *Through the Dark Continent* (New York: Harper and Brothers, 1878).

50 For an excellent reading of Stanley, see Adam Hochschild, *King Leopold's Ghost: A Story of Greed, Terror, and Heroism in Colonial Africa* (Boston: Houghton Mifflin, 1998).

51 Henry Morton Stanley, *The Autobiography of Henry M. Stanley,* ed. Dorothy Stanley (Boston: Houghton Mifflin, 1909), 296–97.

52 See Freud, "Medusa's Head," *S.E.* 18:273–74.

53 Dorothy Stanley, ed., *The Autobiography of Henry M. Stanley*, vi.

54 Ibid., ix.

55 Henry M. Stanley, *The Autobiography*, 6.

56 Sigmund Freud, "Delusions and Dreams in Jensen's *Gradiva*" (1906 [1907]), *S.E.* 9:40. Freud also uses the image of Pompeii for describing repression. An example of this can be found in "Notes upon a Case of Obsessional Neurosis" (1909), *S.E.* 10:176–77.

57 David Macey, in *Lacan in Contexts*, writes of Freud's use of the metaphor of the "dark continent," saying: "In keeping with a rationalist ideology of enlightenment, he frequently applies metaphors of darkness—often drawn from archaeology and exploration—to areas of ignorance. . . . [Freud] appears to be blissfully ignorant of the political connotations of his metaphor [the dark continent]. Within the discourse of late-nineteenth-century colonialism, Africa is moist, dark, unknown. It is, however, amenable to penetration, providing that the appropriate degree of force is used." David Macey, *Lacan in Contexts* (London: Verso, 1988), 178–79.

58 Freud, "Question of Lay Analysis," *S.E.* 20:254.

59 The letter from Freud to Jung (26 May 1907) can be found in William McGuire, *The Freud/Jung Letters,* trans. Ralph Manheim and R. F. C. Hull (London: Hogarth Press and Routledge and Kegan Paul, 1974), 51.

60 The Freudian superego was not theorized until well after the essay on *Gradiva*. The term first appears in 1923 in "The Ego and the Id," *S.E.* 19:3.

61 Jacobus, *Reading Woman*, 87.

62 Sarah Kofman, *Quatres Roman Analytiques* (Paris: Editions Galilée, 1973), 113.

63 Freud, "Delusion and Dreams in Jensen's *Gradiva,*" *S.E.* 9:85.

64 Ibid., 87–88.

65 Guy Rosolato, "Que contemplait Freud sur l'Acropole?" *Nouvelle Revue de Psychanalyse* 15 (Spring 1977): 135. My translation.

> Avec le Parthénon, le contenant apparaît particulièrement ravagé, n'étant que vestige; mais si on l'imagine intact, se recompose le lieu saint (la *cella*) dans lequel on pénètre par *une* porte (alors qu'on le divine entre les fentes qui ménagent les colonnes), lieu qui contient la statue de la déesse et qui ne réunit pas les fidèles, puisque le culte se déroule devant le temple. L'inconnu est localisé a l'intérieur. . . . La Vierge, comme objet de perspective, corps phallique, déesse de la raison et de l'intelligence, conjure le vide central et fixe l'inconnu.

66 Wilhelm Jensen, *Gradiva*, trans. Helen M. Downey (London: George Allen and Unwin, 1921), 53.

67 Sigmund Freud, *Correspondance 1873–1939* (Paris: Gallimard, 1966), 283. My translation.

68 Harry Slochower, "Freud's *Déjà Vu* on the Acropolis: A Symbolic Relic of '*mater nuda,*'" *Psychoanalytic Quarterly* 1 (1970): 90–102.

69 Sigmund Freud, "Extracts from the Fliess papers: Letter 70, October 3, 1897," *S.E.* 1:261–62.

70 Freud, "A Disturbance of Memory on the Acropolis" (1936), *S.E.* 22:237–48. The letter has echoes of Keats's sonnet "On First Looking into Chapman's Homer" and, in turn, of Homer and Cortez, to whom Keats alludes in the sonnet.

71 Michel Foucault, *The Archaeology of Knowledge* (London: Tavistock, 1972), 12.

72 Ibid., 191.

73 G. C. Spivak, "Postcoloniality and Value," in *Literary Theory Today,* ed. P. Collier and H. Geyer-Ryan (Cambridge, U.K.: Polity Press, 1990), 228.

74 Sigmund Freud, "A Disturbance of Memory on the Acropolis," *S.E.* 22:245–46.

75 J. Moussaieff Masson, *The Oceanic Feeling: The Origins of Religious Sentiment in Ancient India* (Boston: D. Reidel, 1980).

76 See Frederic Morton, *A Nervous Splendour: Vienna 1888–1889* (Harmondsworth: Penguin, 1979), 281.

77 Freud, *The Letters of Sigmund Freud,* 341–42.

78 Freud, "Why War?" (1933), *S.E.* 22:197–215.

79 Freud, "On Transience" (1915), *S.E.* 14:303–7.

80 Freud, *S.E.* 23:301. This was a letter that appeared in *Time and Tide* in 1938 in response to a request for a contribution to a special issue on anti-Semitism.

81 Freud, "Splitting of the Ego in Defence" (1940 [1938]), *S.E.* 23:275–76.

82 Freud, "Disturbance," *S.E.* 22:248.

83 Ibid., 240.

84 Ibid., 247.

85 Ibid., 245.

86 Freud, *S.E.* 5:399.

87 Freud, "Disturbance," *S.E.* 22:241.

88 Freud, "A Comment on Anti-Semitism," *S.E.* 23:292.

89 Dipesh Chakrabarty formulates this concept in his essay "Postcoloniality and the Artifice of History: Who Speaks for 'Indian' Pasts?" *Representations* 37 (Winter 1992): 1–24. He later dismisses the idea.

90 Freud, "Mourning and Melancholia," in *S.E.* 14:247–48.

2. Freud in the Sacred Grove

Epigraphs are taken from Sigmund Freud, *Totem and Taboo,* in *The Standard Edition of the Complete Psychological Works of Sigmund Freud,* trans. and ed. James Strachey, 24 vols. (London: Hogarth Press and the Institute of Psychoanalysis, 1953–74), 13:1 [hereafter referred to as *S.E.*]; Freud, *Totem and Taboo, S.E.* 13:131; Michel Foucault, *The Order of Things,* trans. A. Sheridan Smith (New York: Pantheon Books, 1970), 377.

1 Quoted in Lucille Ritvo, *Darwin's Influence on Freud* (New Haven, Conn.: Yale University Press, 1990), 214.

2 Harold Bloom, "Reading Freud: Transference, Taboo, and Truth," in *Centre and Labyrinth: Essays in Honour of Northrop Frye,* ed. Eleanor Cook et al. (Toronto: University of Toronto Press, 1983), 310.

3 Mary Ann Doane, *Femmes Fatales* (London: Routledge, 1991), 211.

4 Ernest Gellner's chapter, "Freud's Social Contract," makes a similar point in relation to "Moses and Monotheism." See his *Anthropology and Politics* (Oxford: Blackwell, 1996).

5 E. B. Tylor, *Primitive Culture* (London: John Murray, 1891), 2 vols.

6 Jean-Antoine-Nicolas Condorcet, *Sketch for a Historical Picture of the Progress of the Human Mind,* trans. June Barraclough (London: Weidenfeld and Nicholson Press, 1955).

7   Darwin, disagreeing with this principle, suggested that there was no universal devel-
     opment or advancement because organisms develop as they require, depending on
     need and the things with which they come into contact. Lucille Ritvo's *Darwin's In-
     fluence on Freud* (New Haven, Conn.: Yale University Press, 1990) is extremely instruc-
     tive on the relationship between Lamarck and Darwin and on the significance of this
     for Freud.

8   Freud, *Totem and Taboo*, S.E. 13:75–76.

9   James Frazer, *The Golden Bough: A Study in Magic and Religion* (1911–14), 3d ed. (Evans-
     ton, Ill.: American Theological Library Association, 1992), microfiche, 1:10.

10   For selections by Bastian, see Klaus-Peter Koepping, ed., *Adolf Bastian and the Psychic
     Unity of Mankind: The Foundations of Anthropology in Nineteenth-Century Germany* (St.
     Lucia, N.Y.: University of Queensland Press, 1983).

11   Tylor, *Primitive Culture*, 2:142.

12   Ibid., 2:109.

13   As Willis says, "the renowned self-confidence and unshakeable paternal authority of
     Britain's colonial administrators expressed a deep awareness of their country's awe-
     somely responsible position at the top of the social-evolutionary ladder." Roy Willis,
     "An Indigenous Critique of Colonialism: The Fipa of Tanzania," in *Anthropology and
     the Colonial Encounter*, ed. Talal Asad (Atlantic Highlands, N.J.: Humanities Press, 1973),
     245.

14   Tylor, *Primitive Culture*, 1:26.

15   Ibid., 2:108.

16   Hume, *Natural History of Religion* (section 3), quoted in Tylor, *Primitive Culture*, 1:477;
     see also Freud, *Totem and Taboo*, S.E. 13.

17   Tylor, *Primitive Culture*, 2:142–43.

18   Ibid., 2:453.

19   Emile Durkheim, *Elementary Forms of Religious Life* (London: Allen and Unwin, 1976),
     223.

20   Talal Asad has made this argument concerning the exaggerated role in "Afterword:
     From the History of Colonial Anthropology to the Anthropology of Western Hege-
     mony," in *Colonial Situations: Essays on the Contextualization of Ethnographic Knowledge*,
     ed. George Stocking (Madison: University of Wisconsin Press, 1991), 315.

21   Raymond Williams, *Keywords: A Vocabulary of Culture and Society* (Oxford: Oxford Uni-
     versity Press, 1976).

22   See George Stocking, *Victorian Anthropology* (New York: Free Press, 1987).

23   Robert Young, *Colonial Desire* (London: Routledge, 1995).

24   Johannes Fabian, *Time and the Other* (New York: Columbia University Press, 1983).

25   V. Y. Mudimbe, *The Idea of Africa* (Bloomington: Indiana University Press, 1994), 59.

26   Ibid., 61.

27   Freud, *Totem and Taboo*, S.E. 13:56.

28   Ibid., 4 n.2.

29   Edwin Wallace, *Freud and Anthropology: A History and Appraisal* (New York: Interna-
     tional University Press, 1983).

30   Stocking, *Victorian Anthropology*, 262–66.

31   David Nonini, "Freud, Anteriority, and Imperialism," *Dialectical Anthropology* 17, no. 1

(1992): 26. See also Jacqueline Rose, "Freud in the Tropics," *History Workshop Journal* 47 (1999): 49–67.

32 Stocking, *Victorian Anthropology,* 16.

33 Freud, *Totem and Taboo, S.E.* 13:13.

34 Edwin Wallace has made a very convincing argument about the inaccuracy of Freud's description of primitive mourning. Wallace, *Freud and Anthropology.*

35 Freud, "Mourning and Melancholia," *S.E.* 14:243.

36 James Frazer, *The Golden Bough.* Ernest Gellner offers a useful reading of the politics of Frazer's work in relation to the history of the discipline of anthropology in *Anthropology and Politics.*

37 Some claim that Freud uses the Lamarckian model uncritically in spite of its discrediting by Darwin. (See, for example, Anthony Storr, *Freud* [Oxford: Oxford University Press, 1989], 88.) I, however, concur with Gellner that the transmission and refashioning of a feeling is cultural and social rather than genetic. See Gellner, *Anthropology and Politics,* 80–81.

38 Freud, *Totem and Taboo, S.E.* 13:67–68. The culmination of this comes later in the theorization of the superego. See *Ego and the Id* (1923), *S.E.* 19:3–66.

39 Foucault, *The Order of Things,* 376.

40 Freud, *Totem and Taboo, S.E.* 13:71.

41 Ibid., 73.

42 Ibid., 6.

43 Durkheim, *Elementary Forms of Religious Life,* 225.

44 Freud, *Totem and Taboo, S.E.* 13:29.

45 Ibid., 66.

46 Ibid., 74.

47 Ernest Gellner, *The Psychoanalytic Movement: The Cunning of Unreason* (1985; London: Fontana Press, 1993), 223.

48 Freud, *Group Psychology and the Analysis of the Ego, S.E.* 18:122.

49 Sigmund Freud, *A Phylogenetic Fantasy,* trans. Axel Hoffer and Peter T. Hoffer (1915; Cambridge, Mass.: Harvard University Press, 1987), 19.

50 Freud, *Phylogenetic Fantasy,* 19.

51 Ibid.

52 Freud, "On Narcissism," *S.E.* 14:76–77.

53 Ibid., 101–2.

54 Freud, *Group Psychology, S.E.* 18:116.

55 Ibid., 129.

56 Ibid., 122.

57 Ibid., 127.

58 Ritvo, *Darwin's Influence on Freud,* 61.

59 Sigmund Freud, "On the Grounds for Detaching a Particular Syndrome from Neurasthenia under the Description 'Anxiety Neurosis'" (1895), *S.E.* 3:109.

60 Freud, "Mourning and Melancholia," *S.E.* 14:244.

61 Ibid., 251.

62 Ibid., 247.

63 Ibid., 249.

64 Ibid., 253.

65 Ibid., 254–55.

66 Ibid., 256–57.

67 Ibid., 245.

68 Ibid., 252–53.

69 Ibid., 258.

70 Freud, *Group Psychology, S.E.* 18:125.

71 Ibid., 132.

72 Ibid., 132.

73 Freud, *Three Essays on the Theory of Sexuality, S.E.* 7:177–78.

74 Freud, *Totem and Taboo, S.E.* 13:73.

75 See *Journal des années des guerres, 1914–19* (Paris: Albin Michel, 1952).

76 William Thomas Starr, *Romain Rolland: One against All: A Biography* (The Hague: Mouton, 1971), 204–5.

77 Ibid., 203.

78 Ibid., 201.

79 Romain Rolland, *Mahatma Gandhi*, trans. Catherine D. Groth (New York: Century, 1924), 3–5.

80 Erik H. Erikson, *Gandhi's Truth: On the Origins of Militant Nonviolence* (Toronto: Norton, 1969), 43.

81 Sudhir Kakar, *The Analyst and the Mystic* (Chicago: University of Chicago Press, 1991), x.

82 Ibid., 65.

83 Freud, *On the History of the Psychoanalytic Movement, S.E.* 14:30.

84 Ashis Nandy, *The Savage Freud and Other Essays on Possible and Retrievable Selves* (Delhi: Oxford University Press, 1995), 81–144.

85 Kalpana Seshadri-Crooks, "The Primitive as Analyst: Postcolonial Feminism's Access to Psychoanalysis," *Cultural Critique* (Fall 1994): 175–218.

86 Nandy, *Savage Freud*, 136.

87 Freud, *Civilisation and Its Discontents, S.E.* 21:95.

88 Ibid., 103.

89 McClintock, *Imperial Leather* (New York: Routledge, 1995), 207–31.

90 Freud, *Civilisation and Its Discontents, S.E.* 21:93.

91 Gananath Obeyesekere, *The Work of Culture* (Chicago: University of Chicago Press, 1990).

92 Ibid., 241.

93 Nandy, *Savage Freud*, 82.

94 Catherine Clément and Sudhir Kakar's coauthored book *La Folle et le saint* (Paris: Seuil, 1993) offers a wonderful reading of how symptoms read as pathological in one context could as easily be read as mystical in another.

95 Nandy, *Savage Freud*, 102.

96 Bloom's analogical suggestion that *Totem and Taboo* is Freud's most interesting writing on the subject of transference is here given further credibility, as the transferential relationship, and acknowledgment of it in ethnography, was previously lacking.

97   Georges Devereux, *Ethnopsychoanalysis* (Berkeley: University of California Press, 1978), 66.

3. War, Decolonization, Psychoanalysis

The epigraph is taken from Michel Foucault, "Politics and Ethics: An Interview," in *The Foucault Reader* (New York: Pantheon, 1984), 374.

1   Arthur Rimbaud, *Illuminations,* trans. Louise Varèse, letters to Georges Izambard (13 May 1871) and Paul Demeny (15 May 1871), in "By Way of a Preface" (New York: New Directions, 1946). See also Jean-Paul Sartre, *The Transcendency of the Ego: An Existentialist Theory of Consciousness* (1937), trans. Forrest Williams and Robert Kirkpatrick (New York: Noonday Press, 1957).

2   Sartre, *Notebooks for an Ethics,* trans. David Pellauer (Chicago: University of Chicago Press, 1992), 175.

3   Jacques Lacan, "The Mirror Stage," in *Ecrits,* trans. Alan Sheridan (New York: Norton, 1977), 6.

4   Jean-Paul Sartre, *Being and Nothingness,* trans. Hazel Barnes (Secaucus, N.J.: Citadel Press, 1956), 726–27.

5   Sartre, *Notebooks for an Ethics,* trans. David Pellauer (Chicago: University of Chicago Press, 1992), 434–35.

6   Sartre, *Being and Nothingness,* 728–29.

7   Ibid., 727–28.

8   Sartre, *The Transcendence of the Ego,* 34 and 60.

9   For a further elaboration of Wallon's disciplinary allegiances, see Elisabeth Roudinesco, *Jacques Lacan and Co.: A History of Psychoanalysis in France 1925–198,* trans. Jeffrey Mehlman (Chicago: University of Chicago Press, 1990), 65–71.

10   "Le stade du miroir est bien loin de seulement connoter un phénomène qui se présente dans le développement de l'enfant. Il illustre le caractère conflictuel de la relation duelle." Jacques Lacan, *Le Seminaire livre IV* (1956–57; Paris: Editions du Seuil, 1994), 17.

11   See Emily Apter and William Piets, *Fetishism as Cultural Discourse* (Ithaca, N.Y.: Cornell University Press, 1990); Anne McClintock, *Imperial Leather* (London: Routledge, 1995).

12   See David Macey, *Lacan in Contexts* (London: Verso, 1988), 103.

13   Sartre, *Being and Nothingness,* 257.

14   Ibid., 729–30.

15   Freud, "An Autobiographical Study" (1925), in *The Standard Edition of the Complete Psychological Works of Sigmund Freud,* trans. and ed. James Strachey, 24 vols. (London: Hogarth Press and the Institute of Psychoanalysis, 1953–74), 20:3–76 [hereafter referred to as *S.E.*]; "Selbstdarstellung," in *Gesammelte Werke,* 18 vols. (London: Imago Publishing Co., 1948), 14:31–96.

16   Sartre, *Being and Nothingness,* 734.

17   Freud, *On the History of the Psychoanalytic Movement, S.E.* 14:20.

18   Freud, *Five Lectures on Psychoanalysis, S.E.* 11:33.

19   Freud, *S.E.* 1:271.

20   Freud, "The Future Prospects of Psychoanalytic Therapy" (1910), *S.E.* 11:145.

21 Sartre, *Being and Nothingness,* 728.

22 Ibid., 721.

23 Ibid., 732.

24 Sartre, *Notebooks* . . . , 316–17.

25 Sartre, *Being and Nothingness,* 708.

26 Ibid., 709.

27 Herbert Marcuse, "Sartre's Existentialism" (1948) and "Postscript" (1965), in *From Luther to Popper,* trans. Joris de Bres (London: Verso, 1972), 172, 189.

28 Ann Stoler, *Race and the Education of Desire: Foucault's "History of Sexuality" and the Colonial Order of Things* (Durham, N.C.: Duke University Press, 1995), 22–23.

29 See, for example, "L'idéologie de Vichy contre la pensée française," *Tropiques* 11 (May 1944): 94–103.

30 Lilyan Kesteloot, *Black Writers in French: A Literary History of Negritude* (1963), trans. Ellen Conroy Kennedy (Philadelphia, Pa.: Temple University Press, 1974); Sartre, "Black Orpheus," trans. S. W. Allen (1948; Paris: Présence Africaine, 1976), 34–39.

31 André Breton and Diego Rivera, "Art and Revolution" (1938), in Leon Trotsky, *"Culture and Socialism" and "Manifesto: Towards a Free Revolutionary Art"* (London: New Park Publications, 1975), 32.

32 Ibid.

33 Ibid., 10–23.

34 Sartre, "Black Orpheus," 39.

35 Sartre, *What Is Literature?,* trans. David Frechtman (1948; Bristol: Methuen, 1967), 136–37.

36 Ibid., 134.

37 Ibid., 136.

38 Ibid., 141.

39 Simone de Beauvoir, *The Ethics of Ambiguity,* trans. Bernard Frechtman (1948; Secaucus, N.J.: Citadel Press, 1997), 55.

40 Sartre, "Black Orpheus," 59.

41 Kesteloot, *Black Writers in French,* 45.

42 Frantz Fanon, *Black Skin, White Masks,* trans. Charles Lam Markman (1952; New York: Grove Weidenfeld, 1967); *The Wretched of Earth,* trans. Constance Farrington (1961; New York: Grove Press, 1963).

43 See James Clifford, *The Predicament of Culture* (Cambridge, Mass.: Harvard University Press, 1988), 122.

44 See Jean-Claude Blachère, *Les Totems d'André Breton: Surréalisme et primitivisme littéraire* (Paris: L'Harmattan, 1996).

45 André Breton and André Masson, *Martinique charmeuse des serpents* (1948; Paris: Jean-Jacques Pauvert, 1972), words on unpaginated illustrations.

46 André Breton, "Un grand poète noir," preface to *Memorandum on My Martinique* (New York: Brentano's, 1947), unpaginated.

47 Aimé Césaire and Pablo Picasso, *Corps Perdu* (Paris: Éditions Fragrance, 1950). (*Lost Body,* trans. Clayton Eshelman and Annette Smith [New York: George Brazilier, 1986]. Citations are from this bilingual edition.)

48 Picasso, *Corps Perdu,* 3.

49   Césaire, *Corps Perdu*, 8, 11.

50   See Suzanne Césaire, "Malaise d'une civilisation," *Tropiques* 5 (1942): 46–49.

51   Aimé Césaire, "Liminaire," *Présence Africaine* 57 (1966): 97.

52   Aimé Césaire, "Letter to Lilyan Kesteloot," quoted in Kesteloot, *Black Writers in French*, 262.

53   Frantz Fanon, *Black Skin, White Masks*, 144.

54   René Ménil, "L'Action foudroyante," *Tropiques* (October 1941): 60; "Lightning Effect," in *Refusal of the Shadow*, trans. Michael Richardson and Krzysztof Fijałkowski (London: Verso, 1996), 153.

55   Carl Jung, "The Concept of the Collective Unconscious" (1936), in *The Archetypes and the Collective Unconscious,* trans. R. F. C. Hull (London: Routledge, 1959), 48.

56   A. James Arnold, *Modernism and Negritude: The Poetry and Poetics of Aimé Césaire* (Cambridge, Mass.: Harvard University Press, 1981), 34.

57   André Breton, preface to *Memorandum . . . ,* unpaginated.

58   Fanon was very critical of this. See Fanon, *Black Skin, White Masks,* 39.

59   Sartre, "Black Orpheus," 11.

60   Ibid., 17.

61   Sartre, "Black Presence," in *The Writings of Jean-Paul Sartre, Vol. 2: Selected Prose,* trans. Richard McCleary (Evanston, Ill.: Northwestern University Press, 1974), 188. Originally published as "Présence noire" in the first issue of *Présence Africaine* (November–December 1947).

62   Sartre, "Appendix 2: Revolutionary Violence: The Oppression of Blacks in the United States," in *Notebooks for an Ethics,* trans. David Pellauer (Chicago: University of Chicago Press, 1992), 563.

63   Ibid., 569.

64   Ibid., 572–73.

65   Ibid., 566–67.

66   Marcuse, "Sartre's Existentialism," 175.

67   Aimé Césaire, "Poésie et Connaissance," *Tropiques* 12 (January 1945): 159.

68   Ibid., 157.

69   Ibid., 159. His terms echo Marcuse's language in *Eros and Civilisation.*

70   Ménil, "L'Action foudroyante," 61; Ménil, "Lightning Effect," 153–54.

71   Senghor, "Speech and Image: An African Tradition of the Surreal," trans. John Reed and Chris Wake, in *Poems for the Millennium Volume One: From Fin-de-Siècle to Negritude,* ed. Jerome Rothenberg and Pierre Joris (Berkeley: University of California Press, 1995), 564–65.

72   Césaire, *Cahiers d'un retour au pays natal,* in *Aimé Césaire: The Collected Poems,* trans. Clayton Eshelman and Annette Smith (Berkeley: University of California Press, 1983), 58–59.

73   Herbert Marcuse, *One Dimensional Man: Studies in the Ideology of Advanced Industrial Society* (London: Routledge and Kegan Paul, 1964), 170.

74   Césaire, *Discourse on Colonialism* in *Poems for the Millennium,* 562.

75   René Ménil, *Tracées: Identité, négritude, esthétique dans l'Antilles* (Paris: Éditions Robert Laffont, 1981), 47. "Une psychologie concrète, descriptive de la conscience martiniquaise actuelle, qui révélerait en un tableau synoptique les compressions, refoule-

ments, frustrations, névroses à la limite qui nous travaillent, nous permettrait de comprendre et d'expliquer la nature et la dispersion des visions historiques décrites par nos historiens."

76 Albert Memmi, *The Colonizer and the Colonized*, trans. Howard Greenfeld (Boston: Beacon Press, 1965).

77 Sartre, "For a Theater of Situations," in *The Writings*, 186.

78 When writing *Anti-Semite and Jew*, he did not delimit an audience in any way; the text was written neither for Jews nor anti-Semites.

79 The journal, published from Lagos by the Times Press, was first edited by Ulli Beier, *Black Orpheus* 1, no. 1 (September 1957).

80 Sartre, "Black Orpheus," 46–47.

81 See, for example, the illustrations in *Corps Perdu*. See also the section of the poem by Césaire, "De L'errance," 105–6.

82 Fanon, *Black Skin, White Masks*, 180. Julio Finn, *Voices of Negritude* (London: Quartet, 1988).

83 Sartre, "Black Orpheus," 17.

84 Sartre, *Baudelaire* (Paris: Librairie Gallimard, 1950).

85 Sartre, *Being and Nothingness*, 494–534.

86 See Frantz Fanon, *Studies in a Dying Colonialism. Sociologie d' une révolution (L'an cinq de la Revolution Algerienne)* (Paris: Francois Maspero, 1959 and 1968). (*Studies in a Dying Colonialism*, trans. Haakon Chevalier [London: Earthscan Publications, 1989].)

87 Fanon, *Black Skin, White Masks*, 179–80.

88 Aimé Césaire, *Discourse on Colonialism* (1950; New York: Monthly Review Press, 1972).

89 Fanon, *Black Skin, White Masks*, 192.

90 Césaire, *Cahiers*.

91 Césaire, *Discourse on Colonialism*, 57.

92 Sartre, *Being and Nothingness*, 540.

93 Sartre, "Revolutionary Violence," 573.

94 Fanon, *Black Skin, White Masks*, 135.

95 Jean-Paul Sartre, *Anti-Semite and Jew: An Explanation of the Etiology of Hate*, trans. George Becker (New York: Schocken Books, 1948), 66–69.

96 Sartre, "Revolutionary Violence," 573.

97 Sartre, *Anti-Semite and Jew*, 10–11.

98 Ibid., 105–6.

99 Sartre, "Preface" to *The Wretched of the Earth*, 14.

100 This is contrary to what Lewis Gordon has suggested when writing of Sartre and the situation of blacks. See Lewis Gordon, ed., *Existence in Black: An Anthology of Black Existential Philosophy* (London: Routledge, 1977).

101 Sartre, *Anti-Semite and Jew*, 69.

102 Fanon, *Black Skin, White Masks*, 14.

4. Colonial Melancholy

Epigraphs are taken from Frantz Fanon, *The Wretched of the Earth*, trans. Constance Farrington (New York: Grove Press, 1963), 290; Albert Memmi, *The Colonizer and the*

Colonized, trans. Howard Greenfeld (Boston: Beacon Press, 1965), xiii; Octave Mannoni, "The Decolonisation of Myself," *Race* 7, no. 4 (April 1966): 331.

1 Octave Mannoni, cited in Elisabeth Roudinesco, *Jacques Lacan and Co.: A History of Psychoanalysis in France 1925–1985,* trans. Jeffrey Mehlman (Chicago: University of Chicago Press, 1990), 234.

2 Octave Mannoni, "Je sais bien, mais quand même," in *Clefs pour l'imaginaire* (Paris: Seuil, 1969), 9–35.

3 Sigmund Freud, "The Disturbance of Memory on the Acropolis," *S.E.* 22:246.

4 During the years preceding World War II, this was an "accusation" made by the Nazis against psychoanalysis. More recently, this characterization has not been seen in a negative light. It has ranged from tracing the Talmudic forms of analysis in psychoanalysis, to seeing it as the affective response to anti-Semitism. See, for example, David Bakan, *Freud and the Jewish Mystical Tradition* (Princeton, N.J.: D. Van Nostrand, 1958); Yosef Hayim Yerushalmi, *Freud's Moses* (New Haven, Conn.: Yale University Press, 1991); and Carl Schorske, "Politics and Parricide in Freud's *Interpretation of Dreams*" (1973), in *Fin-de-Siècle Vienna: Politics and Culture* (New York: Knopf, 1980).

5 Octave Mannoni, *Prospero and Caliban: The Psychology of Colonization* (Ann Arbor, Mich.: Ann Arbor Paperbacks, 1990), 161. (*Psychologie de la décolonisation* [Editions de Seuil, 1950]. The book was published in a new edition in 1964 as *Caliban et Prospéro: La Psychologie de la décolonisation.*)

6 Emily Apter has recently written on the strange resistance to Mannoni by Fanon, who seems to share more with him than almost any other writer of the period. See Emily Apter, *Continental Drift* (Chicago: University of Chicago Press, 1999), 222.

7 Antoine Porot and Charles Bardenat, *Anormaux et malades mentaux devant le justice pénale* (Paris: Librairie Maloine, 1960), 15.

8 J. C. Carothers, *The Mind of Man in Africa* (London: Tom Stacey Ltd., 1972), 159–60.

9 Mannoni, *Prospero and Caliban,* 197.

10 Ibid., 132.

11 Ibid., 133.

12 Ibid., 24–25.

13 Ibid., 48.

14 Ibid., 198. See also Carl Jung, "The Relation of the Ego to the Unconscious," in *Two Essays on Analytical Psychology* (London: Builliere, Tindall and Cox, 1928).

15 Frantz Fanon, *Black Skin, White Masks,* trans. Charles Lam Markmann (1952; New York: Grove, 1967), 170.

16 Mannoni, *Prospero and Caliban,* 40.

17 Memmi, *The Colonizer and the Colonized,* 114.

18 Madagascar became a colony of France under the law of 6 August 1896 and gained independence in 1960.

19 Mannoni, *Prospero and Caliban,* 23.

20 We could, perhaps, attribute this to the different notions of assimilation in colonial history attached to the Martiniquan in France or to the Parsi in India. Biographical causality would perhaps miss the larger point; but forms of political and cultural assimilation had, according to Mannoni, different consequences for psychical assimilation.

21 Mannoni, *Prospero and Caliban*, 32–33.

22 Octave Mannoni, *Clefs pour l'imaginaire ou l'autre scène* (Paris: Editions du Seuil, 1969), 99. "Les auteurs de romans de chevalerie (comme aussi Defoe, mais aussi comme Drury!) nous transportaient dans un autre lieu du monde réel, ou un autre temps de l'histoire; ce qui était constituer l'autre scène par des moyens naïvement réalistes qui peuvent, d'ailleurs, aller tout à fait à l'opposé de ce qu'on appelle réalisme en littérature."

23 These are the texts that discuss colonialism directly. In addition Mannoni wrote on many literary texts, including commentaries on authors as diverse as Mallarmé, Rimbaud, Salinger, James, and Proust. See, for example, his collection of essays *Clefs pour l'imaginaire ou l'autre scène*.

24 See Freud, *The Interpretation of Dreams* (1900; Harmondsworth: Pelican, 1976), 112. See also G. T. Fechner, *Elemente der Psychophysik,* 2 vols. (Leipzig, 1860; 2d ed., 1889). See in particular 2:520–21.

25 See Mannoni's preface to *Clefs,* 7–8; and "Decolonisation of Myself," 329.

26 Ashis Nandy, *The Savage Freud and Other Essays on Possible and Retrievable Selves* (Delhi: Oxford University Press, 1995), 82.

27 Mannoni, *Prospero and Caliban*, 134.

28 Ibid., 107.

29 Ibid.

30 Fanon, *Black Skin, White Masks,* 53 n.12.

31 Mannoni, *Prospero and Caliban*, 78 and 111. This is theorized by Mannoni as being a part of the "Prospero Complex."

32 Mannoni, *Prospero and Caliban*, 114.

33 Ibid., 116.

34 Ibid., 60.

35 Ibid., 56.

36 Ibid., 41.

37 Ibid., 56.

38 Freud, "Fetishism," *S.E.* 21:153.

39 Mannoni, "Decolonisation of Myself," 331.

40 Mannoni, *Prospero and Caliban*, 66–67.

41 See the section on the "Fokon'lona" in Mannoni, *Prospero and Caliban*, 177–86.

42 Kobena Mercer, *Mirage: Enigmas of Race, Difference, and Desire* (London: ICA/IVIA, 1994).

43 Cedric Robinson, "The Appropriation of Frantz Fanon," *Race and Class* 35, no. 1 (July/Sept. 1993): 79–91.

44 See Alan Read, *The Fact of Blackness* (London: Institute of Contemporary Arts, 1996), for articles on Fanon by Hall, Vergès, Mercer, and Bhabha.

45 Neil Lazarus, "Disavowing Decolonization," in *Nationalism and Colonial Practice in the Postcolonial World* (Cambridge: Cambridge University Press, 1999), 68–143. See Fanon, *Wretched of the Earth,* 247, for a further discussion on the differences between national consciousness and nationalism.

46 Henry Louis Gates, "Critical Fanonism," *Critical Inquiry* 17, no. 3 (1991): 457–70.

47 Fanon, *Wretched of the Earth,* 312–15.

48   Susan Gearhardt insists that Fanon failed to conceptualize the connection between the individual and the social sentiment voiced also by contributors to *The Fact of Blackness*. See "Colonialism, Psychoanalysis, and Cultural Criticism: The Problem of Interiorization in Albert Memmi," in John Carlos Rowe, *Culture and the Problem of Disciplines* (New York: Columbia University Press, 1998).

49   Frantz Fanon, *Black Skin, White Masks,* 161–64 n.25.

50   Apter, *Continental Drift,* 222. See also Jock McCulloch, *Colonial Psychiatry and the African Mind* (Cambridge: Cambridge University Press, 1995).

51   Françoise Vergès, "Creole Skin, Black Mask: Fanon and Disavowal," *Critical Inquiry* 23, no. 3 (1997): 578–596.

52   Fanon, *Black Skin, White Masks,* 160–61.

53   Ibid., 180.

54   Fanon, "The North African Syndrome," in *Toward the African Revolution: Political Essays,* trans. Haakon Chevalier (New York: Monthly Review Press, 1967), 3–16. (*Pour La Révolution Africaine* [Paris: François Maspero, 1964]. The essay originally appeared in *L'Esprit* [February 1952].)

55   E. Stern, "Médicine psychomatique," *Psyché,* Jan.–Feb. 1949, 128. See Fanon, "North African Syndrome," 10.

56   Léon Mugniery, cited in Fanon, "The North African Syndrome," 11–12.

57   Albert Memmi, "La vie impossible de Frantz Fanon," *Esprit* 39, no. 406 (September 1971): 248–73. Also in translation as "The Impossible Life of Frantz Fanon," *Massachusetts Review* 14, no. 1 (Winter 1973): 9–39.

58   Fanon, "The North African Syndrome," 15.

59   Ibid., 15, 14.

60   Ibid., 15.

61   Freud, "Beyond the Pleasure Principle" (1920), *S.E.* 18:16.

62   Jacques Lacan, *The Ethics of Psychoanalysis,* trans. Dennis Porter (1959–60; London: Tavistock/Routledge, 1992), 19.

63   Ibid.

64   Etienne Balibar, *La crainte des masses* (Paris: Galilée, 1997); Homi Bhabha, "The Postcolonial and the Postmodern: The Question of Agency," in *The Location of Culture* (London: Routledge, 1994), 171–97.

65   Slavoj Žižek, "A Leftist Plea for Eurocentrism," *Critical Inquiry* 24, no. 4 (Summer 1998): 1003.

66   Ibid., 1007–8.

67   Fanon, *Wretched of the Earth,* 247.

68   Ibid., 148.

69   Fanon writes that the colonized man is himself only between the hours he dreams. This suggests that the unconscious is the repository of the colonized man's core subjectivity, politically suppressed, and thus rather like that of the black man as conceived by Sartre in "Black Orpheus." The unconscious does not seem, in that eventuality, inaccessible at all, and is relatively free of the forms of confusion that are so apparent in *Black Skin, White Masks.* There, psychical and theoretical conflict are far more apparent. Fanon, *Wretched of the Earth,* 41.

70 Jacques Lacan, *Ethics of Psychoanalysis*, 325.

71 Ibid., 324.

72 Ibid., 324.

73 Albert Memmi, "The Impossible Life of Frantz Fanon," *Massachusetts Review* (Winter 1973): 9–39; "Frantz Fanon and the Notion of Deficiency," trans. Eleanor Levieux in *Dominated Man* (Boston: Beacon Press, 1969), 84–89.

74 Memmi, "Frantz Fanon and the Notion of Deficiency," 84–89.

75 Memmi, *The Colonizer and the Colonized*, 87–88.

76 See Memmi, "Frantz Fanon and the Notion of Deficiency," 87–88.

77 Memmi, "Negritude and Jewishness," in *Dominated Man: Notes Towards a Portrait* (Boston: Beacon Press, 1969), 38.

78 Memmi, "Frantz Fanon and the Notion of Deficiency," 85; see also *The Colonizer and the Colonized*, 3.

79 See Albert Memmi, "Frozen by Death in the Image of Third World Prophet," *New York Times Book Review* (14 March 1971): 5 and 20. See Peter Geismar, *Frantz Fanon* (New York: Dial Press, 1971).

80 Memmi, "The Impossible Life of Frantz Fanon," 17.

81 Thomas Cassirer notes that Memmi knew Fanon in Tunis in the 1950s. At the time, Memmi was a psychologist and director of an institute of child psychology. Fanon was editor of *El Moudjahid* at the time, and was also a psychiatrist at a local hospital. See Thomas Cassirer's headnotes to "The Impossible Life of Frantz Fanon," 10. Fanon had moved to Tunis in 1957 after he had been expelled from Algeria following his support of striking doctors. He worked in Tunis under a pseudonym.

82 Memmi, "The Impossible Life of Frantz Fanon," 28.

83 Ibid., 29.

84 Ibid., 37.

85 Ibid., 29.

86 Memmi, "A Tyrant's Plea," in *Dominated Man*, 142.

87 Ibid., 145–46.

88 We see this described in as diverse writers as V. S. Naipaul, Jacques Derrida, Ngugi Wa Thiong'o, Edward Said, and Hélène Cixous. See V. S. Naipaul, *A House for Mr. Biswas* and *The Mimic Men;* Jacques Derrida, *Monolingualism of the Other;* Ngugi Wa Thiong'o, *Decolonising the Mind;* Hélène Cixous, "My Algeriance, in Other Words: To Depart Not to Arrive from Algeria," in *Stigmata: Escaping Texts* (London: Routledge, 1998); Edward Said, *Out of Place* (New York: Knopf, 1999).

89 See Guy Dugas, *Albert Memmi: Écrivain de la déchirure* (Sherbrooke: L'Harmattan, 1984).

90 Albert Memmi, *The Pillar of Salt*, trans. Edouard Roditi (New York: Orion Press, 1962), 110.

91 Ibid., 111.

92 Suzanne Gearhart discusses Memmi's interest in psychoanalysis in terms of his *métissage,* in "Colonialism, Psychoanalysis, and Cultural Criticism," 171–97.

93 Memmi, *Pillar of Salt*, 289.

94 Memmi, *The Colonizer and the Colonized*, 149.

95 Memmi, "The Paths of the Revolt," in *Dominated Man*, 14.

96 Ibid., 4.

97 Memmi, *The Colonizer and the Colonized,* 141.

98 Memmi, "The Paths of the Revolt," 15.

99 Memmi, "Postscript," in *Dominated Man,* 209–11.

100 Memmi, "The Colonial Problem and the Left," in *Dominated Man,* 70.

101 Albert Memmi, "The Double Lesson of Freud" (trans. Carol Martin-Sperry), in *Dominated Man.* The essay first appeared under the title "La double leçon de Freud" as the introduction to the French translation of David Bakan's *Freud and the Jewish Mystical Tradition* (Princeton, N.J.: D. Van Nostrand, 1958). It was included in the 1968 edition of *L'homme dominé* (Paris: Payot, 1968), 95–111, under the title "La judéité de Freud."

102 Memmi, "Double Lesson," 95.

103 Ibid., 101.

104 Ibid., 99–101.

105 Ibid., 101.

106 Yerushalmi, *Freud's Moses;* Jacques Derrida, "Archive Fever: A Freudian Impression," *Diacritics* 25, no. 2 (Summer 1995): 9–63.

107 Derrida, "Archive Fever," 47.

108 Memmi, "Negritude and Jewishness," in *Dominated Man,* 31.

109 Memmi, "Zionism, Israel, and the Third World," *Dispersion and Unity* 15–16 (1972): 93–120.

110 Memmi, "Negritude and Jewishness," 36.

5. The Ethical Ambiguities of Transnational Feminism

Epigraphs are taken from Simone de Beauvoir, *A Very Easy Death* (Harmondsworth: Penguin, 1966), 92; Simone de Beauvoir, *Prime of Life* (Harmondsworth: Penguin, 1965), 121; Luce Irigaray, "Equal or Different" (1986), in *The Irigaray Reader,* ed. Margaret Whitford (Oxford: Blackwell, 1991), 32.

1 See Chandra Mohanty, "Cartographies of Struggle," in *Third World Women and the Politics of Feminism,* ed. Chandra Talpade Mohanty, Ann Russo, and Lourdes Torres (Bloomington: Indiana University Press, 1991); Gayatri Chakravorty Spivak, "Can the Subaltern Speak?" in *Marxism and the Interpretation of Culture,* ed. Cary Nelson and Lawrence Grossberg (Urbana: University of Illinois Press, 1988), 271–313; Maria Lugones and Elizabeth Spelman, " 'Have We Got a Theory for You!': Feminist Theory, Cultural Imperialism, and the Demand for 'the Woman's Voice,' " in *Hypatia Reborn: Essays in Feminist Philosophy,* ed. Azizah Y. Al-Hibri and Margaret A. Simons (Bloomington: Indiana University Press, 1990).

2 See Jacques Derrida, *Specters of Marx: The State of the Debt, the Work of Mourning, and the New International,* trans. Peggy Kamuf (New York: Routledge, 1994); Benedict Anderson, *Imagined Communities: Reflections on the Origin and Spread of Nationalism,* 2d ed. (1983; London: Verso, 1991).

3 Bruce Robbins, ed., *The Phantom Public Sphere* (Minneapolis: University of Minnesota Press, 1993), vii–xxvi.

4 Such a concept of haunting draws from Abraham and Torok's understanding of the

distinctions between introjection and incorporation, and transgenerational haunting through a phantom that manifests itself in language. Taking the terms *introjection* and *incorporation* from Ferenczi, they speak of them in terms of losses and their aftermath. Whereas Freud does not distinguish between introjection and incorporation when he writes about mourning and melancholia, Abraham and Torok formulate introjection as a successful assimilation of something lost into the self, a process that goes on constantly through a lifetime, as psychical assimilation is always necessary. Incorporation, on the other hand, is the swallowing whole of something lost. It may appear to be assimilated, but will emerge through symptoms in language. This language, and thus this incorporation, could in theory be carried through generations, resulting in a being haunted by a secret once incorporated. And it could manifest itself at particular historical moments in which events occur that cause the phantom to emerge. In the context of coloniality, we could think, for example, of incorporated colonialist ideals apparently available but actually unavailable to colonized peoples—and which are mourned as a loss of an ideal. The trace of such incorporation would thus be crucial to any understanding of the present or the future because of the specters that haunt. The terms are elaborated upon in Nicolas Abraham and Maria Torok, "Maladie du deuil," in *L'écorce et le noyau* (Paris: Aubier-Flammarion, 1978). See pp. 233–35 in particular, where they elaborate on this idea in a subsection called "La notion ferenczienne de l'introjection des pulsions opposée à celle d'incorporation de l'objet." *The Shell and the Kernel,* vol. 1, trans. Nicholas Rand (Chicago: University of Chicago Press, 1994), 125–38. For more on intergenerational haunting, see their *The Wolf Man's Magic Word: A Cryptonomy,* trans. Nicholas Rand (Minneapolis: University of Minnesota Press, 1986). (*Cryptonomie: Le verbier de l'Homme aux loups* [Paris: Flammarion, 1976].)

5   Drucilla Cornell has written about this extensively, and pits Lacan against Derrida (through Levinas) in this regard. See *The Philosophy of the Limit* (London: Routledge, 1992).

6   See, for example, Judith Butler's *Gender Trouble* (London: Routledge, 1990).

7   Simone de Beauvoir, *The Ethics of Ambiguity,* trans. Bernard Fretchman (1948; Secaucus, N.J.: Citadel Press, 1997).

8   Jean-Paul Sartre, *Being and Nothingness,* trans. Hazel Barnes (1943; New York: Pocket Books, 1956).

9   This has recently received much attention in the field of black studies. See, for example, Lewis Gordon, ed., *Existence in Black: An Anthology of Black Existential Philosophy* (London: Routledge, 1997). Sartre, *Notebooks for an Ethics,* trans. David Pellauer (Chicago: University of Chicago Press, 1992).

10 See Herbert Marcuse, "Sartre's Existentialism" (1948) and "Postscript" (1965), in *From Luther to Popper,* trans. Joris de Bres (London: Verso, 1972), 157–89. Marcuse withdrew his criticism in the postscript.

11 See Sartre, *What Is Literature?,* trans. David Fretchman (1948; Bristol: Methuen, 1967).

12 Sigmund Freud, *Civilization and Its Discontents* (1930), in *Standard Edition of the Complete Works of Sigmund Freud,* vol. 21, trans. James Strachey (London: Hogarth Press, 1953–74), 59–145. [Hereafter referred to as *S.E.*]

13 Jacques Lacan, *The Ethics of Psychoanalysis,* trans. Dennis Porter (1959–60; London: Tavistock/Routledge, 1992).

14 Most recently, see *The Psychic Life of Power* (Stanford, Calif.: Stanford University Press, 1997).

15 See Joan Copjec, *Read My Desire: Lacan against the Historicists* (Cambridge, Mass.: MIT Press, 1994); Renata Salecl, *The Spoils of Freedom: Psychoanalysis and Feminism after the Fall of Socialism* (London: Routledge, 1994); Slavoj Žižek, *The Sublime Object of Ideology* (London: Verso, 1989).

16 Copjec, *Read My Desire,* 4.

17 Foucault, *The Order of Things: An Archaeology of the Human Sciences,* trans. Alan Sheridan (London: Tavistock, 1970), xiii.

18 Copjec, *Read My Desire,* 6.

19 Ibid., 7.

20 Frantz Fanon, *Black Skin, White Masks,* trans. Charles Lee Markmann (New York: Grove Press, 1967), 112. (*Peau Noire, masques blancs* [Paris: Editions du Seuil, 1952].)

21 Homi Bhabha, "How Newness Enters the World," in *The Location of Culture* (London: Routledge, 1994), 227.

22 Freud, *Group Psychology and the Analysis of the Ego* (1921), S.E. 18:69–143; *The Ego and the Id* (1923), S.E. 19:3–66; *Totem and Taboo* (1912–13), S.E. 13:1–161.

23 Slavoj Žižek, "Fantasy as a Political Category," *Journal for the Psychoanalysis of Culture and Society* 1, no. 2 (Fall 1996): 77–86.

24 Lacan, *Ethics of Psychoanalysis* and *Télévision* (Paris: Seuil, 1973).

25 Slavoj Žižek, "A Leftist Plea for Eurocentrism," *Critical Inquiry* 24, no. 4 (Summer 1998): 995.

26 Gayatri Chakravorty Spivak, "Postcoloniality and Value," in *Literary Theory Today,* ed. P. Collier and H. Geyer-Ryan (Cambridge, U.K.: Polity Press, 1990), 228.

27 Fredric Jameson, *The Geopolitical Aesthetic: Cinema and Space in the World System* (Bloomington: Indiana University Press, 1995), 1.

28 Simone de Beauvoir, *The Second Sex,* trans. H. M. Parshley (London: Picador, 1988), 115–16. (*Le Deuxième Sexe* [Paris: Gallimard, 1949].)

29 Debra Bergoffen, "Out from Under: Beauvoir's Philosophy of the Erotic," in *Feminist Interpretations of Simone de Beauvoir,* ed. Margaret Simons (University Park: Pennsylvania State University Press, 1995), 179–92.

30 Beauvoir, *Ethics of Ambiguity,* 135.

31 Simone de Beauvoir and Gisèle Halimi, *Djamila Boupacha* (Paris: Gallimard, 1962). (*Djamila Boupacha: The Story of the Torture of a Young Algerian Girl Which Shocked Liberal Opinion,* trans. Peter Green [London: André Deutsch and Weidenfeld and Nicolson, 1962].)

32 Beauvoir, *Ethics of Ambiguity,* 101.

33 Luce Irigaray, *Ethique de la différence sexuelle* (Paris: Editions de Minuit, 1984); *J'aime à toi: esquisse d'une félicité dans l'histoire* (Paris: B. Grasset, 1992); *Je, tu, nous: pour une culture de la différence* (Paris: B. Grasset, 1990).

34 Mariama Ba, *So Long a Letter* (London: Heinemann, 1981); Rigoberta Menchu, *I, Rigoberta Menchu: An Indian Woman in Guatemala* (London: Verso, 1985); Assia Djebar, *A*

Sister to Scheherazade (London: Heinemann, 1993); Mahasweta Devi, *Imaginary Maps* (London: Routledge, 1994). See also Spivak, "The Politics of Translation," in *Destabilising Theory: Contemporary Feminist Debates,* ed. Michèle Barrett and Anne Phillips (Cambridge, U.K.: Polity Press, 1992), 54–85.

35   Beauvoir, *Ethics of Ambiguity,* 18.

36   I have written on the Djamila Boupacha case more extensively in "The Experience of Evidence: Language, the Law, and the Mockery of Justice," in *Algeria in Others' Languages,* ed. Anne-Emmanuelle Berger (Ithaca: Cornell University Press, 2002).

37   I have written on this issue more extensively in an article on Alice Walker's books and film on clitoridectomy. See Ranjana Khanna and Karen Engle, "Forgotten History: Myth, Empathy, and Assimilated Culture," in *Feminism and the New Democracy,* ed. Jodie Dean (London: Sage Press, 1996).

38   See Frantz Fanon, "Colonial War and Mental Disorders," in *The Wretched of the Earth,* 249–311.

39   Gayatri Chakravorty Spivak, "Scattered Speculations on the Question of Value," in *In Other Worlds* (New York: Methuen, 1987), 154.

6. Hamlet in the Colonial Archive

The epigraph is taken from C. L. R. James, "Notes on *Hamlet,*" in *The C. L. R. James Reader* (Oxford: Blackwell, 1992), 244–45.

1   Sigmund Freud, *The Interpretation of Dreams, S.E.* 4:265. The footnote was later included as part of the main text.

2   Ibid., 264.

3   Ernest Jones, *Hamlet and Oedipus* (New York: Norton, 1949), chap. 3.

4   Ernest Jones, "The Problem of Hamlet and the Oedipus-Complex," in Shakespeare, *"Hamlet," with a Psycho-analytical Study by Ernest Jones, M.D.* (London: Vision Press, 1947), 42.

5   Wulf Sachs, *Psychoanalysis: Its Meaning and Practical Application* (London: Cassell, 1934).

6   Wulf Sachs, "The Mind of a Witch-Doctor," *Book Find News* (August 1947), cited in Saul Dubow, "Introduction: Part One," in *Black Hamlet* (Baltimore, Md.: Johns Hopkins University Press, 1996), 16. All citations from *Black Hamlet* will be taken from this edition.

7   Sachs, *Psychoanalysis,* 197.

8   Freud, *Dreams,* 266.

9   Sachs, *Psychoanalysis,* 211–12.

10   Juliet Mitchell, "Trauma, Recognition, and the Place of Language," *Diacritics* 28, no. 4 (1998): 121–134. Cathy Caruth, *Unclaimed Experience: Trauma, Narrative and History* (Baltimore: Johns Hopkins University Press, 1996).

11   James Joyce, *Ulysses* (1922; New York: Vintage, 1961), 188.

12   Ibid., 189.

13   I am, of course, reformulating the beginning of *The Communist Manifesto:* "A specter is haunting Europe—the specter of communism." For a further discussion of Joyce and colonialism, see Ranjana Khanna, " 'Araby' (*Dubliners*): Women's Time and the Time of

the Nation," in *Joyce, Feminism, Colonialism/Postcolonialism,* ed. Ellen Carol Jones, Joyce Studies 5 (Amsterdam: Rodopi, 1998).

14　Nicolas Abraham, "The Phantom of *Hamlet,* or the Sixth Act," in Nicolas Abraham and Maria Torok, *The Shell and the Kernel,* ed. Nicholas T. Rand (Chicago: University of Chicago Press, 1994), vol. 1.

15　The most sustained of such spectral musings is Jacques Derrida's *Specters of Marx: The State of the Debt, the Work of Mourning, and the New International* (New York: Routledge, 1994), 6. (*Spectres de Marx* [Editions Galilée, 1993].)

16　Joyce, *Ulysses,* 184–89.

17　Sybille Yates, "Review: *Black Hamlet,*" *International Journal of Psychoanalysis* 19, no. 2 (1938): 251–52.

18　Sachs, *Psychoanalysis,* 161.

19　See Sigmund Freud, *Totem and Taboo* (1912–13), *S.E.* 13:43.

20　See the two introductions, by Saul Dubow and Jacqueline Rose respectively, in *Black Hamlet.* See also Jacqueline Rose's chapter entitled "Black Hamlet" in *States of Fantasy* (Oxford: Oxford University Press, 1996), 38–55.

21　Sachs, *Black Hamlet,* 71.

22　Ibid., 235.

23　Rose, "Black Hamlet," 49.

24　Bronislaw Malinowski, *Sex and Repression in Savage Society* (1927; Chicago: University of Chicago Press, 1985).

25　See Bronislaw Malinowski, *The Dynamics of Culture Change: An Inquiry into Race Relations in Africa* (1945; New Haven: Yale University Press, 1961). The work was published posthumously, but represents interests of Malinowski that were based on earlier analytical techniques, most famously those that concentrated upon social organization, belief, material circumstances, and language.

26　Ernest Gellner, *Anthropology and Politics* (Oxford: Blackwell, 1995), 103.

27　Saul Dubow, "Introduction: Part One," in *Black Hamlet,* 15–16. See also, Megan Vaughan, *Curing Their Ills: Colonial Power and African Illness* (Stanford, Calif.: Stanford University Press, 1991), 100–128.

28　Ellen Hellmann, *Rooiyard: A Sociological Survey of an Urban Native Slum Yard* (Cape Town: Oxford University Press, 1948), 114. (My emphasis.)

29　See, for example, her comment on the decrease of tribal educational institutions, and the inadequacy of school instruction as a substitute: "In Rooiyard the informal training of the tribe is lacking altogether for the boy and but partially substituted for the girl. School instruction is but an inadequate substitute for the wide context of tribal education. But tribal institutions provide for one period of intensive formal training during the course of the initiation rites. . . . In an urban area, this final period which sets a seal on all training that has preceded it is lacking. . . . A natural outcome of this loss of strength of Native educational institutions is the emergence of an undisciplined younger generation." And then, quoting Freud from the *New Introductory Lectures on Psychoanalysis,* " 'Education has . . . to steer its way between the Scylla of giving instincts free play and the Charybdis of frustrating them.' The native populace may well be heading for disaster in the direction of Scylla." Hellmann, *Rooiyard,* 75.

See also her comments on Roheim's psychoanalytic study of training of children and lactation in South Africa (Hellmann, *Rooiyard*, 115).

30 Ibid., 115.

31 Frantz Fanon, *The Wretched of the Earth*, trans. Constance Farrington (New York: Grove Press, 1963), 290.

32 Antonio Gramsci, "History of the Subaltern Class: Methodological Criteria," in *Selections from Prison Notebooks*, trans. and ed. Quintin Hoane and Geoffrey Nowell Smith (London: Lawrence and Wishart, 1971), 52–55. Gayatri Chakravorty Spivak, "Subaltern Studies: Deconstructing Historiography," in *In Other Words* (New York: Methuen, 1987), 197–221.

33 Wulf Sachs, *Black Anger* (New York: Grove Press, 1947). Saul Dubow has written extensively on the distinctions between the two in his "Introduction: Part One."

34 For a discussion of the relationship between private and public spheres and political and civil society, see Karen Engle and Ranjana Khanna, "Forgotten History: Myth, Empathy, and Assimilated Culture," in *Feminism and the New Democracy*, ed. Jodie Dean (New York: Sage Press, 1996).

35 For a further discussion of this personalization of memory, see Pierre Nora, "Preface to the English Language Edition" and "Between Memory and History," in *Realms of Memory*, vol. 1 (New York: Columbia University Press, 1996).

36 See Sigmund Freud, "The Uncanny," *S.E.* 17:217–52 and "Medusa's Head," *S.E.* 18:273–74.

37 Sachs, *Black Hamlet*, 250.

38 Ibid., 250–51.

39 Ibid., 251.

40 Derrida, *Specters of Marx*, 6.

41 Sachs, *Black Hamlet*, 274.

42 Ibid., 91.

43 Ibid., 197.

44 Ibid.

45 For a discussion of the use and meaning of the "secret" and the withholding of information in anthropological work, see Doris Sommer, "No Secrets: Rigoberta's Guarded Truth," *Women's Studies* 20 (1991): 51–72.

46 Homi Bhabha, "Of Mimicry and Man," in *Location of Culture* (London: Routledge, 1994), 86.

47 Walter Benjamin, "Theses on the Philosophy of History," in *Illuminations*, trans. H. Zohn (London: Cape, 1970), 253–64.

48 For more on the distinction, and the slipperiness of it, see Jacques Derrida, "Me —Psychoanalysis: An Introduction to the translation of *The Shell and the Kernel* by Nicolas Abraham," *Diacritics* (March 1979): 4–12.

49 In fact, Hellmann's own presentation of the methodological problems shares much with feminist anthropology today. See Hellmann, "Method of Work," in *Rooiyard*, 1–5.

50 Laura Mulvey, in an essay on Freud's use of the Oedipus myth, also notes the structure of interrogation implicit in the psychoanalytic process, comparing the psychoanalytic investigation to the police questioning and the archaeological dig:

Archaeology depends on the preservation of actual objects in time, and the fossilisation of these objects in a medium that preserves their reality intact. In semiological terms, its signs are indexical. They come to the surface as a challenge to the erosion of time and provide a point of contact with, and traces of, a remote and almost lost epoch. Detection, too, makes use of indexical signs in the traces and clues which have to be interpreted and read to make sense. This leads, once again, to the psychoanalytic process.

The "process of revealing . . . a process that can be likened to the process of psychoanalysis" allows the detective to piece together the signs available. Laura Mulvey, "The Oedipus Myth: Beyond the Riddles of the Sphinx" (1987), in *Visual and Other Pleasures* (Bloomington: Indiana University Press, 1989), 189. See also Donald P. Spence, "The Sherlock Holmes Tradition: The Narrative Metaphor," in *The Freudian Metaphor* (New York: Norton, 1987), 113–60.

51 Sachs, *Black Hamlet,* 214–15.

52 Ibid., 237.

53 Ibid., 238.

54 Ibid., 77.

55 Ibid., 80.

56 Ibid., 79.

57 Ibid.

58 Ibid., 90.

59 Ibid., 337–38.

60 Ibid., 271.

61 Ibid., 87.

62 E. R. Dodds, *Les Grecs et l'irrationel,* trans. Michael Green (Paris: Aubier, 1965).

63 Marie-Cécile Ortigues and Edmund Ortigues, *Oedipe Africain* (Paris: Plon, 1966), 91–92.

64 Francis Fukuyama, *The End of History and the Last Man* (New York: Free Press, 1992).

65 Ibid., 72.

66 Peggy Kamuf, Translator's Note to Derrida, *Specters of Marx,* 177–78 n. 2.

67 For a discussion of the archive in the context of psychoanalysis, see Jacques Derrida, "Archive Fever: A Freudian Impression," *Diacritics* (Winter 1998): 68–81.

68 This is reminiscent of what Benedict Anderson (in an unpsychoanalytic sense), following José Rizal, calls the "spectre of comparison" (*el demonio de las comparaciones*), a vertiginous, dizzying feeling that arises when, for example, one looks through a telescope only to find, unexpectedly, someone looking back through another. Benedict Anderson, *The Spectre of Comparisons: Nationalism, Southeast Asia, and the World* (London: Verso, 1999), 2. Anderson quotes from José Rizal, *Noli Me Tangere* (1887; Manila: Instituto Nacional de Historia, 1978).

69 For examples of this type of scholarship, see Joan Copjec, *Read My Desire;* Slavoj Žižek, "Love Thy Neighbor? No Thanks!" in *The Psychoanalysis of Race,* ed. Christopher Lane (New York: Columbia University Press, 1998), 154–75; Renata Salecl, *The Spoils of Freedom: Psychoanalysis and Feminism after the Fall of Socialism* (New York: Routledge, 1994).

70 Nicolas Abraham and Maria Torok, *The Shell and the Kernel* (Chicago: Chicago University Press, 1994), vol. 1, 126–27.

71 See Benedict Anderson, *Imagined Communities* (London: Verso, 1991); Bruce Robbins, ed., *The Phantom Public Sphere* (Minneapolis: University of Minnesota Press, 1993); Derrida, "Archive Fever."

72 Walter Benn Michaels, "Race into Culture: A Critical Genealogy of Cultural Identity," *Critical Inquiry* 18, no. 4 (1992): 655–686.

73 See David Lloyd and Paul Thomas, *Culture and the State* (London: Routledge, 1998), 145–50, for a recent interesting contribution to the debates on cultural interest and the culture of disinterestedness.

74 Abraham, "The Phantom of *Hamlet*," 204. Nicolas Abraham and Maria Torok, *The Wolfman's Magic Word: A Cryptonymy* (Minneapolis: University of Minnesota Press, 1986).

75 Ania Loomba, "*Hamlet* in Mizoram," in *Cross-Cultural Performances: Differences in Women's Re-visions of Shakespeare,* ed. Marianne Novy (Urbana: University of Illinois Press, 1993), 227–50.

76 Sigmund Freud, "On Narcissism" (1914), in *S.E.* 14:94–95.

77 Sachs, *Black Anger,* 288.

78 Ibid., 289.

79 Ranajit Guha, *Dominance without Hegemony: History and Power in Colonial India* (Cambridge, Mass.: Harvard University Press, 1997).

80 Annette Weiner's *Women of Value, Men of Renown: New Perspectives in Trobriand* (Austin: University of Texas Press, 1976) is interesting to read in this light, as she revisits Malinowski and the Trobriand Islands and sees very different politics there.

Coda: The Lament

1 Derrida, *Specters of Marx: The State of the Debt, the Work of Mourning, and the New International* (New York: Routledge, 1994), xxxv.

2 Walter Benjamin, *Origin of German Tragic Drama* (London: Verso, 1998); Jacques Derrida, "Archive Fever," *Diacritics* 25, no. 2 (1995): 9–63; Ernest Renan, "What Is a Nation?" in *Nation and Narration,* ed. Homi Bhabha (London: Routledge, 1990), 8–22.

Index

Abraham, Karl, 83

Abraham, Nicolas, and Maria Torok, 257–60, 270, 294 n.4; "The Phantom of *Hamlet,* or the Sixth Act" (Abraham), 236, 243, 259–60, 266–67. *See also* De-metaphorization; Incorporation and introjection

Affect, xi–xii, 24–25, 29, 146, 159, 162–64, 167–68, 170, 174, 176, 178, 180, 185, 190, 196, 198–99, 212, 218–22, 227–30, 245, 254–57, 263, 272

Althusser, Louis, x–xi, 179, 219

Ambiguity, 89, 108, 143, 186, 203, 208, 210, 215–22, 225–26, 247. *See also* Beauvoir, Simone de: *Ethics of Ambiguity*

Ambivalence, 76–79, 86–89, 109–10, 115, 143, 182, 186, 198, 200, 203, 212, 226

Anderson, Benedict, 14–15

Animism, 70–72, 74–77

Annales, 14

Anthropology, 8, 26–27, 34, 37, 40, 64–95, 100, 123, 129, 131, 146, 155, 248, 249, 257, 272; as ethnography, 59, 64–65, 68, 77, 94–95; as ethnology, 33–37, 66–67, 71; as ethnopsychology, 93

Anti-Semitism, 1, 13, 101, 127, 198, 201;

against Freud, 7, 27–28, 36, 38, 99–100, 148, 178; Freud on, 9, 59–65

Apter, Emily, 162–63, 171, 178, 277 n.39, 290 n.6

Archaeology, 8, 26–27, 33–65, 68, 75, 100, 104–5, 123–24, 129, 244, 249, 255, 257, 299 n.50; Foucault on, 33–37

Archive, 15, 17, 20, 202–4, 212, 224, 228, 244, 254, 256, 261, 265, 268–73; as official narrative, 13; as public history, 76. *See also* Derrida, Jacques: "Archive Fever"

Arnold, Matthew, 73, 267

Assimilation: and the inassimilable, 25, 162–64, 170, 190, 198, 200, 204, 233–34, 249, 254, 257, 261–63, 267–68, 271; political, 12, 123, 151–52, 161, 164, 166, 196, 198–99, 201, 243, 255, 261–66, 271; psychical, 22, 24–25, 60, 76, 151–57, 161, 164, 166, 181, 199, 229, 246–48, 253, 257, 265–66, 271. *See also* Incorporation and introjection

Astavakrasamhita, 59

Autobiography, 39–46, 49–52, 113–15, 195–99, 202, 256; and self-analysis, 55

Ba, Mariama, 226
Bakan, David, 201
Balibar, Etienne, 188–89
Bastian, Adolph, 69
Baudelaire, Charles, 137
Beauvoir, Simone de, 30, 99, 195, 196, 199,
    207–8; *Ethics of Ambiguity,* 122, 167–68,
    199, 215–16, 224–29; *The Second Sex,*
    108, 167, 172, 208, 224
Benjamin, Walter, 14–16, 220, 271
Bentham, Jeremy, 215, 216, 221
Bergoffen, Debra, 225
Berkeley-Hill, Owen, 93
Bernal, Martin, 45, 279 n.37
Bernays, Martha, 39, 42, 56
Bernays, Minna, 39, 42
Bhabha, Homi, 15, 155–56, 168, 169, 188,
    219–20, 222, 247, 260
Bhâgavata Purana, 91
Bible, 183–84, 189
Bloch, Maurice, 154–55
Bloom, Harold, 67, 285 n.96
Bose, Grindrasekhar, 93–94
Boupacha, Djamila, 224–25, 227
Breton, André, 120–25, 128, 131–32, 157
Breuer, Josef, 36
Burnouf, Eugène, 91
Buthalia, Pankaj, 260–61
Butler, Judith, 37, 48, 217

Capécia, Mayotte, 157, 160
Carothers, J. C., 150–52, 178
Caruth, Cathy, 14, 233–35, 265, 268
Césaire, Aimé, xi, 29, 102, 119, 123–34, 136,
    138, 157, 171
Césaire, Suzanne, 29, 119, 124–26
Chakrabarty, Dipesh, 11, 100; on the
    politics of despair, 64, 282 n.89
Charcot, Jean-Martin, 42
Chatterjee, Partha, 11
Civilization, 6, 11–12, 90–95, 100; and
    culture, 72–78; and evolution, 165;
    and modernity, 16, 80, 153. *See also*
    Modernity; Tylor, E. B.

Cixous, Hélène, 265
Clark, Grahame, 45
Collective unconscious, 76–77, 81, 89,
    126–28, 138, 140–42, 152–53, 161. *See also*
    Césaire, Aimé; Jung, Carl
Colonial discipline: psychoanalysis as a,
    x, 6–12, 16, 26–27, 65, 100, 260. *See also*
    Worlding
Condensation and displacement, 20,
    53, 146, 158. *See also* Freud, Sigmund:
    Interpretation of Dreams
Condorcet, Jean-Antoine Nicolas, 69
Copjec, Joan, 218–19, 221
Cornell, Drucilla, 226
Cure: status in psychoanalysis, 24–25, 36,
    55, 72, 95, 104–5, 109, 115, 255–56
Cuvier, Georges, 75

Daly, Claud Dangar, 94
Damas, Léon Gontran, 102
"Dark Continent," ix–xii, 6, 46–53, 62, 68,
    104, 128, 136–37, 249–50
Darwin, Charles, 27, 42, 48, 67, 68, 75, 80,
    86, 89, 150, 282 n.7
Decolonization, 100–104, 108, 118–44,
    145–204
Deleuze, Gilles, and Guattari, Félix, 95
De Man, Paul, 110, 220
Demetaphorization, 24–25, 43, 153, 166–67,
    176, 179, 189–90, 191, 199, 254–59, 263,
    270, 272. *See also* Abraham, Nicolas, and
    Maria Torok; Melancholia
Derrida, Jacques, 18, 29, 164, 212, 220, 255,
    265, 276 n.23; "Archive Fever," 203–4,
    271–72; *Geopsychoanalysis,* 1–2; on intro-
    jection and incorporation, 24, 252–54,
    257, 260; *Specters of Marx,* 212, 245–46,
    269–71
Descartes, René, 101
Detribalization, 237–40, 246–47, 250–51,
    254, 256, 263, 267. *See also* Hellmann,
    Ellen
Devereux, George, 94–95
Devi, Mahasweta, 226

214, 228, 243, 252; and impossibility, 199, 209, 212–15, 227, 230; and the law, 210, 212–13, 224, 252, 267; and the police, 249

Kakar, Sudhir, 14, 92; and Catherine Clément, 285 n.94
Kamuf, Peggy, 254
Kant, Immanuel, 123, 184–85, 216
Kesteloot, Lilyan, 119, 122, 138
Kofman, Sarah, 54, 110
Kohut, Heinz, 93
Kojève, Alexander, 101
Kuspit, Donald, 40–41

Lacan, Jacques, xii, 36–37, 102, 106, 108–12, 117, 119, 139, 146–48, 158, 164, 178–87, 216–19, 221, 222, 229, 233, 253, 271, 272; *Ethics of Psychoanalysis,* 183–90; *Four Fundamental Concepts of Psychoanalysis,* 111, 172; "Function and Field of Speech and Language," 37; "The Mirror Stage," 101, 103, 108–9, 169–76, 187, 224; *Seminar IV,* 109
Lamarck, Jean-Baptiste, 68, 69, 75, 80, 81, 86, 150
Lament. *See* Melancholia
Laub, Dori, 13
Lazarus, Neil, 168–69
Le Bon, Gustave, 85, 89
Légitime Défense, 99, 120
Lenin, Vladmir, 120
Léro, Étienne, 120
Levinas, Emmanuel, 225–26
Leys, Ruth, 277 n.28
Lloyd, David, and Paul Thomas, 19
Loomba, Ania, 260–61
Lubbock, Sir John, 42
Lugones, Maria, 209

Macey, David, 52, 281 n.57
Malinowski, Bronislaw, 29, 74, 239–41, 253, 298 n.25
Mania. *See* Melancholia

Mannoni, Octave, 23, 26, 29, 99, 119, 145–67, 169, 175, 178, 272; "Decolonisation of Myself," 145–46, 159, 162–67; "Je sais bien, mais quand même," 147, 162–67, 177–78; *Prospero and Caliban,* 146, 149–50, 152–61, 165, 179, 192
Marcuse, Herbert, 117, 126, 130, 132–33, 139, 142–44, 216
Marx, Karl, x–xi, 120, 212, 245, 254, 271
Marxism, x, 9, 29, 121, 179, 188, 200, 247; and communism, 120, 122, 188, 222; Memmi on, 134, 145, 243. *See also* Gramsci, Antonio; Marx, Karl
Masson, André, 123, 124
Masson, Jeffrey Moussaieff, 59
McClintock, Anne, 48, 93, 110
McCulloch, Jock, 171
McDougall, William, 85, 89
Melancholia, x–xii, 15–27, 30, 38, 64–65, 86–91, 95, 191, 208, 230–31, 242–55, 257, 261–63, 267–73; as colonial melancholy, 21, 23, 145–204; critical agency in, 21–23, 65, 85, 89, 95, 149, 166, 199–200, 203–4, 248, 261–63, 265–66, 272–73; as lament, 201, 208, 245, 268–73; and mania, 23, 71, 81, 88–89; as morbidity, 71, 175–79, 189, 191; nostalgia, contrast to, 13, 257; and remainder or trace, 4, 13–14, 21, 24–25; work of, 25. *See also* Freud, Sigmund: "Mourning and Melancholia"; Haunting
Memmi, Albert, 9, 26, 28, 29, 118, 119, 148, 157, 159, 162, 178, 179, 190–204, 243, 272; *The Colonizer and the Colonized,* 102, 134, 135, 139, 142–43, 145–46, 154, 191, 192, 196, 199; *Dominated Man,* 191, 192, 195, 199; "The Impossible Life of Frantz Fanon," 176, 190–95; *Pillar of Salt,* 102, 146, 196–98; *Portrait of a Jew,* 191
Memory, 13, 222, 228, 271; collective, 140, 243, 256, 261, 268; and forgetting, 12, 13, 65, 271; and genealogy, 13
Menchú, Rigoberta, 226
Meng, Heinrich, 175

Responsibility, 12–13, 79, 85, 101, 106, 112–18, 141, 143, 186, 209, 222, 231, 267. *See also* Ethics; Justice

Robinson, Cedric, 168

Rimbaud, Arthur, 101, 120, 146

Ritvo, Lucille, 86

Rivera, Diego, 120

Rivière, Joan, 48

Robbins, Bruce, 212

Rolland, Romain, 59–65, 91–95. *See also* Oceanic feeling

Rose, Jacqueline, 237–38, 265, 283 n.31

Rosolato, Guy, 55–57, 59

Rothschilds family, 44

Rowlands, Michael, and Roland Robertson, 38, 41

Roy, Dilip Kumar, 91

Rudnytsky, Peter, 46

Sachs, Wulf, 29, 30, 160, 234, 240, 241; *Black Anger,* 243, 263–64, 267–68; *Black Hamlet,* 236–69; "Hamletism," 237–38, 242, 245, 249, 252; *Psychoanalysis: Its Meaning and Practical Application,* 233, 236

Said, Edward, 9, 17, 20, 21, 108, 164

Salecl, Renata, 218

Sartre, Jean-Paul, 28–29, 99–144, 160, 163, 169, 170, 171, 173, 178, 187, 192, 196, 216, 225, 227, 272; *Anti-Semite and Jew,* 99, 101, 118, 136, 139–42, 154, 172; *Being and Nothingness,* 99, 101, 103, 111, 116, 137, 216, 225; "Black Orpheus" (preface to Senghor,) 29, 99, 102, 118, 120–21, 135–38; *Notebooks for an Ethics,* 102, 129–30, 216; preface to Fanon, 102, 135, 138–42; preface to Memmi, 135, 142–43; *Transcendence of the Ego,* 101, 108; *What Is Literature?,* 121–22, 130, 132, 135

Saussure, Ferdinand de, 38, 111

Schliemann, Heinrich, 38–46, 48, 57–58, 62, 65, 75, 124; and Minna, 43–44, 46; and Sophia, 44, 46, 58

Schorske, Carl, 7–8

Self and subjectivity: anthropological structure of, 66–95; archaeological

structure of, 33–65; modern, national, and colonial, 2, 6, 9, 26–28, 30, 67–72, 75–78, 83–85, 100, 190; and psychoanalytic imperialism, xii, 1–2, 7, 10, 239–40; splitting of, 54, 60–65; Western models of, ix, xi, 106

Sen, Mrinal, 261

Senghor, Léopold Sédar, 28, 102, 119, 120, 126, 132, 135–38

Seshadri-Crooks, Kalpana, 93–95

Shakespeare, William, 9, 149, 157, 160, 232–35, 238, 245, 261, 266, 268; *The Tempest,* 159–61. See also *Hamlet*

Silverman, Kaja, xi, 275 n.5

Singularity, 12, 162, 194, 210, 221, 260, 269–73

Slochower, Harry, 55–57, 59

Soyinka, Wole, 13

Specter. *See* Haunting

Spelman, Elizabeth Victoria, 209

Spirit. *See* Animism; Haunting

Spivak, Gayatri Chakravorty, 4, 22, 58, 209, 223, 228, 242

Stanley, Henry Morton, 38, 49–52, 57–58, 62; and Alice Pike, 49–50; and Dorothy Stanley, 51–52, 58

Starr, William Thomas, 91

Stern, E., 175

Stocking, George, 73, 75

Stoler, Ann, 118, 119, 132

Strachey, James, 41

Strümpell, Ludwig, 40

Subaltern, 17–21, 242–44, 247–48, 254, 268, 271. *See also* Gramsci, Antonio; Guha, Ranajit; Spivak, Gayatri Chakravorty

Super-ego, 87, 94–95, 164–66, 233, 252–53. *See also* Freud, Sigmund: "Ego and the Id"

Surrealism, 99, 102, 118–34, 146

Taboo, 67, 77, 86, 90, 110. *See also* Incest taboo

Temporality, xii, 4, 6, 180, 215, 224, 247, 261, 270; biblical, 75; and evolution, 12,

Ranjana Khanna is Assistant Professor of English and Literature at
Duke University. She is also affiliated with women's studies.

Library of Congress Cataloging-in-Publication Data
Khanna, Ranjana.
Dark continents : psychoanalysis and colonialism / Ranjana Khanna.
p. cm. — (Post-contemporary interventions)
Includes index.
ISBN 0-8223-3055-5 (cloth : alk. paper)
ISBN 0-8223-3067-9 (pbk. : alk. paper)
1. Social sciences and psychoanalysis. 2. Imperialism–Psychological
aspects. I. Title. II. Series.
BF175.4.S65 K43 2003   150.19'5–dc21   2002152607